S ECRETS

O F

H EAVEN

S ECRETS

O F

H EAVEN

The Portable New Century Edition

EMANUEL SWEDENBORG

Volume 7

Translated from the Latin by Lisa Hyatt Cooper

SWEDENBORG FOUNDATION

Royersford, Pennsylvania

Originally published in Latin as *Arcana Coelestia*, London, 1749–1756. The volume contents of this and the original Latin edition, along with ISBNs of the annotated version, are as follows:

Volume number in this edition	Text treated	Volume number in the Latin first edition	Section numbers	ISBN (hardcover)
1	Genesis 1–8	1	§§1–946	978-0-87785-486-9
2	Genesis 9–15	1	§§947–1885	978-0-87785-487-6
3	Genesis 16–21	2 (in 6 fascicles)	§§1886–2759	978-0-87785-488-3
4	Genesis 22–26	3	§§2760–3485	978-0-87785-489-0
5	Genesis 27–30	3	§§3486–4055	978-0-87785-490-6
6	Genesis 31–35	4	§§4056–4634	978-0-87785-491-3
7	Genesis 36–40	4	§§4635–5190	978-0-87785-492-0
8	Genesis 41–44	5	§§5191–5866	978-0-87785-493-7
9	Genesis 45–50	5	§§5867–6626	978-0-87785-494-4
10	Exodus 1–8	6	§§6627–7487	978-0-87785-495-1
11	Exodus 9–15	6	§§7488–8386	978-0-87785-496-8
12	Exodus 16–21	7	§§8387–9111	978-0-87785-497-5
13	Exodus 22–24	7	§§9112–9442	978-0-87785-498-2
14	Exodus 25–29	8	§§9443–10166	978-0-87785-499-9
15	Exodus 30–40	8	§§10167–10837	978-0-87785-500-2

ISBN of e-book of library edition, vol. 7: 978-0-87785-734-1
ISBN of Portable Edition, vol. 7, containing translation only: 978-0-87785-423-4
ISBN of e-book of Portable Edition, vol. 7: 978-0-87785-729-7

(The ISBN in the Library of Congress data shown below is that of volume 1.)

Library of Congress Cataloging-in-Publication Data

Swedenborg, Emanuel, 1688–1772.
 [Arcana coelestia. English]
 Secrets of heaven / Emanuel Swedenborg ; translated from the Latin by
Lisa Hyatt Cooper. — Portable New Century ed.
  p. cm.
 Includes bibliographical references and indexes.
 ISBN 978-0-87785-408-1 (alk. paper)
 1. New Jerusalem Church—Doctrines. 2. Bible. O.T. Genesis—Commentaries—Early works to 1800. 3. Bible. O.T. Exodus—Commentaries—Early works to 1800. I. Title.
 BX8712.A8 2010
 230'.94—dc22
                                                                              2009054171

Ornaments from the first Latin edition, 1749–1756
Text designed by Joanna V. Hill
Senior copy editor, Alicia L. Dole
Typesetting by Mary M. Wachsmann and Sarah Dole
Cover design by Karen Connor
Cover photograph by Magda Indigo

Further information about the New Century Edition of the Works of Emanuel Swedenborg can be obtained directly from the Swedenborg Foundation, 70 Buckwalter Road, Suite 900 PMB 405, Royersford, PA 19468 U.S.A.
Telephone: (610) 430-3222 • Web: www.swedenborg.com • E-mail: info@swedenborg.com

Contents

Volume 7

Conventions Used in This Work   VII

Genesis Chapter 36

§§4635–4638 / [Matthew 25:1–13]   3

Text of Genesis Chapter 36   7

§4639 / Summary of Genesis 36   10

§§4640–4651 / Inner Meaning of Genesis 36   10

§§4652–4660 / Correspondence with the Universal Human, or Heaven (Continued): Correspondence of Sound and the Ears   17

Genesis Chapter 37

§§4661–4664 / [Matthew 25:31–46]   23

Text of Genesis Chapter 37   25

§4665 / Summary of Genesis 37   27

§§4666–4790 / Inner Meaning of Genesis 37   28

§§4791–4806 / Correspondence with the Universal Human (Continued): Correspondence of Taste and the Tongue, and of the Face   124

Genesis Chapter 38

§§4807–4810 / [Matthew 25:31–33]   133

Text of Genesis Chapter 38   135

§§4811–4812 / Summary of Genesis 38   137

§§4813–4930 / Inner Meaning of Genesis 38   137

§§4931–4953 / Correspondence with the Universal Human (Continued): Correspondence of the Hands, Arms, Feet, and Lower Torso   212

Genesis Chapter 39

§§4954–4959 / [Matthew 25:34–36]   221

Text of Genesis Chapter 39   223

§§4960–4961 / Summary of Genesis 39   225

§§4962–5049 / Inner Meaning of Genesis 39   225

§§5050–5062 / Correspondence with the Universal Human (Continued): Correspondence of the Lower Torso and the Reproductive Organs   278

Genesis Chapter 40

§§5063–5071 / [Matthew 25:37–46]   285

Text of Genesis Chapter 40   289

§5072 / Summary of Genesis 40   290

§§5073–5170 / Inner Meaning of Genesis 40   291

§§5171–5190 / Correspondence with the Universal Human (Continued): Correspondence of the Internal Organs   380

Biographical Note   391

Conventions Used in This Work

MOST of the following conventions apply generally to the translations in the New Century Edition Portable series. For introductory material on the content and history of *Secrets of Heaven,* and for annotations on the subject matter, including obscure or problematic content, and extensive indexes, the reader is referred to the Deluxe New Century Edition volumes.

Volume designation *Secrets of Heaven* was originally published in eight volumes; in this edition all but the second original volume have been divided into two. Thus Swedenborg's eight volumes now fill fifteen volumes, of which this is the seventh. It corresponds to approximately the second half of Swedenborg's volume 4.

Section numbers Following a practice common in his time, Swedenborg divided his published theological works into sections numbered in sequence from beginning to end. His original section numbers have been preserved in this edition; they appear in boxes in the outside margins. Traditionally, these sections have been referred to as "numbers" and designated by the abbreviation "n." In this edition, however, the more common section symbol (§) is used to designate the section numbers, and the sections are referred to as such.

Subsection numbers Because many sections throughout Swedenborg's works are too long for precise cross-referencing, Swedenborgian scholar John Faulkner Potts (1838–1923) further divided them into subsections; these have since become standard, though minor variations occur from one edition to another. These subsections are indicated by bracketed numbers that appear in the text itself: [2], [3], and so on. Because the beginning of the first *subsection* always coincides with the beginning of the *section* proper, it is not labeled in the text.

Citations of Swedenborg's text As is common in Swedenborgian studies, text citations of Swedenborg's works refer not to page numbers but to section numbers, which unlike page numbers are uniform in most editions. In citations the section symbol (§) is generally omitted after the title of a work by Swedenborg. Thus "*Secrets of Heaven* 29" refers to section 29 (§29) of Swedenborg's *Secrets of Heaven,* not to page 29 of any edition.

Subsection numbers are given after a colon; a reference such as "29:2" indicates subsection 2 of section 29. The reference "29:1" would indicate the first subsection of section 29, though that subsection is not in fact labeled in the text. Where section numbers stand alone without titles, their function is indicated by the prefixed section symbol; for example, "§29:2".

Citations of Swedenborg's unnumbered sections Some material in *Secrets of Heaven* was not given a section number. Swedenborg assigns no section numbers to his quoting of a biblical chapter before he takes up each verse in turn. He also gives no section numbers to occasional prefatory material, such as his author's table of contents in *Secrets of Heaven* (before §1), his prefaces to Genesis 16 and 18 (before §§1886 and 2135, respectively), and his preface to Genesis 22 (before §2760). The biblical material needs no section number, as it is referred to simply by chapter and verse. In this edition, references to the author's unnumbered prefaces follow these models: "(preface to Genesis 22)"; "see the preface to Genesis 18."

Citations of the Bible Biblical citations in this edition follow the accepted standard: a semicolon is used between book references and between chapter references, and a comma between verse references. Therefore "Matthew 5:11, 12; 6:1; 10:41, 42; Luke 6:23, 35" would refer to Matthew chapter 5, verses 11 and 12; Matthew chapter 6, verse 1; Matthew chapter 10, verses 41 and 42; and Luke chapter 6, verses 23 and 35. Swedenborg often incorporated the numbers of verses not actually represented in his text when listing verse numbers for a passage he quoted; these apparently constitute a kind of "see also" reference to other material he felt was relevant. This edition includes these extra verses and also follows Swedenborg where he cites contiguous verses individually (for example, John 14:8, 9, 10, 11), rather than as a range (John 14:8–11). Occasionally this edition supplies a full, conventional Bible reference where Swedenborg omits one after a quotation.

Quotations in Swedenborg's works Some features of the original Latin text of *Secrets of Heaven* have been modernized in this edition. For example, Swedenborg's first edition generally relies on context or italics rather than on quotation marks to indicate passages taken from the Bible or from other works. The manner in which these conventions are used in the original suggests that Swedenborg did not belabor the distinction between direct quotation and paraphrase; but in this edition, directly quoted material is indicated by either block quotations or quotation marks, and paraphrased material is usually presented without such indicators. In passages of dialog as well, quotation marks have been introduced that were not present as such in the original. Furthermore, Swedenborg did not mark his omissions from or changes to material he quoted, a practice in which this edition generally follows him. One exception consists of those instances in which Swedenborg did not include a complete sentence at the beginning or end of a Bible quotation. The omission in such cases has been marked in this edition with added points of ellipsis.

Grammatical anomalies Swedenborg sometimes uses a singular verb with certain dual subjects such as love and wisdom, goodness and truth, and love and charity. The wider context of his works indicates that his reason for doing so is that he understands the two given subjects as forming a unity. This translation generally preserves such singular verbs.

Italicized terms Any words in indented scriptural extracts that are here set in italics reflect a similar emphasis in the first edition.

Special use of vertical rule The opening passages of the early chapters of *Secrets of Heaven,* as well as the ends of all chapters, contain material that derives in some way from Swedenborg's experiences in the spiritual world. Swedenborg specified that the text of these and similar passages be set in continuous italics to distinguish it from exegetical and other material. For this edition, the heavy use of italic text was felt to be antithetical to modern tastes, as well as difficult to read, and so such passages are instead marked by a vertical rule in the margin.

Changes to and insertions in the text This translation is based on the first Latin edition, published by Swedenborg himself (1749–1756); it also reflects emendations in the third Latin edition, edited by P. H. Johnson, John E. Elliott, and others, and published by the Swedenborg Society (1949–1973). It incorporates the silent correction of minor errors, not only in the text proper but in Bible verse references and in section references to this and other volumes of *Secrets of Heaven.* The text has also been changed without notice where the verse numbering of the Latin Bible cited by Swedenborg differs from that of modern English Bibles. Throughout the translation, references or cross-references that were implied but not stated have been inserted in brackets; for example, [John 3:27]. In many cases, it is very difficult to determine what Swedenborg had in mind when he referred to other passages giving evidence for a statement or providing further discussion on a topic. Because of this difficulty, the missing references that are occasionally supplied in this edition should not be considered definitive or exhaustive. In contrast to such references in square brackets, references that occur in parentheses are those that appear in the first edition; for example, (1 Samuel 30:16), (see §42 above). Occasionally square brackets signal an insertion of other material that was not present in the first edition. These insertions fall into two classes: words likely to have been deleted through a copying or typesetting error, and words supplied by the translator as necessary for the understanding of the English text, though they have no direct parallel in the Latin. The latter device has been used sparingly, however, even at the risk of some inconsistency in its application. Unfortunately, no annotations concerning these insertions can be supplied in this Portable edition.

Biblical titles Swedenborg refers to the Hebrew Scriptures as the Old Testament and to the Greek Scriptures as the New Testament; his terminology has been adopted in this edition. As was the custom in his day, he refers to the Pentateuch (Genesis, Exodus, Leviticus, Numbers, and Deuteronomy) simply as "Moses"; for example, in §4925:5 he writes "as recorded in Moses" and then quotes passages from Exodus and Numbers. Similarly, in sentences or phrases introducing quotations he sometimes refers to the Psalms as "David," to Lamentations as "Jeremiah," and to the Gospel of John, the Epistles of John, and the Book of Revelation as simply "John." Conventional references supplied in parentheses after such quotations specify their sources more precisely.

Problematic content Occasionally Swedenborg makes statements that, although mild by the standards of eighteenth-century theological discourse, now read as harsh, dismissive, or insensitive. The most problematic are assertions about or criticisms of various religious traditions and their adherents—including Judaism, ancient or contemporary; Roman Catholicism; Islam; and the Protestantism in which Swedenborg himself grew up. These statements are far outweighed in size and importance by other passages in Swedenborg's works earnestly maintaining the value of every individual and of all religions. This wider context is discussed in the introductions and annotations of the Deluxe edition mentioned above. In the present format, however, problematic statements must be retained without comment. The other option—to omit them—would obscure some aspects of Swedenborg's presentation and in any case compromise its historicity.

Allusive References in Expositional Material

Swedenborg's use of pronouns that refer back to vague or distant antecedents may cause confusion for readers. Such allusive references occur in two situations in his expositions:

In mentions of Jesus If the pronoun *he* without a nearby antecedent appears in a proposition, the reader can assume that it refers to Jesus, the main topic of the exegesis as a whole.

In preview material Swedenborg's preview sections (see the Deluxe edition of *Secrets of Heaven*, vol. 1, pages 30–35) feature a series of propositions, each of which consists of a phrase of biblical text followed by a brief assertion of its inner meaning. These glimpses of the inner meaning quite often use pronouns that point back to other inner meanings mentioned earlier in the preview section. For instance, in §4962, a preview section, we read this:

> *And Joseph* symbolizes spiritual heavenliness drawing on rationality. *Was taken down to Egypt* means to religious learning. *And Potiphar, Pharaoh's chamberlain, bought him* means that **it** had a place among items of inner knowledge. *The chief of the bodyguards* means **that** were of primary importance in interpretation. *An Egyptian man* symbolizes earthly truth.

The words "it" and "that" (shown here in boldface) are confusing: *What* had a place among items of inner knowledge? *What things* were of primary importance in interpretation? The answers lie in the fragments of inner meaning given in propositions earlier in the preview section: The "it" refers back to the "spiritual heavenliness" mentioned in the first proposition. The referent of "that" is the "items of inner knowledge" mentioned at the end of the immediately preceding proposition. Thus Swedenborg has laid the propositions out in such a way that if put together, the five statements might read as follows:

> *And Joseph was taken down to Egypt, and Potiphar, Pharaoh's chamberlain, the chief of the bodyguards, an Egyptian man, bought him* means that spiritual heavenliness drawing on rationality was brought to religious learning and given a place among items of inner knowledge and earthly truth that were of primary importance in interpretation.

SECRETS
OF
HEAVEN

Genesis 36

[Matthew 25:1–13]

THE Lord's predictions in Matthew 24 about the church's final days have already been explained in sections introducing some Genesis chapters [§§3353–3356, 3486–3489, 3650–3655, 3751–3757, 3897–3901, 4056–4060, 4229–4231, 4332–4335, 4422–4424, 4535]. The subject continues in Matthew 25, so let me also explain the inner meaning of that material in order. Here it is in its literal form: **4635**

> Then the kingdom of the heavens will become like ten young women who, taking their lamps, went out to meet the bridegroom. And five of them were prudent, but five were stupid. Those who were stupid, taking their lamps, did not take oil with them. But the prudent took oil in their vessels with their lamps. And the groom being late, they all slumbered and slept. And in the middle of the night a shout was raised: "Look! The groom is coming! Go out to meet him!" Then all the young women woke up and adorned their lamps. But the stupid said to the prudent, "Give us some of your oil, because our lamps are going out." And the prudent answered, saying, "[No,] or there might not be enough for us and you. But rather go to the vendors and buy for yourselves." As they went to buy, though, the groom came, and the well-prepared ones went in with him to the wedding, and the door was closed. And later the other young women also come, saying, "Lord! Lord! Open up to us!" But he, answering, said, "Truly, I say to you: I do not know you." Be watchful, therefore, because you do not know the day or the hour in which the Son of Humankind is to come. (Matthew 25:1–13)

The Lord used this parable to depict his Coming, as can be seen from the details and from the ending, where he says, "Be watchful, therefore, because you do not know the day or the hour in which the Son of Humankind is to come." He says something similar in the previous chapter, Matthew 24, where he talks explicitly about his Coming: "Be **4636** watchful, then, because you do not know at what hour your Lord is to come" (verse 42). I have already shown that his Coming is the close of the age, or the final days of the church [§§931, 1850, 2118, 2243, 3353, 4422, 4535].

4637   Absolutely everything the Lord said in parable represented and symbolized the spiritual and heavenly qualities of his kingdom and (in the highest sense) divine qualities in himself. This is quite plain. People who do not know it cannot grasp that the Lord's parables are anything more than common metaphors or that they conceal anything further in their inmost recesses. That is how they look at this parable about the ten young women, for instance, unless they know what is symbolized on an inner level by the young women, by ten, five, lamps, vessels, oil, vendors, a wedding, and so on. It is the same for all the other parables.

What the Lord said in these stories appears in its outward form like everyday metaphors, as just mentioned, but in its inward form it is such that it fills the whole of heaven. Present in every detail is an inner meaning whose spiritual and heavenly content spreads throughout the heavens in every direction like fire and light. It exists high above the literal meaning and flows from each sentence, each word, and even every jot.

What this parable involves in its inner meaning becomes clear from the following comments.

4638   *Then the kingdom of the heavens will become like ten young women* symbolizes the last days of the old church and the first stage of a new one, the church being the Lord's kingdom on earth. The ten young women mean everyone in the church—both those committed to what is good and true and those committed to what is evil and false. In an inner sense, ten means a remnant, and also completeness, and therefore everyone. Young women mean people in the church. This holds true elsewhere in the Word, too.

[2] *Who, taking their lamps,* symbolizes spiritual qualities holding what is heavenly—in other words, true ideas holding what is good, or faith holding charity for one's neighbor, and charity holding love for the Lord. (Oil means a loving goodness, as will be discussed below.) Lamps *without* oil, though, mean those same things not holding any goodness.

[3] *Went out to meet the bridegroom* symbolizes their welcome.

And five of them were prudent, but five were stupid symbolizes the portion of them whose true ideas are full of goodness and the portion whose true ideas hold no goodness. The first group is the prudent women, and the second is the stupid ones. In an inner sense, five means some, so in this case it means a portion of them.

Those who were stupid, taking their lamps, did not take oil with them means that they did not have charitable goodness in their truth. Oil in an inner sense means good done out of charity and love.

But the prudent took oil in their vessels with their lamps means that their truth did hold a charitable, loving goodness. Vessels mean religious teachings.

[4] *And the groom being late, they all slumbered and slept* symbolizes a delay and consequent doubt. In an inner sense, slumbering means becoming lazy in religious matters as a result of the delay. Sleeping means experiencing doubt—for the prudent, doubt behind which there is an affirmative attitude, and for the stupid, doubt behind which there is a negative attitude.

And in the middle of the night a shout was raised symbolizes a period that was the last stage of the old church and the first stage of a new one. This period is what the Word refers to as night, when treating of the church's state. The shout means a change.

"Look! The groom is coming! Go out to meet him!" has the same symbolism as a judgment, namely, acceptance and rejection.

[5] *Then all the young women woke up, they adorned their lamps,* symbolizes preparation by all of them. People with truth that is empty of goodness trust that they will be accepted just as much as people with truth that is full of goodness. They think faith by itself brings salvation, not realizing that where charity is lacking there is no faith.

But the stupid said to the prudent, "Give us some of your oil, because our lamps are going out," means that they want other people to lend goodness to their empty truth, their hollow faith. In the other world, everyone shares everything spiritual and heavenly with each other, but only through the medium of goodness.

[6] *And the prudent answered, saying, "[No,] or there might not be enough for us and you,"* means that it cannot be lent, because the little goodness they have would be taken from them. In the other life, when goodness is shared with people committed to truths devoid of goodness, they in effect rob the goodness from the giver and claim it as their own. They do not share it with others but defile it. As a result, no one ever lends goodness to them. A description of my experience of these people will appear at the end of the next chapter, Genesis 37 [§§4804–4805].

[7] *"But rather go to the vendors and buy for yourselves"* symbolizes self-righteous goodness. Vendors mean people who boast of their goodness. People who possess truth that is devoid of goodness are more likely than others in the next life to take credit for everything they have done that looked good on the outside, even if it was evil on the inside. As the Lord says in Matthew,

> Many will say to me on that day, "Lord! Lord! Haven't we prophesied in your name and cast out demons in your name and exercised many powers in your name?" But then I'll proclaim to them, "I do not know you. Leave me, you evildoers!" (Matthew 7:22, 23)

And in Luke:

> From the time the householder rises and shuts the door, then you will start to stand outside and knock on the door, saying, "Lord! Lord! Open up to us!" But answering, he will say to you, "I do not know you, where you are from." Then you will start to say, "We ate in front of you, and drank, and in our streets you taught." But he will say, "I tell you I do not know you, where you are from. Leave me, all you evildoers!" (Luke 13:25, 26, 27)

They are the kind of people meant by the stupid young women. That is why something similar is said here of these: "They also came, saying, 'Lord! Lord! Open up to us!' But he, answering, said, 'Truly, I say to you: I do not know you.'"

[8] *As they went to buy, though, the groom came* symbolizes a completely backward approach.

And the well-prepared ones went in with him to the wedding means that people with goodness and therefore with truth are taken into heaven. Heaven is compared to a wedding because of the heavenly marriage, the marriage of goodness and truth. The Lord is compared to a bridegroom because these people are then united with him. That is why the church is called a bride.

And the door was closed means that others cannot go in.

[9] *And later the other young women also come, saying, "Lord! Lord! Open up to us!"* means that they want to go in on the basis of faith by itself without charity, and good deeds filled not with the Lord's life but with self-centered life.

But he, answering, said, "Truly, I say to you: I do not know you," symbolizes rejection. In an inner sense, not knowing them means their not having any charity for their neighbor or any bond with the Lord through charity. People who do not have this bond are being described as unknown.

[10] *Be watchful, therefore, because you do not know the day or the hour in which the Son of Humankind is to come* symbolizes being intent on living a life in keeping with faith's precepts. This is what being watchful means. We do not know when or in what state we will be taken [to the other world], and this is symbolized by "you do not know the day or the hour in which the Son of Humankind is to come."

There is also another place in Matthew where the Lord ascribes prudence to people who have goodness—people who live by the commandments—but stupidity to those who know what is true and do not live by it:

> Everyone who hears my words and does them, I will compare that person to a *prudent* man. And everyone hearing my words and yet not doing them will be compared to a *stupid* man. (Matthew 7:24, 26)

Genesis 36

1. And these are the births of Esau, that is, Edom.

2. Esau took his women from the daughters of Canaan: Adah daughter of Elon the Hittite, and Oholibamah, daughter of Anah son of Zibeon the Hivite,

3. and Basemath, daughter of Ishmael, sister of Nebaioth.

4. And Adah bore Eliphaz to Esau, and Basemath bore Reuel.

5. And Oholibamah bore Jeush and Jalam and Korah. These were the sons of Esau who were born to him in the land of Canaan.

6. And Esau took his women and his sons and his daughters and all the souls of his household, and his gain and every animal of his and all his purchases that he had acquired in the land of Canaan and went to a land away from Jacob his brother,

7. because their acquisitions were too much for living together and the land of their immigrant journeys could not bear them because of their gains.

8. And Esau lived on Mount Seir. Esau is Edom.

9. And these are the births of Esau, father of Edom, on Mount Seir.

10. These are the names of the sons of Esau: Eliphaz, son of Adah wife of Esau; Reuel, son of Basemath wife of Esau.

11. And the sons of Eliphaz were Teman, Omar, Zepho, and Gatam, and Kenaz.

12. And Timna was a concubine of Eliphaz son of Esau, and she bore Amalek to Eliphaz. These were the sons of Adah wife of Esau.

13. And these were the sons of Reuel: Nahath and Zerah, Shammah and Mizzah. These were the sons of Basemath wife of Esau.

14. And these were the sons of Oholibamah, daughter of Anah son of Zibeon, wife of Esau; and she bore Jeush and Jalam and Korah to Esau.

15. These were the commanders of the children of Esau, the sons of Eliphaz, Esau's firstborn: the commander Teman, the commander Omar, the commander Zepho, the commander Kenaz,

16. the commander Korah, the commander Gatam, the commander Amalek. These were the commanders of Eliphaz in the land of Edom. These were Adah's sons.

17. And these were the sons of Reuel son of Esau: the commander Nahath, the commander Zerah, the commander Shammah, the commander Mizzah. These were the commanders of Reuel in the land of Edom. These were the sons of Basemath wife of Esau.

18. And these were the sons of Oholibamah wife of Esau: the commander Jeush, the commander Jalam, the commander Korah. These were the commanders of Oholibamah, daughter of Anah, wife of Esau.

19. These were the sons of Esau, and these were their commanders; he is Edom.

20. These were the sons of Seir the Horite, inhabitants of the land: Lotan and Shobal and Zibeon and Anah

21. and Dishon and Ezer and Dishan. These were the commanders of the Horite, the sons of Seir, in the land of Edom.

22. And the sons of Lotan were Hori and Heman; and the sister of Lotan was Timna.

23. And these were the sons of Shobal: Alvan and Manahath and Ebal, Shepho and Onam.

24. And these were the sons of Zibeon: both Aiah and Anah. This is the Anah who found the mules in the wilderness as he was pasturing the donkeys for Zibeon his father.

25. And these were the children of Anah: Dishan and Oholibamah daughter of Anah.

26. And these were the sons of Dishan: Hemdan and Eshban and Ithran and Cheran.

27. These were the sons of Ezer: Bilhan and Zaavan and Akan.

28. These were the sons of Dishan: Uz and Aran.

29. These were the commanders of the Horite: the commander Lotan, the commander Shobal, the commander Zibeon, the commander Anah,

30. the commander Dishon, the commander Ezer, the commander Dishan. These were the commanders of the Horite, by their commanders, in the land of Seir.

31. And these are the monarchs who reigned in the land of Edom, before the reigning of a monarch for the children of Israel.

32. And Bela son of Beor reigned in Edom, and the name of his city was Dinhabah.

33. And Bela died, and in his place reigned Jobab son of Zerah from Bozrah.

34. And Jobab died, and in his place reigned Husham from the land of the Temanites.

35. And Husham died, and in his place reigned Hadad son of Bedad, who struck Midian in the field of Moab; and the name of his city was Avith.

36. And Hadad died, and in his place reigned Samlah from Masrekah.

37. And Samlah died, and in his place reigned Saul from Rehoboth of the River.

38. And Saul died, and in his place reigned Baal-hanan son of Achbor.

39. And Baal-hanan son of Achbor died, and in his place reigned Hadar, and the name of his city was Pau, and the name of his wife was Mehetabel, daughter of Matred daughter of Me-zahab.

40. And these are the names of the commanders of Esau by their clans, by their places, as to their names: the commander Timna, the commander Alvah, the commander Jetheth,

41. the commander Oholibamah, the commander Elah, the commander Pinon,

42. the commander Kenaz, the commander Teman, the commander Mibzar,

43. the commander Magdiel, the commander Iram. These are the commanders of Edom by their dwellings in the land of their possession. He is Esau, father of Edom.

Summary

4639 IN an inner sense this has to do with the Lord's divine goodness on the earthly plane. The names describe the pattern in which all that goodness is arranged. Esau means the Lord's divine goodness on the earthly plane.

Inner Meaning

4640 GENESIS 36:1. *And these are the births of Esau, that is, Edom.*

These are the births of Esau symbolizes developments in the divine goodness on the Lord's earthly level. *That is, Edom* symbolizes the earthly and bodily aspects of the Lord as a divine-human being.

4641 *These are the births of Esau* symbolizes developments in the divine goodness on the Lord's earthly level, as the following shows: *Births* symbolize what develops—what develops out of goodness and truth—as discussed in §§1330, 3263, 3279, 3860, 3868, 4070. And *Esau* represents divine goodness on the Lord's earthly level, as discussed in §§3302, 3322, 3494, 3504, 3576, 3599. This goodness is the theme of the current chapter. However, by nature it is inaccessible to any person's intellect and only barely accessible to any angel's, so it is portrayed by names alone.

Divine goodness on the Lord's earthly level, which Esau represents, is the goodness that was divine in him from birth. He was conceived by Jehovah, so from birth he had divine beingness. This beingness served as his soul and consequently as the core of his life. [2] On the outside it was clothed with attributes he inherited from his mother, and because these were not good but intrinsically evil, he banished them by his own power, particularly through the struggles of spiritual trial. Then, having recreated this humanity in himself, he united it with the divine goodness he had from birth. Jacob represented the goodness the Lord acquired by his own power (as described in previous chapters). This is the goodness he united with his divine goodness. In doing so he made the humanity in himself completely divine.

The goodness that Esau represents flowed directly into the Lord's earthly plane by an inner route, through goodness on the rational plane. The goodness that Jacob and Israel represents flowed in by an outer route. It was met by a divine inflow into the earthly plane through goodness on the rational plane, but indirectly, through truth on the rational plane. Isaac represents this rational type of goodness, and Rebekah represents this rational type of truth; see the earlier discussion of this subject at §§3314, 3573, 4563 at the end.

That is, Edom symbolizes the earthly and bodily aspects of the Lord as a divine-human being. This can be seen from the representation of *Edom* as earthly goodness in the Lord's divine humanity, to which doctrinal truth is linked (discussed in §§3302, 3322, 4241). Edom therefore represents the earthly and bodily aspects, since doctrines are like a physical body for truth. To put it in spiritual terms, doctrines are the bodily level of earthly truth. That is why Edom represents the earthly and bodily aspects of the Lord as a divine human. Doctrine is like an embodiment of truth because doctrine itself is not truth; it has truth within it, like a soul in its body.

[2] The theme of the verses that follow is divine goodness on the Lord's earthly plane, and what developed out of that goodness is portrayed by the names, for the reason given above: that such offshoots exceed the grasp of any person and even of an angel. Angels are finite, and what is finite cannot comprehend what is infinite. Still, when people read this chapter, the developments contained in the names are represented to angels in a general way, through the inflow of divine love from the Lord by means of heavenly fire that touches their hearts with divine goodness.

[3] Some people doubt that the Word was inspired down to its smallest jot. They do not believe it was inspired in such a way that every series represents divine and therefore heavenly and spiritual things, or that every word symbolizes those things. Such people inevitably doubt that these names involve anything more than Esau's genealogy. But what does a genealogy have to do with the Word? What is divine in it? On the point that all names in the Word have symbolic meaning, see §§1224, 1264, 1876, 1888, 4442, and any other place where the symbolism of names is explained.

Genesis 36:2, 3, 4, 5. *Esau took his women from the daughters of Canaan: Adah daughter of Elon the Hittite, and Oholibamah, daughter of Anah son of Zibeon the Hivite, and Basemath, daughter of Ishmael, sister of Nebaioth. And Adah bore Eliphaz to Esau, and Basemath bore Reuel. And Oholibamah bore Jeush and Jalam and Korah. These were the sons of Esau who were born to him in the land of Canaan.*

Esau took his women from the daughters of Canaan symbolizes the initial union of earthly goodness with a desire for what appears to be true. *Adah daughter of Elon the Hittite, and Oholibamah, daughter of Anah son of Zibeon the Hivite,* symbolizes the nature of that desire, that it came from the ancient church. *And Basemath, daughter of Ishmael, sister of Nebaioth,* symbolizes a second union, with a desire for truth from divine stock. *And Adah bore Eliphaz to Esau, and Basemath bore Reuel* symbolizes the initial offshoots. *And Oholibamah bore Jeush and Jalam and Korah* symbolizes a second offshoot. *These were the sons of Esau who were born to him in the land of Canaan* means from what is good in the Lord's kingdom.

4644   Again, the theme here is the goodness that was divine in the Lord from birth; the bond that kind of goodness had with the truth and goodness he obtained for himself as a person born on earth; and resulting developments. These subjects are inaccessible even to the angelic mind, as noted [§§4641, 4642], so they cannot be explained individually. Besides, this divine goodness with its offshoots is being portrayed simply by names. To explain names by themselves, without any narrative context to shed confirmatory light, would be to cast the matter into doubt. Not many people can believe that names in the Word have symbolic meaning, even if it is demonstrated to them. For these reasons let me just copy out the contents of the chapter and add some general explanation in terms that might be accessible to human understanding, although it will be no more than an outline. What exists in the Divine is never visible to anyone, but what emerges from the Divine does appear, though in a very general form (depending on the type of mind it falls into) and only in its outlines.

It is also important to realize that not a soul is born with any goodness, only with evil—inward evil from the father, and outward evil from the mother. Everyone's heredity is bad. Only the Lord was born with goodness—divine goodness itself—so far as he was born from the Father. This divine goodness that the Lord was born with is the current topic of discussion. Its offshoots are qualities that emerged in the Lord's human nature when he made it divine and that he used in glorifying that nature.

That is why I am able to add a certain amount of broad explanation.

4645   *Genesis 36:6, 7, 8. And Esau took his women and his sons and his daughters and all the souls of his household, and his gain and every animal of his and all his purchases that he had acquired in the land of Canaan and went to*

*a land away from Jacob his brother, because their acquisitions were too much
for living together and the land of their immigrant journeys could not bear
them because of their gains. And Esau lived on Mount Seir. Esau is Edom.*

*Esau took his women and his sons and his daughters and all the souls
of his household, and his gain and every animal of his and all his purchases
that he had acquired in the land of Canaan and went to a land away from
Jacob his brother* symbolizes everything involved in the resulting divine
goodness and truth that the Lord nonetheless possessed. All of it had
counterparts in heaven, so these words also symbolize heaven. Esau was
withdrawing from Jacob for the sake of the representation. *Because their
acquisitions were too much* means on account of its infinite extent. *For
living together* symbolizes representations. *And the land of their immigrant
journeys could not bear them because of their gains* means that none of it
is capable of being described. *And Esau lived on Mount Seir* symbolizes
truth developing out of earthly goodness. *Esau is Edom* symbolizes the
Lord's divine humanity.

Genesis 36:9, 10, 11, 12, 13, 14. *And these are the births of Esau, father
of Edom, on Mount Seir. These are the names of the sons of Esau: Eliphaz,
son of Adah wife of Esau; Reuel, son of Basemath wife of Esau. And the sons
of Eliphaz were Teman, Omar, Zepho, and Gatam, and Kenaz. And Timna
was a concubine of Eliphaz son of Esau, and she bore Amalek to Eliphaz.
These were the sons of Adah wife of Esau. And these were the sons of Reuel:
Nahath and Zerah, Shammah and Mizzah. These were the sons of Basemath
wife of Esau. And these were the sons of Oholibamah, daughter of Anah son
of Zibeon, wife of Esau; and she bore Jeush and Jalam and Korah to Esau.*

4646

These are the births of Esau, father of Edom, symbolizes developments
in divine goodness on the earthly level—*father of Edom* meaning the divine
goodness from which offshoots developed. *On Mount Seir* means in regard
to truth that comes of goodness. *These are the names of the sons of Esau* symbolizes the nature of the offshoots. *Eliphaz, son of Adah wife of Esau; Reuel,
son of Basemath wife of Esau,* symbolizes their state, resulting from a marriage of goodness and truth. *And the sons of Eliphaz were Teman, Omar,
Zepho, and Gatam, and Kenaz* symbolizes a first outgrowth from goodness. *And Timna was a concubine of Eliphaz son of Esau* symbolizes what
was subservient to those things. *And she bore Amalek to Eliphaz* symbolizes the sensory level. *These were the sons of Adah wife of Esau* symbolizes a
second outgrowth. *And these were the sons of Reuel: Nahath and Zerah,
Shammah and Mizzah; these were the sons of Basemath wife of Esau* symbolizes a third outgrowth. *And these were the sons of Oholibamah, daughter of*

Anah son of Zibeon, wife of Esau; and she bore Jeush and Jalam and Korah to Esau symbolizes subsequent developments.

4647   Genesis 36:15, 16, 17, 18, 19. *These were the commanders of the children of Esau, the sons of Eliphaz, Esau's firstborn: the commander Teman, the commander Omar, the commander Zepho, the commander Kenaz, the commander Korah, the commander Gatam, the commander Amalek. These were the commanders of Eliphaz in the land of Edom. These were Adah's sons. And these were the sons of Reuel son of Esau: the commander Nahath, the commander Zerah, the commander Shammah, the commander Mizzah. These were the commanders of Reuel in the land of Edom. These were the sons of Basemath wife of Esau. And these were the sons of Oholibamah wife of Esau: the commander Jeush, the commander Jalam, the commander Korah. These were the commanders of Oholibamah, daughter of Anah, wife of Esau. These were the sons of Esau, and these were their commanders; he is Edom.*

These were the commanders of the children of Esau symbolizes the main truths that come of goodness. *The sons of Eliphaz, Esau's firstborn: the commander Teman, the commander Omar, the commander Zepho, the commander Kenaz, the commander Korah, the commander Gatam, the commander Amalek* symbolizes a first category of truths, and their nature here, and their nature in the Lord's kingdom. *These were the commanders of Eliphaz in the land of Edom; these were Adah's sons* symbolizes the main ones in the first category. *And these were the sons of Reuel son of Esau: the commander Nahath, the commander Zerah, the commander Shammah, the commander Mizzah* symbolizes another category of truths and their nature, as they exist in heaven. *These were the commanders of Reuel in the land of Edom* symbolizes the second category. *These were the sons of Basemath wife of Esau* means resulting from a marriage of goodness and truth. *And these were the sons of Oholibamah wife of Esau* symbolizes the main truths of a third category. *The commander Jeush, the commander Jalam, the commander Korah* symbolizes their nature here, and consequently their nature in the Lord's kingdom. *These were the commanders of Oholibamah, daughter of Anah, wife of Esau,* symbolizes the main ones resulting from the union of goodness and truth. These twelve *commanders* are like the twelve tribes, according to the pattern in which goodness arranges them. *These were the sons of Esau, and these were their commanders* means that among truths that come of goodness, these are the main ones. *He is Edom* means in the Lord as a divine human.

4648   Genesis 36:20–28. *These were the sons of Seir the Horite, inhabitants of the land: Lotan and Shobal and Zibeon and Anah and Dishon and Ezer* *and Dishan. These were the commanders of the Horite, the sons of Seir, in the land of Edom. And the sons of Lotan were Hori and Heman; and the sister of Lotan was Timna. And these were the sons of Shobal: Alvan and Manahath and Ebal, Shepho and Onam. And these were the sons of Zibeon: both Aiah and Anah. This is the Anah who found the mules in the wilderness as he was pasturing the donkeys for Zibeon his father. And these were the children of Anah: Dishan and Oholibamah daughter of Anah. And these were the sons of Dishan: Hemdan and Eshban and Ithran and Cheran. These were the sons of Ezer: Bilhan and Zaavan and Akan. These were the sons of Dishan: Uz and Aran.*

[2] *These were the sons of Seir the Horite, inhabitants of the land,* symbolizes the resulting truths, in order. *Lotan and Shobal and Zibeon and Anah and Dishon and Ezer and Dishan* symbolizes their nature. *These were the commanders of the Horite, the sons of Seir,* symbolizes the main truths-from-goodness that grow out of the earlier ones. *In the land of Edom* means in the Lord as a divine human. *And the sons of Lotan were Hori and Heman; and the sister of Lotan was Timna* symbolizes a second category of truths. *And these were the sons of Shobal: Alvan and Manahath and Ebal, Shepho and Onam* symbolizes a third category and [some of] its qualities. [3] *And these were the sons of Zibeon: both Aiah and Anah* symbolizes [other] qualities of the third category. *This is the Anah who found the mules in the wilderness* symbolizes truth rising out of learning. *As he was pasturing the donkeys for Zibeon his father* means when the Lord was intent on knowledge. *And these were the children of Anah: Dishan and Oholibamah daughter of Anah* symbolizes [still other] qualities of the third category. *And these were the sons of Dishan: Hemdan and Eshban and Ithran and Cheran* symbolizes [some] qualities of a fourth category. *These were the sons of Ezer: Bilhan and Zaavan and Akan* symbolizes [other] qualities of the fourth category. *These were the sons of Dishan: Uz and Aran* symbolizes qualities of a fifth category.

Genesis 36:29, 30. *These were the commanders of the Horite: the commander Lotan, the commander Shobal, the commander Zibeon, the commander Anah, the commander Dishon, the commander Ezer, the commander Dishan. These were the commanders of the Horite, by their commanders, in the land of Seir.*

These were the commanders of the Horite symbolizes the main secondary [truths]. *The commander Lotan, the commander Shobal, the commander Zibeon, the commander Anah, the commander Dishon, the commander Ezer, the commander Dishan* symbolizes their nature. *These were the commanders of the Horite, by their commanders, in the land of Seir* symbolizes the main derivative ones.

4650   Genesis 36:31–39. *And these are the monarchs who reigned in the land of Edom, before the reigning of a monarch for the children of Israel. And Bela son of Beor reigned in Edom, and the name of his city was Dinhabah. And Bela died, and in his place reigned Jobab son of Zerah from Bozrah. And Jobab died, and in his place reigned Husham from the land of the Temanites. And Husham died, and in his place reigned Hadad son of Bedad, who struck Midian in the field of Moab; and the name of his city was Avith. And Hadad died, and in his place reigned Samlah from Masrekah. And Samlah died, and in his place reigned Saul from Rehoboth of the River. And Saul died, and in his place reigned Baal-hanan son of Achbor. And Baal-hanan son of Achbor died, and in his place reigned Hadar, and the name of his city was Pau, and the name of his wife was Mehetabel, daughter of Matred daughter of Me-zahab.*

These are the monarchs who reigned in the land of Edom symbolizes the primary truths the Lord possessed as a divine human. *Before the reigning of a monarch for the children of Israel* means at a point when spiritual truth deep within the earthly dimension had not yet arisen. *And Bela son of Beor reigned in Edom* symbolizes a first truth. *And the name of his city was Dinhabah* symbolizes a theology springing from it. *And Bela died, and in his place reigned Jobab son of Zerah from Bozrah* symbolizes what grew out of this first truth, as from its essential element, and the nature of it. *And Jobab died, and in his place reigned Husham* symbolizes what grew out of this. *From the land of the Temanites* symbolizes where it came from. *And Husham died, and in his place reigned Hadad son of Bedad* symbolizes what grew out of this. *Who struck Midian in the field of Moab* symbolizes purification from falsity. *And the name of his city was Avith* symbolizes the doctrines springing from it. *And Hadad died, and in his place reigned Samlah from Masrekah* symbolizes what grew out of this, and its nature. *And Samlah died, and in his place reigned Saul* symbolizes what grew out of this. *From Rehoboth of the River* symbolizes its nature. *And Saul died, and in his place reigned Baal-hanan son of Achbor* symbolizes what grew out of this, and its nature. *And Baal-hanan son of Achbor died, and in his place reigned Hadar* symbolizes what grew out of this. *And the name of his city was Pau* symbolizes a theology. *And the name of his wife was Mehetabel, daughter of Matred daughter of Me-zahab* symbolizes the goodness in it.

Genesis 36:40, 41, 42, 43. *And these are the names of the commanders of*  *Esau by their clans, by their places, as to their names: the commander Timna, the commander Alvah, the commander Jetheth, the commander Oholibamah, the commander Elah, the commander Pinon, the commander Kenaz, the commander Teman, the commander Mibzar, the commander Magdiel, the commander Iram. These are the commanders of Edom by their dwellings in the land of their possession. He is Esau, father of Edom.*

These are the names of the commanders of Esau by their clans, by their places, as to their names, symbolizes the resulting doctrines teaching what is good, and their origin, state, and nature. *The commander Timna, the commander Alvah, the commander Jetheth, the commander Oholibamah, the commander Elah, the commander Pinon, the commander Kenaz, the commander Teman, the commander Mibzar, the commander Magdiel, the commander Iram* symbolizes the nature of these doctrines. *These are the commanders of Edom* symbolizes the main ones. *By their dwellings in the land of their possession* means in regard to truth and goodness. *He is Esau, father of Edom* symbolizes divine goodness on the earthly level of the Lord as a divine human.

Correspondence with the Universal Human, or Heaven (Continued): Correspondence of Sound and the Ears

WHAT kind of correspondence exists between the soul and the body, or between the attributes of the spirit inside a person and those of the body outside? The answer is plain from the way thought and awareness (which belong to the spirit) correspond to, act on, and communicate with speech and hearing (which belong to the body).

The thoughts we have when we are talking are nothing but the speech of our spirit, and our mental awareness of another's words is nothing but our spirit's capacity to hear. Admittedly, the thoughts we have when talking do not seem like speech to us, because they unite with the speech of our body and exist inside it. The mental impression we receive when listening does not seem any different from the sound in our ears. That is why most people, who have not reflected on it, cannot help thinking that all sensation is located in the physical organs. They inevitably believe that when death demolishes these organs, no sensation remains. That is actually the moment, though, when real, genuine sensation comes alive for us, or for our spirit.

[2] My conversations with spirits have made it obvious to me that the spirit is what speaks and hears. When their speech was conveyed to my spirit, it dropped into my own inner speech and from there into the corresponding organs, where it ended up as an impulse, which I plainly sensed several times. Their words, then, were as audible to me as the words of people on earth.

Once, some spirits talked to me while I was in the company of other people. The spirits' speech was so clearly audible that some of the spirits thought my companions would also be able to hear it. I countered that they could not hear it, because the spirits' words reach my ear by an inner route, and human speech by an outer route.

This shows how the Spirit spoke with the prophets—not the way one person talks to another but the way a spirit talks to a person: inside the person (Zechariah 1:9, 13, 19; 2:3; 4:1, 4, 5; 5:5, 10; 6:4; and other places).

However, I know that these ideas are incomprehensible to people who do not believe that a human being is a spirit, or that the body [merely] serves as a tool for useful activity in the world. People who have hardened themselves in this disbelief do not even want to hear about a supposed correspondence. If they do hear, their attitude is so negative that they reject it. In fact, the idea that *any* capacity is attributed to anything other than the body depresses them.

4653   Spirits who correspond to the power of hearing, or who constitute the area of the ear, are those given to simple obedience. They do not figure out whether an idea is true but believe it because others have said so. They can be called the epitome of obedience.

The reason they are like this is that hearing is to speech as a passive force is to its active force, or like a listener who agrees with a speaker. As a consequence, even in everyday language, hearing someone or listening to someone's voice means obeying. The inner depths of human language have risen mostly from correspondence, because the spirit of a person on earth lives among spirits in the other world and does its thinking there, although we do not know it in the least. A body-centered person does not even want to know.

[2] There are many different kinds of spirits corresponding to the ear, or rather to its purposes and functions. Each substructure of the ear has spirits that relate to it. Some relate to the outer ear; some to the membrane called the eardrum; to the deeper membranes called windows; and to the malleus, stapes, incus, canals, and cochlea. Some relate to components still deeper, all the way to substance-based structures that are closer to the spirit and finally that are in the spirit. Ultimately there are ear spirits who are tightly connected with the spirits belonging to the inner eye, differing from them in having less insight, but passively offering their support.

There were spirits with me who were flowing quite strongly into my thoughts while I was writing about the effects of providence, especially when I thought that what I was waiting and longing for would never happen. The angels described the spirits as ones who when they lived in the body grew angry if their prayers for something were not answered and therefore brought themselves into doubt about providence. Even so, when they were outside that state, they followed whatever religious path others told them to follow. They were obedient in a simple way, then.   4654

I heard that such spirits belong to the vicinity of the outer ear, or auricle. That is also where they showed up when talking with me.

Many other times too I noticed spirits around my ear, and also inside it, so to speak. When I noticed them inside, it was due to appearances. Conditions in the other world are what create the appearance.   4655

All of these spirits were unsophisticated and obedient.

There was a spirit who talked with me in my left ear, at the back, where the muscles that lift the ear are. He told me he was sent to say that he does not reflect on anything others say, as long as he catches it with his ears.   4656

When he spoke, he more or less belched the words. That is how he talks, he said. From this I could tell that his words had nothing inside them and therefore little life, which is why he belched as he did. I was told that spirits like this, who pay little attention to the meaning of a thing, belong to the outer ear, the part made of cartilage and bone.

Certain spirits talked with me several times in a whisper. They spoke near my left ear, as if they wanted to talk directly in my ear to prevent anyone from overhearing. I was allowed to tell them that this is not helpful in the other life, because it reveals that they had been gossips and that   4657 a gossip's character was now ingrained in them. Many of them like to watch for flaws and blemishes in others and report these to their friends when no one is listening; or when the victim is present, they speak in their friend's ear. They look at everything the wrong way, misinterpret it all, and consider themselves better than others. As a result they cannot possibly live among good spirits, whose nature prevents them from hiding their thoughts.

I learned that this kind of talk sounds louder in the other world than open speech.

4658   To the inner parts of the ear belong those who are farsighted because they listen inwardly, who obey what the spirit of their inner hearing speaks there, and who faithfully make known what it says. Their nature was shown to me.

A certain sound spreading from down on the left side of my torso up to my left ear became audible. I noticed there were spirits working to climb up this way, but could not tell what kind of spirits they were. When they made it to my ear, they talked with me, saying they were students of logic and metaphysics. That is what they immersed their minds in, their only goal being to develop their reputations as scholars and in this way obtain status and wealth. They now lived a wretched life, they complained, because they had steeped themselves in that study for no other purpose and therefore had not used it to develop their ability to reason. Their speech was slow and muffled.

[2] In the meantime there were two spirits talking to each other above my head. When I asked who they were, I was told that one of them was an extremely famous figure in the academic world, and I was given to believe that it was Aristotle. The other one was not identified. Then the first one was sent back into the frame of mind in which he had lived in the world. (Anyone can easily be returned to the state of life that had been his or hers in the world, because we take all the states of our life with us.) To my surprise, he positioned himself at my right ear, where he talked, hoarsely but intelligently. From the drift of his words I could tell that his character was entirely different from that of the scholars who had appeared first. To be specific, his own thoughts had been the source of his writings, and from them he produced his philosophy. The terms he came up with and applied to the subjects he was thinking about, then, were expressions for describing deep ideas. What is more, the pleasure of a desire and longing to learn about the realm of thought stirred him to this activity, and he obediently followed the inner call of his spirit. That

is why he was at my right ear. It is different with his followers, who are called Scholastics. They do not go from thoughts to terms but from terms to thoughts and therefore go backward. Many of them do not even make it as far as thoughts but stick exclusively to terms. If they put the terms to use, it is only to justify whatever they want and to plaster falsity with the appearance of truth, in keeping with their passion for persuading others. In their case, philosophy is a means of going insane rather than becoming wise and brings them darkness instead of light.

[3] Next I spoke with him about the science of analytical reasoning and was given the opportunity to say that what a child spontaneously utters in half an hour follows more rules of philosophy, analytical reasoning, and logic than *he* could describe in several volumes. This is because all human thought and speech is analytical, and the laws governing it come from the spiritual world. When people try to think artificially, on the basis of terms, they bear some resemblance to dancers who want to learn dancing by studying motor fibers and muscles. If that were what they focused on when dancing, they would hardly be able to move a toe. Without any knowledge of the science, though, they move all the motor fibers throughout their body and, by extension, their lungs, diaphragm, trunk, arms, neck, and so on, as would require more than a few volumes to describe. It is the same with people who want to think from terms. He agreed with all this, saying that people who learn this way are going about it backward. Those who want to be fools, he added, are welcome to continue in this fashion; but they should always be thinking about the purpose, and thinking deeply.

[4] Then he demonstrated for me the idea he had had of the Supreme Deity, whom he portrayed to himself as having a human face and a halo around the head. He now realizes that the Lord is the quintessential human being and that the halo is divinity radiating from the Lord, flowing into not just heaven but the entire universe, managing and governing it. Whoever manages and governs heaven, he said, manages and governs the universe as well. The one cannot be separated from the other. He added that he had believed in only one God, whose attributes and qualities were designated by various names, each of which was worshiped by others as a god.

[5] I saw a woman stretching out her hand, wanting to stroke my cheek. When I wondered about it, he said that when he lived in the world such a woman had often appeared to him and caressed his cheek, so to speak, and that her hand was beautiful. Some angelic spirits said that

the ancients sometimes saw such beings, whom they called Pallases. The vision had come to him, the angelic spirits said, from spirits who relished ideas and reveled in thought while living as people on earth in antiquity but did not use philosophy. Because he had such spirits with him and delighted them with his deep thinking, they presented such a woman to him as a representation.

[6] Last of all he told me how he had pictured the human soul or spirit, which he called the pneuma. He had viewed it as invisible but full of life, like something made of ether. He knew his spirit would live on after death, he said, because it was his inner essence, which cannot die, since it can think. He could not ruminate any further on it in a distinct way, only vaguely, because he had nowhere to learn about it except from himself and to some slight extent from other ancients.

Aristotle is among the sane spirits in the other world. Many of his devotees are among the idiots.

4659 At the end of §4652 I said that a human being is a spirit and that the body [merely] serves as a tool for useful activity in the world. In several other places I have said that the spirit is our inner part, and the body, our outer part. People who do not understand what the situation is with a person's spirit and body might suppose that this means the spirit dwells inside the body, and the body more or less envelops and clothes it. It needs to be known, though, that our spirit is in our body, in the whole and in every part of it. It is our purer substance, in both our motor and our sensory organs and everywhere else. Our body is the matter attached to it at every point and suited to the world in which we now are. That is what I mean by saying that a human being is a spirit, that the body serves as a tool for useful activity in the world, that the spirit is our inner part, and that the body is our outer part.

These comments also show that after death we have a similar life of action and sensation, and that we are in a human shape as in the world, but a more perfect one.

4660 There is more about correspondence with the universal human, or heaven, at the end of the next chapter, where the subject is the correspondence of taste and the tongue [§§4791–4806].

Genesis 37

[Matthew 25:31–46]

A T the head of the previous chapter I continued with the explanation of the Lord's prediction concerning the church's last days and the meaning of the parable about the ten young women in Matthew 25:1–13 [§§4635–4638]. What follows it is another parable—the parable of the slaves given talents by a person going abroad. This person gave five talents to one slave, two talents to another, and one talent to a third for them to do business with. The one who received five talents used them to make five more, the one who received two used them to make two more, and the one who received one talent hid it in the earth. This parable involves almost the same meaning as the parable of the ten young women, so let me jump ahead and explain the end of the same chapter. Here is how Matthew 25:31–end reads in the text:

4661

> When the Son of Humankind comes in his glory, and all the holy angels with him, then he will sit on his glorious throne. And all nations will assemble before him, and he will separate them from each other, as a shepherd separates the sheep from the goats. And he will indeed set the sheep on his right but the goats on the left. Then the King will say to those on his right, "Come, you who are blessed by my Father! Take possession of the kingdom prepared for you from the foundation of the world. For I was hungry and you gave me something to eat. I was thirsty and you gave me a drink. I was a foreigner and you gathered me in; naked and you clothed me. I was sick and you visited me. I was in jail and you came to me." Then the righteous will answer him, saying, "Lord, when did we see you hungry and feed you? Or thirsty and give you a drink? But when did we see you as a foreigner and gather you in? Or naked and clothe you? But when did we see you sick or in jail and come to you?" But answering, the King will say to them, "Truly, I say to you: so far as you did it for one of these least consequential brothers and sisters of mine, you did it for me." Then he will also say to those on

4662

the left, "Go away from me, you cursed ones, into eternal fire prepared
for the Devil and the Devil's angels! For I was hungry and you did not
give me something to eat. I was thirsty and you did not give me a drink.
I was a foreigner and you did not gather me in; naked, and you did not
clothe me; sick and in jail, and you did not visit me." Then these also
will answer him, saying, "Lord, when did we see you hungry or thirsty
or a foreigner or naked or sick or in jail and not tend to you?" Then he
will answer them, saying, "Truly, I say to you: so far as you did not do
it for one of these least consequential, you also did not do it for me."
And these will go away into eternal punishment, but the righteous into
eternal life. (Matthew 25:31–46)

4663   People who do not know the inner meaning cannot help imagining
that the Lord said all this about some doomsday on which everyone everywhere in the world will assemble before the Lord and that we are then to
be judged. They think that the process of judgment will happen exactly
the way it is depicted in the text—that he will set us on the right and
left and say these words to us. Some people do know the inner meaning,
however. Some have also learned from other passages in the Word that
the Lord never condemns anyone to eternal fire but that we each condemn ourselves, or cast ourselves into that fire. And some have learned
that we each have our own last judgment when we die. All these people
can to some extent see what the passage generally involves. Those who
know from the inner meaning and from correspondence what lies inside
the words can also see the specific symbolism of them, which is that we
receive our reward in the other life according to our life in the world.

[2] People who promote the idea that we are saved by faith alone can
explain this passage only by stating that what the Lord says about good
deeds refers to the fruits of faith. He mentioned these fruits, they claim,
only for the sake of the uneducated, who are unacquainted with religious
mysteries. Suppose their opinion is correct, though; the passage still makes
it plain that the fruits of faith are what bless and gladden us after death.
The fruits of faith are actually a life in keeping with the precepts of faith.
Living according to them is what saves us, then. Believing without living
does not. We take all the states of our life with us after we die, so that we
are the same as we had been in the body. Those who despised others in
comparison with themselves during bodily life also despise others in the
next life. Those who hated their neighbor during bodily life also hate their
neighbor in the next life. Those who deceived their companions during
bodily life also deceive them in the next life. And so on. The nature we

took on in physical life stays with us in the other life. People recognize that we cannot rid ourselves of our nature, and that if we do, no life remains.

[3] That is why the Lord mentions only deeds of neighborly love [in this passage], because people who do such deeds, in other words, who live a life of faith, can be granted faith—in the other life if not in this one. People who do not do charitable deeds, or do not live a life of faith, though, are completely unable to be granted faith, in either this life or the next. After all, evil is never compatible with truth. The one rejects the other. If people who subscribe to evil speak the truth, they speak from their lips, not from the heart; their evil and the truth are still polar opposites.

What is involved in the inner meaning of the Lord's words here concerning the Last Judgment (that is, everyone's last judgment after death) is too abundant to explain at the head of this chapter. With the Lord's divine mercy, then, it will be explained in sequence at the head of the chapters that follow [§§4807–4810, 4954–4959, 5063–5071].

4664

Genesis 37

1. And Jacob settled in the land of his father's immigrant journeys in the land of Canaan.

2. These are the births of Jacob: Joseph, a son of seventeen years, was pasturing the flock with his brothers (and he was a youth)—with the sons of Bilhah and with the sons of Zilpah, his father's women. And Joseph brought a bad report of them to their father.

3. And Israel loved Joseph above all his children, because he was the son of his old age; and he made him a coat of many colors.

4. And his brothers saw that their father loved him above all his brothers, and they hated him and could not speak to him in peace.

5. And Joseph dreamed a dream and told his brothers, and they added further to their hatred of him.

6. And he said to them, "Please listen to this dream that I dreamed.

7. And look! We were binding sheaves in the middle of the field, and look! My sheaf rose and even stood, and look! Your sheaves circled around and bowed down to my sheaf!"

8. And his brothers said to him, "Will you really rule over us? Are you really to dominate us?" And they added further to their hatred of him over his dreams and over his words.

9. And he dreamed still another dream and recounted it to his brothers and said, "Look! I dreamed another dream, and look! The sun and the moon and eleven stars bowing down to me!"

10. And he recounted it to his father and to his brothers, and his father scolded him and said to him, "What is this dream that you dreamed? Will we really come, I and your mother and your brothers, to bow down to you to the earth?"

11. And his brothers envied him, and his father kept the word [in mind].

12. And his brothers went to pasture their father's flock in Shechem.

13. And Israel said to Joseph, "Aren't your brothers shepherding in Shechem? Go, and let me send you to them." And [Joseph] said to him, "Here I am."

14. And [Israel] said to him, "Go, please; see the peace of your brothers and the peace of the flock and bring word back to me." And he sent him from the valley of Hebron, and [Joseph] came to Shechem.

15. And a man found him, and here, he was wandering in the field, and the man asked him, saying, "What are you looking for?"

16. And he said, "I am looking for my brothers; please tell me where they are shepherding."

17. And the man said, "They traveled on from here, because I heard them saying, 'Let's go to Dothan.'" And Joseph went after his brothers and found them in Dothan.

18. And they saw him from far off, and before he came close to them they plotted against him to put him to death.

19. And they said, a man to his brother, "Look: that lord of dreams comes!

20. And now come, and let's kill him and put him into one of the pits and say, 'A bad wild animal ate him up,' and we will see what his dreams will be!"

21. And Reuben listened and rescued him from their hand and said, "Let's not strike his soul."

22. And Reuben said to them, "Don't shed blood; put him into that pit that is in the wilderness and don't put a hand on him"—in order to rescue him from their hand, to return him to his father.

23. And it happened as Joseph came to his brothers that they stripped Joseph of his coat, the coat of many colors that was on him.

24. And they took him and put him into the pit; and the pit was empty, with no water in it.

25. And they sat to eat bread and lifted their eyes and looked, and here, a company of Ishmaelites came from Gilead, and their camels were carrying perfumes and resin and stacte as they went to take them down to Egypt.

26. And Judah said to his brothers, "What gain if we kill our brother and cover up his blood?

27. Come, and let's sell him to the Ishmaelites, and let our hand not be on him, because he is our brother, our flesh." And his brothers took heed.

28. And Midianite trader men came through and drew out and brought up Joseph from the pit and sold Joseph to the Ishmaelites for twenty pieces of silver, and they took Joseph to Egypt.

29. And Reuben returned to the pit and look, no Joseph in the pit; and he tore his clothes.

30. And he returned to his brothers and said, "The child is no more, and I, where do I go?"

31. And they took Joseph's coat and slaughtered a buck of the goats and dipped the coat in the blood.

32. And they sent the coat of many colors and took it to their father and said, "This we found; please recognize whether it is your son's coat or not."

33. And he recognized it and said, "My son's coat. A bad wild animal ate him up; Joseph has surely been mauled."

34. And Jacob tore his clothes and put sackcloth on his hips and mourned over his son many days.

35. And all his sons and all his daughters rose to comfort him, and he refused to comfort himself and said, "Because I will go down to my son mourning, to the grave." And his father cried for him.

36. And the Midianites sold him into Egypt, to Potiphar, Pharaoh's chamberlain, the chief of the bodyguards.

Summary

THE inner meaning of this chapter has to do with divine truth from the Lord's divine humanity, which the church rejected more and more

4665

over time, eventually accepting falsity instead. Specifically, it has to do with people possessing a faith detached from neighborly love and their opposition to the Lord's divine humanity.

Inner Meaning

4666 GENESIS 37:1, 2, 3. *And Jacob settled in the land of his father's immigrant journeys in the land of Canaan. These are the births of Jacob: Joseph, a son of seventeen years, was pasturing the flock with his brothers (and he was a youth)—with the sons of Bilhah and with the sons of Zilpah, his father's women. And Joseph brought a bad report of them to their father. And Israel loved Joseph above all his children, because he was the son of his old age; and he made him a coat of many colors.*

Jacob settled in the land of his father's immigrant journeys in the land of Canaan symbolizes the Lord's earthly divinity, living in harmony under divine goodness on the rational plane. *These are the births of Jacob* means that which follows. *Joseph* symbolizes the Lord's divine humanity on the spiritual plane. *A son of seventeen years* symbolizes its state. *Was pasturing the flock with his brothers* means that it was present among people of faith who were teaching. *And he was a youth* symbolizes the first stage. *With the sons of Bilhah and with the sons of Zilpah, his father's women,* means that he was rejected by them. *And Joseph brought a bad report of them to their father* means that [divine truth] showed what they were like. *And Israel loved Joseph above all his children* symbolizes the union of spiritual divinity on the rational level with spiritual divinity on the earthly level. *Because he was the son of his old age* symbolizes its life within that. *And he made him a coat of many colors* symbolizes resulting manifestations of truth by which the spiritual side of the earthly level is recognized and identified.

4667 *Jacob settled in the land of his father's immigrant journeys in the land of Canaan* symbolizes the Lord's earthly divinity, living in harmony under divine goodness on the rational plane, as the following shows: *Settling* symbolizes living, as discussed in §§1293, 3384, 3613, 4451. *Jacob* in the highest sense represents the Lord's earthly divinity, as discussed in §§3305, 3509, 3525, 3546, 3576, 3599, 3775, 4009, 4234, 4286, 4538, 4570. Isaac, the *father,* represents goodness in the Lord's divine rationality, as discussed in §§1893, 2066, 2630, 3012, 3194, 3210. And the *land of Canaan* in the highest sense symbolizes the Lord's divine humanity, as discussed in §§3038, 3705. As a result of all this, "Jacob settled in the land of his father's *immigrant journeys* in the land of Canaan" means the Lord's earthly divinity living together with and harmoniously under divine goodness on the rational plane in the Lord's divine humanity.

Earlier, at Genesis 35:22, 23, 24, 25, 26, there was a discussion of the Lord's earthly level and the fact that everything in it was now divine (see §§4602–4610). At the next verses, Genesis 35:27, 28, 29, there was a discussion of the union between the Lord's earthly divinity and his divine rationality (see §§4611–4619). This sentence, then, sums up by saying that the Lord's earthly divinity led a harmonious life under divine goodness on the rational plane.

[2] I use the phrase "under divine goodness on the rational plane" because the earthly plane lives under that goodness. The rational plane is higher, more inward, or to use the conventional term, prior, while the earthly plane is lower, more outward, and therefore subsequent. So the earthly plane is subordinate to the rational. In fact, when they are in tune with each other, the earthly level is just a generalized form of the rational level, because whatever the earthly level then possesses belongs not to itself but to the rational level. The only difference between them is like that between subcategories and their general category, or between individual components and their overall pattern, in which they appear as a single whole. As scholars know, the purpose is everything to a cause, and the cause is everything to an effect, so that a cause is the expression of a purpose, and an effect is the expression of a cause. The effect disappears completely if you take away the cause, and the cause disappears completely if you take away the purpose. The cause comes under the purpose, and the effect comes under the cause. It is the same with earthliness and rationality.

These are the births of Jacob means that which follows. This is established by the symbolism of *births* as developments in attributes belonging to the church—specifically, in truth that comes from goodness, or in faith that comes from love. No other births are meant in the Word's inner sense. These are the theme of the text that follows, which is the reason for saying that the *births of Jacob* mean that which follows.

4668

Another piece of evidence that births have this meaning is the failure of subsequent verses to mention any genealogical births. The subject matter is Joseph, his dreams, his brothers' plots against him, and his abduction into Egypt. For births meaning developments in these areas, see §§1145, 1255, 1330, 3263, 3279, 3860, 3868, 4070.

4669   *Joseph* symbolizes the Lord's divine humanity on the spiritual plane. This can be seen from the representation of *Joseph* in the highest sense as the Lord's divine spirituality (discussed in §3969). The church realizes that Joseph represents the Lord, because when people speak of the heavenly Joseph, they mean no one else. What it is about the Lord that Joseph represents is not as well known, however. It is divine spirituality radiating from the Lord's divine humanity. Divine spirituality radiating from the Lord's divine humanity is the divine truth from him in heaven and in the church. Spirituality in its essence is exactly that.

Divine spirituality, or divine truth, is also what is called the Lord's royalty, and it is also symbolized by Christ, or the Messiah. (See §§2015 at the end, 3009, 3670.) That is why Joseph became like a king in Egypt, in order to represent attributes of the Lord's role as monarch.

4670   *A son of seventeen years* symbolizes its state. This can be seen from the ages in years of people mentioned in the Word, since these symbolize attributes or states, as any other number does. For the idea that all numbers in Scripture symbolize attributes and states, see §§575, 647, 648, 1988, 2075, 2252, 3252, 4264, 4495. For the idea that years do too, see §§487, 488, 493, 893.

[2] It does appear as though numbers of years or ages given in years have no further meaning, since they seem to be more a part of the story than other numbers. Even so, they also contain attributes and states, as shown in the explanations at Genesis 5, and in the remarks on Abraham's age at Genesis 17:1; 25:7 and on Isaac's at Genesis 35:28. The same thing can also be seen from the fact that the Word never includes any narrative detail that does not involve something heavenly. It even changes into this heavenly thing when it passes from the thoughts of the person reading it to the angels with the person, and through the angels to heaven, where every bit of scriptural narrative produces a spiritual meaning.

[3] The symbolism of Joseph's age, seventeen, can be seen from the symbolism of the number in other passages, where it symbolizes a beginning. Here it symbolizes the start of Joseph's representational role. For the meaning of seventeen as a beginning and something new, see §§755, 853. The same number also has in general the ability to involve everything Joseph represents, because seven symbolizes holiness, and ten symbolizes a remnant. For seven in the Word adding something holy, see §881. For

ten meaning a remnant, see §§576, 1906, 2284. The Lord's remnant was divine, was his own, and was the means by which he made his human and divine natures one (§1906).

Was pasturing the flock with his brothers means that [divine truth] was present among people of faith who were teaching. This can be seen from the symbolism of *pasturing a flock* as teaching people in the church, especially teaching them doctrine. One who pastures a flock—a shepherd— means one who teaches; see §§343, 3772, 3795. In this case it means being present among people who were teaching, since it says that he was pasturing *with his brothers.* In this chapter *his brothers* represent a religion that turns aside from neighborly love to faith, then to a detached faith, and so to falsity, as the following will make plain. **4671**

And he was a youth symbolizes the first stage. This can be seen from the symbolism of a *youth,* when the term refers to a new religion, as a first stage, or its first state. A church resembles a child, youth, adult, or old person because it goes through those stages the way a person does. The church as a whole is in fact like a person and is referred to as one. **4672**

In a church that is called a youth (owing to its stage of development) and that by its very nature rapidly turns aside, the Lord is present at first, both with those who teach and with those who learn, but later they push him away. This is also represented by Joseph, in that his brothers put him into a pit and sold him.

[2] Every religion that starts with faith is like this, but a religion that starts with neighborly love is different. One that starts with faith has only the intellect to regulate it, and the intellect has only human inheritance, which is self-love and materialism, as a guide. These persuade the intellect to find justification for them in the Word and to reinterpret anything that does not provide justification. Not so in a religion that starts with charity. This religion has goodness to regulate it, and within goodness, the Lord. Bridging between the Lord and faith is good that is done out of charity and love. Without this middle ground spiritual communication does not take place between the two; nothing flows in without a conduit. If evil is substituted for this goodness, it drives the Lord away. It also rejects or perverts everything belonging to him and therefore everything connected with faith, since faith comes from him by way of what is good.

With the sons of Bilhah and with the sons of Zilpah, his father's women, means that he was rejected by them. This is indicated by the symbolism of **4673** the *sons of Bilhah* and the *sons of Zilpah* as shallower or lowlier desires for truth, which serve as means (discussed in §§3849, 3931). *With the sons of Bilhah and with the sons of Zilpah,* then, means that divine truth (Joseph) was relegated to a lower realm, which is relatively slavelike.

Divine truth is said to be relegated to a lower realm when faith comes before charity, or leads the way in people's hearts, and when charity follows and comes second in people's hearts. All divine truth comes from divine goodness, you see. Divine goodness is its source. If something similar is not the case in us, we are not in the Lord. This divine truth is nothing less than the holy operation of the spirit, which emanates from the Lord and is called the Paraclete and the Spirit of Truth (John 14:16, 17).

4674   *And Joseph brought a bad report of them to their father* means that [divine truth] showed what they were like, as the following indicates: *Joseph* represents spiritual divinity, or divine truth from the Lord, as discussed in §§4286, 4675. A *father* symbolizes goodness, as discussed in §§3703, 3704—in this instance the goodness of the ancient church. Jacob represents that church, as will be seen at the end of the chapter. And a *bad report* symbolizes blemishes and flaws in the people symbolized by Joseph's brothers, or in those in the church who turn aside from goodness and truth, as noted above in §4671. This shows what the sentence means in its first layer of inner meaning: that the blemishes and flaws symbolized by Joseph's brothers were brought out into the open or into plain view by divine truth, as it looked at them from the standpoint of the ancient church's goodness. In other words, it showed what they were like.

[2] Here is how matters stand: The falsity and evil of a church, or rather of the people in a church, are invisible to the ones in whom they exist. Falsity does not expose falsity for what it is, nor does evil expose evil. False assumptions throw truth into deep shadow, and a life of evil snuffs it out. Both false assumptions and a life of evil produce the appearance that falsity is true, and truth false, and that goodness is evil, and evil good. Considerable experience makes it plain that this is so. In heaven, though, where there is divine truth from the Lord, the church and its people look entirely different. Divine truth there is the light, and in this light they are seen for what they are. The soul or spirit of every person on earth lives in some angelic or devilish community; that is where our thoughts exist. But our words and deeds come out among the people with whom we interact.

[3] To learn more about the idea that divine truth, or divine light, shows what people in a church are like, consider this: Evil spirits who are

newcomers from the world and have not yet thrown themselves into hell are more eager than anyone else to be accepted into heaven. They think it is simply a matter of being accepted, and that anyone of any character can be allowed into heaven by pure grace. Sometimes they are told that the Lord denies heaven to no one and that they can go to heaven if they are capable of being there. Some of them are even taken up into the first communities, in the entryway to heaven, but when they arrive they start to gasp for air and nearly suffocate. This hampers the vital energy of their thoughts and intentions—of thoughts based on the false principles they held, and of intentions springing from the evil life they led in the world. When they observe themselves in heaven's light, they see themselves as devils and sometimes as corpses or monsters. So they hurl themselves down headlong from that community. They plunge from heaven's light into some hellish thundercloud, where they catch their breath again, and where their fantasies allow them to see themselves as spirits who are not evil. In this way they learn what they are like. From this it is now clear how to understand the statement that divine truth shows what they are like.

And Israel loved Joseph above all his children symbolizes the union of spiritual divinity on the rational level with spiritual divinity on the earthly level, as the following shows: Jacob as *Israel* represents spiritual divinity on the earthly level, or spiritual heavenliness from the earthly plane, as discussed in §§4286, 4598. *Joseph* represents spiritual divinity on the rational level, or spiritual heavenliness from the rational plane, as discussed in §§4286, 4592. And *loving* symbolizes being united, since love is spiritual union. These remarks show that *Israel loved Joseph* symbolizes the union of spiritual divinity on the rational level with spiritual divinity on the earthly level.

4675

Because such a union is the current theme, Jacob is not called Jacob as he was above in verses 1 and 2 but Israel. Even the change of name suggests that the inner meaning here contains some secret.

It is not possible yet to explain what is going on in the union between spiritual divinity on the rational level and spiritual divinity on the earthly level. This is the subject not of the current chapter but of later chapters, where the secret will be explained as far as possible. Here it may simply be said that spirituality is ascribed to both the rational and the earthly dimensions, because the spiritual element is divine truth from the Lord. When it shines on the rational level, or in the inner self, it is called spirituality on the rational level, and when it shines from there on the earthly level, or in the outer self, it is called spirituality on the earthly level.

4676   *Because he was the son of his old age* symbolizes its life within that. This can be seen from the symbolism of *old age* as the shedding of a previous state and putting on of a new state, and also as new life (discussed in §§3492, 4620).

In an inner sense, old age does not mean old age, because our inner self or spirit does not know what old age is. As our body or outer self ages, we pass on to a new stage of life. Our spirit improves with age while our body deteriorates, and it improves even more in the other world. The Lord is constantly leading the inhabitants of that world who are in heaven to a better life and eventually to the bloom of young adulthood—even those who died at a good old age. This shows that on an inner plane, old age symbolizes life.

The meaning of "its life within that" was explained above at §4667.

[2] I just said that our spirit or inner self does not know what old age is, and yet I have stated before that our spirit is what thinks within our body, and that our body receives life from it [§4406].

Why then can this thinking of our spirit not be communicated to our body, teaching us that we live on after death? It is because as long as our spirit remains in our body we cannot help thinking from assumptions that our earthly self has been imbibing. Sometimes there is an assumption and conviction that only our body lives and that when it dies our whole self dies. Under those circumstances the idea cannot flow into us. It reveals its influence nonetheless in the worries most people have about their burial, their eulogy, and in some cases their reputation after death. Some people even build splendid monuments to themselves on this account, to prevent the memory of themselves from dying out. When the idea of everlasting life flows into people who otherwise have no belief in it, that is what it turns into. If there were no such influence they would laugh to scorn all memorializing of themselves after their death.

4677   *And he made him a coat of many colors* symbolizes resulting manifestations of truth by which the spiritual side of the earthly level is recognized and identified. This can be seen from the symbolism of a *coat* as truth on the earthly level (discussed below) and from that of *many colors* as manifestations of truth by which the spiritual side of the earthly level is recognized and identified.

No one can see that this is the symbolism of "many colors" except those who know that color is just as visible in the other life as in the world. In fact, the colors there are far more beautiful and varied than here. One also needs to know where such colors come from. The colors in the other life come from changes in the light there and are modified forms of understanding and wisdom, so to speak. The light that appears there is from divine truth from the Lord; that is, it is divine spirituality from him, or divine understanding and wisdom. This appears as light to the eyes of angels and spirits. Clearly, then, the colors produced by that light symbolize various qualities of truth and therefore manifestations of it; and desires for what is good and true make them visible. On colors in the other world, see §§1042, 1043, 1053, 1624, 3993, 4530.

[2] The meaning of a *coat,* [or tunic,] as earthly truth was mentioned before, in §3301, but since it was not illustrated there, let me support it with other scriptural passages.

In the Jewish religion, monarchs represented the Lord's spiritual divinity, or divine truth (§§2015, 2069, 3009, 3670). The daughter of a monarch consequently wore a coat of many colors, since daughters symbolized desires for what is good and true and therefore symbolized religions (§§2362, 3963). This is mentioned in 2 Samuel:

> There was on Tamar, David's daughter, a *coat of many colors,* because those were the kinds of robes the daughters of a monarch—the unmarried ones—wore. (2 Samuel 13:18)

[3] Since high priests represented the Lord's heavenly divinity, or divine goodness, Aaron wore garments that represented divine truth from the Lord's divine goodness. Divine goodness is in the Lord, but divine truth comes from him. That is what the garments represented. By the same token, when the Lord was transfigured before Peter, James, and John, divine goodness appeared as the sun, and divine truth was revealed in his clothes, which looked like the light (Matthew 17:2). [4] Here is how Moses describes the garments in which Aaron and his sons were dressed:

> For Aaron you shall make a tunic of byssus, a miter of byssus, and you shall make a belt, the work of an embroiderer. And for Aaron's sons you shall make *tunics,* and you shall make belts for them, and you shall make them turbans for glory and for adornment. (Exodus 28:39, 40)

All these things symbolized facets of divine truth from the Lord's divine goodness. The tunic of byssus symbolized divine spirituality in particular. It is similar in another place in the same author:

> You shall take the garments and *put on Aaron the tunic,* and the robe of the ephod, and the ephod, and the breastplate; and you shall wrap him

with the sash of the ephod. Afterward you shall bring his sons near and *clothe them with tunics.* (Exodus 29:5, 8; 40:14)

The symbolism of the details here will be given in the proper place, with the Lord's divine mercy. For the meaning of clothes in general as truth, see §§297, 1073, 2576, 4545.

[5] The prophets also wore coats, but coats of hair, [or hair shirts,] because prophets represented the Lord in regard to doctrinal truth. Since this truth belongs to the earthly, outer self, they had coats of hair, because hair symbolizes something earthly (see §3301).

[6] The symbolism of coats, [or tunics,] as divine truth from the Lord stands out still more plainly from passages in the New Testament referring to them. In John, for instance:

> The soldiers took his garments and made four parts—a part for each soldier—and the *tunic.* But the *tunic* was *seamless, woven from the top throughout the whole.* Therefore they said to each other, "Let's not split it," so that there would be a fulfillment of the scripture saying, "They divided my garments for themselves, and over *my tunic* they cast lots." (John 19:23, 24)

One who reads these words thinks they involve nothing more secret than the fact that the garments were divided among the soldiers and that lots were cast over the tunic. In reality, though, every bit of it represented and symbolized something divine—the dividing of the garments into four parts, the decision not to split the tunic but to cast lots over it, and especially the seamlessness of the tunic woven from the top throughout the whole. The tunic symbolized the Lord's divine truth. The oneness of this truth and its origin in goodness was represented by the fact that the tunic was seamless and woven from the top throughout the whole. [7] The same thing was symbolized by Aaron's tunic, which was woven, or was "the work of a weaver," as Moses shows:

> They made the *tunics of byssus, the work of a weaver,* for Aaron and his sons. (Exodus 39:27)

Also represented was the fact that the Lord did not allow divine truth to be torn in pieces, as was done by Jews to religious truth, which is on a lower level.

[8] Since there is only one divine truth—divine truth arising out of divine goodness—the twelve disciples were commanded not to take two

tunics when they were sent to preach the gospel of the kingdom, as recorded in Luke:

> Jesus sent the twelve disciples to preach the kingdom of God. And he said to them, "Take nothing for the road, not staffs or a bag or bread or silver or *the possession of two tunics* each." (Luke 9:2, 3)

In Mark:

> He commanded them to take nothing for the road except a staff only, not a bag, not bread, not brass in their belt, but shoes on, "*and do not wear two tunics."* (Mark 6:8, 9)

And in Matthew:

> You are not to possess gold or silver or brass in your belts or a bag for the road *or two tunics* or shoes or staffs. (Matthew 10:9, 10)

[9] All the items in these quotations represent heavenly and spiritual qualities of the Lord's kingdom, the kingdom they were sent to preach about. They were not to take gold, silver, brass, bag, or bread with them because those things symbolized goodness and truth, which are from the Lord alone. Gold symbolized goodness (§§113, 1551, 1552); silver symbolized truth growing out of goodness (1551, 2954); brass, earthly goodness (425, 1551); and bread, the good that comes of love, or heavenly goodness (276, 680, 2165, 2177, 3478, 3735, 4211, 4217). A tunic and a shoe symbolized the truth in which they were clothed; and a staff, [or rod,] the power truth receives from goodness. For the meaning of a rod as this power, see §§4013, 4015. For the meaning of a shoe as the bottom of the earthly level, see §1748—in this case, as the truth there. A tunic means an inner kind of earthly truth. Since these attributes must not be twofold but singular, the disciples were forbidden to take two staffs, two pairs of shoes, or two tunics.

These are the secrets contained in the Lord's command above, and they can be seen only from the inner meaning.

[10] Absolutely everything the Lord said represented divine qualities and therefore the heavenly and spiritual qualities of his kingdom, so it was adapted to the grasp of people on earth and at the same time to the genuine understanding of spirits and angels. Consequently the words the Lord spoke filled all of heaven, and still do. From this you can see how important and advantageous it is to know the Word's inner meaning. Without it, we can use the Word to prove any dogma we wish, and since

people immersed in evil view the Word that way, they sneer at it and believe it to be anything but divine.

4678   Genesis 37:4–11. *And his brothers saw that their father loved him above all his brothers, and they hated him and could not speak to him in peace. And Joseph dreamed a dream and told his brothers, and they added further to their hatred of him. And he said to them, "Please listen to this dream that I dreamed. And look! We were binding sheaves in the middle of the field, and look! My sheaf rose and even stood, and look! Your sheaves circled around and bowed down to my sheaf!" And his brothers said to him, "Will you really rule over us? Are you really to dominate us?" And they added further to their hatred of him over his dreams and over his words. And he dreamed still another dream and recounted it to his brothers and said, "Look! I dreamed another dream, and look! The sun and the moon and eleven stars bowing down to me!" And he recounted it to his father and to his brothers, and his father scolded him and said to him, "What is this dream that you dreamed? Will we really come, I and your mother and your brothers, to bow down to you to the earth?" And his brothers envied him, and his father kept the word [in mind].*

His brothers saw symbolizes aspects of faith, and (in the first layer of meaning) Jacob's descendants. *That their father loved him above all his brothers* means that [the Lord] was united with earthly divinity, and (in the first layer of meaning) that he was united with the ancient church (the *father*). *And they hated him and could not speak to him in peace* symbolizes contempt and disdain. *And Joseph dreamed a dream* symbolizes a declaration about him. *And told his brothers* means in the hearing of people who subscribed to a detached faith. *And they added further to their hatred of him* symbolizes still greater contempt and disdain. *And he said to them, "Please listen to this dream that I dreamed,"* symbolizes the content of the declaration. *And look! We were binding sheaves in the middle of the field* symbolizes people who teach doctrine. *And look! My sheaf rose and even stood* symbolizes teachings about the Lord's divine humanity. *And look! Your sheaves circled around* symbolizes people who would focus on faith. *And bowed down to my sheaf* symbolizes reverence. *And his brothers said to him* symbolizes those who subscribed to a detached faith. *Will you really rule over us? Are you really to dominate us?* means, would the workings of their intellect and will be subordinate? *And they added further to their hatred of him over his dreams and over his words* symbolizes still greater contempt and disdain because of truth's declaration. *And he dreamed still another dream* symbolizes a further declaration.

And recounted it to his brothers and said, means in the hearing of people dedicated to a detached faith. *Look! I dreamed another dream* symbolizes the content. *And look! The sun and the moon* symbolizes earthly goodness and earthly truth. *And eleven stars* symbolizes knowledge of what is good and true. *Bowing down to me* symbolizes reverence. *And he recounted it to his father and to his brothers* means that they were permitted to know this. *And his father scolded him and said to him, "What is this dream that you dreamed?"* symbolizes outrage, the *father* meaning the Jewish religion springing from the ancient church. *Will we really come, I and your mother and your brothers, to bow down to you to the earth?* means, is the church going to offer reverence? *And his brothers envied him* symbolizes their disdain. *And his father kept the word [in mind]* means that their religious tradition retained some truth.

His brothers saw symbolizes aspects of faith, and (in the first layer of meaning) Jacob's descendants. This can be seen from the symbolism of *seeing* as perceiving and understanding (dealt with in §§2150, 2325, 2807, 3764, 3863) and from the representation of Joseph's *brothers* as aspects of faith. In this chapter Joseph represents the Lord's divine spirituality, or divine truth, and his brothers represent a religion that turns aside from charity to faith, then to faith detached from charity, and finally to falsity; see above at §§4665, 4671. That is why they now symbolize aspects of faith. Since Jacob's descendants were like this, they are symbolized in the first layer of meaning.

4679

That their father loved him above all his brothers means that [the Lord] was united with earthly divinity, and (in the first layer of meaning) that he was united with the ancient church (the *father*). This can be seen from the explanation above in §4675, where similar words occur.

4680

The reason the first level of meaning is that [the Lord] was united with the ancient church, and the reason that church is meant on this level by the father, is that Joseph's brothers in the most immediate sense symbolize Jacob's descendants, as was said just above in §4679. As a result they represented the religion that existed among them.

The situation in all this has been explained several times before but needs to be gone over again briefly here because of the series of ideas in what follows. [2] The ancient church, which the Lord established after the Flood, was a representative religion. Its nature was such that all its outward signs of worship represented heavenly and spiritual qualities of the Lord's kingdom, and in the highest sense, even the Lord's divine qualities. The inner depths of its worship all related to charity.

The ancient church extended through much of the Near East and many of the countries there. Even though they differed over faith's doctrines it was a single religion, because everyone everywhere considered charity essential to religion. In those days people who separated faith from charity and considered faith the essential ingredient of religion were called Ham.

After a while, though, this church turned aside to idolatry, and to magic in Egypt, Babylon, and elsewhere. People started to worship superficialities apart from any inward significance. Since this drew them away from neighborly love, heaven drew away from them, and spirits from hell arrived to lead them instead.

[3] When the ancient church had been ruined, Eber started a new religion called the Hebrew religion, which existed in Syria and Mesopotamia and also among other nations in the land of Canaan. What made it different from the ancient church was the fact that it viewed sacrifice as the essential element in outward worship. It did acknowledge that charity was the inner core of worship, though not in as heartfelt a way as the ancient church did. It too became idolatrous, however.

[4] Finally, it pleased the Lord to establish a new religion among Abraham's descendants through Jacob and to introduce into their nation the ancient church's visible signs of worship. By their very nature, though, since their hearts absolutely opposed neighborly love, they could not accept any inner dimension of religion, so only a representation of a religion was set up among them.

This then is why Jacob's sons, Joseph's brothers, symbolize such a religion in the most immediate sense, and why Jacob, their father, symbolizes the ancient church. Jacob often means the ancient church in other parts of the Word as well, especially the prophetic books. Sometimes the ancient church is also called a father or mother—a father as to the goodness in it, and a mother as to the truth in it.

This discussion now shows that *their father loved Joseph above all his brothers* means that the Lord's divine truth was united with the ancient church.

4681 *And they hated him and could not speak to him in peace* symbolizes contempt and disdain—contempt and disdain for the divine truth that Joseph represents—as the following shows: *Hating* means having contempt. In an inner sense hatred does not mean the hatred we feel when we hate, because the meaning of the term softens as it rises into heaven. In heaven they do not know what hatred is, so contempt is what it symbolizes. And *not being* *able to speak to him in peace* means disdaining. *Speaking in peace* means wishing a person well, because in its highest sense the ancients understood *peace* to mean the Lord himself; in an inward sense, to mean his kingdom and life there, or salvation; but on the surface, to mean worldly salvation, or wellness. The opposite is *not* being able to speak to him in peace, which means not wishing someone well and therefore disdaining the person, or in this case divine truth.

And Joseph dreamed a dream symbolizes a declaration about him. This can be seen from the symbolism of *dreaming a dream* as making a declaration. Since the dream is about Joseph, it means declaring the Lord's divine humanity. The reason this dream symbolizes a declaration is that Joseph's two dreams summarize all that was foreseen and provided for in relation to Joseph, or (in an inner sense) in relation to divine truth in the kind of religion Joseph's brothers represent—the kind that starts with faith. Besides, divine truth was revealed in ancient times by speech, visions, or dreams, from which people of that day preached. That is why the prophets in the Word, to whom divine truth was revealed by speech, visions, or dreams, symbolize people who teach truth, and in an abstract sense, doctrinal truth itself (§2534). Seeing visions and dreaming dreams, then, have the same meaning. [2] In Joel, for instance:

> I will pour out my spirit on all flesh, and your sons and your daughters will *prophesy,* your elders will *dream dreams,* your young adults will *see visions.* Also on male slaves and female slaves in those days I will pour out my spirit. (Joel 2:28, 29)

Pouring out his spirit on them stands for instructing people about truth. Prophesying stands for teaching and preaching truth, and so does dreaming dreams. Elders stand for people with wisdom; young adults stand for people with understanding; and slaves stand for people with knowledge. [3] In Jeremiah:

> This is what Jehovah Sabaoth has said: "Do not pay attention *to the words of the prophets prophesying to you;* they cause you to be deluded. The vision of their own heart they speak, not [what comes] from Jehovah's mouth. I have heard what the *prophets* have said, who *prophesied* a lie in my name, saying, '*I dreamed! I dreamed!*' Let the *prophets with whom there is a dream* tell the *dream,* but let those with whom my word exists tell my word in truth. Look: I am *against those who prophesy dreams that are lies,*" says Jehovah. "They tell [the dreams] and lead my people astray with their lies." (Jeremiah 23:16, 25, 28, 32)

4682

Again prophesying stands for teaching and preaching, but teaching and preaching from dreams that are the lies that form the basis of their preaching. Likewise in other places, such as Jeremiah 29:8, 9; Zechariah 10:2. [4] In Moses:

> When *prophets* or *dreamers of dreams* rise in your midst to give you a sign or portent, and should there come to pass the sign or portent that they spoke to you, saying, "Let's go to other gods whom you do not know, and serve them," you shall not obey the *words of those prophets* or those *dreamers of dreams*. And *those prophets* and those *dreamers of dreams* shall be killed because they spoke for deserting Jehovah your God. (Deuteronomy 13:1, 2, 3, 5)

Prophets and dreamers of dreams both stand for people who teach and preach, and in this instance, who teach and preach falsity.

4683   *And told his brothers* means in the hearing of people who subscribed to a detached faith. This can be seen from the representation of Joseph's *brothers* as a religion that turns aside from charity to faith, or in an abstract sense, as aspects of faith itself (discussed above in §§4665, 4671, 4679). Here they represent people who subscribe to a faith detached from charity, because the text goes on to say that they added further to their hatred of him, which symbolizes still greater contempt and disdain.

Here is the situation in that kind of religion: At its start it preaches charity, but only at the urging of doctrine and so from mere knowledge, not from neighborly love itself and therefore not from a warm feeling or from the heart. As time passes, and charity and warmth is erased from their heart, the people of that religion turn to preaching faith. Eventually, when charity ceases to exist, they preach faith alone, which they claim saves us without our doing good deeds. They no longer describe good deeds as works of neighborly love but as works of faith, which they call the fruits of faith. They do unite [faith and deeds], then, but only in their doctrine, not in their lives. [2] Although they can see clearly from the Word and also from their own intellect that doctrine is nothing without life, or that faith is nothing without its fruits, they do not believe that a religious life or goodness brings any salvation, only that faith does. As a result they equate faith's saving power with trust, which allows them to continue backing away from the fruits of faith. They fail to realize that all trust derives its essence from the purpose of our life. Genuine trust is impossible except in a context of goodness; but artificial and false trust can exist in a context of evil.

In order to divorce faith still more decisively from charity, they also argue that we are saved by a single moment of trust, even at the very end of life, no matter how we lived beforehand. Yet they know that our life awaits every one of us after death and that we will each be judged according to the deeds of our life.

These brief remarks show what faith is like when it is separated from charity and therefore what a religion is like when it deems faith but not a faith-based life to be essential.

The false beliefs that pour from this attitude as their wellspring will be discussed later, by the Lord's divine mercy [§§4721, 4730, 4783, 4925].

And they added further to their hatred of him symbolizes still greater contempt and disdain. This can be seen from the comments above at §4681 where similar words occur.

4684

And he said to them, "Please listen to this dream that I dreamed," symbolizes the content of the declaration. This can be seen from the symbolism discussed above at §4682 of *dreaming a dream* as making a declaration, and here as the content of the declaration, since a description of the dream he had now follows.

4685

And look! We were binding sheaves in the middle of the field symbolizes people who teach doctrine. This can be seen from the symbolism of a *sheaf* as doctrine, and therefore of *binding sheaves* as teaching doctrine (discussed below), and from the symbolism of a *field* as the church (discussed in §§2971, 3766, 4440, 4443). The *middle of a field* means an inner level of the church, so it means people with a faith marked to some extent by neighborly love. In an inner sense, the middle means an inward or inmost part (§§1074, 2940, 2973). Every religion has people who are at its core or inmost part, and they are the ones with charity, or in this case, the ones whose faith is based to some extent on charity. With them the Lord is present, because he is present in charity, and through charity in faith (§4672). That they are the ones symbolized is also evident from what follows, where Joseph's sheaf rose and the other sheaves circled around it. Joseph's sheaf symbolizes the teachings of the Lord's divine truth.

4686

[2] A sheaf means doctrine because (to repeat) a field means the church, and the crop in a field means truth in the church. The sheaves holding the crops, then, mean the doctrines holding truth.

Sheaves have the same symbolism in David:

> Those who sow in tears, in song will reap. They will certainly go weeping, carrying a casting's worth of *seed,* but they will certainly come with song, carrying *their sheaves.* (Psalms 126:5, 6)

This verse is about people in spiritual captivity who were freed. Carrying a casting's worth of seed stands for being taught truth. Coming with song stands for gladness brought on by a desire for truth. Carrying sheaves stands for the teachings of that truth.

4687   *And look! My sheaf rose and even stood* symbolizes teachings about the Lord's divine humanity. This can be seen from the symbolism of a *sheaf* as a doctrine (discussed just above) and from the symbolism of *rising* and *standing* as that which is to reign supreme and which people are to revere. This is the Lord's divine humanity, as the details that follow show: the eleven sheaves bowed down to this sheaf, and in the second dream the sun, moon, and eleven stars bowed down to Joseph. These things symbolize that which was to reign supreme and which people were to revere. That is why Jacob says, "Are we to come, I and your mother and your brothers, to bow down to you to the earth?" The Lord's divine truth is what Joseph represents, as noted above [§4669]. Its highest form is the Lord himself, and the supreme teaching is that his humanity is divine.

[2] A word about this highest doctrinal teaching: The earliest church, which was heavenly and above all others was called Humankind, revered the infinite reality and the resulting infinite presence. The people of that religion could not have any perception of the infinite reality, but they could perceive the resulting infinite presence to some extent from perceptible features of their inner self, palpable features of their outer self, and visible features of the world around them. As a consequence, they revered the infinite presence containing the infinite reality.

The way they perceived infinite presence containing the infinite reality was as a divine human, because they knew that the infinite presence emerged from the infinite reality through heaven. Heaven is a universal human corresponding to everything in a person in whole and in part, as has been shown at the end of previous chapters and will be shown at the end of several subsequent ones. Accordingly, the earliest people were unable to perceive or picture the infinite presence in its emergence from infinite reality as anything but a divine human. Whatever comes from infinite reality and passes through heaven as a universal human carries this human image with it in every aspect.

When this heavenly church began to fall, its people foresaw that the infinite presence would no longer be able to flow into human minds and that the human race would be destroyed as a result. Therefore they received a revelation that one would be born who would make the humanity in himself divine. In the process he would become the same infinite presence that had existed before, and at the last he would become one with the infinite reality that had also existed before. From this came their prophecy about the Lord in Genesis 3:15.

[3] The same thing is described this way in John:

> In the beginning there was the Word, and the Word was with God, and the Word was God. This was with God in the beginning. Everything was made by him, and nothing that was made was made without him. In him was life, and the life was the light of humankind. And the Word became flesh and resided among us, and we saw his glory, like that of the Only-Born of the Father, who was full of grace and truth. (John 1:1, 2, 3, 4, 14)

The Word is divine truth, which in its essence is infinite presence emerging from infinite reality and is the Lord himself in his humanity. The Lord's humanity is the source from which divine truth now emanates and flows into heaven and through heaven into human minds. So it is what controls and governs the universe, as it has controlled and governed the universe from eternity. It is one and the same with the infinite reality, because [the Lord] united humanity with divinity and did so by making the humanity in himself divine.

Clearly, then, the highest form of divine truth is the Lord's divine humanity, and consequently the supreme doctrinal teaching in the church is that his humanity is divine.

And look! Your sheaves circled around symbolizes people who would **4688** focus on faith, and specifically on a faith marked to some extent by neighborly love, as the following shows: In this case *circling around* means coming close in order to offer reverence, because the next clause says that they bowed down to Joseph's sheaf, which symbolizes reverence. And a *sheaf* symbolizes doctrine, as discussed just above in §4686. Here it symbolizes all of doctrine, or all of faith. The reason the sheaves have this symbolism is that Jacob's sons as a whole, in a positive sense, represent everything involved in faith (§§3858, 3926). The sheaves have the same representation because in the dream they stood for Jacob's sons and because the setting of the dream was the middle of a field. The middle of a field symbolizes an inner level or people at an inner level in the church, as described in §4686, so it symbolizes people focusing on faith that is marked to some extent by neighborly love. They are the sheaves that circled around Joseph's sheaf and bowed down to it. People who are on the outside, or farther from the middle—the ones who are Joseph's brothers here, properly speaking—are not meant. This is clear from assertions before and after that they hated him more and more. That is, they had contempt and disdain for him, because the hating, the not speaking in peace, and the envying attributed to Joseph's brothers symbolize contempt and disdain.

4689   *And bowed down to my sheaf* symbolizes reverence. This is established by the symbolism of *bowing down* as an outward effect of humility (discussed at §2153) and consequently as reverence, and from that of Joseph's *sheaf* as teachings about the Lord's divine humanity (discussed at §4687). Divine humanity, then, is what was revered by the people on the inner plane of the church. People on the outer plane—in other words, people who subscribe to a detached faith—do anything but offer reverence. This is a natural consequence of a faith detached from charity, because as noted above [§4686] the Lord is present in charity but not in faith except through charity. Charity is the uniting medium. What is truth without goodness, or intellect without will? What is faith, then, without charity, or trust without its vital essence?

[2] People arriving in the other life from the Christian world who are under the sway of faith detached from charity have enabled me to see plainly that their type does anything but revere the Lord's divine humanity. I have spoken with many of them there, where the heart speaks—not the mouth, as in this world. Everyone's thoughts are shared much more openly in that life than by any kind of talking in the world, and to speak differently than one thinks or therefore than one believes is not allowed there. Many of the ones who in fact proclaimed the Lord in this world flatly deny him there. When you ask what their reason or purpose was for proclaiming him and even piously venerating him, at least on the surface, you find that their job demanded it of them, and that it earned them high rank and wealth. People who did not preach the Lord but still claimed to believe in him did so because they were born into the church and would have been libeled if they had spoken against religion. Not even one person from the Christian world knows that the Lord's humanity is divine, and hardly anyone knows that he alone rules heaven and the universe, let alone that his divine humanity is the all-in-all in heaven. The truth of the matter could not be openly revealed, because the Lord foresaw that the Christian religion would turn aside from neighborly love to faith and consequently distance itself from him. In doing so it would not only reject but even profane anything holy coming from his divine humanity. Faith detached from neighborly love cannot do otherwise.

[3] Clearly faith is divorced from charity at the present day. Churches distinguish themselves from each other by their dogmas, and anyone who believes differently than the dogma teaches is thrown out of the communion and slandered. However, those who steal, heartlessly swindle others (provided they do not do so openly), plot fraud against their neighbor, scoff at acts of neighborly kindness, or commit adultery—these people are still called Christians, as long as they attend religious services and talk doctrine. Doctrine rather than life is obviously what makes a church these days, then, and the fruits that people tack on to faith exist only in their doctrine, not in their minds.

And his brothers said to him symbolizes those who subscribed to a detached faith. This is established by the representation of Joseph's *brothers* as a religion that turns aside from charity to faith and finally detaches faith from charity (discussed in §§4665, 4671, 4679). People on the inner level of that religion, though, are symbolized by the sheaves in the dream (§§4686, 4688).

4690

Joseph's brothers represent that religion because in the first layer of meaning they symbolize the representation of a religion (or the religiosity) that was instituted among Jacob's descendants. Admittedly they did not know anything about the faith that the Christian religion knows, but they did know truth. Truth was to them what faith is to Christians. The original language uses the same word for both. The Jewish religion took "truth" to mean the Ten Commandments, however, and also the laws, judgments, testimonies, and statutes handed down by Moses. Deeper layers of truth they did not know and did not want to know. [2] The Christian religion, on the other hand, refers to its deeper doctrines—the ones that it says have to be accepted—as faith. Most people take the term *faith* simply to mean a creed, or the faith the creedal books teach. Then there are those who doubt that anyone can be saved by religious teachings or the knowledge of them and think that few live a life in accord with faith. They label faith as *trust,* but they are above the common herd and are more scholarly than others.

These considerations show that the inner meaning here deals not only with the representation of a religion that was instituted among Jacob's descendants but also with the Christian religion that came after it. The Lord's Word is universal and includes every religion in general. The Lord foresaw what would happen with the Christian religion just as much as with the Jewish, but more immediately with the Jewish. That is why this meaning is called the most immediate layer of meaning, or the inner narrative meaning, while the other is called the inner meaning.

4691   *Will you really rule over us? Are you really to dominate us?* means, would the workings of their intellect and will be subordinate? This can be seen from the symbolism of *ruling* as being subordinate in matters of the intellect, and from that of *dominating* as being subordinate in matters of the will.

Ruling over us and *dominating us* plainly mean being made subordinate, but the reason both terms are used is that one relates to matters of the intellect and the other to matters of the will. It is common for the Word and especially the prophetic books to express a single concept in two ways. People who do not know the secret involved cannot help supposing that it is mere repetition for the sake of emphasis; but this is not so. In every part of the Word there is a heavenly marriage, a marriage of truth with goodness and of goodness with truth, just as there is a marriage of intellect and will in the human being. One expression has to do with truth; the other, with goodness. So one relates to the intellect, whose province is truth, and the other, to the will, whose province is goodness. Such words form expressions in Scripture that consistently have this symbolism. That is the secret hidden in the use of two terms for one idea; see §§683, 793, 801, 2173, 2516, 2712, 4137 at the end.

Likewise here with ruling over them and dominating them. "Ruling" has regard to truth, the province of the intellect, and "dominating" has regard to goodness, the province of the will. In addition, "kingship" is used to portray truth (§§1672, 2547), and "dominion" to portray goodness. This is the case in Daniel, in another passage whose theme is the Lord's divine humanity:

> To him was given *dominion* and glory and *kingship,* so that all peoples, nations, and tongues would worship him. His *dominion* is an *eternal dominion* that will not pass away, and his *kingship* one that will not perish. (Daniel 7:14)

And in David:

> Your *kingship* is a *kingship* to all eternity, and your *dominion* is for all generations. (Psalms 145:13)

4692   *And they added further to their hatred of him over his dreams and over his words* symbolizes still greater contempt and disdain because of truth's declaration—in this instance, concerning the Lord's divine humanity—as the following shows: *Adding* means more greatly; *hatred* means showing contempt and disdain, as discussed above in §4681; a *dream* symbolizes a declaration, as also discussed above in §§4682, 4685; and *words* symbolize truth. Words symbolize truth because every word in heaven is from the Lord. On an inner level, then, individual words symbolize truth, and the Word as a whole symbolizes all divine truth.

[2] As for the subject matter itself, the main object of contempt and disdain in a religion that has detached faith from charity is the supreme truth that the Lord's humanity is divine.

Everyone in the ancient church who did not separate charity from faith believed that the God of the universe was a divine human and that he was the divine reality. That is why they named him Jehovah. They knew this from the earliest people and from the fact that he had appeared as a person to many of their number. They also knew that all the rituals and outward signs of their church represented him.

Those who subscribed to a detached faith could not believe it, though. They could not comprehend how a human nature could be divine or accept that divine love glorified that nature. If they could not grasp a concept with the help of any idea formed through their outward, physical senses, you see, they dismissed it. This is a natural consequence of faith isolated from neighborly love. In people with such a faith, deep perception is shut off, because there is no conduit through which it can flow in.

[3] The Jewish religion, which came next, did believe that Jehovah was both a person and God, because he had appeared to Moses and the prophets as a person. That is why the people of that religion applied the name Jehovah to every angel who appeared. Still, their idea of him was no different from the idea the surrounding nations had of their own gods. The people of the Jewish religion considered Jehovah God better because he could do miracles (§4299), not knowing that Jehovah was the Lord in the Word (§§2921, 3035) or that his divine humanity was what all their rituals represented. They thought of the Messiah or Christ only as the future greatest prophet (greater than Moses) and greatest monarch (greater than David), who was to lead them into the land of Canaan with wondrous miracles. His heavenly kingdom was not something they wanted to hear about, because worldly subjects were all they grasped. After all, they were detached from neighborly love.

[4] The Christian religion reveres the Lord's humanity as divine in its outward worship, especially in the Holy Supper, because he said that the

bread was his body and the wine was his blood [Matthew 26:26–28; Mark 14:22–24; Luke 22:19–20]. However, Christians do not make his humanity divine in their theology, because they distinguish between his divine and human natures. This too is because the church has turned aside from charity to faith and finally to a detached faith. In failing to acknowledge his humanity as divine, many put stumbling blocks in their own way and deny him at heart (§4689). The fact of the matter is that the Lord's divine humanity is the divine presence emerging from the divine reality (discussed above in §4687), and he is the divine reality itself. The divine reality and the divine presence are one, as the Lord also teaches explicitly in John:

> Jesus said to Philip, "So much time I've spent with you, and you do not know me? Whoever has seen me has seen the Father. Don't you believe that I am in the Father and the Father is in me? Believe me that I am in the Father and the Father is in me." (John 14:9, 10, 11; and other places)

The divine presence is divinity itself radiating from the divine reality. Humankind is in its image, because heaven, to which [the divine presence] is everything, takes the form of a universal human. (This is noted above at §4687 and at the ends of some chapters, where the correspondence of everything in us with the universal human has been demonstrated.)

[5] It is true that the Lord was born like any other human and received human frailty from his mother; but he banished this human nature so thoroughly that he was no longer Mary's son. He made the humanity in him divine, which is what is meant by saying that he was glorified. He also showed Peter, James, and John when he was transfigured that he was a divine human.

4693   *And he dreamed still another dream* symbolizes a further declaration, which can be seen from the discussion above in §4682 of the symbolism of a *dream* as a declaration.

4694   *And recounted it to his brothers and said,* means in the hearing of people dedicated to a detached faith. This is established by the representation of Joseph's *brothers* as people with a detached faith (discussed above in §§4665, 4671, 4679, 4690).

4695   *Look! I dreamed another dream* symbolizes the content—the content of the declaration—as the remarks above in §4685 show.

4696   *And look! The sun and the moon* symbolizes earthly goodness and earthly truth. This can be seen from the symbolism of the *sun* as heavenly goodness (dealt with in §§1529, 1530, 2120, 2441, 2495, 3636, 3643, 4060) and from that of the *moon* as spiritual goodness, or truth (dealt with in §§1529, 1530, 2495).

At the highest level the sun symbolizes the Lord, because he appears as the sun to those in heaven who have heavenly love. The moon at the highest level also symbolizes the Lord, because he appears as the moon to those in heaven who have spiritual love. This is the source of all light in heaven. Consequently the light from the sun there is the heavenly side of love, or goodness, and the light from the moon there is the spiritual side of love, or truth. In the current verse, then, the sun means earthly goodness, and the moon means earthly truth. This is because the sun and moon refer to Jacob and Leah, as is evident from verse 10, where Jacob says, "Will we really come, I and your mother and your brothers, to bow down to you to the earth?" Jacob represents earthly goodness, and Leah represents earthly truth, as demonstrated a number of times before.

Anything divine that comes from the Lord is in the highest sense the divinity in him, but in a secondary sense the divinity from him. The divine goodness that comes from him is what is called heavenly, and the divine truth that comes from him is what is called spiritual. When the rational plane receives these things, goodness and truth on the rational plane are symbolized. When the earthly plane receives them, goodness and truth on the earthly plane are symbolized. Goodness and truth on the earthly plane are symbolized here because they are connected with Jacob and Leah.

And eleven stars symbolizes knowledge of what is good and true. This can be seen from the symbolism of *stars* as knowledge of what is good and true. Stars have this symbolism in the Word because they are tiny lights that shine at night. They shed a twinkling light in our night sky, just as knowledge sheds bits of goodness and truth.

4697

The symbolism of stars as knowledge of what is good and true can be seen from many Scripture passages. In Jeremiah, for example:

> The word spoken by Jehovah, who gives the *sun as light for the day, the statutes of moon and stars as light for the night,* who disturbs the sea, so that its waves heave. (Jeremiah 31:35)

This is about a new religion. Giving the sun as light for the day symbolizes good done out of love and charity. The statutes of moon and stars as

light for the night symbolize truth and knowledge. [2] The meaning is
similar in David:

> . . . Jehovah, who made the *great lights—the sun for ruling in the day, the
> moon and stars for ruling in the night.* (Psalms 136:7, 8, 9)

Anyone who does not know the Word's inner meaning will believe that
this sun means the sun in this world, and that the moon and stars mean
the moon and stars. This does not give rise to any spiritual or heavenly
meaning, though—and the Word is heavenly at every point. Here too is
evidence that what is symbolized is good done out of love and charity, the
truth that leads to faith, and the knowledge of both.

[3] Likewise with the contents of Genesis 1, which treats of a heavenly
person being created anew:

> God said, "Let there be *lights* in the expanse of the heavens to make a
> distinction between day and night; and they will act as signals and will
> be used for seasons both for the days and for the years. And they will act
> as *lights* in the expanse of the heavens to shed light on the earth"; and
> so it was done. And God made the *two great lights: the greater light to
> rule by day and the smaller light to rule by night; and the stars.* And God
> placed them in the expanse of the heavens, to shed light on the earth,
> and to rule during the day and during the night, and to make a distinc-
> tion between light and darkness. (Genesis 1:13, 14, 15, 16, 17, 18)

See §§30–38. [4] In Matthew:

> Immediately after the affliction of those days, *the sun will go dark,* and
> *the moon will not shed its light,* and *the stars will fall down from the sky,*
> and the powers of the heavens will be shaken. (Matthew 24:29)

The sun and moon symbolize love and charity, or goodness and truth, and
the stars symbolize knowledge (see §4060). Since this verse is about the
church's final days, or final state, the fact that the sun will go dark and the
moon will not shed its light means that any loving, charitable goodness
will then die out. The fact that the stars will fall down from the sky means
that any knowledge of goodness and truth will also die out. [5] This symbolism becomes clear in the prophetic parts of the Word, where similar
things are said about the end of the church. In Isaiah, for instance:

> Look—the day of Jehovah will come as a cruel one, to make the earth
> a wasteland; and sinners he will destroy from it. For the *stars of the*

heavens and *their constellations* will not shed their light; *the sun will go dark in its rising,* and *the moon will not radiate light.* (Isaiah 13:9, 10)

In Joel:

Near is the day of Jehovah; the *sun* and *moon* have gone black, and the *stars* have withdrawn their rays. (Joel 3:14, 15)

In Ezekiel:

When I blot you out, I will cover the heavens and *blacken their stars; the sun I will cover with a cloud,* and *the moon will not make its glimmer shine.* All the *lamps of light* in the sky I will blacken above you, and I will bring darkness over your land. (Ezekiel 32:7, 8)

And in John:

The fourth angel trumpeted and a *third of the sun* was struck and a *third of the moon* and a *third of the stars,* so that a third of them was *shadowed over* and the day did not shine for a third of it and the night likewise. (Revelation 8:12)

[6] The following passages also show that stars mean knowledge of goodness and truth. In Daniel:

From one horn of the buck of the goats one horn went out a bit, and it grew immensely toward the south and toward the sunrise and toward the ornament [of Israel] and grew right to the *armies of the heavens* and threw down to the ground *some of the army* and some of the *stars* and trampled them. (Daniel 8:9, 10)

And in John:

A big dragon dragged a *third of the stars in heaven* with its tail and threw them onto the earth. (Revelation 12:4)

Stars obviously are not meant here. Daniel and John are talking about the condition of the church in its final days. [7] The meaning is similar in David:

Jehovah counts the number of the *stars;* to them all he gives names. (Psalms 147:4)

In the same author:

Praise Jehovah, *sun* and *moon!* Praise him, all you *shining stars!* (Psalms 148:3)

In John:

> A great sign was seen in heaven: a woman enveloped in the *sun,* and the *moon* under her feet, and on her head a crown of *twelve stars.* (Revelation 12:1)

[8] Because stars symbolize knowledge of what is good and true, they symbolize the church's doctrines, since these are concepts to know. A doctrine detaching faith from charity in the [church's] final days is depicted by a star this way in John:

> The third angel trumpeted, and there *fell from the sky a large star* burning like a lamp, and it fell onto a third of the rivers and onto the springs of water. *The name of the star is called Wormwood,* and many people died in the water, because it was embittered. (Revelation 8:10, 11)

The water embittered by the star means truth, so the rivers and springs of water mean understanding and wisdom acquired from the Word. For the meaning of water as truth, see §§2702, 3058, 3424. For that of rivers as understanding, [or intelligence,] §3051. For that of springs as wisdom from the Word, §§2702, 3424.

4698   *Bowing down to me* symbolizes reverence. This is established by the discussion above in §4689 of the symbolism of *bowing down* as reverence.

4699   *And he recounted it to his father and to his brothers* means that they were permitted to know this, as can be seen without explanation.

4700   *And his father scolded him and said to him, "What is this dream that you dreamed?"* symbolizes outrage. This can be seen from the symbolism of *scolding* as being outraged—outraged by truth's declaration concerning the Lord's divine humanity (the symbolism of *dreaming a dream,* as noted at §§4682, 4693, 4695). Joseph's *father* and brothers at this point mean the Jewish religion springing from the ancient church. For the most part the outer level of that religion resembled the outer level of the ancient church, but the people of the ancient church had an inner level within that. Not so the people of the Jewish religiosity, because Jews did not acknowledge anything internal and still do not. Nonetheless there was an inner level in it.

This outer level with its inner level is what is being called the father, and the outer without the inner, the brothers. That is why the next verse says that his brothers envied him and his father kept the word [in mind]. The first part symbolizes the disdain of people with an outer level and no inner level. The second part means that their religious tradition retained some truth anyway.

[2] The situation resembles that of the Christian religion. Christians who engage on the surface but not at a deeper level eat the bread and drink the wine of the Holy Supper merely with the thought that they should do so because it was commanded and is the custom in the church. Some of them believe that the bread and wine are holy without realizing that the holiness is due to bread's symbolism as the holy quality of love and charity in heaven and to wine's symbolism as the holy quality of charity and faith there (§§3464, 3735). People who engage in both outward and inward worship do not revere the bread and wine but the Lord whom these represent and who is the source of holy love, charity, and faith. They revere him not from doctrine but from love, charity, and a faith applied to life.

Will we really come, I and your mother and your brothers, to bow down to you to the earth? means, is the church going to offer reverence? This can be seen from the following: *Coming to bow* means being about to offer reverence, as discussed at §§4689, 4698. A father—*I*—and *mother* and *brothers* symbolize a church, and in this case the Jewish religion, as just above.   **4701**

And his brothers envied him symbolizes disdain of him. This can be seen from the symbolism of *envying,* which is also disdain, like the symbolism of hating him and not speaking to him in peace, as above at §4681. The word "envy" in the original language also means to strive and wrangle with. Since strife and wrangling result from hatred, the word symbolizes disdain.   **4702**

And his father kept the word [in mind] means that their religious tradition retained some truth, as the following shows: The *father* here symbolizes the Jewish religion springing from the ancient church, as discussed above at §4700. *Keeping [in mind]* means preserving within and therefore retaining. And the *word* symbolizes truth, as discussed above in §4692. For a fuller explanation of the idea that their religiosity retained some truth, see above at §4700.   **4703**

Genesis 37:12–17. *And his brothers went to pasture their father's flock in Shechem. And Israel said to Joseph, "Aren't your brothers shepherding in Shechem? Go, and let me send you to them." And [Joseph] said to him, "Here I am." And [Israel] said to him, "Go, please; see the peace of your brothers and the peace of the flock and bring word back to me." And he sent him from the*   **4704** *valley of Hebron, and [Joseph] came to Shechem. And a man found him, and here, he was wandering in the field, and the man asked him, saying, "What are you looking for?" And he said, "I am looking for my brothers; please tell me where they are shepherding." And the man said, "They traveled on from here, because I heard them saying, 'Let's go to Dothan.'" And Joseph went after his brothers and found them in Dothan.*

His brothers went to pasture the flock means people who teach of faith. *Of their father* symbolizes [the faith] of the ancient church and of the early [Christian] church. *In Shechem* symbolizes the first rudiments of it. *And Israel said to Joseph* symbolizes a perception from divine spirituality. *Aren't your brothers shepherding in Shechem?* means that they are teaching. *Go, and let me send you to them* means that he would teach about divinely spiritual goodness. *And [Joseph] said [to him], "Here I am,"* means saying yes. *And [Israel] said to him, "Go, please; see the peace of your brothers,"* symbolizes every coming of the Lord, and perceiving how things stood with the people who were teaching. *And the peace of the flock* means how things stood with the people learning, or the church. *And bring word back to me* symbolizes knowledge. *And he sent him from the valley of Hebron* means [teaching] of the earthly and sensory planes of divinity. *And [Joseph] came to Shechem* symbolizes knowledge of general doctrines. *And a man found him, and here, he was wandering in the field* means that they had fallen away from the church's general truth. *And the man asked him, saying, "What are you looking for?"* symbolizes foresight. *And he said, "I am looking for my brothers; please tell me where they are shepherding,"* means knowing how the situation stood and what state they were in. *And the man said, "They traveled on from here, because I heard them saying, 'Let's go to Dothan,'"* means that they turned from broad outlines of theology to specifics. *And Joseph went after his brothers and found them in Dothan* means that they focused on specifics involving false assumptions.

4705   *His brothers went to pasture the flock* means people who teach of faith. This can be seen from the symbolism of Joseph's *brothers* as people in the church who concentrate on faith (discussed above at §§4665, 4671, 4679, 4690) and from that of *pasturing the flock* as teaching (discussed at §§343, 3767, 3768, 3772, 3783).

4706   *Of their father* means [the faith] of the ancient church and of the early [Christian] church. This can be seen from the symbolism of the *father,* Jacob, as the ancient church (discussed above in §4680 at the end). Jacob also symbolizes the early Christian church (see §4690 at the end), "the early [Christian] church" meaning the Christian church in its very beginnings.

There are in general four distinct churches that the Word talks about. There is the one that existed before the Flood and was named Humankind, which is called the earliest church. Then there is the one that existed after the Flood, which is called the ancient church. There is the one that existed among Jacob's descendants, which was not a church but a representation of a church; this one I also refer to as a religiosity. And there is the one established after the Lord's Coming, which is called the Christian church. This is the one whose beginnings are called the early [Christian] church.

In Shechem symbolizes the first rudiments of it. This is established by the symbolism of *Shechem* as truth of an ancient, divine stock (discussed in §§4399, 4454) and as theology (§§4472, 4473). Here it symbolizes first rudiments of it—the first rudiments of a theology concerning faith. What nuance is implied by a name depends on the subject matter in its context. The first rudiments are general doctrines, the general ones being learned first, and specific ones later.

4707

And Israel said to Joseph symbolizes a perception from divine spirituality. This can be seen from the symbolism of *saying* in the narratives of the Word as perception (discussed in §§1791, 1815, 1819, 1822, 1898, 1919, 2080, 2619, 2862, 3395, 3509) and from the representation of *Joseph* as divine spirituality (discussed at §4669).

4708

Aren't your brothers shepherding in Shechem? means that they are teaching. This can be seen from the symbolism of *shepherding* as teaching (noted just above at §4705) and from that of *Shechem* as the first rudiments of a theology concerning faith (discussed just above at §4707).

4709

Go, and let me send you to them means that he would teach about divinely spiritual goodness. This can be seen from the representation of Joseph as the Lord's divine spirituality (discussed at §§4669, 4708). When this is said to be *sent,* it means teaching about divinely spiritual goodness. In an inner sense, being sent means coming from and radiating out (§2397) and also teaching. In this verse, then, it means teaching about the divinely spiritual goodness that radiates from the Lord's divine spirituality.

4710

Divinely spiritual goodness is the goodness associated with love and charity, while divinely spiritual truth is truth associated with the resulting faith. One who teaches this truth teaches about such goodness, because this truth develops out of such goodness and describes it.

Many passages in the Word show that in an inner sense being sent means radiating out and also teaching. For instance, the Word often says that the Lord was sent by the Father, meaning that he came forth from the Father, which is to say from divine goodness; or that the Lord would send the Paraclete, the Spirit of Truth, meaning that holy truth radiates from him. The prophets were also sent, which symbolized the fact that they taught about qualities that radiate from the Lord. Anyone can confirm these things from the Word, since they are found in many places there.

4711   *And [Joseph] said [to him], "Here I am,"* means saying yes, as is self-evident.

4712   *And [Israel] said to him, "Go, please; see the peace of your brothers,"* symbolizes every coming of the Lord, and perceiving how things stood with the people who were teaching. This is indicated by the symbolism of *saying* as perception (noted just above at §4708); from that of *peace* as salvation (mentioned at §4681), and therefore how matters stood; and from the representation of the *brothers* as people who teach of faith (noted above at §4705). These comments show that the sentence symbolizes a perception of the way things stood with the people teaching.

It also symbolizes every coming of the Lord because Joseph represents the Lord as to divine spirituality (§§4669, 4708, 4710). When the text says that Joseph went and saw the peace of his brothers, then, a coming of the Lord is symbolized. It is called a coming when truth from the Word flows into one's thinking.

4713   *And the peace of the flock* means how things stood with the people learning, or the church. This is indicated by the symbolism of *peace* as the way matters stood (dealt with just above at §4712) and from that of the *flock* as people who are learning. A shepherd, or pasturer, is one who teaches people and leads them to a goodness inspired by neighborly love, while a flock is one who learns and is led (discussed in §343) and is therefore the church.

4714   *And bring word back to me* symbolizes knowledge. This can be seen from the meaning of *bringing word back* as reporting how things stood and therefore as knowledge.

4715   *And he sent him from the valley of Hebron* means [teaching] of the earthly and sensory planes of divinity. This can be seen from the symbolism of being *sent* as radiating out and as teaching (discussed above in §4710); from that of a *valley* as something down low (discussed in §§1723, 3417); and from that of *Hebron* as goodness in the Lord's church (discussed at §2909). The sentence, then, means that he would teach about the lowlier aspects of the church, since people would not grasp higher aspects.

People who teach faith and not charity can never discern the higher, inner dimensions of the religion, because they have nothing to guide them. They have nothing telling them whether such and such is consonant with the faith, or whether such and such is true. If they teach charity, though, they have goodness. Goodness is their inner dictate and guide. All truth comes from goodness, you see, and has to do with goodness. In other words, all faith comes from charity and has to do with charity. Anyone can see just from earthly illumination that all theology is about life.

[2] In a higher sense, these words mean [that he would teach] of divine rationality. The lowlier aspects of the church are said to be from the earthly and sensory planes of the Lord's divinity. Not that they are lowlier in the Lord, because everything in the Lord and in his divine humanity is infinite. He is Jehovah in regard to both natures (§§2156, 2329, 2921, 3023). Rather, it is because they are lowlier in humankind. People who are sense-oriented have a sensory grasp of everything in and from the Lord. People who are limited to the earthly plane have an earthly grasp. It is because of the nature of the people on the receiving end that these descriptions are used. People who are heavenly and therefore truly rational, though, perceive inner levels. They are said to be taught of the Lord's divine rationality. This is the higher meaning symbolized by the sentence, as just mentioned.

[3] The meaning of a valley as a lowlier plane of the church can be seen from other places in the Word, such as Isaiah:

> An *oracle of the Valley of Vision:* What is going on for you here, that you have all gone up onto the roofs? It is a day of upheaval and trampling and chaos to the Lord Jehovih Sabaoth in the *Valley of Vision.* (Isaiah 22:1, 5)

The Valley of Vision stands for fanciful notions of the spiritual dimension based on sense impressions and consequently on a lower dimension. In the same author:

> The *choicest* of your *valleys* were filled with chariots, and riders positioned [themselves] firmly at the gate. (Isaiah 22:7)

The choicest of the valleys stands for goodness and truth in the earthly, outer self. In the same author:

> The voice of one shouting in the wilderness, "Prepare the way for Jehovah! Level in the desert a path for our God!" *Every valley* will be raised up. (Isaiah 40:3, 4)

The valley stands for the humble. [4] In Jeremiah:

> How can you say, "I am not defiled; I have not gone after the baals"? Look at *your path in the valley;* acknowledge what you have done! (Jeremiah 2:23)

The valley stands for secular and sense-based knowledge, lowly kinds of information by which people have twisted the truth. In the same author:

> "I am against you, *inhabitant of the valley,* rock of the plain," says Jehovah, "who are saying, 'Who will come down against me?'" (Jeremiah 21:13)

The inhabitant of the valley and the rock of the plain stand for faith in which there is no charity. In the same author:

> A destroyer will come over every city, and no city will escape, but *the valley will perish* and the plain be destroyed. (Jeremiah 48:8)

The meaning is similar. In the same author:

> You will not glory in the *valleys; your valley* has flowed down, wayward daughter! (Jeremiah 49:4)

The valley stands for the superficial aspects of worship, which are also the lowliest. [5] In Ezekiel:

> I will give Gog a place for a grave in Israel: the *valley of passersby.* They will there bury Gog and all its horde. So they will call it the *Valley of Gog's Horde.* (Ezekiel 39:11, 15)

Gog stands for people who engage in an outward display of worship that lacks inner content (§1151). That is why its grave is called the valley of passersby and the Valley of Gog's Horde. In David:

> Even when I walk in the *valley of shadow* I will not be afraid of evil. (Psalms 23:4)

The valley of shadow stands for lower planes, which are in comparative shadow.

[6] Since valleys lie between mountains and hills and are at their feet, they symbolize lower or more superficial features of the church. This is because hills and mountains symbolize its higher, inner features—hills symbolizing anything connected with charity, and mountains, anything connected with love for the Lord (§§795, 1430, 2722, 4210). Because the

land of Canaan symbolizes the Lord's kingdom and church, it is called a "*land of mountains and valleys,* drinking up water at the raining of the sky" (Deuteronomy 11:11).

The text says that Joseph was sent from the valley of Hebron because it is saying he was sent to people who taught about faith (§4705), since people with faith but not charity are on a low level. With these individuals, faith lives just in the memory and on the lips, not in the heart and therefore in deeds.

And [Joseph] came to Shechem symbolizes knowledge of general doctrines. This can be seen from the discussion in §4707 of the symbolism of *Shechem* as first rudiments—in other words, as general doctrines.

4716

And a man found him, and here, he was wandering in the field means that they had fallen away from the church's general truth. This can be seen from the symbolism of *wandering in the field* as falling away from the church's general truth. A *field* means the goodness in a church (§§2971, 3196, 3766), and "a man of the field" means a good life resulting from doctrine (§3310). The word *man* is used because a man symbolizes truth belonging to the church (§3134).

4717

People are said to fall away from the church's general truth when they acknowledge the Lord but not his divine humanity, and when they acknowledge faith as essential but not charity. Each of these is a general truth that is part of the church, and when people in the church back away from it, they fall away from general truth. Those who fall away from general truth, later fall away from specific truth, as dealt with below [§§4720, 4721]. Likewise, when people start with a false assumption and draw conclusions from it, the conclusions turn out false. The assumption governs everything that follows from it, which in turn corroborates the false premise.

And the man asked him, saying, "What are you looking for?" symbolizes foresight. This can be seen from context, because the context involves foresight.

4718

And he said, "I am looking for my brothers; please tell me where they are shepherding," means knowing how the situation stood and what state they were in. In the layer of meaning that most nearly tracks the words, it symbolizes how the situation stood with people teaching faith and how [the Lord] knew their state. *Brothers* symbolize people who teach of faith (§4712). *Looking for* them ("seeing their peace") symbolizes the way things stood with them (§§4712, 4713). *Where* symbolizes their state, since in an inner sense everything having to do with place means state (2625, 2837,

4719

3356, 3387, 4321). And people *shepherding* symbolize those who teach (343, 3767, 3768, 3772, 3783).

4720   *And the man said, "They traveled on from here, because I heard them saying, 'Let's go to Dothan,'"* means that they turned from broad outlines of theology to specifics, as the following shows: *Traveling on* means turning or resorting to. From Shechem—*from here*—means from the broad outlines of theology (§§4707, 4716). And *Dothan* symbolizes the specifics of theology.

The meaning of *Dothan* as the specifics of theology cannot be confirmed very well by other Scripture passages, because it is mentioned only in 2 Kings 6:13. The account there is that the king of Syria sent chariots and riders and a large army to Dothan to seize Elisha, who had them struck with blindness and led them to Samaria. [2] Since all narratives in the Word represent heavenly and spiritual components of the Lord's kingdom, this one does too. The king of Syria represents people with concepts that are true (§§1232, 1234, 3249, 3664, 3680, 4112), though here, in a negative sense, he represents people with concepts that are not true. Elisha represents the Lord's Word (2762). Dothan represents doctrines from the Word. The chariots, riders, and large army that Syria's king sent symbolizes falsehood in theology. The horses and fiery chariots filling the mountain all around Elisha, which were seen by his boy [2 Kings 6:17], symbolize goodness and truth in theology, acquired from the Word (2762). The blindness that struck the troops sent there by Syria's king symbolizes the falsities themselves (2383). The fact that Elisha led them to Samaria, where their eyes were opened, symbolizes instruction through the Word. That is what the story involves, and Dothan, where Elisha was, symbolizes doctrines about goodness and truth from the Word.

The symbolism is the same in the current verse, since that is exactly what the specifics of theology are. In this verse, though, Dothan symbolizes specifics based on false assumptions, since the theme is a religion that starts with faith, detaching it from charity right at the outset. Any doctrines formed after that all smack of the overall starting point and therefore of faith without charity, so they give rise to falsities, which are specifics based on false premises.

[3] No religion starts off knowing anything but the broad outlines of its theology because it is then in its simplicity and its youth, so to speak. As time passes it brings in specifics. In part these are confirmations of the general doctrines, and in part they are additions to it, but additions that do not clash with the overall theology. They are also explanations

intended to take open contradictions and draw them into agreement, to prevent them from violating the dictates of common sense. Nonetheless they are all specifics that involve false assumptions. In any theology, all the elements interrelate, as if they formed a community. They are united by a kind of blood relationship and family tie, acknowledging a shared premise as their ancestor. Obviously they all smack of falsity, then, if the overall starting point is false.

And Joseph went to his brothers and found them in Dothan means that they focused on specifics involving false assumptions, as the following shows: *Joseph* represents the Lord's divine truth, as discussed in §4669. *His brothers* represent a religion that turns aside from charity to faith and eventually to a detached faith, as discussed in §§4665, 4671, 4679, 4680, 4690. And *Dothan* symbolizes specifics based on false assumptions, as discussed just above in §4720. The sentence as a whole, then, means that he found them focusing on specifics involving false assumptions.

[2] To see what is meant by specifics involving false assumptions, take as illustration several doctrines of a religion acknowledging faith alone as a premise, specifically these: We are absolved by faith alone. All our sins are then erased. We are saved by faith alone even in the last hour of our life. Salvation is simply getting into heaven by grace. Even babies are saved by faith. People outside the religion are not saved, because they do not have the faith. And so on. These doctrines and others like them are specifics based on a premise of faith alone.

However, if the church acknowledged a *life* of faith as a starting point, it would acknowledge charity for one's neighbor and love for the Lord and therefore deeds of charity and love. Then all those specifics would tumble down. Rather than absolution the church would acknowledge rebirth, of which the Lord says in John, "Unless one is born anew, one cannot see the kingdom of God" (John 3:3). It would recognize that rebirth is accomplished through a life of faith, not through a detached faith. It would not hold that on being absolved we are washed clean of all our sins but instead that the Lord's mercy holds us back from our sins and anchors us in goodness and accordingly in truth. So it would acknowledge that everything good is from the Lord, and everything evil from oneself. The church would not hold that we are saved by faith in the last hour of our life but that we are saved by a life of faith, this being what awaits us [after death]. It would not hold that salvation is simply getting into heaven by grace, since the Lord does not deny heaven to anyone. Rather, it would recognize that if our life is not such that we can be together with angels, we spontaneously flee the place (§4674). The church would not hold that babies are saved by faith but would acknowledge that the Lord teaches them charitable goodness and religious truth in the other world and that they are welcomed into heaven as a result (§§2289–2309). And it would not hold that people outside the religion are not saved because they do not have the faith. Instead, it would acknowledge that their life equally awaits them, that the ones who had lived lives of neighborly love for each other learn about the goodness connected with the faith, and that they are equally welcomed into heaven. The ones who live good lives want this and believe it. See §§2589–2605. The same holds true for many other doctrines as well.

[3] A church that acknowledges faith alone as its premise can never see what charity is, or our neighbor, or heaven. Such a church is inevitably puzzled to hear anyone say that a happy life after death and joy in heaven is the Divine flowing into our good wishes and good deeds toward others. The resulting happiness and bliss outstrips all perception, and no one can possibly receive it who had not lived a life of faith—in other words, had not exercised neighborly kindness. All this is astounding to such a church.

The Lord also openly teaches in Matthew 25:31–end and many other places that a life according to faith saves people. The creed called Athanasian teaches the same, when it says at the end, "All will offer an accounting of their deeds. Those who had done good will enter eternal life, but those who had done evil will enter eternal fire."

4722 Genesis 37:18, 19, 20, 21, 22. *And they saw him from far off, and before he came close to them they plotted against him to put him to death. And they said, a man to his brother, "Look: that lord of dreams comes! And now come, and let's kill him and put him into one of the pits and say, 'A bad wild animal ate him up,' and we will see what his dreams will be!" And Reuben listened and rescued him from their hand and said, "Let's not strike his soul." And Reuben said to them, "Don't shed blood; put him into that pit that is in the wilderness and don't put a hand on him"—in order to rescue him from their hand, to return him to his father.*

They saw him from far off symbolizes a perception of the Lord's divine humanity at a distance. *And before he came close to them they plotted against him to put him to death* means that they wanted to extinguish the divine spirituality radiating from the Lord's divine humanity. *And they said, a man to his brother,* symbolizes their shared thought. *Look: that lord of dreams comes* means that those things were worthless. *And now come, and let's kill him* symbolizes snuffing out the essential doctrine of the Lord's divine humanity. *And put him into one of the pits* means accounting it as falsity. *And say, "A bad wild animal ate him up,"* symbolizes a lie resulting from the life within their cravings. *And we will see what his dreams will be* means that the declarations about him therefore seemed false, too. *And Reuben listened* symbolizes a confession of the church's faith in general. *And rescued him from their hand* symbolizes deliverance. *And said, "Let's not strike his soul,"* means that it was not to be extinguished, because it was the very life of their religion. *And Reuben said to them* symbolizes a plea. *Don't shed blood* means not to violate what was sacred. *Put him into that pit that is in the wilderness* means that meanwhile they would hide it among their falsities. *And don't put a hand on him* means to avoid violating it. *In order to rescue him from their hand, to return him to his father,* means so that he could reclaim it for the church.

They saw him from far off symbolizes a perception of the Lord's divine humanity at a distance. This can be seen from the symbolism of *seeing* as perception (discussed at §§2150, 3764); from that of *from far off* as distantly; and from the representation of Joseph, the one they saw from far off, as the Lord in respect to divine truth (discussed at §4669). Joseph means the Lord's divine humanity here because this is the highest form of divine truth. There are two essential components of the church and therefore two main points of theology. One is that the Lord's humanity is divine. The other is that love for the Lord and charity for one's neighbor (not faith in isolation from these) make the church. Because these are the most important points of divine truth, they are represented by Joseph. One who represents divine truth in general also represents particular points of divine truth. Context reveals what Joseph represents specifically.

4723

And before he came close to them they plotted against him to put him to death means that they wanted to extinguish the divine spirituality radiating from the Lord's divine humanity, as the following shows: *Plotting* means wanting something with sinister intent, since when people want something this way they plot to achieve it. *Putting to death* means extinguishing. And Joseph represents divine spirituality, or divine truth (discussed several times above). Divine truth comes from the Lord's divine humanity, which is the reason for speaking of the divine spirituality radiating from his divine humanity.

4724

[2] Here is the situation: All divine truth throughout heaven comes exclusively from the Lord's divine humanity. Nothing that comes from divinity itself can possibly flow directly into any angel, because it is infinite. The inflow has to come indirectly through the Lord's divine humanity,

which is what the Lord meant by these words: "God has never been seen by anyone; the only-born Son, who is in the Father's embrace, is the one who has revealed him" (John 1:18). For this reason the Lord is called a mediator in regard to his divine humanity [1 Timothy 2:5; Hebrews 8:6; 9:15; 12:24].

[3] The Lord's divine humanity has also existed from eternity. If the divine reality had not flowed in through heaven, giving rise to the divine presence, it could not have been communicated to any angel, let alone any spirit, not to mention any person on earth. The Lord's divinity itself is the divine reality, and his divine humanity is the divine presence (see §4687).

What is more, not even the Lord's humanity could have received any inflow of the divine reality if that humanity had not become divine in him, because a thing has to be divine to receive the divine reality.

These brief remarks show that divine truth cannot radiate directly from divinity itself, only from the Lord's divine humanity.

[4] People extinguish divine truth in themselves when they do battle for faith alone without living a life of faith. They consider the Lord's human nature purely human, little different from the nature of any other person. Many of them consequently deny the Lord's divinity, no matter how vocally they claim to believe in him. On bent knees, however, with a humble heart, people who live a life of faith revere the Lord as God the Savior, and while praying, they do not think from doctrine about the difference between his divine and human natures. Likewise during the Holy Supper. For them, then, the Lord's divine humanity clearly lives in their heart.

4725 *And they said, a man to his brother,* symbolizes their shared thought. This can be seen from the symbolism of *saying* as perceiving and thinking (discussed in §3395) and from the meaning of a *man to his brother* as mutually.

It was idiomatic for the ancients to say "a man to his brother" when they meant something mutual because a *man* symbolized truth (§§3134, 3459) and a *brother* symbolized goodness (§4121). Between these two exists a relationship epitomizing mutuality, because truth unites mutually and reciprocally with goodness, and goodness with truth (§2731).

4726 *Look: that lord of dreams comes* means that those things were worthless. This can be seen from the symbolism of *dreams* as declarations (discussed at §4682), and in the current verse, which is talking about Joseph, as declarations about divine truth. People devoted to faith alone reject the essential points of divine truth, as I have demonstrated concerning the Lord's divine humanity and charity [§§4692, 4717]. The dreams here, then, symbolize something worthless. To people like this, falsity seems true and truth false, or if not false, still worthless. The *lord* of the dreams is one who makes declarations about those points.

There is much evidence that divine truth appears worthless to such people. For example, it is a divine truth that the Word is holy, and divinely inspired down to every jot. The Word is holy and divinely inspired because everything in it represents and symbolizes the heavenly and spiritual qualities of the Lord's kingdom. However, if you open up Scripture's inner meaning, teaching the representation and symbolism of the individual words, the type of people who subscribe to faith alone reject those ideas as worthless, denying that they are of any use. Yet such things are the very model of all that is heavenly and spiritual, and they please the inner self more than worldly objects please the outer self. The same is true for many other examples.

And now come, and let's kill him symbolizes snuffing out the essential doctrine of the Lord's divine humanity. This is established by the symbolism of *killing* as extinguishing, and by the representation of Joseph, the one they wanted to kill, as the Lord's divine truth—specifically, the doctrine of his divine humanity (§4723). This is the essential teaching of theology (see the same section).

It is recognized that the church, in acknowledging faith alone, has blotted out this essential truth. After all, who in the church considers the Lord's humanity divine? Does the mere suggestion not rouse opposition? The ancient churches, though, believed that the Lord who was destined to come into the world was a divine human, and when they saw this person, they called him Jehovah, as numerous passages in the Word show. For the time being take just this one quotation from Isaiah:

> The voice of one shouting in the wilderness, "Prepare the way for *Jehovah*, and level in the desert a path for *our God!*" (Isaiah 40:3)

These words were said of the Lord, for whom John the Baptist prepared the way and leveled a path, as the Gospels make quite plain (Matthew 3:3; Mark 1:3; Luke 3:4; John 1:23). The same point can also be seen from the Lord's own words, that he was one with the Father, that the Father was in him, and that he was in the Father [John 10:30, 38; 14:10, 11, 20; 17:21–23]; that he was given all power in the heavens and on earth [Matthew 28:18]; and that he was given the power to judge [John 5:22, 26–27]. Anyone who knows just a little about power in heaven and on earth and about the power to judge can see that these things are meaningless unless the Lord was divine even on the human level.

[2] People devoted to faith alone also have no idea what makes us a new person, or sanctifies us, let alone what made the Lord's human nature divine, because they know nothing about love and charity. Love for the Lord and charity for our neighbor make us new and sanctify us, but divine love itself made the Lord divine. Love is our very being, so it is our life. It forms us in its image. Love works the same way as our soul, which is our inner being. Our soul forms the body in its image, so to speak, and in such a way that it uses the body to act and sense exactly as it wills and thinks. The body, then, is like an effect, and the soul is like a means containing a purpose. The soul is therefore everything to the body, just as the means of achieving a purpose is everything to the effect. One whose soul was Jehovah himself, as the Lord's was (since he was conceived by Jehovah), could not have had a human nature that was anything but [divine], once it had been glorified.

These considerations show how big a mistake people make in equating the humanity of the Lord after his glorification with anyone else's humanity, when in reality it is divine. Moreover, the Lord's divine humanity is the source from which all wisdom, all understanding, and all light radiates in heaven. Whatever emanates from him is holy. Anything holy that does not come from the Divine is not actually holy.

4728   *And put him into one of the pits* means accounting it as falsity, which can be seen from the symbolism of *pits* as falsity. Pits mean falsity because people whose basic assumptions have been false are kept in an underground region for a while after death until their falsities have been removed and more or less cast aside. Those places are called pits. The people who go there are the ones who have to undergo spiritual devastation, as described in §§1106–1113, 2699, 2701–2704. That is why on an abstract level pits symbolize falsity.

The underground realm is an area just below the feet and a little beyond them all around. Many people find themselves there after death before being lifted into heaven. This realm is mentioned several times in the Word. Beneath it are the places of devastation called pits. Below these and stretching far beyond them in all directions are the hells.

[2] This shows to some extent what is meant by hell, the underground realm, and the pit when they are mentioned in the Word, as in Isaiah:

To *hell* you were sent down, *to the sides of the pit.* You were thrown out of your grave like a despicable offshoot, [like] the garment of the slain,

[who were] stabbed with a sword, *who drop to the stones in the pit.*
(Isaiah 14:15, 19)

This is about the monarch of Babylon, who represents profanation of truth.
A monarch means truth (§§1672, 2015, 2069, 3009, 4581), and Babylon
profanation (1182, 1326). Hell is where the damned are. Their damnation is
being compared here to an abominable offshoot and to the garment of the
slain and of those stabbed with a sword, who drop to the stones in the pit.
The garment of the slain is profaned truth. Those stabbed with a sword are
people in whom truth has been wiped out. The pit means falsity that needs
to be purged. The stones mean the outer limits and are therefore called the
sides too, since all around the pits lie the hells. (A garment means truth,
2576. The garment of the slain means profaned truth because the blood
staining it means what is profane, 1003. Those stabbed with a sword are
people in whom truth has been wiped out, 4503.) This evidence also shows
that without the inner sense it is impossible to tell what these things mean.
[3] In Ezekiel:

> When I make you go down *with those going down into the pit,* to an
> ancient people, and settle you *in the underground realm*—to prevent
> you from settling in *places desolate* for ages, *with those going down into
> the pit*—then I will set beauty in the land of the living. (Ezekiel 26:20)

Those going down into the pit stand for people put into spiritual devastation. Not settling with those who go down into the pit stands for being
delivered from falsity. [4] In the same author:

> To prevent all the trees of the water from vaunting because of their
> height and sending their branch in among the thickets, and to prevent
> all those drinking the water from standing over them because of their
> height, they will all be handed over to death, *to the underground realm,*
> in the midst of the children of humankind, *to those going down into the
> pit.* At the sound of its wreckage I will make the nations tremble *when
> I make it go down into hell with those going down into the pit.* And *in
> the underground realm* all the trees of Eden will comfort themselves,
> the choice and foremost of Lebanon, all drinking the water. (Ezekiel
> 31:14, 16)

This is about Egypt, which symbolizes learning that relies on its own
resources to solve faith's mysteries; that is, it symbolizes people who do so
(§§1164, 1165, 1186). The remarks above clarify what is symbolized by hell,
the pit, and the underground realm, as mentioned here in this prophet.

In addition, only the inner meaning can show what is symbolized by the trees of the water, the trees of Eden, the branch sent in among the thickets, the choice and foremost of Lebanon, and the ones drinking the water. [5] In the same author:

> Son of humankind, lament over the throng of Egypt, and *bring [Egypt] itself* and the daughters of the majestic nations *down to the underground realm, with those going down into the pit.* There lies Assyria, which has been given graves *on the sides of the pit,* everyone who was stabbed by the sword. (Ezekiel 32:18, 22, 23)

The meaning of these things can be seen from the explanations above. In David:

> Jehovah, you brought my soul up *from hell;* you brought me to life *from among those going down into the pit.* (Psalms 30:3)

In the same author:

> I have been reckoned *with those going down into the pit.* I have been reckoned like a man [who has] no strength. You have put me *in a pit underground,* in dark places, in the depths. (Psalms 88:4, 6)

In Jonah:

> To the *excavations of the mountains* I had gone down; the poles of the earth lay above me forever; nonetheless *you brought my life up out of the pit.* (Jonah 2:6)

This is about the Lord's trials and deliverance from them. The excavations of the mountains are the places of the deeply damned, because the inky clouds that seem to surround them are mountains.

[6] The meaning of a pit as the purging away of falsity, and in an abstract sense as falsity itself, is further evident in Isaiah:

> The prisoners at the pit will be gathered in a gathering and will be shut up in jail, but after a multitude of days they will be visited. (Isaiah 24:22)

In the same author:

> Where is the anger of the oppressor? The one who leads [you] out will hurry to open [the oppressor's grip] and will not die *at the pit,* nor will the bread fail. (Isaiah 51:13, 14)

In Ezekiel:

> Look: I am bringing foreigners on you, the violent among the nations, who will unsheathe their swords over the beauty of your wisdom and profane your radiance; *down into the pit they will send you,* and you will die the deaths of the stabbed in the heart of the seas. (Ezekiel 28:7, 8)

This is about the chieftain of Tyre, who symbolizes people with false assumptions. [7] In Zechariah:

> Rejoice immensely, daughter of Zion; cheer aloud, daughter of Jerusalem! See: your king comes to you, honorable, afflicted, and riding on a donkey, and on a young animal, the foal of jennies. By the blood of the pact I will *let your prisoners out of a pit in which there is no water.* (Zechariah 9:9, 11)

A pit that has no water stands for falsity containing no truth. The same thing is said below in verse 24: "They sent Joseph into the pit, and the pit was empty, with no water in it." In David:

> To you, Jehovah, I shout; my Rock, do not be silent toward me, for fear that if you are silent toward me *I would seem like those going down into the pit.* (Psalms 28:1)

In the same author:

> Jehovah *brought [me] up out of the pit of devastation,* out of the muddy clay, and set my feet on a rock. (Psalms 40:2)

In the same author:

> May a wave of water not overwhelm me, nor the deep swallow me, *nor the pit close its mouth over me!* (Psalms 69:15)

[8] In the same author:

> He sent his word and healed them and rescued them *from their pits.* (Psalms 107:20)

From pits means from falsity. In the same author:

> Hurry; answer me, Jehovah! My spirit has been consumed; do not hide your face from me so that *I become like those going down into the pit.* (Psalms 143:7)

Since a pit symbolizes falsity, and the blind symbolize people caught up in falsity (§2383), the Lord says:

> Let them be; they are blind leaders of the blind, and if a blind person leads a blind person, *both fall into a pit.* (Matthew 15:13, 14; Luke 6:39)

The prophet Jeremiah had a representation similar to Joseph's, a situation he writes of in this way:

> They took Jeremiah and threw him *into the pit* that was in the courtyard of the prison and let Jeremiah down by ropes *into the pit, where there was no water.* (Jeremiah 38:6)

In other words, they rejected divine truth, accounting it as falsity empty of truth.

4729   *And say, "A bad wild animal ate him up,"* symbolizes a lie resulting from the life within their cravings. This can be seen from the symbolism of a *wild animal* as a feeling or craving (discussed at §§45, 46). In a positive sense a wild animal means something living (§§774, 841, 908), so this *bad* wild animal symbolizes the life within their cravings. The fact that it is a lie is obvious.

This meaning relates to what comes before, which is to say that their rejection of divine truth as falsity was a lie resulting from the life within their cravings.

There are three sources of falsity: (1) the theology of one's religion; (2) the illusions of the senses; (3) the force of one's cravings. Falsity springing from a religion's theology takes control only of our intellectual side, because we are persuaded from childhood on that it represents the truth, and eventually we find proof for it. Falsity produced by the illusions of the senses does not affect the intellectual side as strongly, because people who buy into this kind of falsity do not apply their intellect much, since they think on the lower plane of the senses. But falsity rising out of the life within our cravings pours out from our actual will, or what is the same, from our heart. What we seek from the heart is what we crave. This falsity is the worst sort, because it clings and is eradicated only by a new kind of living energy from the Lord.

[2] People recognize that we have two inner capacities: the intellect and the will. Just because the intellect takes something in and absorbs it does not mean it passes into the will. What the will absorbs, on the other hand, does pass into the intellect, because what we intend, we think. So when we willfully crave some evil, we think it and justify it. The justification of

evil in our thoughts is what is called falsity resulting from the life within our cravings. This falsity seems true to us, and when we have proved it to ourselves, truth seems false to us, because we have then shut off any inflow of light through heaven from the Lord. If we have *not* proved it to ourselves, the truth our intellect had previously absorbed stands in the way and prevents us from confirming it.

And we will see what his dreams will be means that the declarations about him therefore seemed false, too. This is established by the symbolism of *dreams* as declarations (discussed at §4682). Because the declarations appeared false in their eyes (§§4726, 4729), these dreams symbolize declarations about divine truth that in their opinion were false, especially the declaration that the Lord's humanity was divine. The fact that these too seemed false to them is symbolized by their saying, *we will see what they will be.* The discussion just above in §4729 shows that to people intent on faith alone, declarations about the Lord's divine humanity appeared false, as they still do today. That is how things confirmed by our cravings appear.

[2] Another reason the force of their cravings leads people to confirm falsity is that they do not know what heaven is, what hell is, what love for their neighbor is, and what love for themselves and for worldly advantages is. If they did know, or even if they merely wanted to know, they would think very differently. Who today has any idea that love for our neighbor does not mean giving our things to the poor, helping everyone with our wealth, and benefiting people in every way without regard to their goodness or evil? If we did such things, we would be deprived of our own resources and end up impoverished and wretched ourselves. That is why people reject the doctrine of charity and embrace the doctrine of faith. Afterward they harden themselves against charity with many arguments. We were born in sin, they think to themselves, so we can do no good on our own; and if we do charitable, pious deeds, we cannot help taking credit for them. Under the inspiration of these ideas on one hand and the stimulus of their cravings on the other, they take sides with those who say faith alone saves us. Armed with this belief, they harden themselves still further, until they deny that acts of neighborly love are necessary to salvation. Once those deeds are dismissed they fall into the new idea that because we are like this, the Lord has provided a means of salvation, which is called faith. Finally they arrive at the concept that we are saved if we have the confidence or assurance to say, even at the moment of death, that God takes pity on us when he looks on his Son, who suffered

4730

for us. They neglect to consider what the Lord said in John 1:12, 13 and a thousand other places.

This then is why the churches have deemed faith alone essential— though not to the same extent everywhere, because the church leaders cannot profit off faith alone, only off the preaching of good deeds.

[3] If these same people had known what charity toward one's neighbor was, they never would have fallen into that false theology. The foundation of charity is our doing what is right and fair in every arena in which we have any duty or responsibility. For instance, when judges punish wrongdoers in accord with the law, acting with zeal, they are exercising charity toward their neighbor. They seek their neighbor's reform, so they want what is good for her or him. They also wish well to society and their country in trying to stop the criminal from doing more harm to either of these. They can love the evildoer who straightens out, just as parents can love the child they discipline. At the same time they love society and their country, which is their overall neighbor. The same holds true for all other instances.

These ideas will be explored in greater depth elsewhere, the Lord in his divine mercy willing [§8121].

4731   *And Reuben listened* symbolizes a confession of the church's faith in general. This is established by the representation of *Reuben* as a faith that belongs to the intellect, or doctrinal faith, which is the first step of rebirth, and all doctrinal truth as a whole through which we can attain a good life (discussed at §§3861, [3863,] 3866). In the current verse, then, he represents a confession of the church's faith in general.

Reuben interferes at this point because a religion that starts with faith ceases to be a religion unless it holds on to the divine truth that the Lord's humanity is divine. This is the highest, inmost truth in the church. Reuben therefore wanted to rescue Joseph (who represents that truth here) from the hand of his brothers to return him to his father, meaning that he wanted to reclaim that truth for the church. Furthermore, when Reuben returned to the pit and saw no Joseph there, he tore his clothes and said to his brothers, "The child is no more, and I, where do I go?" (verses 29, 30), meaning that there was no longer any faith in the Lord and consequently no religion.

[2] People in the church who are devoted to faith alone deny this highest, inmost truth that the Lord's humanity is divine. However, since they know from the Word that the Lord has divinity and do not grasp

how his humanity can be divine, they credit him with both a divine and a human nature, distinguishing between the two.

By contrast, people who live a life of faith—in other words, exercise charity—revere the Lord as their God and Savior. While they are worshiping, they think about his divinity without dividing it from his humanity. In doing so they acknowledge at heart that everything about the Lord is divine. When they think from doctrine, though, they too are unable to understand how his humanity can be divine, so they repeat what the doctrines teach.

And rescued him from their hand symbolizes deliverance, as is evident without explanation.

And said, "Let's not strike his soul," means that it was not to be extinguished, because it was the very life of their religion. This can be seen from the symbolism of *striking* as extinguishing, and from that of the *soul* as life (discussed in §§1000, 1005, 1436, 1742)—here, as the life of their religion.

Acknowledgment and worship of the Lord's divine humanity is the lifeblood of religion. This can be seen from the comments just above in §4731 and from the fact that by our very nature we want to worship something of which we can form some picture in perception and thought. In fact, people who are limited to the sensory plane want to worship something they can sense in some way. They are unwilling to worship anything divine except in tangible form. This is common to the whole human race. That is why people outside the church venerate idols, which they believe have something divine in them. Others venerate the deceased whom they believe to be either gods or saints. Nothing in us can be stirred unless it moves our senses. [2] Most people who say they acknowledge a supreme being that they cannot picture or perceive actually acknowledge no God. They recognize nature instead, and they recognize nature because they can grasp it. Many well-educated Christians are like this, partly because they do not accept the divinity of the Lord's humanity.

There was a danger, then, that people who had alienated themselves from the Divine to this extent and become so body-centered would worship wood and stone. They might adulate someone who had died and therefore a devil in that person's guise. They might not worship God himself because they had no way of perceiving him. Then the whole church would have been destroyed, and with the church, the human race. To prevent all this, the Divine itself decided to adopt a human nature and make it divine.

[4732]

[4733]

Scholars should therefore be careful not to think about the Lord's humanity without also believing in its divinity. Otherwise they trip themselves up and eventually believe nothing.

4734   *And Reuben said to them* symbolizes a plea. In the first layer of meaning it symbolizes a confession of the church's faith in general—or *Reuben* (§4731)—pleading with them or dictating to them from within not to commit violence, as in the next section.

4735   *Don't shed blood* means not to violate what was sacred. This can be seen from the symbolism of *blood* as something sacred (dealt with below). Accordingly, *shedding blood* means violating it.

Everything sacred in heaven comes from the Lord's divine humanity, so everything sacred in the church does as well. To keep people from violating it, the Lord established the Holy Supper, in which it is explicitly said that the bread is his flesh, and the wine his blood. That is, ever since then his divine humanity is the source of what is sacred.

To the ancients, flesh and blood symbolized human selfhood, because a person consists of flesh and blood. That is why the Lord said to Simon, "Fortunate are you, because *flesh and blood* did not reveal this to you but my Father who is in the heavens" (Matthew 16:17). The flesh and blood meant by the bread and wine in the Holy Supper therefore means the Lord's human sense of self. His true selfhood, which he acquired for himself by his own power, is divine. The selfhood he received by conception was the one he had from Jehovah, his Father, and was Jehovah himself, so the sense of self he acquired as a human being was divine. This divine selfhood in his human side is what is called flesh and blood. The flesh is his divine goodness (§3813). The blood is the divine truth belonging to his divine goodness.

[2] Now that the Lord's human nature has been glorified, or made divine, it cannot be conceived of as human but as divine love in human form. This is far truer of the Lord than it is of angels, and yet when they are seen—as I have seen them—they too look like forms of love and charity in human shape. It is from the Lord that they have this appearance. Divine love was what the Lord used in making his humanity divine, just as heavenly love is what turns people into angels after death, so that they look like forms of love and charity in human shape, as noted.

These remarks show that, in a heavenly sense, the Lord's divine humanity means divine love itself, which is love for the whole human race. It consists in his wanting to save us, make us blissful and happy forever, and give his divinity to us as our own so far as we can receive it. This love, and our reciprocal love for the Lord, as well as love for our neighbor, are what are symbolized and represented in the Holy Supper. Divine heavenly love is meant by the flesh or bread, and divine spiritual love, by the blood or wine.

[3] From these considerations you can now see what is meant in John by the eating of the Lord's flesh and the drinking of his blood:

> I am the *living bread* who came down from heaven. If anyone eats *of this bread,* that person will live forever. But the *bread* that I will give is *my flesh.* Truly, truly, I say to you: *unless you eat the flesh of the Son of Humankind* and *drink his blood* you will not have life in you. Whoever *eats my flesh* and *drinks my blood* has eternal life. And I will revive that person on the last day, because *my flesh* is truly food, and *my blood* is truly drink. Those who *eat my flesh* and *drink my blood* remain in me, and I in them. This is the *bread* that came down from heaven. (John 6:50–58)

As noted, the flesh and blood symbolize heavenly divinity and spiritual divinity from the Lord's divine humanity—in other words, the divine goodness and divine truth belonging to his love. Eating and drinking them, then, means adopting those things as our own. We adopt them by living a life of love and charity, which is also the life of faith. For the idea that eating means adopting what is good as our own, and that drinking means adopting what is true, see §§2187, 3069, 3168, 3513, 3596, 3772, 3832, 4017, 4018.

[4] Since blood on a heavenly plane symbolizes spiritual divinity, or divine truth radiating from the Lord's divine humanity, it symbolizes the holy [operation of the spirit]. Divine truth emanating from the Lord's divine humanity is this holy influence itself. The holy [operation of the spirit] has no other identity or source.

[5] The equation of blood with this holy influence can be seen from many places in the Word. Let me quote just the following. In Ezekiel:

> Son of humankind, this is what the Lord Jehovih has said: "Say to every bird of the sky, to every wild animal of the field, 'Gather and come! Gather from round about to my sacrifice that I am sacrificing for you, a grand sacrifice on the mountains of Israel, so that you can *eat flesh* and *drink blood. The flesh of the mighty you will eat,* and *the blood of the*

chieftains of the earth you will drink, rams, lambs, and he-goats, all fattened animals of Bashan; and you will eat fat to fullness and *drink blood* to drunkenness from my sacrifice that I sacrifice for you. You will be sated at my table on horse and on chariot, on mighty one and on every man of war. So will I set my glory among the nations.'" (Ezekiel 39:17, 18, 19, 20, 21)

This is about calling everyone to the Lord's kingdom, and in particular about establishing the church among the nations, or people outside the church. Eating flesh and drinking blood means adopting divine goodness and truth and therefore the holy influence from the Lord's divine humanity. Who can fail to see that the flesh does not mean flesh, and the blood does not mean blood? Consider, for instance, the statements that they would eat the flesh of the mighty, drink the blood of the chieftains of the earth, and be sated on horse, chariot, mighty one, and every man of war. [6] Likewise in John:

I saw an angel standing in the sun, who shouted in a loud voice, saying to all the birds flying in midair, "Come, gather to the supper of the great God, so that you can eat the *flesh* of monarchs and the *flesh* of commanders, and the *flesh* of the mighty, and the *flesh* of horses and of the people sitting on them, and the *flesh* of all, free people and slaves, small and great." (Revelation 19:17, 18)

Who is ever going to understand this passage without knowing the inner-level symbolism of flesh, or of monarchs, commanders, the mighty, horses, the people sitting on them, free people, and slaves? [7] Again, in Zechariah:

He will speak peace to the nations. His rule will be from sea to sea, and from the river to the ends of the earth. And you: by the *blood of your pact* I will let your prisoners out of the pit. (Zechariah 9:10, 11)

This is about the Lord. The blood of the pact means divine truth coming from his divine humanity, and the holy operation itself that emanated from him after he had been glorified. This holy influence is what is also called the Holy Spirit, as John reveals:

Jesus said, "If any are thirsty, let them come to me and *drink.* Any who believe in me, as the scripture said, from their belly will flow rivers of living water." This he said about the spirit that believers in him were about to receive, for there was not the Holy Spirit yet because Jesus was not yet glorified. (John 7:37, 38, 39)

To see that the holy influence coming from the Lord is the Spirit, read John 6:63. [8] Further evidence that blood stands for a holy influence radiating from the Lord's divine humanity occurs in David:

> From deceit and violence drive back their soul, and *their blood will be precious* in his eyes. (Psalms 72:14)

Precious blood stands for the holy influence they will be subject to. In John:

> These are the ones coming out of great affliction, and they washed their robes and whitened their robes *in the Lamb's blood*. (Revelation 7:14)

In the same author:

> They conquered the dragon *through the Lamb's blood* and through the word of their testimony. And they declined to love their soul, even to the point of death. (Revelation 12:11)

[9] The church today is fully convinced that the Lamb's blood here symbolizes the Lord's suffering. This is because people believe they are saved by the mere fact that the Lord suffered, which they view as the purpose of his mission in the world. Leave that idea for the unsophisticated, though, who cannot grasp deeper secrets. The Lord's Passion was the final stage of his trials and was the means by which he fully glorified his humanity (Luke 24:26; John 12:23, 27, 28; 13:31, 32; 17:1, 4, 5). The Lamb's blood here is the same thing as divine truth, or holy influence emanating from his divine humanity. It is the same, then, as the blood of the pact mentioned just above.

[10] Moses also mentions the blood of the pact:

> Moses took the book of the pact and read it in the ears of the people, who said, "Everything that Jehovah has spoken we will do and hear." Then Moses took the *blood* and spattered it on the people and said, "Look: the *blood of the pact* that Jehovah struck with you over all these words." (Exodus 24:7, 8)

The book of the pact was the divine truth they then received, as confirmed by the blood, which testified that it came from his divine humanity.

[11] In the rituals of the Jewish religion, blood actually symbolized a holy influence from the Lord's divine humanity. So when the people of that religion were being consecrated, it was done with blood. For example, when Aaron and his sons were being *consecrated*, *blood* was spattered on the horns of the altar, the rest [was poured out] at the base of the altar,

and some was put on the tip of their right ear, on their right thumb and their right big toe, and on their clothes (Exodus 29:12, 16, 20, 21; Leviticus 8:[15, 19, 23, 30]). And when Aaron entered inside the veil to approach the appeasement cover, then too he spattered *blood* with his finger toward the east onto the appeasement cover seven times (Leviticus 16:12, 13, 14, 15). Likewise with the other ceremonies of consecration and with atonements and cleansings, as described in Exodus 12:7, 13, 22; 30:10; Leviticus 1:5, 11, 15; 3:2, 8, 13; 4:6, 7, 17, 18, 25, 30, 34; 5:9; 6:27, 28; 14:14–19, 25–30; 16:12, 13, 14, 15, 18, 19; Deuteronomy 12:27.

[12] Since blood symbolizes something holy in a positive sense, in a negative sense blood symbolizes agents of violence against anything holy. The reason is that the shedding of innocent blood symbolizes the violation of something holy. That is why criminal lives and profane worship were referred to as blood. This meaning of blood can be seen from the following passages. In Isaiah:

> . . . when the Lord has washed off the excrement of Zion's daughters and rinsed away the *blood of Jerusalem* from its midst, through a spirit of judgment and through a spirit of cleansing. (Isaiah 4:4)

In the same author:

> The waters of Dimon are full of *blood.* (Isaiah 15:9)

In the same author:

> Your hands have been defiled with *blood,* and your fingers with wickedness. Their feet run to evil, and they hurry *to shed innocent blood.* Their thoughts are thoughts of wickedness. (Isaiah 59:3, 7)

In Jeremiah:

> Yes, on your hems *is found the blood* of innocent paupers' souls. (Jeremiah 2:34)

[13] In the same author:

> On account of the sins of the prophets, the transgressions of the priests, *who shed the blood of the just* in Jerusalem's midst, [those same prophets and priests] have wandered blind in the streets, *they are defiled with blood;* things that they themselves cannot touch they touch with their clothes. (Lamentations 4:13, 14)

In Ezekiel:

> I passed right by you and saw you trampled *in your blood,* and I told you, "Live *in your blood!*" And I told you, "Live *in your blood!*" I washed you with water and cleaned *your blood* off you. And I anointed you with oil. (Ezekiel 16:6, 9)

In the same author:

> You, son of humankind, will you enter into controversy with the *blood-soaked city?* Let it know all its abominations: "*By your blood that you shed* you have become guilty, and by the idols that you made you have been defiled. Here, now, the chieftains of Israel, each according to [the strength of] his arm, have been in you and have *shed blood.* Men of slander have been in you *to shed blood* and have eaten on the mountains in you." (Ezekiel 22:2, 3, 4, 6, 9)

In Moses:

> If anyone sacrifices anywhere else than on the altar at the tent, *it will be blood[guilt]* and will be as if the person had *shed blood.* (Leviticus 17:1–9)

[14] Truth falsified and profaned is symbolized in the following passages about blood. In Joel:

> I will give portents in the heavens and on earth: *blood* and fire and pillars of smoke. The sun will turn to darkness and the *moon to blood* before the great and fearsome day comes. (Joel 2:30, 31)

In John:

> The sun turned black as sackcloth made of hair, and *the whole moon became like blood.* (Revelation 6:12)

In the same author:

> The second angel trumpeted, and what seemed to be a large mountain burning with fire was thrown into the sea, *and a third of the sea became blood.* (Revelation 8:8)

In the same author:

> The second angel poured out his bowl onto the sea, and *it became blood like that of a dead person,* so that every living soul in the sea died. The

third angel poured out his bowl onto the rivers and onto the springs of water, and *there was blood.* (Revelation 16:3, 4)

[15] Likewise with the fact that rivers, and gatherings and pools of water turned to *blood* in Egypt (Exodus 7:15–22). After all, Egypt symbolizes learning that relies on its own resources to pry into secrets of heaven, twisting, denying, and profaning divine truth in the process (§§1164, 1165, 1186). All the miracles in Egypt were divine and therefore involved a similar meaning. The rivers that were turned to blood mean the truth characterizing intelligence and wisdom (108, 109, 3051). So do water (680, 2702, 3058) and springs (2702, 3096, 3424). Seas mean whole bodies of secular truth (28). The moon, which the text says would also turn to blood, means divine truth (1529, 1530, 1531, 2495, 4060). Clearly, then, the moon, sea, springs, water, and rivers that were turned to blood symbolize truth falsified and profaned.

4736 *Put him into the pit that is in the wilderness* means that meanwhile they would hide [divine truth about the Lord's divine humanity] among their falsities—that is, they would consider it false but keep it anyway because it matters to the church. This can be seen from the symbolism of a *pit* as falsity (discussed above at §4728) and from that of a *wilderness* as a place where there is no truth. A wilderness has a broad range of meaning. It is an uninhabited and therefore undeveloped area, and applied to the church it means a place where there is no goodness and consequently no truth (§§2708, 3900). The pit in the wilderness accordingly means falsity that contains no truth because it contains no goodness.

The reason I am saying it contains no truth because it contains no goodness is this: When salvation is attributed to faith without deeds, truth can indeed exist, but it is not true in the person who thinks that way, because the person is not looking toward goodness or taking the side of goodness. This truth is not living, because it harbors a false premise. As a result, in people who accept it, such truth is nothing but falsity based on the premise that reigns supreme in it. The premise is like a soul that gives life to everything else.

On the other hand, there exists a kind of falsity that is accepted as truth, when it contains goodness, especially the goodness of innocence, as is found among people outside the church and also among many within the church.

4737 *And don't put a hand on him* means to avoid violating it, as is self-evident.

In order to rescue him from their hand, to return him to his father, means **4738**
so that he could reclaim it for the church. This can be seen from the symbolism of *rescuing from their hand* as delivering, as above at §4732, and
from that of *returning him to his father* as reclaiming for the church—
Jacob, the *father,* representing the Jewish religion that developed out of
the ancient church, as above at §§4700, 4701.

What the church would reclaim was divine truth about the Lord's
divine humanity. That is what Joseph symbolizes in a specific way, as
mentioned before.

[2] It needs to be further realized in regard to this truth that it was
acknowledged by the ancient church and also by the early Christian church.
Eventually, though, the papal throne grew powerful enough to rule all
human souls and exalted itself the way Isaiah says the king of Babylon did:

> You have said in your heart, "I will climb into the heavens; I will raise
> my throne above the stars of heaven and sit on the mountain of assem-
> bly; I will climb onto the loftiest parts of the cloud and become like the
> Highest One." (Isaiah 14:13, 14)

At that point the Lord's humanity started to be stripped of its divinity;
in other words, a distinction began to be drawn between his divinity and
his humanity. [3] The way the issue was decided in a certain council was
also revealed to me.

I saw a group of people out front and to the left on a level with the
sole of the foot, some distance away. They were talking together, but I
could not hear what it was about. I was told that they were some of the
ones who had been together on the council when it decided on the Lord's
dual nature, divine and human. Soon I was also allowed to talk with them.
They said that the council members with the greatest influence, highest
in rank and authority, had gotten together in a dark room and decided
to ascribe both divinity and humanity to the Lord—mainly because the
papal throne would not have survived otherwise. If they had acknowledged that the Lord was one with the Father, as he himself said, no vicar
of his could have been acknowledged on earth. Rifts were developing at
the time that could have sunk papal power and dispersed it if they had
not made the distinction. In order to shore it up they looked for scriptural
proof and persuaded the others.

[4] They added that the move enabled them to rule heaven and
earth, because they had it from the Word that all power in the heavens

and on earth had been given to the Lord, and this power could not have been attributed to a vicar of his if they had acknowledged that the Lord's humanity was also divine. They knew, after all, that none of us are allowed to make ourselves God's equal. They also knew that divinity would have this power on its own but humanity would not unless the power had been given to it, as it was later given to Peter.

They said there were some brilliant dissenters in those days whom they were able to subdue in this way, shoring up the pope's power in the process.

Plainly, then, the distinction was invented purely for the sake of control. In consequence, the people involved did not want to know that the power given to the Lord's humanity in the heavens and on earth is evidence that this humanity was also divine. Nor did they want to know that the Peter to whom the Lord gave the keys of heaven is not Peter but faith born of charity. This faith comes from the Lord alone, so the power is the Lord's alone; see the preface to Genesis 22.

4739   Genesis 37:23–30. *And it happened as Joseph came to his brothers that they stripped Joseph of his coat, the coat of many colors that was on him. And they took him and put him into the pit; and the pit was empty, with no water in it. And they sat to eat bread and lifted their eyes and looked, and here, a company of Ishmaelites came from Gilead, and their camels were carrying perfumes and resin and stacte as they went to take them down to Egypt. And Judah said to his brothers, "What gain if we kill our brother and cover up his blood? Come, and let's sell him to the Ishmaelites, and let our hand not be on him, because he is our brother, our flesh." And his brothers took heed. And Midianite trader men came through and drew out and brought up Joseph from the pit and sold Joseph to the Ishmaelites for twenty pieces of silver. And they took Joseph to Egypt. And Reuben returned to the pit and look, no Joseph in the pit; and he tore his clothes. And he returned to his brothers and said, "The child is no more, and I, where do I go?"*

It happened as Joseph came to his brothers means when a declaration was made about the Lord. *That they stripped Joseph of his coat* means that they did away with manifestations of truth and obliterated them. *The coat of many colors that was on him* symbolizes the nature of the manifestations in regard to the truth that comes of goodness. *And they took him and put him into the pit* means accounting it as falsity. *And the pit was empty, with no water in it,* means that there was then no truth. *And they sat to eat bread* symbolizes adoption of the evil that comes of falsity. *And lifted their eyes and looked* symbolizes further thoughts. *And here, a company of Ishmael-ites came from Gilead* symbolizes people with a simple goodness, such as people outside the church possess. *And their camels were carrying per-fumes and resin and stacte* symbolizes inner earthly truth. *As they went to descend into Egypt* symbolizes instruction in knowledge. *And Judah said to his brothers* symbolizes the wicked in the church who oppose each and every kind of goodness. *What gain if we kill our brother and cover up his blood?* means that its total extinction would bring no profit or preeminence. *Come, and let's sell him to the Ishmaelites* means that people of simple goodness acknowledge the Lord. *And let our hand not be on him* means that they are blameless. *Because he is our brother, our flesh,* means because what came from them was acceptable. *And his brothers took heed* symbolizes compliance. *And Midianite trader men came through* symbol-izes people focusing on the truth that goes with that goodness. *And drew out and brought up Joseph from the pit* symbolizes their help in keeping it from being accounted false. *And sold Joseph to the Ishmaelites* symbolizes acceptance by people of simple goodness and estrangement from people committed to a detached faith. *For twenty pieces of silver* symbolizes its value. *And they took Joseph to Egypt* means consulting knowledge. *And Reuben returned to the pit* symbolizes the church's faith in general. *And look, no Joseph in the pit* means that there was no longer any faith. *And he tore his clothes* symbolizes mourning. *And he returned to his brothers* sym-bolizes people who teach. *And said, "The child is no more,"* means that faith in the Lord is nonexistent. *And I, where do I go?* means, where is the church now?

It happened as Joseph came to his brothers means when a declaration was made about the Lord. This can be seen from the representation of *Joseph* as divine truth, especially divine truth about the Lord's divine humanity. When this truth is described as *coming to* them, the meaning is that it was declared to them. *His brothers* represent a religion clinging to detached faith, and it was to the adherents of this religion that such truth was preached.

That they stripped Joseph of his coat means that they did away with man-ifestations of truth and obliterated them, as the following shows: *Strip-ping* something off, when it happens to divine truth, which is *Joseph* here, means doing away with it and obliterating it. And the *coat,* since it was of many colors, symbolizes manifestations of truth, as discussed in §4677.

Manifestations of truth are done away with and obliterated after truth itself has been rejected, because truth itself naturally gleams in the mind.

4740

4741

No matter how fully it is extinguished, it still makes itself visible, especially in people with goodness. Even individuals who have annihilated truth in themselves see clearly that this is so and accordingly try to dispel and obliterate any manifestation of it.

[2] Take the following example as illustration: Who fails to see that wishing well and doing good is the very epitome of a Christian life? If you tell someone that this is neighborly love, he or she cannot help but agree. In fact, those who agree will say they know what it is because it is part of their life. But to suppose that some concept or other is true and feel confident about it, as people devoted to faith alone wish to do, may cause these others to say they do not know what that is and cannot conceive of it as anything but a puff of smoke that vanishes.

Since that is how faith alone, and the confidence it hopes to inspire, appears to anyone who thinks seriously about it, and especially to the good, its supporters endeavor to do away with the manifestations of truth and obliterate them. In this manner they cut away anything that touches on the truth or is found anywhere near it. That is what is symbolized by stripping Joseph of the coat that was on him.

[3] The same people also consider the wisest of all to be those who are able in various ways to prove a dogma—any dogma—once it has been accepted, and to use various arguments in giving it the appearance of truth. Such a deed is anything but the mark of a sage, however. The feat can be accomplished by anyone with a bit of ingenuity, and the evil are more skilled at it than the upright. The ability is not the mark of a rational being. Rational people can see from a kind of height whether the idea being confirmed is true or false, and this being so, they completely discount confirmations of falsity. Such "proof" they regard for their own part as ludicrous and hollow, despite the others' belief that it was plucked from the great debates of wisdom itself.

In short, to be able to prove falsity is anything but sagelike and even anything but rational. What is sagelike and rational is first to see that a thing is true and then to confirm it. In fact, the sight of truth comes from heaven's light, which the Lord supplies, but the sight of falsity as true comes from the swamp light that hell supplies.

4742 *The coat of many colors that was on him* symbolizes the nature of the manifestations in regard to the truth that comes of goodness. This is established by the symbolism of the *coat of many colors* as manifestations of truth used in recognizing and identifying the spiritual side of the earthly level (discussed at §4677). In this case it therefore symbolizes the nature of those manifestations, which is why the text uses the word "coat" twice ("They stripped Joseph of his coat, the coat of many colors").

The fact that the nature of the manifestations depends on the truth that comes of goodness can be seen from the manifestations of truth as presented visually in heaven's light. That is, it can be seen in the other world, where there is no light that does not come through heaven from the Lord and arise from his divine truth. Divine truth appears to angels' eyes as light, you see (§§2776, 3190, 3195, 3222, 3339, 3340, 3636, 3643, 3993, 4302, 4413, 4415). This light differs from person to person according to the way it is received. All of an angel's thinking results from the variegation of that light. So does the thinking of people on earth, although we do not realize it, since in us the light filters down into physical images or ideas, which are produced in our earthly, outer self by the world's light. Heaven's light is therefore so dim in us that we hardly know that our intellectual light and sight come from there. In the other world, though, when our eyes no longer see by the world's light but by heaven's, it becomes plain that this light is the source of our thoughts.

[2] When heaven's light passes from heaven into the world of spirits, it appears in the form of various colors, which vastly outdo the colors produced by the world's light in beauty, variety, and appeal. See the lessons of my experience with color reported earlier, in §§1053, 1624, 3993, 4530, 4677.

Since this is what produces colors in the other life, in their origin they are actually manifestations of the truth that comes from goodness. Truth has no light of its own, because in itself it contains nothing fiery; it has light only from goodness. Goodness is like a flame that gives off light. The nature of the goodness, then, determines how the truth appears; and the nature of the truth determines how it shines from goodness.

These remarks show what the coat of many colors symbolizes on an inner level: the nature of the manifestations in regard to truth that rises out of goodness. Joseph, the owner of the coat, represents divine truth, as shown before.

And they took him and put him into the pit means accounting it as falsity. This can be seen from the discussions above at §§4728, 4736, where similar words occur. **4743**

And the pit was empty, with no water in it, means that there was then no truth. This can be seen from the meaning of a *pit* as falsity (discussed in §4728); from that of *empty* as a place where there is no truth because there is no goodness (discussed below); and from that of *water* as truth (discussed in §§680, 739, 2702, 3058, 3424). **4744**

The meaning of "empty" as a place where there is no truth because there is no goodness can be seen from other places in the Word as well, as in Jeremiah:

> The nobles have sent the young ones for *water;* they came to the *pits* and did not find *water.* They returned with *empty vessels;* they felt shame and embarrassment and covered their head. (Jeremiah 14:3)

The empty vessels stand for a type of truth devoid of the truth that springs from goodness. In the same author:

> Nebuchadnezzar, monarch of Babylon, has devoured me, has churned me up. He has rendered me an *empty vessel;* he has swallowed me down. (Jeremiah 51:34)

The empty vessel stands for a place where there is no truth. Babylon stands for ravagers, people who deprive others of truth (§1327 at the end). In the same author:

> I looked at the earth, and there—it was *empty* and *void;* and to the heavens, and these had no light. (Jeremiah 4:23)

In Isaiah:

> Spoonbill and harrier and owl and raven will possess it; they will live in it and stretch over it a *line measuring its emptiness* and a *plummet measuring the void.* (Isaiah 34:11)

[2] In the same author:

> The *empty city* will be broken; every house will be closed, so that no one will be able to enter. A shouting over the wine in the streets! The joy of the land will go into exile; what is left in the city will be a wasteland. (Isaiah 24:[10,] 11, 12, 13)

The idea of emptiness here is expressed by a different word in the original language, but one with the same significance. The inner meaning of the individual words—the symbolism of city, house, shouting, wine, streets—shows that "empty" means a place where there is no truth because there is no goodness. In Ezekiel:

> The Lord Jehovih has said, "Doom to the blood-soaked city! Yes, I will build up the fire, placing the *pot* on the coals *empty,* so that its bronze will heat up and get hot and its uncleanness will dissolve in it, its scum will be consumed." (Ezekiel 24:9, 11)

This passage indicates what "empty" means. The empty pot is what holds the uncleanness and scum, or evil and falsity. [3] Likewise in Matthew:

> When the unclean spirit leaves a person, it goes through dry places seeking a resting place but does not find one. Then it says, "Let me go back to my house that I left," and when it comes and discovers *it empty* and swept and prepared for itself, it then goes and attaches to itself seven other spirits worse than it and, entering, they settle there. (Matthew 12:43, 44, 45)

The unclean spirit stands for uncleanness in our life and also for the unclean spirits with us (since unclean spirits make a home in the unclean part of our life). The dry places, or places where there is no water, stand for places where there is no truth. The empty house stands for our inner depths full of uncleanness, or of falsity that comes of evil. In Luke:

> God has filled the starving with good [food] and *sent the rich away empty.* (Luke 1:53)

The rich stand for people who know a lot, since riches in a spiritual sense mean secular knowledge, doctrines, and the knowledge of what is good and true. These people are called rich but empty because they possess information but do not act on it. For them, the truth is not true, because it lacks goodness (§4736).

And they sat to eat bread symbolizes adoption of the evil that comes of falsity. This can be seen from the symbolism of *eating* as adopting (discussed at §§3168, 3513, 3596, 3832) and from that of *bread* as a loving goodness (discussed at §§276, 680, 2165, 2177, 3464, 3478, 3735, 3813, 4211, 4217, 4735; bread also means all food in general, §2165). In the current case it symbolizes the opposite, or evil. People recognize that those who eat the bread of the Holy Supper unworthily are taking in evil rather than goodness as their own. The negative symbolism of eating bread, then, is plainly the adoption of evil. 　**4745**

It was customary for the ancients to eat together when they had made a noteworthy decision ratified by everyone else involved. This shared meal was a sign that they approved the decision and accordingly that they adopted it as their own. In Ezekiel, for instance:

> Here, now, the chieftains of Israel, each according to [the strength of] his arm, have been in you and have shed blood. Men of slander have been in you to shed blood and *have eaten on the mountains* in you. (Ezekiel 22:6, 9)

It also needs to be known that evil has two general sources: life and doctrine. Evil rising out of false doctrine is called the evil that comes of falsity. That is the evil meant here.

4746   *And lifted their eyes and looked* symbolizes further thoughts. This can be seen from the symbolism of *lifting the eyes and looking* as focusing and thinking, or as focused thought (discussed in §§2789, 2829, 3198, 3202, 4339). In this verse it symbolizes further thoughts, as the context suggests.

4747   *And here, a company of Ishmaelites came from Gilead* symbolizes people with a simple goodness, such as people outside the church possess. This can be seen from the following: *Ishmaelites* represent people whose lives are marked by simple goodness and whose theology is therefore filled with earthly truth (discussed in §3263). And *Gilead* symbolizes the shallow goodness that starts us off when we are being reborn (discussed in §§4117, 4124). A *company of Ishmaelites from Gilead,* then, clearly symbolizes the kind of goodness that exists among people outside the church, or people who have this simple goodness.

[2] The situation in all this can be seen from the discussion so far and the remarks to follow. Just one thing needs to be mentioned first: Some people in the church have hardened themselves against divine truth, particularly against the idea that the Lord's humanity is divine and that we need to do deeds of neighborly love in order to be saved. If they have hardened themselves against these truths not only in their beliefs but also in their life, they have reduced their inner depths to such a condition that they cannot possibly be led to accept the truth later. Once we have confirmed something in both theology and life, it stays forever. People who do not know the inner human condition might imagine that we can easily accept these truths after turning against them, no matter how rigidly, as long as someone convinces us. The feat is impossible, though, as I have been allowed to learn through a great deal of experience with this type of person in the other world. What we confirm in our theology permeates our intellect, and what we confirm in our life permeates our will. Anything that takes root in both kinds of life—the life of our intellect and the life of our will—cannot be dug out. Our very soul, which lives on after death, is formed of such things and by its nature is utterly incapable of withdrawing from them.

That is why the fate of people in the church with whom this happens is worse than the fate of people outside the church. The latter, called Gentiles, do not disprove these ideas to themselves, because they do not know them. The ones who have lived lives of mutual charity, then, readily accept divine truth—in the next life if not in the world. See the report from experience in §§2589–2604 on the condition and lot of [non-Christian] nations and peoples in the other life.

[3] That is the reason the Lord, when he starts a new religion, does not do so among people in the church but among those outside, or Gentiles. The Word speaks of this many times.

I have made these remarks first to show what is involved in Joseph's being thrown into a pit by his brothers, drawn out of it by Midianites, and sold to Ishmaelites. Joseph's brothers represent people in the church who have hardened themselves against divine truth not only in theology but also in life, particularly against the two ideas that the Lord's humanity is divine and that we need to do deeds of neighborly love in order to be saved. The Ishmaelites represent people of simple goodness, and the Midianites represent people devoted to the truth accompanying that goodness. The Midianites are said to have drawn Joseph out of the pit, and the Ishmaelites to have bought him. The symbolism of their taking him down to Egypt and selling him to Potiphar, Pharaoh's chamberlain, will be told below [§§4760, 4787–4790].

And their camels were carrying perfumes and resin and stacte symbolizes inner earthly truth, as the following shows: In general *camels* symbolize parts of the earthly self that serve the spiritual self. In particular they symbolize general knowledge in the earthly self. This is discussed at §§3048, 3071, 3114, 3143, 3145, 4156. And *perfumes, resin,* and *stacte* symbolize inner earthly truth united with the goodness on that level, as discussed below.

4748

In their sacred worship the ancients made use of sweet scents and fragrances and therefore of frankincense and other kinds of incense, and they mixed these substances into their anointing oils. Nobody today knows why they did, though. Nobody knows because nobody has any idea that the various components of worship among the ancients rose out of spiritual and heavenly phenomena existing in heaven and corresponded to them. Humankind has wandered so far from such origins, immersing itself in earthly, worldly, and bodily concerns, that it is in the dark, and many people deny that anything spiritual or heavenly exists.

[2] The ancients used frankincense and other incenses in their sacred practices because smell corresponds to perception. The fragrant smell of different types of perfume corresponds to a pleasing, welcome perception of truth that is based on goodness, or of faith that is based on neighborly

love. In fact, the correspondence is such that perceptions actually turn into scents in the other world whenever the Lord pleases. See previous descriptions from experience in §§925, 1514, 1517, 1518, 1519, 3577, 4624–4634.

The precise symbolism of the perfumes, resin, and stacte can be seen from other places where they are named. In general they symbolize inner truth on the earthly plane, but truth that comes from the goodness there. Truth by itself does not [turn into a fragrance in the other world]; goodness does so through truth. The different types of fragrance consequently relate to the nature of the truth that is united to goodness and therefore to the nature of the goodness (since goodness takes its quality from truth).

[3] Gilead symbolizes an outer kind of goodness such as belongs to the senses and is called physical pleasure (§§4117, 4124). Egypt in a positive sense symbolizes knowledge that consists of the outer truths of the earthly self and that corresponds to that goodness, or harmonizes with it (§1462). So Ishmaelites from Gilead on camels taking these perfumes down to Egypt symbolize people who take the inner truths they glean from what they know and carry them down to the knowledge that Egypt symbolizes, as explained below.

Inner truths are the conclusions we draw from outer truths, or knowledge. Facts known to the earthly self are means we use in drawing conclusions and therefore in looking more deeply. It is like seeing someone's character in that person's face, in the gleam of the person's eyes, in the vital energy of the sound when the person speaks and of the movements when the person acts.

[4] Because this truth is the means of improving and correcting our earthly self, such perfumes are credited with the power to heal. Take *resin,* for example. In Jeremiah:

> *Is there no balsamic resin in Gilead?* Is there no doctor there? Why has the health of my people not improved? (Jeremiah 8:22)

In the same author:

> Go up to *Gilead* and take *resin,* virgin *daughter of Egypt!* In vain have you multiplied medicines; there is no healing for you. (Jeremiah 46:11)

In the same author:

> Suddenly Babylon has fallen and been broken; wail over her! Take *resin* for her pain; maybe she will be healed. (Jeremiah 51:8)

[5] Other substances of a similar kind have a spiritual symbolism, as is quite plain in John:

> The merchants of the earth will cry and mourn over Babylon, that no one buys their wares anymore—wares of *gold* and *silver* and *precious stone* and *pearl* and *fine linen* and *red-violet fabric* and *silk* and *scarlet fabric,* and all *thyine wood* and every *ivory* vessel and every vessel of the *most precious wood* and of *bronze* and of *iron* and of *marble,* and *cinnamon* and *incense* and *ointments* and *frankincense* and *wine* and *oil* and *flour* and *wheat* and *beasts of burden* and *sheep* and *horses* and *coaches* and bodies and human souls. (Revelation 18:11, 12, 13)

These items would never have been listed so specifically if they had not each symbolized something in the Lord's kingdom and church. Otherwise they would have been a string of meaningless words. Babylon, as is well known, symbolizes people who have deflected all worship of the Lord to themselves and who therefore engage in inward profanation while practicing outward piety. Their wares accordingly symbolize fictions they have invented with energy and skill in order to secure adulation for themselves. The wares also symbolize teachings and concepts from the Word relating to goodness and truth that they have twisted to their own advantage. Everything mentioned, then, symbolizes something specific of this kind. The cinnamon, incense, ointments, and frankincense symbolize truth stemming from goodness, although in these people it symbolizes twisted truth and falsity stemming from evil.

[6] It is similar with statements about Tyre's wares in Ezekiel:

> Judah and the land of Israel were your dealers in minnith wheat and pannag; for honey and oil and *resin* they sold your trade goods. (Ezekiel 27:17)

Here too the resin symbolizes truth from goodness. To anyone who disbelieves in an inner meaning to Scripture, these all have to be mere words and therefore vessels with nothing inside, when in reality they have divine, heavenly, and spiritual content.

As they went to take them down to Egypt symbolizes instruction in knowledge. This can be seen from the symbolism of *Egypt* as knowledge (discussed at §§1164, 1165, 1462). Since the perfumes, resin, and stacte symbolize inner truth taken from facts known to people with the kind of simple goodness those outside the church have, *as they went to take them down* there means their being taught.

Here is the situation: The knowledge symbolized by *Egypt* is a type that contributes to spiritual life and corresponds to spiritual truth. The ancient church once existed in Egypt but eventually turned toward sorcery there, and ever since then, the knowledge meant has been a kind that perverts the spiritual qualities symbolized by Egypt. As a result, Egypt symbolizes knowledge in a positive and a negative sense in the Word. See §§1164, 1165, 1462. In this case it has a positive sense.

The facts giving rise to the inner truth symbolized by the Ishmaelites on camels carrying perfumes, resin, and stacte are the kind that do not belong to the church—the kind people outside the church have. This truth from these facts is corrected and cured only through the knowledge belonging to a genuine religion and therefore through instruction in it.

That is what is symbolized here.

4750   *And Judah said to his brothers* symbolizes the wicked in the church who oppose each and every kind of goodness, as the following shows: *Judah* in a positive sense represents the goodness that goes with heavenly love, as noted in §§3654, 3881, and in a negative sense, opposition to every kind of goodness, as discussed below. And *his brothers* symbolize religious people who subscribe to a detached faith.

Judah represents people who oppose each and every kind of goodness here because in a positive sense in the Word he represents people who do the good called for by heavenly love. Heavenly love is love for the Lord and the resulting love for one's neighbor. People with this love are closely united to the Lord and are therefore in the inmost heaven. They live in a state of innocence, which makes them look like little children to everyone else and like embodiments of love through and through. No others can go near them, so when they are sent to anyone else, they are densely surrounded by a different set of angels, who tone down the atmosphere of love around them. Otherwise it would cause the individuals receiving their visits to faint, since the atmosphere of their love penetrates right to the marrow.

[2] Since Judah in a positive sense represents this love, or this loving goodness, which is called heavenly, in a negative sense he represents something opposed to heavenly goodness and therefore opposed to every kind of goodness. Most things in the Word have two meanings, one positive and one contrary to it. From their positive meaning we can tell what kind of negative meaning they have, because the contents of the negative sense are diametrically opposed to those of the positive sense.

[3] The goodness that comes from love is of two general types: the goodness from heavenly love and the goodness from spiritual love. Opposite and contrary to the goodness from heavenly love is the evil that comes from self-love. Opposite and contrary to the goodness from spiritual love is the evil that comes from love of materialism. People given to the evil of self-love oppose everything good, but people given to materialistic evil do not. In the Word, Judah in a negative sense represents people with self-love, while Israel in a negative sense represents materialistic people. This is because Judah represents the Lord's heavenly kingdom, and Israel his spiritual kingdom.

[4] The hells also divide along the lines of these two loves. Since spirits caught up in self-love oppose everything good, they are in the deepest and therefore the grimmest hells. Since spirits caught up in materialism are not as radically opposed to everything good, they are in hells that are not as deep and are therefore less grim.

[5] The evil of self-love is not the outward conceit called pride, as it usually appears to be. Rather it is hatred for one's neighbor and consequently a burning lust for revenge and pleasure in cruelty. These are the inner depths of self-love, and its outer surface consists in contempt for others and a loathing for anyone with spiritual goodness. It is sometimes accompanied by visible conceit or pride and sometimes not.

People who hate their neighbor this way love themselves alone inside. The only other people they love are those whom they view as one with themselves, so they see the other in themselves and themselves in the other, with an eye solely to their own advantage.

[6] This is the type represented by Judah in a negative sense. The Jewish nation had been given to this kind of love right from the beginning. Its people had viewed everyone in the entire world as the vilest slaves and worthless in comparison with themselves. They had hated everyone, and what is more, when self-love and materialism did not bind them together, they attacked their own friends and relations with the same kind of hatred. The situation still holds today among the people of that nation, but since they live in foreign lands and their status is precarious, they hide their natural urges.

What gain if we kill our brother and cover up his blood? means that its total extinction would bring no profit and no preeminence, as the following shows: *What gain?* means that no profit would result, and no preeminence either, as discussed below. *Killing* symbolizes extinction—in

4751

this instance, extinction of divine truth, particularly as it concerns the Lord's divine humanity, meant by the *brother,* Joseph. And *covering up the blood* means hiding sacred truth away completely. For the meaning of *blood* as sacred truth, see above at §4735. What follows will clarify all this.

[2] The *gain* symbolizes not only profit but also preeminence—or rather "What gain?" means no resulting profit or preeminence—because it was said out of greed and avarice. Avarice and a craving for money contains the desire not only to possess the whole world but also to despoil and even kill everyone in the quest for gain. It *would* kill over very little, too, if the law did not stand in the way. In addition, people with this greed see the gold and silver they possess as giving them great power, however different the superficial appearance is. Avarice, then, clearly contains not only love of worldly gain but also self-love, and in fact the grossest form of self-love. In misers, self-importance or pride is not very obvious on the outside, because avarice does not always care about the use of wealth for impressing others. Neither is it the type of self-love that usually unites with sensual indulgence, because misers have little interest in their body or the feeding and clothing of it. It is a purely earthly kind of love, holding no other goal in mind but money, which these people see as placing them in charge of everyone—not actually but potentially. So avarice plainly holds within itself the lowest, shabbiest form of self-love. As a result, they seem to themselves to be living among pigs in the other world (§939), and more than anyone else, they oppose each and every kind of goodness.

They are therefore in such deep darkness that they cannot possibly see what is good and what is true. The existence of something inside us that lives on after death they cannot conceive of at all. In their heart they mock people who say it exists.

[3] This is what the Jewish nation had been like from the start. Nothing internal could be openly revealed to them, then, as the Old Testament Word makes plain. Because the people of that nation are deeply immersed in this worst form of self-love, they would pollute inner truth and goodness and profane it more than anyone else if greed did not put the inner realm far out of their reach and therefore keep them in dense darkness. They cannot profane it as long as they do not acknowledge it, after all (§§1008, 1010, 1059, 2051, 3398, 3402, 3479, 3898, 4289, 4601).

That is why the Lord says of them in John:

> You are from your father, the Devil, and your father's desires you wish to do; he was a murderer from the start. (John 8:44)

And in the same author, concerning Judas Iscariot, who represented the Jewish religion:

> Did I not choose you twelve? But one of you is a devil. (John 6:70)

Judas, in selling the Lord, represented the same thing represented here by Judah, who said, "Come, and let's sell Joseph."

Come, and let's sell him to the Ishmaelites means that people of simple goodness acknowledge the Lord, as the following establishes: *Selling* means disowning something and therefore its being accepted by others, as mentioned in §4098. When it applies to truth, as it does here, it means being acknowledged by others. And the *Ishmaelites* represent people of simple goodness, as mentioned above in §4747. The fact that people with simple goodness acknowledge divine truth, especially concerning the Lord's divine humanity, has already been shown [§§3263, 4747].

4752

And let our hand not be on him means in order to be blameless. This is established by the symbolism of *let our hand not be on someone* as seeking to avoid violating anything, as above at §4737. To avoid violating anything is to seek blamelessness, so this too is a symbolism of the clause.

4753

Because he is our brother, our flesh, means because what came from them was acceptable. This can be seen from the symbolism of the *brother* as something related through goodness (discussed at §3815), and from that of *flesh* as selfhood, in both senses (discussed at §3813). Flesh, then, symbolizes something that is acceptable because it comes from people in the church, and it is acceptable to them because it comes from people with simple goodness.

4754

The Ishmaelites represent people with simple goodness, and Joseph's brothers represent a religion intent on a faith divided from neighborly love. People of simple goodness acknowledge that the Lord's humanity is divine and that we need to do deeds of neighborly love in order to be saved. People intent on a detached faith know this, so they do not press the point to others (and scarcely mention it at all to those of simple goodness), mainly because they do not dare contradict common sense. To do so would be to undermine their own status and wealth, since if they denied these ideas, a person of simple goodness would call them fools. The simplehearted know what love is, and what deeds of love are, but not what faith separated from love and good deeds is. If they heard arguments for faith against deeds, or arguments about the distinction between the Lord's humanity and his divinity, they would describe them as sophistries beyond their grasp. So devotees of a detached faith freely yield in order to be acceptable, and also because what comes from the simple-hearted is acceptable. After all, if the truth [about good deeds and the Lord's divine humanity] were obliterated, they would lose all profit and preeminence (§4751).

4755   *And his brothers took heed* symbolizes compliance, as is self-evident.

4756   *And Midianite trader men came through* symbolizes people focusing on the truth that goes with that goodness. This can be seen from the symbolism of *Midianites* as people with truth born of simple goodness (discussed at §3242) and from that of *traders* as people with concepts of goodness and truth. These concepts are riches, wealth, and goods, in a spiritual sense, so trading means acquiring and sharing this knowledge (§§2967, 4453). In this case concepts of truth rather than goodness are being symbolized, because Midianites mean people who focus on the truth that goes with simple goodness, as said above. Accordingly, they are also called *men,* because people who are focused on truth are referred to as men (§§3134, 3309 at the beginning).

The story line makes it clear that Joseph was sold to the Ishmaelites but that the Midianites drew him out of the pit and also sold him to Potiphar in Egypt. The final verse of the chapter says, "And the Midianites sold him into Egypt, to Potiphar, Pharaoh's chamberlain." It might be supposed, since Joseph was sold to the Ishmaelites, that they rather than the Midianites would have sold him in Egypt. But it happened this way so that the subject matter of the inner meaning could be represented. Joseph, or divine truth, you see, cannot be sold by people devoted to goodness but by people devoted to the truth associated with that goodness. The reason will appear in the explanation of the chapter's final verse.

4757   *And drew out and brought up Joseph from the pit* symbolizes their help in keeping it from being accounted false. This can be seen from the symbolism of *drawing out and bringing up* as delivering and so as helping (discussed below) and from that of the *pit* as falsity (dealt with in §4728) and therefore as keeping [divine truth] from being accounted false.

The *drawing out and bringing up* means helping because truth is what helps goodness. Truth is credited with power, because goodness exercises power through truth (§§3091, 3563). Besides, truth is what enables falsity to be recognized, so it is what helps keep [divine truth] from being counted as false. That is why the Midianites were the ones who drew out and brought up Joseph from the pit and the Ishmaelites were the ones who bought him.

And sold Joseph to the Ishmaelites symbolizes acceptance by people of simple goodness and estrangement from people committed to a detached faith. This is established by the symbolism of *selling* as disowning, in respect to people with a detached faith (meant by Joseph's brothers here, since they sold him), and as accepting, in respect to people of simple goodness (meant by the Ishmaelites, since they bought him). Ishmaelites are people with simple goodness, as shown above in §§3263, 4747. For a discussion of this, see above in §4756.

4758

For twenty pieces of silver symbolizes its value. This can be seen from the symbolism of *twenty* as goodness and truth stored away by the Lord in the inner self. This goodness and truth is called a remnant, as discussed at §2280. So twenty also symbolizes holy goodness or truth, and in this case, holy truth, because the text says *twenty pieces of silver,* silver meaning truth (§§1551, 2954). The same number symbolizes what is not holy too, because most things in the Word have a negative meaning as well. Here it symbolizes what is unholy in relation to the people who disowned divine truth (that is, who sold Joseph, §4758) but holy in relation to the people who accepted it (that is, who bought Joseph). It therefore means [truth] that is unholy in relation to Joseph's brothers (that is, people in the church who believe in a detached faith) but holy in relation to the Ishmaelites (people with a simple goodness). That is what is meant by its value.

4759

[2] The reason *twenty* also symbolizes what is not holy is that it means a remnant, as noted above. To people who do not have remaining traces of goodness and truth in their inner self but evil and falsity instead, holiness is not holy but either impure or profane, depending on the type of evil and falsity.

The alternate meaning of twenty as something unholy can be seen in Zechariah:

> I looked, and here, a scroll flying. And he said to me, "What do you see?" To which I said, "I see a scroll flying, its length *twenty* cubits, its width, ten cubits." And he said to me, "This is the *curse* issuing over the face of the whole earth." (Zechariah 5:1, 2, 3)

In Haggai:

> When one came to the winepress to draw fifty from the press, there were *twenty.* I struck you with blight; and with mildew, all the work of your hands. (Haggai 2:16, 17)

[3] In Ezekiel:

> "Your food that you eat by weight shall be *twenty shekels* per day; from period to period you shall eat it. And in fact you shall eat it as a cake of barleycorns. With human dung you shall make a cake in their eyes. For in this way," Jehovah has said, "the children of Israel shall eat their bread unclean among the nations." (Ezekiel 4:10, 12, 13)

In these passages, twenty stands for what is unholy, unclean, and profane.

The decree that everyone in the wilderness who was over *twenty years* old would die (Numbers 14:29; 32:11) similarly represented something holy in relation to anyone below that age and something unholy in relation to anyone above it.

For the idea that all numbers in the Word have symbolic meaning, see §§482, 487, 575, 647, 648, 755, 813, 1963, 1988, 2075, 2252, [3252,] 4264, 4495, 4670. For the idea that a remnant consists of goodness and truth stored away by the Lord in the inner self, see §§468, 530, 560, 561, 576, 660, 798, 1050, 1738, 1906, 2284.

4760   *And they took Joseph to Egypt* means consulting knowledge. This can be seen from the symbolism of *Egypt* as knowledge (discussed in §§1164, 1165, 1186, 1462). When divine truth is carried to knowledge, it means consulting it—*Joseph* representing divine truth, as shown above.

A few words need to be said about the consultation of knowledge in regard to divine truth. To consult knowledge in regard to divine truth is to see in it whether divine truth is true, but this is done two ways. One way, followed by people with the affirmative attitude that truth is true, is to consult knowledge in order to substantiate the truth and strengthen their faith. People with a negative attitude proceed another way. When they consult knowledge, they cast themselves further into falsity. A negative attitude reigns supreme in them, but a positive attitude in the others.

The situation also depends on every individual's mental abilities. If people who have no higher, inner insight consult knowledge, they do not see any confirmation of truth there, so the knowledge carries them off into denial. People who do have higher, inner insight do see confirmation, though. They see it through correspondence, if in no other way.

[2] Take for example the idea that humans live on after death. People with a negative attitude toward the truth of this confirm their opposition to it by countless pieces of information, if they consult them. For instance, brute animals also live, also feel, and also act. In many areas they are more skilled than people. The ability to think, in which we have the

upper hand, is something we acquire by taking longer to mature. That is the kind of animal we are. And there are a thousand other arguments. Clearly, then, if people with a negative attitude consult knowledge, they cast themselves further into falsity, until finally they have no belief at all in eternal life.

[3] People with an affirmative attitude toward the truth of the idea that humans live on after death use knowledge to confirm themselves, if they consult it, and likewise have an endless supply. They see that everything in the physical world lies below humans, that brute animals act from instinct where people act from rationality, that animals have to look down but people can look up. By using our mind, we can comprehend what belongs to the spiritual world and be affected by it. We can even be united in love with God himself and so make life from the Divine our own. We mature later so that we can be led and lifted to that world. This and everything else in the physical world they see as confirmation. And finally they see a representation of the heavenly kingdom in the whole physical world.

[4] It is common and familiar for the educated to believe less than the uneducated in life after death and to see less of divine truth generally than the uneducated. That is because the educated consult knowledge—which they possess in greater abundance than others—from a negative standpoint. In doing so they destroy any higher, inner insight in themselves. Once it has been destroyed, they no longer see anything by heaven's light but by the light of the world. Facts exist in worldly light, and if they are not illuminated by heavenly light, they generate darkness, even if it appears otherwise to such people.

That was why the uneducated believed in the Lord when the scribes and Pharisees, who were the scholars of that nation, did not. So says the following passage in John:

> Many from the crowd heard this word; they said, "This is truly the Prophet!" Others said, "This is the Christ [Messiah]." The Pharisees answered them, "Has any of the rulers believed in him, or any of the Pharisees?" (John 7:40, 41, 47, 48)

In Luke:

> Jesus said, "I praise you, Father, Lord of heaven and earth, that you have hidden such things from the wise and understanding but revealed them to babies." (Luke 10:21)

Babies stand for the uneducated. And in Matthew:

> Therefore I speak to them in parables, because seeing, they do not see, and hearing, they do not hear or understand. (Matthew 13:13)

4761 *And Reuben returned to the pit* symbolizes the church's faith in general. This can be seen from the representation of *Reuben* as a confession of the church's faith in general (discussed in §§4731, 4734) and from the symbolism of the *pit* as falsity (discussed in §4728). *Reuben returned to the pit,* then, means that the church's faith in general came and looked at the falsity belonging to detached faith.

4762 *And look, no Joseph in the pit* means that there was no longer any faith. This can be seen from the representation of *Joseph* as divine truth. When divine truth appears to be among falsities—the *pit* symbolizing falsity (§4728)—there is no longer any faith.

4763 *And he tore his clothes* symbolizes mourning. This can be seen from the symbolism of *tearing one's clothes* as mourning—mourning for lost truth, or the death of faith.

The Word, especially in its narrative portions, often says that people tore their clothes, but today the source of the practice is unknown, as is the fact that it was a way of representing grief over the loss of truth. The representation came from the fact that clothes symbolized truth, as you may see in §4545.

Later on, the current chapter also says that when Jacob recognized his son's coat, *he tore his clothes* (verse 34), which symbolizes mourning for lost truth.

The same thing occurs elsewhere in the Word, as for instance when the Rabshakeh, sent by Sennacherib, king of Assyria, hurled insults at Jerusalem. Eliakim, who was over the royal household, and Shebna the scribe, and Joah the historian, *their clothes torn,* reported these things to King Hezekiah. On hearing it the king also *tore his clothes* and covered himself in sackcloth (Isaiah 36:22; 37:1; 2 Kings 18:37; 19:1). The insults were directed against God, the king, and Jerusalem and therefore against divine truth, as can be seen more clearly from the inner sense. It was in mourning for these things, then, that they tore their clothes.

[2] When Jehudi had read before the king the scroll of the book that Jeremiah had written, the text says that he threw it into the fire, and the king and his servants listening to all these words *did not rip their clothes* (Jeremiah 36:23, 24). Their failure to rip their clothes was a failure to mourn the fact that divine truth was not welcome.

When the scouts gave a bad report about the land of Canaan, Joshua, son of Nun, and Caleb, son of Jephunneh, *tore their clothes* and contradicted them (Numbers 14:6). This involves something similar. The land of Canaan symbolizes the Lord's kingdom, and speaking against it means opposing divine truth with falsity.

When the Philistines captured the ark of God and Eli's two sons died, a man ran from the battle line to Shiloh with *torn clothes* and with dirt on his head (1 Samuel 4:11, 12). This symbolized mourning over the loss of divine truth and divine goodness. The ark represented the Lord's kingdom, and in the highest sense the Lord himself, so it represented what was holy in religion. The torn clothes therefore symbolized mourning over the loss of divine truth, while the dirt on the man's head symbolized mourning over the loss of divine goodness.

[3] Of Samuel and Saul we read, "When Samuel turned to go, Saul grabbed the *hem of his coat, which tore off.* So Samuel said to him, 'Jehovah has torn the kingdom of Israel from you today and given it to your companion. I will not go back with you, because you have rejected Jehovah's word, and Jehovah has rejected you from being king over Israel'" (1 Samuel 15:26, 27, 28). When Saul ripped off the hem of Samuel's coat, it represented exactly what Samuel said, that the kingdom would be torn from Saul and he would no longer be king of Israel. On an inner level, a kingdom symbolizes divine truth (§§1672, 2547, 4691), as do a king and monarchy (§§1672, 1728, 2015, 2069, 3009, 3670, 4575, 4581). The kingdom and king of Israel in particular have this symbolism, because Israel represented the Lord's kingliness.

It is similar with the story of Jeroboam and Ahijah the prophet: "When Jeroboam left Jerusalem, and Ahijah the prophet found him on the way, when [Ahijah] was covered with a new garment and the two were alone in the field, *Ahijah grabbed his new garment* that was on him and *tore it into twelve pieces* and said to Jeroboam, 'Take yourself ten pieces, because this is what Jehovah, God of Israel, has said, "Watch: I am tearing the ten tribes from the hand of Solomon and will give them to you"'" (1 Kings 11:29, 30, 31).

[4] Again, there was ripping of clothes when Saul was killed in battle, as reported in 2 Samuel: "When Saul was killed in battle, on the third day a man *whose clothes were torn* came from the camp. And when David heard about Saul's death, *David grabbed his clothes and ripped them,* as did all the servants who were with him" (2 Samuel 1:2, 10, 11, 12). This too represented mourning on account of divine truth, which had been

lost and cast off by people dedicated to a detached faith. Monarchy represented divine truth, as noted above, and the Philistines, Saul's killers, represented people with a detached faith (§§1197, 1198, 3412, 3413). This is also evident from David's lament over him in verses 18–27 of that same chapter.

[5] When Absalom had struck his brother Ammon, and the report came to David that Absalom had struck all the king's sons, *he ripped his clothes* and lay on the ground, and all his servants were *standing there, their clothes ripped* (2 Samuel 13:28, 30, 31). This too happened for the sake of what it represented: that truth from the Divine disappeared from memory. Such truth is what a monarch's children symbolize on an inner level.

When David fled from Absalom, Hushai the Archite met him, *his coat ripped* (2 Samuel 15:32). The meaning is the same, because in the Word a monarch (especially David) represents divine truth.

Likewise when Elijah repeated to Ahab, king of Israel, Jehovah's message that he would be blotted out for the evil he had done, Ahab *ripped his clothes* and put sackcloth on his flesh (1 Kings 21:27, 28, 29).

[6] The following passage also shows that the ripping or tearing of clothes represented mourning for lost truth: "Hilkiah the priest found the Book of the Law in the house of Jehovah, whereupon Shaphan read it before King Josiah, and when the king heard the words of the Book of the Law, *he ripped his clothes*" (2 Kings 22:[8–]11). Quite explicitly, this was over the Word, or divine truth, which had been lost for so long, erased from people's hearts and lives.

When the Lord acknowledged that he was the Christ, the Son of God, the high priest *ripped apart his clothes,* saying, "He spoke utter blasphemy!" (Matthew 26:63, 64, 65; Mark 14:63, 64). This symbolized the high priest's conviction that the Lord's words had violated Scripture and therefore divine truth.

[7] When Elijah went up in the whirlwind, and Elisha was watching, Elisha *grabbed his own clothes and ripped them into two pieces;* and he took up Elijah's *coat,* which had fallen off him, and struck the water, and it parted this way and that, and Elisha crossed (2 Kings 2:11, 12, 13, 14). Elisha ripped his clothes into two pieces on that occasion for grief that the Word, or divine truth, had been lost. Elijah represents the Lord as the Word—that is, divine truth (§2762). The fact that the coat fell from Elijah and was snatched up by Elisha represented the continuance of the representation in Elisha, a coat meaning divine truth (see §4677).

The garment that was torn in such grief was a coat, then, as some of the passages cited show.

Since clothing symbolized the church's truth and in the highest sense divine truth, it was extremely disrespectful to go around with torn clothing except during such mourning. This is plain from the deed done to David's servants by Hanun, king of the children of Ammon. He cut off half their beard and cut *their clothes in the middle, right to the buttocks.* As a result they were not admitted to David's presence (2 Samuel 10:4, 5).

And he returned to his brothers symbolizes people who teach. This can be seen from the representation of Joseph's *brothers* as people who espouse a detached faith and also (since they were shepherds) as people who teach about faith, as above in §4705.

And said, "The child is no more," means that faith in the Lord is nonexistent. This can be seen from the symbolism of a *child* as the truth espoused by faith. Truth is symbolized by a son (§§489, 491, 533, 1147, 2623, 2803, 2813, 3373, 3704) and therefore by male offspring—in this case Joseph, who has been shown to represent divine truth. All truth belongs to faith, because what the ancient churches called truth, the contemporary church calls faith (§4690). *The child is no more* consequently means that faith in the Lord is nonexistent.

And I, where do I go? means, where is the church now? This can be seen from the representation of Reuben as the church's faith in general (discussed at §§4731, 4734, 4761). Since Reuben says of himself, *And I, where do I go?* the meaning is, where now is the church's faith—in other words, the church?

There is no religion where there is no heavenly Joseph—that is, where the Lord's divine truth does not exist. Of particular importance is the divine truth that the Lord's humanity is divine and that charity and therefore deeds of charity are essential to religion. All this can be seen from demonstrations of both points in the current chapter.

[2] If one does not accept the divine truth that the Lord's humanity is divine it necessarily follows that we are to revere the Trinity rather than a unity. It also follows that we are to worship half the Lord—namely, his divinity and not his humanity. Who worships anything that is not divine? But does a church exist where the Trinity is revered, one part separately from another? That is, does it exist where three are worshiped equally? Even though the three are said to be one, the thinking behind it distinguishes and creates three. Only the words on the lips refer to them as one. Think about it: If you say you acknowledge and believe in one

God, are you thinking about three? If you say that the Father is God, the Son is God, and the Holy Spirit is God, and that they are distinct persons with distinct functions, can you think that there is one God? The only way to do so is to make the three distinct gods into one through harmony among them and also through hierarchy, so far as one originates in another. So when three gods are worshiped, where is the church then?

[3] However, the Christian church does exist if it worships the Lord alone, in whom the whole Trinity exists, the Father in him and he in the Father, as he himself says:

> Even if you do not believe me, believe my deeds, so that you may know and believe that the Father is in me and I am in the Father. (John 10:38)

> Whoever has seen me has seen the Father. Don't you believe, Philip, that I am in the Father and the Father is in me? Believe me that I am in the Father and the Father is in me. (John 14:9–11)

> Whoever sees me sees him who sent me. (John 12:45)

> Everything of mine is yours and of yours is mine. (John 17:10)

The Christian church also exists when it abides by this statement of the Lord's:

> The first of all the commandments is "Listen, Israel: *The Lord our God is one Lord.* Therefore you shall love *the Lord your God* with all your heart and with all your soul and with all your mind and with all your powers." This is the first commandment. The second, similar one is this: "You shall love your neighbor as yourself." *There is no other commandment greater than these.* (Mark 12:29, 30, 31)

"The Lord our God" is the Lord; see Matthew 4:7, 10; 22:43, 44; Luke 1:16, 17; John 20:28. Jehovah in the Old Testament is called the Lord in the New; see §2921.

[4] If we do not also accept it as divinely true in both our theology and our life that love for our neighbor and therefore neighborly deeds are essential to religion, it necessarily follows that to contemplate truth is part of religion but to contemplate goodness is not. The thinking of a religious person can accordingly contradict and oppose itself; we can think what is evil and what is true at the same time. By thinking what is evil, we can be with the Devil, and by thinking what is true, with the Lord. Yet truth and evil never harmonize. "No one can serve two masters; the person will either

hate the one and love the other . . ." (Luke 16:13). When people who believe in detached faith settle on this idea and confirm it by living according to it, although they may talk about the fruits of faith, where is the church then?

Genesis 37:31, 32, 33, 34, 35. *And they took Joseph's coat and slaughtered a buck of the goats and dipped the coat in the blood. And they sent the coat of many colors and took it to their father and said, "This we found; please recognize whether it is your son's coat or not." And he recognized it and said, "My son's coat. A bad wild animal ate him up; Joseph has surely been mauled." And Jacob tore his clothes and put sackcloth on his hips and mourned over his son many days. And all his sons and all his daughters rose to comfort him, and he refused to comfort himself and said, "Because I will go down to my son mourning, to the grave"; and his father cried for him.* **4767**

They took Joseph's coat symbolizes appearances. *And slaughtered a buck of the goats* symbolizes external truth rising out of pleasures. *And dipped the coat in the blood* means that they defiled [appearances] with falsity and evil. *And they sent the coat of many colors* symbolizes the appearances defiled as a result. *And took it to their father* symbolizes comparison with the goodness and truth taught by the ancient church and the early [Christian] church. *And said, "This we found,"* means that this is how it appears to them. *Please recognize whether it is your son's coat or not* means whether there was a similarity. *And he recognized it* means yes, there was. *And said, "My son's coat,"* means that it was truth known to the church. *A bad wild animal ate him up* means that cravings for evil snuffed it out. *Joseph has surely been mauled* means that falsity turned it into something completely nonexistent. *And Jacob tore his clothes* symbolizes mourning for lost truth. *And put sackcloth on his hips* symbolizes mourning for lost goodness. *And mourned over his son many days* symbolizes the state. *And all his sons* symbolizes people devoted to falsity. *And all his daughters rose* symbolizes people dedicated to evil. *To comfort him* means in order to interpret the Word's literal meaning. *And he refused to comfort himself* means that it was impossible. *Because I will go down to my son mourning, to the grave,* means that the ancient church perished. *And his father cried for him* symbolizes inner mourning.

They took Joseph's coat symbolizes appearances. This can be seen from the symbolism of a *coat,* and in this case a coat of many colors, as appearances, [or manifestations,] of truth (discussed at §§4677, 4741, 4742). **4768**

The next few verses deal with [the brothers'] efforts to absolve themselves of the crime they had committed. In an inner sense the text is about validating falsity in its opposition to divine truth (discussed above in §4760) through the use of appearances presented by rational arguments based on the literal meaning of the Word. Any interpretation of the Word's literal meaning to prove something false is an appearance. Such appearances tend to lead the unsophisticated astray, presenting falsity as true, and truth as false. That is what the inner meaning is talking about in the next verses.

4769   *And slaughtered a buck of the goats* symbolizes external truth rising out of pleasures. This can be seen from the symbolism of a *buck of the goats* in the Word as earthly truth—that is, truth known to the outer self that brings pleasure to a person's life—and also as external truth rising out of pleasures (discussed below). Truth known to the outer self that brings pleasure to a person's life is the divine truth found in the Word's literal meaning, from which the doctrines of a genuine religion develop. This truth is what a *buck* properly symbolizes, and the resulting pleasures are symbolized by *goats.* So in a positive sense a buck of the goats symbolizes people with this type of truth and the resulting pleasures. In a negative sense, a buck of the goats symbolizes people with external truth, or appearances of truth from the literal meaning that conform with their life's pleasures (such as the physical pleasures generally called creature comforts and the psychological pleasures generally consisting in position and wealth). They are the ones symbolized by the buck of the goats in a negative sense. In short, a buck of the goats in this sense symbolizes people under the sway of faith detached from neighborly love. The only truth they glean from the Word, you see, is that which suits their life's pleasures—in other words, which promotes self-love and materialism. As for any other truth, they reduce it to the same thing by their interpretations and consequently present falsity under the appearance of truth.

[2] The symbolism of a buck of the goats as people with a detached faith can be seen in Daniel:

> Look: a *buck of the goats* came from the west onto the face of all the earth and was not touching the earth, and *this buck* had a conspicuous horn between its eyes. From one of the four horns one horn went out a bit and grew immensely toward the south and toward the sunrise and toward the ornament [of Israel]. For it grew right to the army of the heavens and threw down to the ground some of the army and some of the stars and trampled them. And it cast truth to the ground. (Daniel 8:5, [9,] 10, 11, 12)

This is about the state of religion in general—not only the state of the Jewish religion but also the state of the next religion, the Christian religion—the

Lord's Word being universal. In relation to the Jewish religion, the buck of the goats symbolizes people who considered internal truth worthless but welcomed external truth so far as it promoted what they loved, which was to be very important and very rich. As a result of this mindset, the only form in which they acknowledged the Christ or Messiah they were awaiting was as a king who would raise them up over all nations and peoples everywhere on the planet. They expected him to place everyone else under them as the lowliest slave. That was the source of their love for him. Love for their neighbor was not something they grasped at all, unless they understood it as a bond through participating in the honors and financial gain just described. [3] In relation to the Christian religion, the buck of the goats symbolizes people committed to the external truth rising out of pleasure, or people with a detached faith. They too have no interest in internal truth. If they teach such truth, it is only to develop a reputation so that they can rise to high rank and attain wealth. These are the pleasures lying in their heart when truth fills their mouth. What is more, by misinterpreting the tenets of a genuine faith they steer them toward favoring their own passions.

These comments show what the passage in Daniel symbolizes on an inner level. The buck of the goats symbolizes people with a detached faith. The buck came from the west, meaning that such people came from evil (the west meaning evil; see §3708). It came onto the face of all the earth, not touching the earth, meaning that they were over the whole church. (In the Word, the earth actually means a land where the church exists and therefore means the church, §§566, 662, 1066, 1262, 1413, 1607, 1733, 1850, 2117, 2118 at the end, 2928, 3355, 4447, 4535.) The horns it had are different kinds of power lent by falsity (§2832). The conspicuous horn between its eyes is the power derived from rationalizations about religious truth (as can be seen from explanations concerning the eye in §§4403–4421, 4523–4534). The one horn that grew toward the south, the sunrise, and the ornament [of Israel] is the power derived from detached faith, reaching all the way to a state of heavenly light, a state of goodness, and a state of truth. (The south is a state of light; see §3708. The sunrise or east is a state of goodness, §§1250, 3249, 3708. An ornament is a state of truth, as various passages in the Word show.) It grew right to the army of the heavens and threw down to the ground some of the army and some of the stars and trampled them, meaning that they trampled the knowledge of what is good and true. (The army of the heavens and the stars mean knowledge of what is good and true, §4697.) From this discussion you can see what is meant by the fact that it cast truth to the ground: they cast down faith itself, which essentially is neighborly love, since faith looks to neighborly love because it originates in that love. What the ancient church called truth, the contemporary church calls faith (§4690).

[4] It is similar with male goats in Ezekiel:

> Here, I am judging between flock member and flock member, between the rams and the *he-goats*. Is it too little for you [that] the good pasture you graze and the rest of your pastures you trample with your feet? The settled water you drink; the rest you churn with your feet. With your horns you strike all the weak until you scatter them outside. (Ezekiel 34:17, 18, 21)

Here again he-goats symbolize people with a detached faith, or people who put theology ahead of life and eventually stop worrying about how they live their lives. Yet our life makes us who we are, not theology detached from it, and our life awaits us after death, but our theology does not, except so far as it draws on our life. Of such people the passage says that they graze the good pasture and the rest of the pastures they trample with their feet, that they drink the settled water and the rest they churn with their feet, and that with their horns they strike the weak until they scatter them.

[5] This evidence now shows who is meant by the goats and who by the sheep the Lord mentions in Matthew:

> All nations will assemble before him, and he will separate them from each other, as a shepherd separates the *sheep from the goats*. And he will set the *sheep* on the right *but the goats on the left,* [and so on]. (Matthew 25:32, 33)

The sheep are people with neighborly love and therefore with religious truth, while the goats are people devoid of neighborly love although they possess religious truth—people with a detached faith, in other words—as every detail of the passage makes plain. They will be described at that point in the text.

[6] The identity and nature of those who have a detached faith and are meant by goats is evident in the following two places. In Matthew:

> *Every tree that does not make good fruit will be cut down* and thrown into the fire. *So from their fruits you will know them.* Not everyone saying

"Lord! Lord!" to me will enter the kingdom of the heavens, *but the one doing the will of my Father* who is in the heavens. Many will say to me on that day, "Lord! Lord! Haven't we *prophesied in your name* and *cast out demons in your name* and *exercised many powers in your name?*" But then I'll proclaim to them, "I do not know you. *Leave me, you evildoers!*" (Matthew 7:19, 20, 21, 22, 23)

And in Luke:

Then you will start to stand outside and knock on the door, saying, "Lord! Lord! Open up to us!" But answering, he will say to you, "*I do not know you, where you are from.*" Then you will start to say, "*We ate in front of you, and drank, and in our streets you taught.*" But he will say, "I tell you *I do not know you, where you are from. Leave me, all you evildoers!*" (Luke 13:25, 26, 27)

These are the people who have a detached faith and are called goats.

Some goats [in the Word], though, such as the ones used in sacrifice and others mentioned in various places in the Prophets, have a positive symbolism, which will be discussed elsewhere, by the Lord's divine mercy.

And dipped the coat in the blood means that they defiled [appearances] with the falsity that comes of evil. This can be seen from the symbolism of *dipping in blood* as defiling with falsity, blood in a negative sense symbolizing falsified truth (§4735). Because the blood came from a goat, which symbolizes external truth rising out of pleasures—the kind of truth adopted by people with a detached faith—it plainly means falsity rising out of evil. The same idea becomes clear from what follows, where Jacob says, "A bad wild animal ate him up; Joseph has surely been mauled." This means that evil cravings snuffed out [the truth] and therefore that falsity turned it into something completely nonexistent.

See §4729 for the idea that there are three sources of falsity—the theology of one's religion, the illusions of the senses, and the force of one's cravings—and that falsity from the last source is the worst.

And they sent the coat of many colors symbolizes defiled appearances. This is established by the symbolism of the *coat of many colors* as appearances (discussed at §§4677, 4741, 4742, 4768). Their defilement is meant by the fact that the coat had been dipped in blood (§4770).

And took it to their father symbolizes comparison with the goodness and truth taught by the ancient church and the early [Christian] church. This can be seen from the representation of Jacob, the *father,* as the ancient church (discussed at §§4680, 4700) and also as the early [Christian] church, or the Christian church at its start (discussed below). *Taking* such a coat to that church, in an inner sense, means undertaking a comparison of falsified goodness and truth with the genuine goodness and truth of the church.

Jacob currently represents not only the ancient church but also the early [Christian] church, or the Christian church at its start, because the two are exactly the same inside. They differ only on the outside. The superficial features of the ancient church all served to represent the Lord and the heavenly and spiritual attributes of his kingdom—love and charity and the resulting faith—and therefore the kinds of things that constitute the Christian church. That is why the unfolding and peeling away of the outer layers of the ancient church (and of the Jewish religion) reveals the Christian church. This fact was also symbolized by the tearing of the veil in the Temple (Matthew 27:51; Mark 15:38; Luke 23:45). Jacob, the father, consequently represents not only the ancient church but the early Christian church as well.

4773   *And said, "This we found,"* means that this is how it appears to them. This can be seen from the context in the inner sense. They did not say that it was Joseph's coat but that they had found it, bringing it back to their father so he could recognize whether it was his son's coat. The symbolism of the sentence, it then follows, is that this is how it appears to them.

4774   *Please recognize whether it is your son's coat or not* means whether there was a similarity. This is indicated by the symbolism of *recognizing whether it is* as recognizing whether it was similar.

This meaning relates to the preceding statements and follows from them. A comparison of falsified goodness and truth with the genuine goodness and truth in the church was undertaken, as symbolized by their taking the coat dipped in blood to their father (§4772). *Please recognize whether it is your son's coat,* then, means that he compared them to see whether they were the same, that is, whether there was a similarity.

4775   *And he recognized it* means yes, there was. *And said, "My son's coat,"* means that it was truth known to the church. This can be seen from the symbolism of a *coat* as truth known to the church (discussed in §4677). It was defiled, though, so it was indeed acknowledged as truth but not as being like the truth known to the ancient and early [Christian] churches. That is the reason for saying yes, there was.

A bad wild animal ate him up means that cravings for evil snuffed it **4776**
out, as the following shows. A *bad wild animal* symbolizes a lie resulting
from the force of one's cravings (discussed in §4729) and therefore symbolizes cravings. And *eating up* means snuffing out, since it applies to the
church's truth.

The church's most central truth is that love for the Lord and love for
one's neighbor are paramount (Mark 12:29, 30, 31). Greedy cravings snuff
it out. That is because a person who lives a life of cravings cannot live a
life of love and charity, since they are diametrically opposed. To live a life
of cravings is to love oneself alone, not one's neighbor, except for selfish
reasons, so people who live this way eliminate charity in themselves. People who eliminate charity also eliminate love for the Lord because charity
is the only means of loving the Lord (the Lord being present in charity).
The feeling of neighborly love is the characteristic feeling of heaven and
comes from the Lord alone. Cravings for evil, then, plainly snuff out the
church's most central truth. Once it is snuffed out, people invent a means
that they describe as "saving," which is faith. When faith is detached
from charity, genuine truth is defiled, because no one any longer knows
what charity is or even what a neighbor is. So no one knows what a person's inner plane is or even what heaven is. Our inner dimension and the
heaven we have inside us is charity, or goodwill toward another individual, our community, our country, the church, the Lord's kingdom, and
consequently the Lord himself. From these remarks a conclusion can be
drawn as to what the church's truths must be like when the essential ones
are unknown and their opposites (cravings) reign supreme. When the life
within these cravings talks about those truths, are they not sullied beyond
recognition?

[2] From the inhabitants of heaven with whom I have been allowed to
talk, it has become quite plain to me that no one can be saved except by
living a life of neighborly kindness and internalizing the desires associated
with such kindness—that is, willing well toward others and doing good
to them out of goodwill. It has also become plain that no one can possibly accept religious truth—or absorb and adopt it—except those who live
a charitable life. Everyone in heaven is a form of charity, endowed with
beauty and goodness according to the nature of the charity.

Angels' pleasure, good fortune, and happiness come from being able
to do good to others out of goodwill. People who have not lived a life
of neighborly love cannot possibly see that heaven and its joy consist in

willing well, and from willing well, doing what is good. That is because their heaven consists in willing well to themselves, and doing good to others only because of willing well to themselves—although this is actually hell. Heaven is distinguished from hell in that heaven (to repeat) consists in doing good from goodwill, whereas hell consists in doing evil from ill will. People who love their neighbor do good from goodwill, but people who love themselves do evil from ill will. This they do because they love no one but themselves. They love others only to the extent that they see themselves in those others and those others in themselves. They even hate them, which comes out in the open as soon as the other withdraws and ceases to be theirs. The situation resembles that with robbers, who love one another as long as they belong to the same gang but secretly want to kill each other if they can profit from it.

[3] Heaven, then, is clearly love for one's neighbor, and hell, love for oneself.

People who love their neighbor are capable of accepting all of faith's truth, absorbing it, and making it their own. Neighborly love contains all of faith because it contains heaven and the Lord. People who love themselves, on the other hand, can never accept faith's truth, because self-love contains hell. Only for the sake of their own advancement and gain can they accept religious truth. Thus they can never absorb or adopt truth. What they absorb and adopt are contradictions to truth. At heart they do not even believe in hell and heaven or a life after death, so they do not believe anything they hear about hell, heaven, or life after death. As a result they utterly disbelieve what they hear from the Word and from doctrine about faith and charity. When they are worshiping, they seem to themselves to believe, but that is because it has been ingrained in them since early childhood to take on such a state at that time. As soon as they step outside of worship they step outside the state, and then when they think privately, they absolutely disbelieve. They think up arguments that favor their passions and call them truths, and these they corroborate from the Word's literal meaning, although they are false. Such is everyone whose life and theology fall under the sway of a detached faith.

[4] In addition, it needs to be known that love holds everything within it. Love is what makes life, so the Lord's life flows only into love. The nature of the love therefore determines the nature of the life, because it determines how the life is received. Neighborly love receives the life of

heaven, and self-love receives the life of hell. All of heaven resides in love for one's neighbor, therefore, and all of hell, in love for oneself.

The fact that love holds everything within it can be illustrated by many examples in nature. All animals, whether they walk on the ground, fly in the air, or swim in the water, go along with their love or passion. Everything that contributes to their life—to their nourishment, shelter, reproduction—acts on their love. As a result, every [bird] species knows what to eat, where to live, how to go about mating. For instance, it knows how to pair up, build nests, lay eggs, and raise chicks. [5] Bees know how to build hives, extract honey from flowers, fill honeycombs with it, and prepare for winter. They even know how to conduct a form of government under a ruler. There are many other wonders besides. All of these activities are accomplished through an inflow into their different types of love; only the specific form of their desires varies the effect on their life. Their love contains it all. What would not be found in heavenly love, if we cultivated it? Does it not contain all the wisdom and understanding that exists in heaven?

A consequence is that those who have lived lives of charity are received into heaven and no others are. Another consequence is that charity gives them the ability to accept and absorb all truth, or everything embraced in faith.

The opposite happens to people who subscribe to a detached faith— in other words, who know some truth but have no charity. Their love accepts what agrees with it; love for themselves and their worldly advantage accepts ideas contrary to truth, such as are found in the hells.

Joseph has surely been mauled means that falsity turned it into something completely nonexistent. This can be seen from the symbolism of being *mauled* as being dispersed by falsity—in other words, being turned by falsity into something completely nonexistent. Falsity rising out of evil, or out of one's cravings, is what is meant here (§4770).

See the discussion of this just above at §4776.

4777

And [Jacob] tore his clothes symbolizes mourning for lost truth. This is established by the discussion in §4763 of the symbolism of *tearing one's clothes,* which used to represent mourning for lost truth.

4778

And put sackcloth on his hips symbolizes mourning for lost goodness. This is established by the symbolism of *putting sackcloth on one's hips,* which used to represent mourning for lost goodness. The *hips* symbolize marriage love and therefore all heavenly and spiritual love (§§3021,

4779

3294, 4277, 4280, 4575), and this is due to correspondence. Just as all the organs, limbs, and viscera of the human body correspond to the universal human (as shown at the ends of the chapters), the genital region corresponds to people in the universal human (or heaven) who had enjoyed true marriage love. Marriage love is fundamental to all love, so broadly speaking, the area of the hips symbolizes all heavenly and spiritual love. That was the reason people had the custom of placing sackcloth on that area when they mourned over lost goodness—all goodness being a matter of love.

[2] The narrative and prophetic portions of the Word give evidence that people used to put sackcloth on their hips when they were witnessing to this grief. In Amos, for example:

> I will turn your feasts *into mourning* and all your songs into a lament; *so will I bring sackcloth on all hips* and baldness over every head, and I will make it all like *mourning* for an only child, and the end of it like a bitter day. (Amos 8:10)

Bringing sackcloth on all hips stands for mourning over good things that have been lost. "All hips" stand for all goodness that comes from love. In Jonah:

> The men of Nineveh believed in God and therefore proclaimed a fast and *put on sackcloth garments, from the greatest to the least.* And when word reached the king of Nineveh, he rose from his throne and took his robe off him and *drew on sackcloth* and sat on the ashes. And he proclaimed that *human and animal should be covered with sackcloth garments.* (Jonah 3:5, 6, 8)

This instance was obviously a symbol representing grief over the evil for which Nineveh was to perish and therefore over lost goodness. [3] In Ezekiel:

> They will cry out over you with their voice and shout bitterly and bring dust up on their heads. In the ashes they will roll, and make themselves bald over you, and *wrap themselves with sackcloth garments.* (Ezekiel 27:30, 31)

This is about Tyre. The individual gestures represented mourning for falsity and evil and consequently for lost truth and goodness. Crying out and shouting bitterly stand for lamentation over falsity or lost truth (§2240).

Bringing dust up on their heads stands for being condemned for evil (§278). Rolling themselves in the ashes stands for being condemned for falsity. Making themselves bald stands for grief that the earthly self knows no truth (§3301 at the end). Wrapping themselves with sackcloth garments stands for grief that the earthly self has no goodness. Likewise in Jeremiah:

> Daughter of my people, *wrap yourself with sackcloth* and roll yourself in dust; carry out *mourning* [as] for an only child for yourself, bitter *keening*, because suddenly the destroyer will come over you. (Jeremiah 6:26)

And in another place in the same author:

> The elders of Zion's daughter will sit on the earth, will keep quiet; the young women of Jerusalem will bring dust on their head, *will wrap themselves in sackcloth garments,* will lower their head to the earth. (Lamentations 2:10)

These are similar representations, according to the types of goodness and truth that have been lost, as above. [4] In Isaiah:

> An oracle *concerning Moab:* [Moab] will go up to Bayith and Dibon into the high places to weep over Nebo; and over Medeba, *Moab* will wail. On all its heads is baldness; every beard has been shaved. *In its streets they wrapped themselves with sackcloth;* on its roofs and in its streets all [Moab] will wail, going down into weeping. (Isaiah 15:2, 3)

Moab stands for people who adulterate what is good (§2468). Mourning over the adulteration symbolized by Moab is depicted by acts that correspond to that type of evil. As a result it is almost the same in Jeremiah:

> Every head is baldness, every beard is shaved; on all hands there are cuts, *and on the hips, sackcloth.* On all the roofs of *Moab* and in its streets, universal *mourning.* (Jeremiah 48:37, 38)

[5] When King Hezekiah heard the blasphemies that the Rabshakeh spoke against Jerusalem, he tore his clothes *and covered himself in sackcloth* (Isaiah 37:1; 2 Kings 19:1). Because [the Rabshakeh] spoke against Jehovah, the king, and Jerusalem, there was mourning. An attack on truth is symbolized by [Hezekiah's] tearing his clothes (§4763). An attack on goodness is symbolized by his putting on sackcloth. Where the Word talks about truth it also talks about goodness, because of the heavenly marriage,

a marriage of goodness with truth and of truth with goodness, at every turn. In David, too:

> You have turned *my mourning* into a dance; you have *undone my sackcloth* and wrapped me in joy. (Psalms 30:11)

The dance has to do with truth, and the joy with goodness, as it does elsewhere in the Word too. Undoing the sackcloth stands for taking away grief over lost goodness. [6] In 2 Samuel:

> David said to Joab and to all the people who were with him, "Tear your clothes and *wrap yourselves with sackcloth garments* and keen before Abner." (2 Samuel 3:31)

Because a crime had been committed against what was true and good, David ordered the people to tear their clothes and wrap themselves with sackcloth garments. Again, Ahab had violated fairness and justice or (in a spiritual sense) truth and goodness, so when he heard Elijah's words, that he would be cut off, he ripped his clothes *and put sackcloth on his flesh* and fasted and *lay in sackcloth* and walked slowly (1 Kings 21:27). [7] The association of sackcloth with lost goodness can also be seen in John:

> When [the Lamb] opened the sixth seal, a huge earthquake occurred! *And the sun turned black as sackcloth,* and the whole moon became like blood. (Revelation 6:12)

The earthquake stands for a change of conditions in the church in regard to goodness and truth (§3355). The sun stands for a loving goodness (1529, 1530, 2441, 2495, 4060, 4300, 4696), so the loss of it is referred to as sackcloth. The moon stands for religious truth (1529, 1530, 2120, 2495, 4060), which is described as bloody because blood means truth falsified and profaned (4735).

[8] Since wearing sackcloth and rolling in ash represented mourning over evil and falsity, it also represented humility and repentance. The first step toward humility is to acknowledge that nothing but evil and falsity comes from us. The same is true for repentance, which does not happen without humility, in the form of a heartfelt confession that this is what we are like on our own. To see that wearing sackcloth was a sign of humility, read 1 Kings 21:27, 28, 29; to see that it was a sign of repentance, read Matthew 11:21; Luke 10:13. It was nothing but a representation, though,

and therefore only an outward act of the body, not an inward act of the heart, as is plain in Isaiah:

> To bow one's head like a rush and *lie in sackcloth and ash*—will you call this a fast and a day of good pleasure for Jehovah? Isn't this the fast that I choose: to open the bonds of evil, to break bread for one starving, [and so on]? (Isaiah 58:5, 6, 7)

And mourned over his son many days symbolizes the state—a state of mourning for lost goodness and truth, as the following shows: Joseph, the *son,* represents divine truth, and specifically the divine truth discussed above in §4776. And *days* symbolize states, as discussed at §§23, 487, 488, 493, 893, 2788, 3785—in this case a state of great mourning, because the text says *many days.* **4780**

And all his sons symbolizes people devoted to falsity. This can be seen from the symbolism of *sons* as truth, and in a negative sense as falsity, or as people devoted to either truth or falsity (discussed in §§489, 491, 533, 1147, 2623, 2803, 2813, 3373, 3704). Here they symbolize people devoted to falsity, because Jacob's sons, Joseph's brothers, represent people with a detached faith and accordingly people who have snuffed out divine truth and are consequently immersed in falsity, as shown above. **4781**

And all his daughters rose symbolizes people dedicated to evil. This can be seen from the symbolism of *daughters* as goodness and in a negative sense as *evil,* or as people dedicated to either goodness or evil, as discussed at §§489, 490, 491, 568, 2362, 3024, 3963. **4782**

To comfort him means in order to interpret the Word's literal meaning. This is established by the symbolism of *comforting* as calming an uneasy mind with hope about something (discussed at §3610). This time the disquiet or grief is over the loss of goodness and truth, which can be calmed only by interpretations of the Word. The verse is talking about Jacob's sons and daughters, who symbolize people caught up in falsity and evil (§§4781, 4782), so the comforting symbolizes interpretations of the Word's literal meaning. Scripture's literal meaning contains generalizations, which are like vessels that can be filled with truth. They can also be filled with falsity, which lets them be explained in a biased way. Since they are general, they are also relatively obscure and cannot be illuminated except by the inner meaning. The inner meaning exists in heaven's light because the inner meaning is the Word for angels, but the literal meaning exists in the world's light because it is the Word for people on **4783**

earth, before the Lord brings them into heaven's light, which then enlight-
ens them. This shows that the literal meaning serves to introduce the
simple to the inner meaning.

[2] The Word's literal meaning can obviously be explained or interpreted in a biased way, since it is used to justify all doctrines, including
heretical ones. For example, the dogma concerning detached faith is justified by these words of the Lord's:

> So much did God love the world that he gave it his only Son, *so that
> anyone who believes in him may not be destroyed but have eternal life.*
> (John 3:16)

From this passage and others people conclude that faith alone without
good deeds is the means to eternal life. Once they have convinced themselves of this, they stop paying attention to what the Lord so often said
about love for him and about charity and good deeds (§§1017, 2373,
3934). So they also ignore what he says in John:

> As many as did accept him, to them he gave the power to be God's
> children, *to those believing in his name,* who had their birth *not from
> blood or from the will of the flesh or from a man's will* but from God.
> (John 1:12, 13)

If you tell them that none can believe in the Lord but those who love
their neighbor, they immediately resort to interpretations like these: the
law has been abolished; we have been born in sin and cannot do good on
our own; and if we do good, we cannot help taking credit for it. They also
prove these ideas from the Word's literal sense—for instance, from what is
said in the parable of the Pharisee and the tax collector in Luke 18:10–14,
and other places. The way the case really stands is very different, though.

[3] People with a detached faith also cannot help believing that anyone can be admitted to heaven as a matter of grace, no matter how she or
he has lived. So they believe that our faith rather than our life awaits us
after death. They prove this from the Word's literal sense, too, although
the Word's spiritual sense actually makes it plain that the Lord shows
mercy to everyone. If heaven were a matter of mercy or grace, no matter
how we have lived, everyone would be saved. People with a detached faith
believe in salvation by grace because they have no idea what heaven is,
and that is because they do not know what charity is. If they knew how
much peace, joy, and happiness dwells in charity, they would know what
heaven is, but this is completely hidden from them.

[4] People with a detached faith cannot help believing they will rise again with their body, which will not happen until Judgment Day. This idea they also confirm with multiple Scripture passages interpreted according to the literal meaning. They fail to consider what the Lord said about the rich man and Lazarus in Luke 16:22–31 and what he said to the robber in Luke 23:43: "Truly, I say to you: today you will be with me in paradise." They ignore many other passages as well. People who subscribe to a detached faith have this belief because if they heard that the body does not rise again, they would deny there is any resurrection at all. What the inner self is they do not know or understand. No one can see what the inner self and its life after death are except those who love their neighbor, because this love characterizes the inner self.

[5] People with a detached faith cannot help believing that charitable deeds consist only in giving to the poor and helping the wretched. Again, they prove this from the Word's literal sense. In reality, though, charitable deeds consist in our doing what is just and fair, each of us in our own job, from a love of justice and fairness and of goodness and truth.

[6] People with a detached faith see nothing in the Word but proofs of their dogmas, because those who are unmoved by neighborly love have no deep insight. All they have is a superficial vision, or a lowly kind of insight, from which no one can possibly observe higher levels. Anything higher looks dark to them. That is why they see falsity as true, and truth as false. As a consequence, they destroy the good pasture and foul the pure waters of the sacred fountain of the Word with their interpretations of its literal meaning, according to these words in Ezekiel:

> Is it too little for you [that] the good pasture you graze and the rest of your pastures you trample with your feet? The settled water you drink; the rest you churn with your feet. With your horns you strike all the weak until you scatter them outside. (Ezekiel 34:17, 18, 21)

And he refused to comfort himself means that it was impossible. This can be seen from the discussion just above. **4784**

Because I will go down to my son mourning, to the grave, means that the ancient church perished, as the following shows: Jacob, who says this of himself, represents the ancient church, as discussed above in §§4680, 4700, 4772. Joseph, *my son,* represents divine spirituality, or divine truth, as discussed above. And *going down mourning to the grave* symbolizes dying. Applied to the church and to divine truth, it means perishing. **4785**

4786   *And his father cried for him* symbolizes inner mourning. This can be seen from the symbolism of *crying* as utmost grief and sorrow and therefore as inner mourning.

In the ancient churches, among the outward signs representing something deeper were keening and tears for the dead, which symbolized inner mourning, even though the mourning was not internal. Concerning the Egyptians who traveled with Joseph to bury Jacob, for instance, we read this:

> When they came to the threshing floor of Atad, which is at the ford of the Jordan, *they keened there a very great* and *heavy keening,* and *he carried out mourning for his father seven days.* And the Canaanite resident of the land saw the mourning on the threshing floor of Atad, and they said, "This [time of] mourning is heavy for the Egyptians." (Genesis 50:10, 11)

And concerning David [in his mourning] over Abner:

> They buried Abner in Hebron, and the king lifted his voice and *cried at the grave* of Abner, and all the people *cried.* (2 Samuel 3:32)

4787   Genesis 37:36. *And the Midianites sold him into Egypt, to Potiphar, Pharaoh's chamberlain, the chief of the bodyguards.*

The Midianites sold him into Egypt means that people with a measure of the truth that goes with simple goodness consulted knowledge. *To Potiphar, Pharaoh's chamberlain,* symbolizes inner knowledge. *The chief of the bodyguards* symbolizes knowledge of primary importance in interpretation.

4788   *The Midianites sold him into Egypt* means that people with a measure of the truth that goes with simple goodness consulted knowledge, as the following shows: *Midianites* represent people with the truth belonging to simple goodness, as noted in §§3242, 4756. *Egypt* symbolizes knowledge, as noted in §§1164, 1165, 1186, 1462, 2588, 4749. *Selling* means disowning, as noted in §§4752, 4758. And Joseph represents divine truth. When people with the truth belonging to simple goodness are said to have sold or disowned divine truth for purchase by knowledge (Egypt), it means they consulted knowledge. People who have the truth that goes with simple goodness usually let themselves be carried away by sensory illusions and therefore by the knowledge gleaned from those illusions.

[2] Verse 28 above said that Midianites drew Joseph out of the pit but that they sold him to Ishmaelites, so it seems as though only the Ishmaelites could have sold him in Egypt. The reason he was sold by the Midianites

rather than the Ishmaelites is that Ishmaelites represent people of simple goodness (§4747), while Midianites represent people focusing on the truth associated with that goodness. Joseph, or divine truth, could not be sold by people intent on goodness but by those intent on truth. People intent on goodness have goodness to teach them what divine truth is, but people intent on truth do not.

[3] Religious people are divided into two kinds: those oriented toward what is good and those oriented toward what is true. Those oriented toward goodness are called heavenly; those oriented toward truth are called spiritual. There is a big difference between the two. People oriented toward goodness like to do good for the sake of goodness, without being repaid. Their reward is the opportunity to do good, because they find joy in this. People oriented toward truth do not like to do good for its own sake but because it has been commanded. They are usually thinking about the reward, because they find joy in this and also in boasting. [4] Those who do good from goodness, then, are clearly acting from inner motivation, while those who do good from truth are acting on a kind of outer motivation. This makes the difference plain: the former are people with depth, but the latter are shallow. People with depth cannot "sell" or disown the divine truth represented by Joseph, because goodness gives them a sense for what is true. As a result, neither sensory illusions nor worldly knowledge lead them astray. The shallow, though, are capable of selling or disowning it, because goodness does not give them a sense for what is true. They merely know truth from their theology and their teachers. If they consult knowledge, they readily let themselves be led astray by illusions, because they have no inner dictate.

So it is that Joseph was sold not by the Ishmaelites but by the Midianites.

To Potiphar, Pharaoh's chamberlain, symbolizes inner knowledge. This can be seen from the symbolism of a *chamberlain* as what is within (discussed below) and from the representation of *Pharaoh* as knowledge. Egypt symbolizes learning in general, as demonstrated in §§1164, 1165, 1186, 1462. Pharaoh has the same symbolism, because whatever a land or nation symbolizes in the Word, its monarch does too, the monarch being the head of the nation.

Pharaoh's chamberlain symbolizes inner knowledge because chamberlains were part of a monarch's inner circle. They were some of the innermost courtiers and highest officers, as the meaning of the word in the original language shows.

4789

4790   *The chief of the bodyguards* symbolizes knowledge of primary importance in interpretation. This can be seen from the symbolism of a *chief* as something of primary importance (discussed in §§1482, 2089). The *chief of the bodyguards* symbolizes [knowledge] of primary importance in interpretation because the subject is divine truth, sold by people devoted to the truth that goes with simple goodness when they consulted knowledge, which led them to stray from and disown divine truth and therefore to interpret the Word's literal sense in various ways (§4783). In addition, *bodyguards* symbolize things that help.

Correspondence with the Universal Human (Continued): Correspondence of Taste and the Tongue, and of the Face

4791   THE tongue provides a point of access to the lungs and also to the stomach, so it represents a kind of entryway to what is spiritual and what is heavenly. It represents an entry to what is spiritual because it helps the lungs and therefore speech. It represents an entry to what is heavenly because it helps the stomach, which feeds the blood and the heart. The lungs correspond to spiritual things, and the heart to heavenly things; see §§3635, 3883–3896. As a consequence, the tongue in general corresponds to a desire for truth, or to individuals in the universal human who have a desire for truth and who come to have a desire for the goodness that grows out of truth.

People who love the Lord's Word and therefore long to know what is true and good belong to this area. However, there are differences among those who belong to the tongue itself, to the larynx and trachea, to the esophagus, to the gums, and to the lips. Not the smallest part of a human being lacks correspondence.

[2] People with a desire for truth belong to the area of the tongue (in the broad sense), as I have been allowed to experience many times through a palpable inflow sometimes into my tongue and sometimes into my lips. I have also been allowed to talk with such people. Some of them, I have observed, correspond to the inner substance of the tongue and lips,

and some to the outer surface. The ones who take pleasure in receiving outer truth only, not inner truth, without actually rejecting inner truth, engage in activity that I have felt on the surface of my tongue rather than inside it.

Since [physical] food and nourishment correspond to spiritual food and nourishment, taste corresponds to a perception of such food and a desire for it. Spiritual food is knowledge, understanding, and wisdom. These keep spirits and angels alive and nourish them. They desire and long for them in the same way starving people long for food, so appetite corresponds to that longing. **4792**

Wonderfully enough, they also grow up on that food. Babies who die look, in the other life, exactly like babies and have a baby's intellect. As they grow in understanding and wisdom, though, they stop looking like babies and start looking older, until finally they appear as adults. I have spoken with some who died as babies but looked like young adults to me because by then they had discernment.

This shows what spiritual food and nourishment are.

Because taste corresponds to perception and to a desire for knowing, understanding, and being wise—a desire that holds human life in it—no spirit or angel is allowed to affect our sense of taste. To do so would be to influence our very life. **4793**

Nonetheless there are some particularly dangerous roving spirits from the crowd in hell who learned during physical life how to worm their way into people's feelings in order to do them harm. In the other world they retain this twisted desire and make every effort to invade the sense of taste in people on earth. When they manage it, they take control of the person's inner depths, or the life of the person's thoughts and feelings. They take control because [thoughts and feelings] correspond [to taste], as noted, and what corresponds acts in unison. Many people today are possessed by these spirits, since inward possession still exists (though the outward possession of former times does not).

[2] Such are the spirits who possess people inwardly. We can tell what they are like if we pay attention to our thoughts and feelings and especially to our deepest intentions, which we may be afraid to expose. In some people these intentions are so insane that if they were not held back by the external restraints of position, wealth, reputation, fear for their life, and fear of the law they would plunge possessed—and more than possessed—into murder and pillage. For the identity and character of the spirits that control the inner depths of people like this, see §1983.

[3] To teach me what the situation is like, they were allowed to try invading my sense of taste, which they worked at most eagerly. I was told at the time that if they should manage to penetrate all the way to my sense of taste, they would also take control of my inner faculties, because correspondence causes the sense of taste to depend on that inner dimension. But this was permitted only for the purpose of teaching me how matters stand with the correspondence of taste. The spirits were sent away immediately afterward.

[4] These pernicious spirits try especially hard to loosen all our internal restraints—the desire for what is good and true, the desire for what is just and fair, fear of God's law, and shame at the thought of harming our community or country. When these internal bonds are undone, such spirits take total possession of us.

When they cannot insert themselves into our inner reaches in this way, through persistence, they try various magical arts that proliferate in the other world but are completely unknown in this. By these arts they corrupt the things we know, bringing forward only those that cater to base desires.

This possession is something we cannot escape unless we have a desire for goodness and a resulting belief in the Lord.

[5] I was also shown how they were driven away. When they thought they had penetrated to the interiors of my head and brain, they were carried down by the excretory conduits there and on toward the surface of the skin. They were then seen being thrown into a pore full of sloughed-off waste matter. I was told that such spirits correspond to dirty pits in the outermost layer of skin where scabies develops, and therefore to scabies itself.

4794   Spirits, or people after death, have all the senses they had in the world—sight, hearing, smell, and touch—but not taste. Instead, they have something analogous to taste that is connected with smell.

The reason they lack a sense of taste is to remove the possibility that they will invade the taste of people on earth and take control of their inner depths. It also prevents the sense of taste from distracting a spirit from the desire to learn and grow wise, or spiritual appetite.

4795   This evidence also shows why the tongue is dedicated to twin functions: aiding in speech and aiding in nourishment. As an aid to nourishment, it corresponds to the desire for knowing truth, understanding it, and gaining wisdom about it. That is why the [Latin] word for wisdom or being wise comes from a word for flavor. And as an aid to speech, the tongue corresponds to the desire for thinking and expressing truth.

When angels show themselves, all their inner feelings appear clearly **4796**
in their face and beam from it. Their face, then, is the outward form of
their feelings and an image representing those feelings. To present a face
at odds with one's feelings does not happen in heaven. People who put on
some other, false face are ousted from society. It is clear, then, that a face
corresponds to everything inward in general, both our feelings and our
thoughts, or the contents of both our will and our intellect.

In the Word, therefore, a "face" and "faces" symbolize emotions. The
Lord's "lifting his face" on someone means that a divine feeling, which
comes of love, moves the Lord to have mercy on the person.

Changes in the state of an angel's emotions show vividly in the angel's **4797**
face. When angels are in their own community, they wear their own face,
but when they go to another community, their face changes in accord
with that community's desire for goodness and truth. Still, their real face
is like a background that is recognizable through all the changes.

I have seen whole series of changes reflecting the desires of the communities with which the angels were communicating. Every angel is
in a certain region of the universal human and has broad and general
contact with everyone else in the same region, even though the individual angel stays in that part of the region to which he or she properly
corresponds.

I have seen angels alter their faces with changes that cover the whole
range of an emotion. Yet I have noticed that they still kept the same face
in general, so that their dominant desire with all its variations was always
gleaming from it. What were shown to me, then, were the faces of an
entire emotion in all its breadth.

[2] What is even more amazing, facial changes were also used to show
me how emotions develop from infancy to adulthood. I was able to recognize how much of the child remained in the adult and that the childlike
quality was the person's very humanity. A baby has the outward appearance of innocence, and innocence is humanity itself, because love and
charity from the Lord flow into it as their foundation. When we are reborn
and become wise, our childhood innocence, which was shallow, deepens.
That is why genuine wisdom has no home but innocence (§§2305, 2306,
3183, 3994) and why no one can enter heaven except one who has some
innocence. As the Lord said, "Unless you become like little children, you
will not enter the kingdom of the heavens" (Matthew 18:3; Mark 10:15).

I was also able to recognize evil spirits from their faces, because all **4798**
their cravings or evil desires are written on their faces. Their faces also

indicate what hells they communicate with, since there are many hells, all of them distinguished by the genera and species of their evil cravings.

As a whole, when their faces appear in heaven's light, they look almost devoid of life, drained of color like a corpse's face. Some have black faces, and some have faces that are grotesque. They are forms of hatred, cruelty, deceit, hypocrisy. In their own light, though, among themselves, their delusions give them a different appearance.

4799   There were spirits with me from another planet (described elsewhere), whose faces were different from the faces of people on our planet. Their faces jutted out, especially around the lips, and were free moving. I talked with these spirits about their lifestyle and the way they socialize with each other. They said their main way of talking together was by variations in their face, particularly around the lips, and that they expressed emotion through the parts around their eyes. Their companions were fully able to understand from this both what they were thinking and what they wanted. They even tried to demonstrate this for me by acting on my lips, bending and curving the area around my mouth in various ways, but I was not susceptible to their changes, because I had not started to learn moving my lips that way as a baby. I could nevertheless tell what they were saying, by the communication of their thoughts.

Language is generally capable of being expressed by the lips, though, as I can see from the multiple intertwining series of muscle fibers in the lips. If they were teased apart and could act in a free and unrestricted way, they could produce many changing movements that are unfamiliar to people in whom the fibers lie crowded together.

[2] The reason the spirits' speech was like this on their planet is that they cannot dissemble, or think one thing and show something else on their face. They live together in such honesty that they hide nothing at all from their companions. No, everyone sees instantly what they are thinking, what they are intending, what they are like, and even what wrongs they have done, since people governed by sincerity are conscious of their missteps. At a glance others can make out their inner face, or their attitude.

[3] They showed me that they do not contract their face but relax it, unlike those who since youth have become accustomed to putting on false appearances, speaking and acting otherwise than they think and intend. These tense their face to be ready for any adjustment their cunning advises. Anything we want to hide tightens our face, although we release the tension when expressing fictitious sincerity.

[4] When I was reading about the Lord in the New Testament Word, spirits from the planet in question were present, as were some Christians. I perceived that the Christians were privately fostering slanders against the Lord and wanting to communicate them nonverbally. The spirits from the other planet were amazed at them, but I was allowed to tell the spirits that in the world the Christians had been like this in their heart, not in explicit words. I was also able to tell them that some people preach about the Lord despite their negativity, and when they preach, they move the crowd to sighs and sometimes to tears with the zeal of their pretended piety, breathing not a whisper of what lies in their hearts.

The spirits were dumbfounded at this—that such a discrepancy could exist between a person's insides and outside, or thoughts and words. They said they knew absolutely nothing of such a discrepancy. It was impossible for them to say anything with their mouth or show anything on their face that did not agree with the feelings in their heart. Otherwise they would be torn in two and be destroyed.

Very few can believe that spirits and angels live in communities, and that everything in a person corresponds to those communities. Few can believe that the more communities there are, and the more members in a community, the better and stronger the correspondence, because there is strength in unanimous numbers. **4800**

To learn that this was so, I was shown how spirits and angels act on and affect the face, how they affect the muscles of the forehead, cheeks, chin, and throat. The ones who belonged to that region were allowed to flow in, and when they did, each part changed in response to their inflow. Some of them also spoke with me. However, these did not know they were assigned to the region of the face. What area they are assigned to is hidden from spirits, though not from angels.

There was one who talked with me who had known outer religious truth better than others during the time he lived in the world but had not lived a life of faith in keeping with the commandments. He had loved himself alone, despising others in comparison with himself, and had believed he would be prominent in heaven. Because he was like this, he had been unable to think of heaven except as resembling a worldly kingdom. **4801**

In the other world he found that heaven was not like this at all. The leading figures, he discovered, were people who had not put themselves ahead of others and especially who had not considered themselves worthy of mercy but last in line when it came to merit. He was then very angry, and what he had accepted as part of his faith in bodily life he now rejected.

He was constantly trying to hurt anyone who came from the area of the tongue. Over the course of many weeks I was allowed to sense his efforts, which taught me the identity and characteristics of those who correspond to the tongue, and the identity of those who oppose them.

4802   There are also spirits who to some extent let in heaven's light and accept faith's truth although they are evil, so that they have some perception of truth. They even welcome truth eagerly, but not in order to live according to it, only to glory in seeming more intelligent and sharp-sighted than others. The human intellect is such that it can accept truth, but we do not make it our own unless we live according to it. If our intellect were not like this, we could not be reformed.

[2] People who have been like this in the world—who have understood what is true and yet lived an evil life—remain so in the other life, but there they misuse their ability to understand truth in order to control others. They know that in the other world truth puts them in touch with certain heavenly communities, which means that they can take up with evil companions and still have clout (since truth carries power with it in the next life). Because their life is wicked, though, they live in hell.

[3] I have spoken with two who were such in bodily life, and they were surprised to find themselves in hell despite their having believed the truths of the faith with conviction. "The light you have, which gives you your understanding of truth," I told them, "is like winter light in the world. Objects look just as beautiful and colorful in that light as they do in summer light, but they are all dormant. Nothing sweet or cheerful comes to view.

"Your aims in discerning the truth have been boastful and therefore self-serving, so when the aura of your purposes rises to the angels in the inner heavens, who perceive only purposes, it cannot be tolerated. It is rejected, and that is why you are in hell.

[4] "People like you were once the main people to be called snakes in the tree of knowledge," I added, "because when you base your reasoning on your life, you contradict the truth.

"What is more, you are like a woman with a beautiful face but a horrible smell that gets her thrown out of society wherever she goes." In the other world such people actually do stink when they arrive in angelic communities, as they themselves can smell when they draw near those communities.

These remarks also show what faith is like without a life of faith.

It is worth mentioning, and completely unknown in the world, that **4803** good spirits and angels continually change and progress in regard to their state. As a result they move deeper into the interior of the region they inhabit and therefore into higher-ranking jobs. In heaven there is a continual process of purification and, as the saying goes, a new creation [2 Corinthians 5:17; Galatians 6:15]. However, it is still the case that no angel can ever achieve absolute perfection to eternity. The Lord alone is perfect. All perfection exists in him and comes from him.

Those who correspond to the mouth are always wanting to talk. They take the greatest pleasure in speaking. When they are being perfected, they are reduced to saying nothing but what is useful to their associates, society in general, heaven, and the Lord. Their delight in speaking this way increases as they lose the compulsion to focus on themselves when they talk and to seek wisdom for selfish ends.

In the other world there is a large number of groups called friend **4804** groups consisting of friends who during physical life preferred social gatherings to any other kind of pleasure. They loved the friends with whom they mingled, not caring whether their friends were good or evil as long as they were fun to be with. As a result they were not friends to goodness or truth.

People who were like this during physical life remain the same in the next life. They form attachments solely on the basis of social pleasure.

Many groups of this kind were present with me at a distance, mainly appearing a little to the right above my head. I could tell they were there by my lethargy and dullness and by the withdrawal of the pleasure I was feeling. That is the effect such groups have. Wherever they go, they rob others of their enjoyment and, surprisingly, take it into themselves as their own. They divert spirits who are present with others and turn those spirits toward themselves, so they transfer another's delight to themselves. Since this practice disturbs and injures anyone intent on doing good, the Lord keeps them from going near heavenly communities.

From this I was able to learn how much damage a bond of friendship can inflict on a person's spiritual life if the focus is on personality rather than on what is good. We can all be friends to others, but we have to be best friends with goodness.

There are also even tighter friend groups. They steal and usurp not **4805** the outer but the inner pleasure of another, or the blessedness the person feels when moved by what is spiritual. The members of these groups are in front to the right, just above the underground realm, and some of them are quite high up. Several times I talked with the ones lower down, and when I did, the ones higher up exerted their combined influence.

In bodily life they were such that they bore a heartfelt love for the others within their common association, who embraced each other in mutual fellowship. They considered themselves alone to be alive and enlightened, and people outside the group to be relatively unalive and unenlightened. As a consequence of this attitude, they also imagined that the Lord's heaven was populated just from their small numbers.

[2] But I was allowed to tell them that the Lord's heaven is immense and consists of people of every population and language. It contains everyone who [in earthly life] did what is good out of love and faith. I showed them that there are individuals in heaven who relate to all the regions of the body, inside and out. "If you aspire to rise higher than the level corresponding to your life," I said, "you cannot be given heaven, especially if you condemn others outside your group. If you do, your group is a tighter friend group, and on your approach, by your very nature, you deprive others of the blessings of spiritual feelings"—as mentioned above. These spirits regard others as nonchosen and not alive, and when this thought is shared with the others, it depresses them. In keeping with a law of order in the other life, though, the depression returns to those who caused it.

4806 There is more on correspondence with the universal human at the end of the next chapter [§§4931–4953].

Genesis 38

[Matthew 25:31–33]

AT the head of the previous chapter, in §§4661, 4662, 4663, 4664, I started to explain what the Lord said in Matthew 25:31–end about a judgment on the good and the evil, whom he calls sheep and goats. The inner meaning of his words has not yet been unfolded, but it will be, here at the beginning of the current chapter and the next two [§§4954–4959, 5063–5071]. The explanation will show that the Last Judgment mentioned there does not mean the world's last days, when the dead will finally rise again, gather before the Lord, and be judged. Instead, it means the last days of everyone who passes from this world into the other life, since that is when we are judged. This is the judgment that is meant. **4807**

The truth of this is apparent not in the literal meaning but in the inner meaning. The Lord spoke this way because he was using representation and symbolism, as he did everywhere else in the Word's Old and New Testaments. To speak in representations and symbols is to speak to both the world and heaven, or to both people and angels. This kind of speech is divine, because it is universal, and it is therefore the kind used in the Word.

People who live in the world and care only about worldly matters, then, glean nothing from these words of the Lord's concerning the Last Judgment except this: Resurrection will happen at the same time for everybody, the Lord will then sit on a glorious throne, and he will address the assembled crowd in the words of that passage. People who care about heavenly matters, though, realize that resurrection always comes at the time of death. They see what is involved in the Lord's words, which is that we are each judged by our life. We all take our judgment with us, because we take our life with us.

An explanation of the inner meaning of the individual words will show that this is the message involved in that meaning. At present, though, the explanation will cover only verses 31, 32, 33: **4808**

> When the Son of Humankind comes in his glory, and all the holy angels with him, then he will sit on his glorious throne, and all nations will

assemble before him. And he will separate them from each other, as a
shepherd separates the sheep from the goats. And he will indeed set the
sheep on his right and the goats on the left. (Matthew 25:31, 32, 33)

4809   *When the Son of Humankind comes in his glory* means when divine
truth appears in its own light, which happens to each of us when we
die. We then enter heaven's light, in which we can perceive what truth
and goodness are and what we ourselves are like. The Son of Humankind,
in the Word's inner sense, means the Lord in regard to divine truth, so it
means divine truth from the Lord. The glory means consequent understanding and wisdom, which appears as a light, and to angels as the radiance of that light. This radiance containing wisdom and understanding
based on divine truth from the Lord is what the Word calls glory. For the
idea that in an inner sense the Son of Humankind means divine truth, see
§§2159, 2803, 2813, 3704.

[2] *And all the holy angels with him* symbolizes heaven with its angels.
The holy angels mean truth stemming from the Lord's divine goodness.
In the Word, angels do not mean angels but something from the Lord;
see §§1925, 4085. Angels themselves are receptive to the living truth that
comes from the Lord's divine goodness, and the more receptive the angels
are to it, the more angelic they are. This shows that angels here mean
these kinds of truth.

Since the passage is talking about the state we each experience after
death and the judgment we each face on our life, it says that all the holy
angels will be with him. This means that judgment comes through heaven,
because all inflow of divine truth takes place through heaven. No one
could handle a direct inflow of it [from the Lord].

[3] *Then he will sit on his glorious throne* symbolizes judgment. A throne
is mentioned in connection with the Lord's role as monarch, and his monarchy is divine truth (§§1728, 2015, 3009, 3670). Divine truth is the source
and standard of judgment.

[4] *And all nations will assemble before him* means that everyone's goodness and evil will lie open. In the Word's inner meaning, nations symbolize goodness, and in a negative sense, evil (§§1259, 1260, 1416, 2588 at the
end, 4574). So "all nations will assemble before him" means that goodness
and evil will be visible in divine light, or the light of divine truth.

[5] *And he will separate them from each other, as a shepherd separates
the sheep from the goats* symbolizes the separation of goodness from evil.
Sheep mean people intent on goodness, and goats, people intent on evil.
Strictly speaking, *sheep* is the word for people who possess neighborly

love and therefore faith, while *goats* is for people who possess faith but no neighborly love. These are the two groups being dealt with. For the meaning of sheep as people with charity and therefore faith, see §§2088, 4169. For that of goats as people with faith and no charity, §4769.

[6] *And he will indeed set the sheep on his right and the goats on the left* means a separation based on truth that comes of goodness and falsity that comes of evil. What is more, people focused on truth-from-goodness actually appear on the right in the other world, and people focused on falsity-from-evil on the left. To be set on the right and on the left, then, means to be arranged according to one's life.

These remarks show what the Lord's words above involve and that they are not meant literally. The meaning is not that the Lord is going to come in glory on some final day, that all the holy angels will be with him, and that he is going to sit on a glorious throne to judge the nations, all assembled before him. No, the meaning is that we will each be judged by the way we have lived, whenever we pass from life in this world to eternal life.

4810

Genesis 38

1. And it happened in that time that Judah went down from among his brothers and turned aside to an Adullamite man, and his name was Hirah.

2. And Judah saw there the daughter of a Canaanite man, and his name was Shua; and he took her and came to her.

3. And she conceived and bore a son, and he called his name Er.

4. And she conceived again and bore a son and called his name Onan.

5. And she went on to bear another son and called his name Shelah. And he was in Chezib when she gave birth to him.

6. And Judah took a woman for Er, his firstborn, and her name was Tamar.

7. And Er, Judah's firstborn, was evil in the eyes of Jehovah, and Jehovah put him to death.

8. And Judah said to Onan, "Come to your brother's wife and perform the levirate for her and raise up seed for your brother."

9. And Onan knew that the seed would not be his, and it happened when he came to his brother's wife that he wasted it on the earth so that he would not give seed to his brother.

10. And what he did was evil in Jehovah's eyes, and [Jehovah] put him to death too.

11. And Judah said to Tamar, his daughter-in-law, "Stay a widow at your father's house till Shelah my son grows up"; for he said, "Or he too might die like his brothers." And Tamar went and stayed at her father's house.

12. And the days multiplied, and Shua's daughter, Judah's wife, died, and Judah was comforted; and he went up to the shearers of his flock, he and Hirah, his companion, the Adullamite, to Timnah.

13. And it was told to Tamar, saying, "Look—your father-in-law is going up to Timnah to shear his flock."

14. And she took the clothes of her widowhood off her and covered up in a veil and cloaked herself and sat in the gateway of the springs that are on the way to Timnah, because she saw that Shelah had grown up and she had not been given to him as his woman.

15. And Judah saw her and accounted her a prostitute because she had covered her face.

16. And he turned aside to her on the way and said, "Grant, please, that I come to you"—because he did not know that she was his daughter-in-law; and she said, "What are you giving me, that you should come to me?"

17. And he said, "I will send a kid of the goats from the flock," and she said, "If you give an earnest against your sending it."

18. And he said, "What is the earnest that I shall give you?" and she said, "Your signet, your lanyard, and your staff that is in your hand"; and he gave them to her and came to her, and she conceived to him.

19. And she rose and went and took her veil off her and put on the clothes of her widowhood.

20. And Judah sent a kid of the goats in the hand of his companion, the Adullamite, to receive the earnest from the hand of the woman, and he did not find her.

21. And he asked the men of that place, saying, "Where is that harlot at the springs along the way?" and they said, "There wasn't a harlot there."

22. And he went back to Judah and said, "I didn't find her, and in addition the men of the place said, 'There wasn't a harlot there.'"

23. And Judah said, "Let her take it for herself, [though] we might be held in contempt. Look, I sent the kid but you did not find her."

24. And it happened in about three months that it was told to Judah, saying, "Tamar your daughter-in-law whored, and here, now, she is also

pregnant from her whoredoms," and Judah said, "Bring her out and let her be burned."

25. She was brought out, and she sent to her father-in-law, saying, "By the man to whom these belong I am pregnant." And she said, "Recognize, please, whose the signet and the lanyard and the staff are."

26. And Judah recognized [them] and said, "She is more justified than I, because I did not give her to Shelah my son." And he did not know her ever again.

27. And it happened in the time when she gave birth that here, there were twins in her womb!

28. And it happened when she gave birth that [one of them] put out his hand, and the midwife took and tied double-dyed [scarlet thread] on his hand, saying, "This one came out first."

29. And it happened as he took back his hand that here, his brother came out! And she said, "Why have you breached yourself a breach?" and called his name Perez.

30. And afterward his brother came out, on whose hand was the double-dyed [scarlet thread], and they called his name Zerah.

Summary

IN its inner meaning, this chapter is about the Jewish religion and a genuine religion. Judah depicts the Jewish religion, and Tamar, the genuine one. **4811**

The sons of Tamar symbolize the two essential factors in the church: faith and love. Perez symbolizes faith, and Zerah love. Their birth represents the fact that love is actually the church's firstborn and that faith only appears to be so. **4812**

Inner Meaning

GENESIS 38:1, 2, 3, 4, 5. *And it happened in that time that Judah went down from among his brothers and turned aside to an Adullamite man, and his name was Hirah. And Judah saw there the daughter of a Canaanite* **4813** *man, and his name was Shua; and he took her and came to her. And she con-ceived and bore a son, and he called his name Er. And she conceived again and bore a son and called his name Onan. And she went on to bear another son and called his name Shelah. And he was in Chezib when she gave birth to him.*

It happened in that time symbolizes the state involved in what follows. *That Judah went down from among his brothers* symbolizes Jacob's descen-dants, and specifically the tribe of Judah, which was separate from the rest. *And turned aside to an Adullamite man* means to falsity. *And his name was Hirah* symbolizes its nature. *And Judah saw there the daughter of a Canaanite man* symbolizes a desire for evil resulting from a false teaching with evil origins. *And his name was Shua* symbolizes its nature. *And he took her and came to her* means that the tribe of Judah attached itself to this. *And she conceived and bore a son* means that religious falsity resulted. *And he called his name Er* symbolizes its nature. *And she conceived again and bore a son* symbolizes evil. *And called his name Onan* symbolizes its nature. *And she went on to bear another son* symbolizes something idolatrous. *And called his name Shelah* symbolizes its nature. *And he was in Chezib when she gave birth to him* symbolizes the state.

4814   *And it happened in that time* symbolizes the state involved in what follows. This can be seen from the symbolism of a *time* as a state (dis-cussed in §§2625, 2788, 2837, 3254, 3356, 3404, 3938). Its being the state involved in what follows is symbolized by the wording "it *happened* in that time," because what follows tells what happened. In any progression, later elements flow from earlier ones. The previous chapter told how Jacob's sons sold Joseph and how Judah advocated it. The text put it this way in verses 26, 27: "Judah said to his brothers, '*What gain* if we kill our brother and cover up his blood? Come, and *let's sell him* to the Ishmaelites.'" This meant that divine truth was disowned by them, especially by Judah, who in the first layer of meaning symbolizes the tribe of Judah, and in general, the wicked in the church who oppose each and every kind of goodness; see §§4750, 4751. The words *in that time* center on this idea, because the subject now is Judah and his sons by the Canaanite woman and then by Tamar, his daughter-in-law. In an inner sense these depict the tribe of Judah and the religious qualities that were established in it.

[2] The idea that a time symbolizes a state, and that *it happened in that time* therefore symbolizes the state involved in what follows, cannot help seeming strange. It seems strange because of the difficulty in under-standing how a concept of time can turn into a concept of state, that is, in understanding that any mention of time in the Word means something

related to state. It is important to realize, though, that angels' thoughts do not draw at all on time or space, because they are in heaven. When they left the world behind, they also left behind any notions of time and space and adopted the idea of state—specifically, of the state of goodness and truth. Consequently, when we on earth read the Word and think about it in terms of time and time's effects, the angels with us do not perceive anything about time but about state instead. The two also correspond.

In fact, not even we on earth perceive time in our inner thinking, only in our outer thinking. The proof is the state we are in when our outer mind has been put to rest (that is, when we sleep) and many other experiences as well.

[3] Be advised that in general there are two kinds of state: a state of goodness and a state of truth. The first is called a state of being; the second a state of emergence. Being has to do with goodness, and the emergence of being has to do with truth. Space corresponds to a state of being, time to a state of emergence. Therefore when we read "and it happened in that time," the angels with us cannot possibly perceive the clause the way we do. Likewise for the rest of Scripture. Everything written in the Word, by its very nature, turns into a corresponding idea among angels, and this corresponding idea is completely invisible in the literal text. The worldly content of the literal meaning changes into the spiritual content of the inner meaning.

That Judah went down from among his brothers symbolizes Jacob's descendants, and specifically the tribe of Judah, which was separate from the rest, as the following shows: *Judah* in a broad sense represents Jacob's descendants, and in a narrow sense, the tribe called Judah. *Going down from among his brothers* means being separated from the rest of the tribes, and in this case, going somewhere worse. *Going down* involves the idea of being thrust down toward evil, since going up involves that of being lifted up toward goodness (§§3084, 4539). The reason for this implication—also mentioned before—is as follows: The land of Canaan represented the Lord's kingdom, and the Canaanite sites of Jerusalem and Zion represented the inmost part of that kingdom. Anything outside the land's borders represented something outside the Lord's kingdom—in other words, falsity and evil. One was therefore said to go down from Zion or Jerusalem toward the borders, and up from the borders to Jerusalem or Zion. That is why going up suggests a rise toward truth and goodness, while going down suggests a lowering toward falsity and evil. The current topic of discussion is the falsity and evil to which the tribe of Judah stooped, so

4815

the text says that Judah went down. It also says that he turned aside to an Adullamite man, and turning aside means turning to falsity and then to evil.

[2] Everyone knows that the tribe of Judah separated from the other tribes. The purpose of its separation was so that it could represent the Lord's heavenly kingdom, the rest of the tribes representing his spiritual kingdom. As a result, Judah in a representative sense means a heavenly person, and in a universal sense the Lord's heavenly kingdom (§§3654, 3881). The rest of the tribes were called by the single name "Israelite," Israel in a representative sense meaning a spiritual person, and in a universal sense the Lord's spiritual kingdom (§§3654, 4286).

[3] "That Judah went down from among his brothers and turned aside" means in specific that the tribe of Judah went in a worse direction than the others. The fact that it did so can be seen from many passages in the Word, particularly in the Prophets. In Jeremiah, for instance:

> Her *treacherous* sister *Judah* saw it when, for all the ways in which *rebellious Israel* committed adultery, I sent her away and gave her document of divorce to her; yet *treacherous Judah,* her sister, was not afraid but went and whored, she too, so that the land was profaned with the sound of her whoredom. She committed adultery with stone and wood. Yet in all these things, *treacherous Judah* did not turn back to me. *Rebellious Israel absolved her soul more than treacherous Judah.* (Jeremiah 3:7–11)

And in Ezekiel:

> Her sister did see but *corrupted her love more than she,* and *her whoredoms above her sister's whoredoms.* (Ezekiel 23:11 and following verses to the end)

This is about Jerusalem and Samaria—in other words, the tribe of Judah and the tribes of Israel. There are many other passages besides.

[4] The inner meaning [of the current chapter] describes the way that tribe slid into falsity, then into evil, and finally into something entirely idolatrous. Of course this is being described in the inner meaning before the tribe ever separated from the others or developed such a character. But what is found in the inner meaning is divine, and to the Divine the future is here and now. See the predictions about that nation in Deuteronomy 31:16–22; 32:15–44.

 And turned aside to an Adullamite man means to falsity, as the following shows: *Turning aside* means going badly astray, because turning aside, like going down, has to do with moving away from goodness to evil, and from truth to falsity. A *man* symbolizes a person with understanding, and in an abstract sense it symbolizes truth. This is because a genuine ability to understand is based on truth, as discussed in §§265, 749, 1007, 3134, 3309. In a negative sense a man symbolizes a person without understanding, and therefore falsity. This falsity is represented by the *Adullamite*. Adullam was on the border of Judah's inheritance (Joshua 15:35), so it symbolized truth that grows out of goodness, as it does in Micah:

> Again I will bring the heir to you, inhabitant of Mareshah. *To Adullam* will come the glory of Israel. (Micah 1:15)

Since most things in the Word also have a negative meaning, so does Adullam, and it symbolizes falsity that grows out of evil.

The reason most things also have a negative meaning is that until the land of Canaan became an inheritance to the children of Jacob, it was occupied by non-Jewish nations, which symbolized falsity and evil. Later, when the children of Jacob became defiant, [they symbolized falsity and evil] too. Different lands take on the representation of the nations and peoples living there, in keeping with the character of those people.

And his name was Hirah symbolizes its nature. This can be seen from **4817** the symbolism of a *name* and calling a name as the quality of something (discussed in §§144, 145, 1754, 1896, 2009, 2724, 3006, 3421). It is the nature of the falsity mentioned just above that is being symbolized. In the Word, the names of both places and people symbolize states and qualities; see §§1224, 1264, 1876, 1888, 1946, 2643, 3422, 4298, 4442.

And Judah saw there the daughter of a Canaanite man symbolizes a **4818** desire for evil resulting from a false teaching with evil origins, as the following shows: A *daughter* symbolizes a desire for goodness, as discussed at §2362, and in a negative sense, a desire for evil (§3024). A *man* symbolizes a person with understanding, and in an abstract sense truth, but in a negative sense it symbolizes a person without understanding, and falsity, as discussed just above in §4816. And a *Canaanite* symbolizes evil, as discussed at §§1573, 1574. The *daughter of a Canaanite man,* then, symbolizes evil resulting from a false teaching with evil origins. Evil resulting from a false teaching with evil origins will be defined below.

[2] The first thing is to talk about the origins of the tribe of Judah, which are the subject of the current chapter. That tribe, or the Jewish nation, has three origins. The first is Shelah, Judah's son by his Canaanite wife. The second is Perez, and the third is Zerah, Judah's sons by Tamar,

his daughter-in-law. These three sons of Judah produced the whole Jewish nation, as is clear from the list in Genesis 46:12 of the sons and grandsons of Jacob who went to Egypt with him. It is also clear from the classification of tribe members according to their families, as reported in Moses:

> The children of Judah, according to their families, were, for *Shelah,* the family of the Shelanite; for *Perez,* the family of the Perezite; for *Zerah,* the family of the Zerahite. (Numbers 26:20; 1 Chronicles 4:21)

This evidence shows what kind of origin the nation has. One third of its members are from a Canaanite mother, and two thirds from Judah's daughter-in-law, so all of them come from an illicit bed. Marriage with the daughters of Canaanites was strictly forbidden, as is apparent in Genesis 24:3; Exodus 34:16; Deuteronomy 7:3; 1 Kings 11:2; Ezra 9, 10; and sleeping with one's daughter-in-law was a capital crime, as is plain in Moses:

> As for a man who lies *with his daughter-in-law,* both shall definitely be killed. They made a mingling; their blood is on them. (Leviticus 20:12)

As verse 26 of the current chapter shows, Judah drew a connection between what he did with his daughter-in-law and the law about the levirate— which regulates the behavior of a [dead man's] brother, not his father. This connection with the levirate means that children produced by Tamar would be recognized as the children of Er, the firstborn, son of a Canaanite mother, and he was evil in the eyes of Jehovah and was therefore put to death (verse 7). After all, the first children born through the levirate did not belong to the man from whom they were conceived but to the man whose seed those children raised up. This can be seen from Deuteronomy 25:5, 6 and from verses 8, 9 of the current chapter. Besides, the children born of Tamar were born through whoredom, because when Judah went in to Tamar he was under the impression that she was a harlot (verses 15, 16, 21). This evidence clarifies the origin of the Jewish nation and the nature of that origin. It also shows that the Jews lied in John:

> The Jews said to him, "We were not born of whoredom." (John 8:41)

[3] The significance and representation of this origin is that their inner depths had a similar quality, or a similar source, as later parts of the story show. The fact that Judah took a Canaanite as his wife involves an evil resulting from a false teaching with evil origins, this being the inner-level symbolism of the daughter of a Canaanite man. His lying with his

daughter-in-law involves and represents damnation through the falsification of truth at the urging of evil, since whoredom throughout the Word symbolizes the falsification of truth; see §2466.

Evil resulting from a false teaching with evil origins is evil in a person's life growing out of doctrinal falsity, when this falsity is hatched out of the evil of self-love (or hatched by people with this evil) and confirmed from the Word's literal meaning. Such is the source of evil in the Jewish nation, and it is also the source of evil among some in the Christian world, especially those meant by Babylon in the Word. By its very nature, this evil completely blocks the way to the inner self—so completely that no trace of conscience can form in the inner self. The evil we do on the basis of doctrinal falsity is evil we believe to be good because we believe it to be true. In consequence we do such evil with license, freedom, and pleasure. Heaven accordingly closes so tightly to us that it cannot open.

[4] Let an example explain what this evil is like. The evil of self-love inspires some to believe there is only one nation that Jehovah ever chose. They view everyone else in the world as a comparative slave, and so worthless that she or he can be murdered at will or tortured. They also confirm this belief from the literal sense of the Word. Such was the belief of the Jewish nation, and such is the belief of the modern-day Babylon. Any evil done as a result of this false doctrine, or of any other doctrine built and founded on it, is an evil resulting from a false teaching with evil origins. It destroys the inner self, and shuts it off so that no conscience can ever form in it. People who do such evil are the ones the Word describes as standing in blood, because they are awash in savagery against all humankind, which fails to adulate them and their creed or to offer gifts on their altar.

[5] As another example, take people who have been led by the evil of love for themselves and for worldly advantages to believe that anyone would be the Lord's deputy on earth, with the authority to open and close heaven and therefore to control everyone's mind and conscience. This falsity they confirm from the Word's literal meaning. Any evil they do as a consequence is an evil resulting from a false teaching with evil origins. It is equally destructive to the inner self in people who claim such authority for themselves and exert such power, at the call of this evil. It destroys the inner self so thoroughly that they no longer know what that self is, or that anyone really has a conscience. Consequently they no longer believe there is any life after death, or hell, or heaven, no matter how often they speak about these things.

[6] In the world, we are unable to distinguish the nature of this evil from other kinds, but angels in the other life spot it as clear as day. In that life, evil and falsity are seen for what they are and recognized by where they are from, in all their variations, which are countless. The types and subtypes of evil and falsity also determine how the hells are divided up. We on earth know hardly anything about the countless variations. We simply believe evil exists; its nature we do not see. The only reason for this ignorance is that we do not know what goodness is, and that is because we do not know what neighborly love is. If we recognized the goodness sought by neighborly love, we would recognize its opposite, or evil in all its permutations.

4819   *And his name was Shua* symbolizes its nature. This can be seen from the symbolism of a *name* as the quality (discussed above at §4817)—here, the nature of evil resulting from a false teaching with evil origins (also discussed above, at §4818).

4820   *And he took her and came to her* means that the tribe of Judah attached itself to this—that is, to an evil resulting from a false teaching with evil origins. This can be seen from the symbolism of *taking her*—taking her as his woman—and *coming to her,* or going in to her, as uniting (noted several times before [§§1900, 1909, 2465, 3834, 3850, 3914, 3918]).

In an inner sense, marriage represents the union of what is good and true, because it rises from that union (§§2727–2759), but in a negative sense it represents the union of what is evil and false. Here it represents the union of the tribe of Judah to [evil and falsity], because it applies to Judah, who symbolizes the tribe named for him; see above at §4815.

The text here does not say that Judah took her as his wife, only that he took her and came to her. That is because their coupling was illicit (§4818). It is also because this would imply that the coupling was not a marriage but whoredom and therefore that the children from this woman were born of harlotry. That is exactly what the union of evil with falsity is.

Later she was referred to as Judah's wife, in these words at verse 12: "And the days multiplied, and Shua's daughter, Judah's wife, died." This fact will be discussed below [§4852].

4821   *And she conceived and bore a son* means that religious falsity resulted. This can be seen from the symbolism of *conceiving and bearing* as acknowledging in faith and deed (discussed in §§3905, 3915, 3919) and from that of a *son* as a religion's truth, but in a negative sense as its falsity (discussed in §§489, 491, 533, 1147, 2623, 3373, 4257). *She conceived and bore a son* in this case, then, means that the religion existing with the tribe of Judah acknowledged falsity in faith and deed.

The reason this son symbolizes religious falsity is that he was a firstborn, and in the ancient churches a firstborn symbolized religious truth (§§352, 3325). In a negative sense it symbolized falsity, and this included the firstborn children and animals of Egypt (§3325). What follows shortly [§§4832–4833] shows that this son symbolized falsity rather than truth, because in verse 7 it says, "Er, Judah's firstborn, was evil in the eyes of Jehovah, and Jehovah put him to death." The name of the son, Er, also embraces the nature of [the falsity], just as the name of the second son, Onan, embraces the nature of its own attribute, which is wickedness, or evil.

And he called his name Er symbolizes its nature. This is established by the symbolism of *calling a name* as the quality (discussed at §§144, 145, 1754, 1896, 2009, 2724, 3006, 3421)—specifically, the nature of the religious falsity discussed just above at §4821.

I mention the nature of the falsity because falsities differ from each other, just as truths do. There are so many differences that even the major types can hardly be listed, and each type of falsity has its own character, which distinguishes it from another. There are general falsities that reign supreme among the wicked in every religion, and this falsity varies from person to person there in keeping with the individual life. The falsity in the Jewish religion that the current text deals with was falsity coming from the evil of self-love and consequent materialism; see §4818.

And she conceived again and bore a son symbolizes evil. This can be seen from the symbolism of a *son* as truth and also as goodness (discussed in §264) and therefore in a negative sense as falsity and also as evil, but as evil that develops out of falsity. In its essence, this evil *is* falsity, because it comes from falsity. Anyone who does evil at the urging of false doctrine is putting falsity into practice, but because it has been turned into action, it is called evil.

The symbolism of the firstborn as falsity and of this son as evil is evident from the fact that verses 9, 10 say that the second son actually did evil: "He wasted his seed on the earth so that he would not give seed to his brother. *And what he did was evil in Jehovah's eyes,* and [Jehovah] put him to death too." The text also makes it plain that the evil came out of falsity. What is more, in the ancient churches a second-born symbolized religious truth put into practice, so this particular second-born symbolizes falsity put into practice, which is the same as evil. The symbolism of this son as evil is also evident from the fact that the firstborn, Er, was named by his father, Judah, but this one, Onan, by his mother, Shua's daughter. This can be seen in the original language. In the Word, a man

4822

4823

symbolizes falsity, and his woman, evil (see §§915, 2517, 4510; for the symbolism of Shua's daughter as evil, see §§4818, 4819). Since Er was called that name by his father, then, he symbolizes falsity, and since Onan was called that name by his mother, he symbolizes evil. It is as if the first son was the father's child and the second the mother's.

[2] The Word often speaks of man and wife, and of husband and wife. When it says "man and wife," the man symbolizes truth, and the wife goodness. In a negative sense the man symbolizes falsity, and the wife evil. When it says "husband and wife," though, the husband symbolizes goodness, and the wife truth. In a negative sense the husband symbolizes evil, and the wife falsity. Here is the reason for this mystery: In the heavenly church, a husband was intent on goodness, and a wife on the truth belonging to that goodness. In a spiritual church, a man is intent on truth, and a wife on the goodness belonging to that truth. They actually are and were such, too, because the inner depths of a human changed in this way. That is why the Word speaks of a husband and wife when it is talking about heavenly goodness and the heavenly truth it produces, but of a man and wife—or more likely a man and his woman—when it is talking about spiritual goodness and the spiritual truth it produces. These clues, and the words themselves, reveal what kind of goodness and truth the Word is dealing with in its inner meaning.

[3] That is also why I have already said several times that marriage represents the union of goodness and truth, and of truth and goodness. And marriage love has its source in that union. Marriage love among the heavenly originates in the union of goodness with truth, while marriage love among the spiritual originates in the union of truth with goodness. The [two] kinds of marriage also have an actual correspondence to those kinds of union.

This evidence shows the significance of the fact that their father named the first boy, while their mother named the second and also the third, as is clear in the original language. Their father named the first boy because the first one symbolized falsity, and their mother named the second because he symbolized evil.

4824 *And called his name Onan* symbolizes its nature—the nature of the evil referred to just above in §4823. This can be seen from the symbolism of *calling someone's name* as the quality (discussed at §4822). *Onan* symbolizes and suggests the nature of that evil.

4825 *And she went on to bear another son* symbolizes something idolatrous. This can be seen from the symbolism of this *son* as something idolatrous. The ones born earlier symbolized falsity and evil (§§4821, 4823), so it follows that the third one symbolizes something idolatrous. Falsity and evil together produce idolatry and lie within it.

Of Judah's three sons by the Canaanite, only this one survived. A third of the Jewish nation descended from him, which in an inner sense means that the Jewish nation had its origin in idolatry.

The narrative and prophetic parts of the Word in their literal sense make it clear that this nation was heavily inclined toward idolatry. The inner sense of the same parts shows that there was never a break in its idolatrous leanings. Idolatry does not just mean worshiping idols and statues or worshiping other gods. It also means worshiping what is external devoid of what is internal, and this was an idolatry the Jewish nation constantly engaged in. It revered external things alone, totally doing away with inner depth, which it did not even want to know about.

The people of that nation did indeed possess holy objects, like the meeting tent, with its ark and the appeasement cover on it, the tables holding the loaves of bread, the lampstand, and the incense. Outside the tent they had the altar, on which burnt offerings and sacrifices were performed. All these things were called holy, and the inmost area in the tent was called either the Holiest Place or the sanctuary. They also had the garments for Aaron and their high priests, and these were called garments of holiness. There was the ephod with its breastplate, containing the Urim and Thummim, and so on. However, these things were not intrinsically sacred. Rather, they were sacred because they represented holy qualities—or the divinely heavenlike and spiritual qualities of the Lord's kingdom—and the Lord himself. Still less were they sacred because of the people among whom they existed. Those people were not touched at all by the inward aspects being represented, only by the outward objects, and to be moved only by outward objects is idolatrous. It is the same as worshiping wood and stone, and the gold and silver plating on them, from a delusion that these items are holy in themselves. That is what the Jewish nation was like then, and that is what it is like today.

[2] Still, a representation of a religion could exist among such people, because a representation does not look to personality, only to some spiritual quality; see §§665, 1097 at the end, 3670, 4208, 4281, 4288. Their worship consequently did not make them blissful and happy in the next life; it only caused them to prosper in the world, as long as they kept with their representative role. They had to avoid turning aside to the idols of other nations and becoming flagrant idolaters, because then the church could no longer be represented at all among that nation.

This, then, is the meaning of the idolatrous quality symbolized by Judah's third son by the Canaanite woman.

Such idolatry among the people of that nation traced its origin to their inward idolatry, because they were more deeply immersed in self-love and materialism than other nations (§§4459 at the end, 4750). People immersed in self-love and materialism engage in inward idolatry, because they worship themselves and the world. They take part in religious ceremonies to win adoration and wealth for themselves—in other words, for selfish goals, not for the sake of the church and the Lord's kingdom, and therefore not for the Lord.

4826   *And called his name Shelah* symbolizes its nature. This is established by the symbolism of *calling someone's name* as the quality (discussed above, where Judah's first two sons, Er and Onan, are dealt with, §§4822, 4824). The nature of the idolatrous quality is what *Shelah* symbolizes, seeing that there are many kinds of idolatry. There is a shallow form and a deep form, and each of the two in general is the worship of falsity and evil.

4827   *And he was in Chezib when she gave birth to him* symbolizes the state. This can be seen from the symbolism of *Chezib* as the state of the idolatry symbolized by Shelah—the idolatry the Jewish nation took up—and from the symbolism of *giving birth* as being united in action (§§3905, 3915, 3919). Since the union was to the evil involved in idolatry, the text says that *she* called his name Shelah (as is clear in the original language), because she, Shua's daughter, symbolizes an evil resulting from a false teaching with evil origins (§§4818, 4819).

4828   Genesis 38:6, 7, 8, 9, 10. *And Judah took a woman for Er, his firstborn, and her name was Tamar. And Er, Judah's firstborn, was evil in the eyes of Jehovah, and Jehovah put him to death. And Judah said to Onan, "Come to your brother's wife and perform the levirate for her and raise up seed for your brother." And Onan knew that the seed would not be his, and it happened when he came to his brother's wife that he wasted it on the earth so that he would not give seed to his brother. And what he did was evil in Jehovah's eyes, and [Jehovah] put him to death too.*

Judah took a woman symbolizes a religion for his descendants. *For Er, his firstborn,* symbolizes falsity in its faith. *And her name was Tamar* symbolizes the nature of the religion, as one representing spiritual and heavenly qualities. *And Er, Judah's firstborn, was evil in the eyes of Jehovah* means that they were caught up in falsity based on evil. *And Jehovah put him to death* means that there was no representation of a religion. *And Judah said to Onan* means in order to preserve the representation of a religion. *Come to your brother's wife and perform the levirate for her* means that this would keep it in existence. *And raise up seed for your brother* means to prevent the church from dying out. *And Onan knew that the seed would not be his* symbolizes loathing and hatred. *And it happened when he came to his brother's wife that he wasted it on the earth* symbolizes opposition to marriage love. *So that he would not give seed to his brother* means that its existence would consequently not be prolonged. *And it was evil in Jehovah's eyes* means that this went against divine order. *And [Jehovah] put him to death too* means that again there was no representation of a religion.

Judah took a woman symbolizes a religion for his descendants. This can be seen from the representation of Tamar, the *woman*, as a religion (discussed below [§4831]). The fact that Judah took her for Er his firstborn so as to acquire descendants means that the religion was for those descendants.

4829

For Er, his firstborn, symbolizes falsity in its faith. This is established by the representation of *Er* as falsity (discussed in §§4821, 4822) and by the symbolism of a *firstborn* as faith (discussed in §§352, 3325, 4821).

4830

And her name was Tamar symbolizes the nature of the religion, as one representing spiritual and heavenly qualities. This can be seen from the symbolism of a *name* as the quality (discussed in §§144, 145, 1754, 1896, 2009, 2724, 3006, 3421). Here, it is the nature of the religion, because in this chapter *Tamar* represents a religion—specifically, the religion representing spiritual and heavenly qualities that was to be established among Judah's descendants. What follows will show that Tamar represents that religion.

4831

The theme of the entire chapter in its inner meaning is the Jewish religion and the fact that it came to represent the spiritual and heavenly attributes of the Lord's kingdom. The ancient church had also filled this role, not only in its outward but also in its inward form, because a religion is a religion not on account of its superficialities (its rituals) but on account of its inner depths. These depths make up the essence. The superficialities merely make up the form. Jacob's descendants refused to accept anything internal, so there was no way to raise up the ancient church among them, only a representation of that church (§§4307, 4444, 4500). Here, the inner level of the church is Tamar; the outer level is Judah with his three sons by the Canaanite woman.

And Er, Judah's firstborn, was evil in the eyes of Jehovah means that they were caught up in falsity based on evil. This can be seen from the representation of *Er* and the symbolism of a *firstborn* as falsity in the faith (discussed just above at §4830). This falsity was the kind based on evil, as

4832

the remarks above at §4818 show. The falsity born of evil in this son was so bad, however, that not even the representation of a religion could be established among any posterity from Er's line. That is why the text says that he was evil in the eyes of Jehovah and that Jehovah put him to death.

Falsity from evil—that is, false doctrine growing out of a wicked life—was present throughout the whole nation right from the start, beginning especially with Judah, but it differed from one of his sons to the next. The purpose that this falsity could serve was foreseen, and in Er, the firstborn, and Onan, the second-born, it was going to be useless. Only the falsity in Shelah would serve. That is why the first two were blotted out and Shelah was saved.

The presence of falsity based on evil throughout the entire nation right from the start is depicted clearly in Moses, in these words:

He has *corrupted* [them] *for himself;* they are not his sons; *the blemish is theirs;* they are a *generation perverted* and *twisted.* When Jehovah saw, for outrage he spurned his sons and his daughters. And he said, "I will conceal my face from them; I will see what *their posterity* is, because *they are a generation of perversities*—offspring in whom there is no faithfulness. I will add evils onto them; my arrows I will use up in them. They will be drained from starvation and devoured with festering and with bitter destruction. It is a *nation that has lost all counsel,* and there is no understanding in them. From the *grapevine of Sodom comes their grapevine* and *from the plowed fields of Gomorrah. Their grapes are grapes of gall;* clusters of bitterness are theirs. The *poison of serpents is their wine,* and the *cruel gall of asps.* Is it not stored up with me, sealed up in my treasuries? Nearby is the day of their ruin, and what is to come hurries on them." (Deuteronomy 32:5, 19, 20, 23, 24, 28, 32, 33, 34, 35)

In an inner sense these words depict the falsity from evil to which that nation was devoted and which was rooted in them.

4833   *And Jehovah put him to death* means that there was no representation of a religion, as the following shows: *Dying* means something's ceasing to be what it was (as discussed at §494) and the end of a representation (§§3253, 3259, 3276). In this case, then, it means that there was no representation of a religion among any descendants from Er's line, in keeping with the remarks just above at §4832.

4834   *And Judah said to Onan* means in order to preserve the representation of a religion. This can be seen from the following clause, toward which this clause looks. After all, Judah told Onan to perform the levirate for his brother, which represented the preservation and prolonged existence of the religion, as the next section will discuss.

Come to your brother's wife and perform the levirate for her means that this would keep it (the representation of a religion) in existence. This can be seen from the symbolism of *coming to his brother's wife* (or going in to her) *and performing the levirate for her* as preserving what belongs to the church and keeping it in existence.

4835

Mosaic law required that if a man died without offspring, his brother would marry the man's widowed wife and raise seed up for his brother. The firstborn would be called by the name of the dead brother, but the rest of the children would be the living man's. This was called the levirate. Events here show that the statute was not something new with the Jewish religion but predated it. So did many other statutes commanded of the Israelites by Moses, such as those in Genesis 24:3, 4; 28:1, 2 forbidding men to take wives from the daughters of Canaanites and requiring them to marry within their clans. From this and much other evidence it is clear that there had been an earlier religion in which customs were started that were then proclaimed to the children of Jacob and enjoined on them. Genesis 8:20, 21 and 22:7, 13 make it clear that altars were used and sacrifices performed even in ancient times. Plainly, then, the Jewish religion was not some new religion but a revival of the ancient church that had died out.

[2] What the law of the levirate had been can be seen in Moses:

> If brothers live together, but one of them dies and has no child, the wife of the dead man shall not wed outside to a man who is a stranger; her brother-in-law shall go in to her and take her to himself as wife, and in this way he shall perform the levirate for her. Then it will happen that the firstborn whom she bears shall carry on the name of the [man's] dead brother, so that his name shall not be wiped out from Israel. But if the man does not want to take his sister-in-law in marriage, his sister-in-law shall come up to the gate to the elders and say, "My brother-in-law refuses to raise up a name for his brother in Israel; he does not want to perform the levirate for me." Then the elders of his city shall call him and speak to him, and if he stands and says, "I do not wish to take her in marriage," his sister-in-law shall come up to him in the eyes of the elders and draw his shoe off his foot and spit in his face. And she shall answer and say, "This is what shall be done to the man who does not build up the house of his brother." So his name in Israel will be called the house of one stripped of his shoe. (Deuteronomy 25:5–10)

[3] People who do not know what the levirate represents cannot help believing that it existed only for the sake of preserving a name and therefore an inheritance. The preservation of a name and inheritance, though, was not an important enough reason for a brother to marry his sister-in-law. No, the practice was commanded so that it could represent the preservation and prolonged existence of the church. Marriage represented the marriage of goodness and truth, which is the heavenly marriage. For this reason it also represented the church, because the marriage of goodness and truth causes the church to be a church. When the church takes part in this marriage, it is at one with heaven, which is the heavenly marriage itself. Because of this representation of marriage, sons and daughters represented and also symbolized truth and goodness. Being childless therefore symbolized being deprived of goodness and truth, so it symbolized that there was no longer any representation of a church in that household and consequently that the household was outside the congregation.

Besides, a brother represented a closely related kind of goodness that would unite with the truth represented by a widowed wife. Truth cannot unite with any other kind of goodness than its own closely related kind, if it is to have life and produce fruit and in the process keep what belongs to the church alive.

This is what heaven perceives the levirate to be.

[4] The fact that a man's sister-in-law was to draw his shoe off his foot and spit in his face if he was unwilling to perform the levirate symbolized his resemblance to a person devoid of goodness and truth, whether external or internal, who would destroy what belonged to religion. A shoe means something external (§1748), and a face means something internal (§§1999, 2434, 3527, 4066, 4796). From this it can be seen that the levirate represented the preservation and prolonged existence of the church.

However, when the Lord's Coming put an end to practices merely *representing* something deeper, this law was abolished. The situation resembles that of our soul or spirit and our body. Our soul or spirit is our inner part, and our body is our outer part. To put the same thing another way, our soul or spirit is our actual likeness; our body is an image representing it. When we rise again, we shed our representative image, or our outer part, which is our body, because we then inhabit our inner part, or our actual likeness.

The situation also resembles that of a person in the dark who views matters of enlightenment in that darkness. Or to say it another way, the situation resembles that of a person in worldly light who views matters of heavenly light in that worldly light. The light of the world is like darkness, compared to the light of heaven. In the dark, or in the world's light, matters of heavenly light are not seen for what they really are. Instead, they are seen in a kind of representative image, just as our mind is seen in our face. When heaven's light appears in its own clarity, therefore, the shadows, or representative images, are dispelled. This was accomplished by the Lord's Coming.

[5] *And raise up seed for your brother* means to prevent the church from dying out. This can be seen from the symbolism of *seed* as the truth that comes of goodness, or the faith that comes of charity (discussed in §§1025, 1447, 1610, 1940, 2848, 3310, 3373, 3671). The firstborn, who was to "carry on the name of" the dead brother, has the same symbolism (§§352, 367, 2435, 3325, 3494). *Raising up* this seed *for one's brother* means keeping what belongs to the church in existence, in accord with the remarks just above in §4834. So it means to prevent the church from dying.

And Onan knew that the seed would not be his symbolizes loathing and hatred. This can be seen from the representation of *Onan* as evil (discussed at §§4823, 4824). Not giving seed to one's brother or performing the levirate means not wanting the goodness and truth in the church to remain in existence (§4835). The clause here, then, symbolizes loathing and hatred. Evil is nothing but loathing and hatred for the goodness and truth in the church. **4836**

And it happened when he came to his brother's wife that he wasted it on the earth symbolizes opposition to marriage love. **4837**

Er, Judah's firstborn, depicts a falsity with evil origins, which the Jewish nation took to first. Onan, the second-born, depicts the evil that comes from that falsity with evil origins, which that nation turned to next. Shelah, the third son, depicts the resulting idolatry, in which that nation constantly engaged from then on (§4826).

Evil that comes from a falsity with evil origins is portrayed by Onan's behavior in not wanting to give seed to his brother and *wasting it on the earth.* This symbolizes opposition to marriage love because in its inner sense, anything relating to marriage means something relating to the church, the church being the marriage of what is good and true. This marriage is utterly opposed by the evil that comes from a falsity with evil origins—that is, by people devoted to such evil.

[2] The people of that nation did not have anything marriagelike about them, whether *marriage* is taken in its spiritual or its earthly sense, as is obvious from the permission the men had to marry more than one wife. This is never allowed where a marital relationship (taken in its spiritual sense) exists—in other words, where the goodness and truth belonging

to the church exist, and therefore where the church itself exists. The true bond of marriage is possible only in people who have the church, or the Lord's kingdom, inside them, and among them it is possible only between two individuals (§§1907, 2740, 3246). Marriage between two people who have genuine marriage love corresponds to the heavenly marriage, or to the union of what is good and true. A husband corresponds to goodness, and a wife to the truth that goes with that goodness. What is more, when they have genuine marriage love, they have that [heavenly] marriage in them. Where the church exists, then, no man is ever allowed to marry more than one wife. The church did not exist among Jacob's descendants, though. Only the representation of a church did, or the outer aspects of a religion without its inner core (§§4307, 4500), so marriage to more than one was tolerated among them.

In heaven, moreover, the marriage of one husband with many wives would present a mental image of one type of goodness united with many truths that are at odds with each other. Consequently it would present the idea that there was no goodness. Discordant truths cause goodness to disappear, because goodness takes its quality from truths and from the harmony among them.

[3] Marriage with many would also present an image not of one church but of many, all distinguished from one another by their religious truth, or doctrine. Yet the church is unified when goodness is the vital factor in it and when truth gives goodness its character and form, so to speak.

The church is an image of heaven, because it is the Lord's kingdom on earth. Heaven is divided into many overall communities and into smaller subgroups, but goodness still unifies them. Religious truth there accords with goodness, because it has goodness as its origin and its goal. If heaven were divided up along the lines of religious truth, not of goodness, it would cease to exist. There would be no unanimity, because the Lord could not give the inhabitants unity of life, or a unified soul. This is possible only where there is goodness, which is to say, where there is love for the Lord and love for one's neighbor. After all, love unites everyone, and when each individual loves what is good and true, it is common ground received from the Lord that unites them all. Therefore it is the Lord himself who does so. Love for goodness and truth is what is called love for one's neighbor, because one's neighbor is a person with goodness and therefore truth. In an abstract sense, one's neighbor is goodness itself and the truth that goes with it.

This discussion shows why marriage within the church has to be between one husband and one wife. It also shows the reason that the men among Jacob's descendants were allowed to marry more than one wife, which was that there was no religion there. As a result, a representation of a religion could not be established through marriage there, since they were opposed to marriage love.

So that he would not give seed to his brother means that its existence **4838** would consequently not be prolonged. This is indicated by the symbolism of *giving seed to one's brother,* or performing the levirate, as keeping what belongs to the church in existence (discussed above at §4835). *Not giving seed to his brother,* then, means that its existence would consequently not be prolonged.

And what he did was evil in Jehovah's eyes means that this went against **4839** divine order. This can be seen from the symbolism of something *evil in Jehovah's eyes,* or something evil against him, as something that goes against what he ordains. It can also be seen from what happened, and from the statute about the levirate. A sister-in-law was to remove the shoe from the foot of [a man who refused to perform the levirate] and spit in his face, and his name in Israel was to be called the house of one stripped of his shoe (Deuteronomy 25:8, 9, 10). The symbolism was that such a person was devoid of outer and inner goodness, and anyone who is without goodness and is set on evil is against divine order.

Every evil that wells up and flows out from evil within, or from an evil intention or aim, such as this evil of Onan's, violates divine order. Sometimes things look evil even when they do not well up and flow out from evil within, from an evil intention or aim, but they are not evil if the aim is not. The purpose gives every deed its character. Our life resides in our goals, since our goals consist in the things we love and therefore think about. That is exactly what the life of our soul is.

[2] Anyone can recognize that evil goes against divine order and goodness follows divine order. Divine order is the Lord himself in heaven. Divine goodness and truth from him go to make up order; in fact, they *are* order. Divine goodness is its essence, and divine truth is its form.

When divine order is presented in a form, it appears as a human being, because the Lord, from whom it comes, is the only human (§§49, 288, 477, 565, 1871, 1894, 3638, 3639). The more that angels, spirits, and people on earth receive from him—that is, the more they are governed by goodness and therefore by truth, and so the more they are in line with divine order—the more human they are. That is why the whole of heaven presents the image of one human, called the universal human, to which absolutely everything in a person corresponds, as demonstrated at the ends of the chapters. It is also why angels in heaven all appear in human form. Evil spirits in hell look like people to each other too, as a result of their delusions, but in heaven's light they look grotesque. How appalling or horrible their deformity is depends on the evil they adopt (§4533). They look like this because evil inherently goes against order, so it goes against the human form, because divine order appears as a human being when it is presented in a form, as noted.

4840   *And [Jehovah] put him to death too* means that again there was no representation of a religion. This can be seen from the explanation above at §4833, where similar words occur.

4841   Genesis 38:11. *And Judah said to Tamar, his daughter-in-law, "Stay a widow at your father's house till Shelah my son grows up"; for he said, "Or he too might die like his brothers." And Tamar went and stayed at her father's house.*

Judah said symbolizes Jacob's descendants in general and those from Judah's line in particular. *To Tamar, his daughter-in-law,* symbolizes a religion representing spiritual and heavenly qualities, which is called a *daughter-in-law* on account of the truth in it. *Stay a widow at your father's house* symbolizes estrangement. *Till Shelah my son grows up* means until the time should come. *For he said* symbolizes the thinking. *Or he too might die like his brothers* symbolizes fear that it would die out. *And she stayed at her father's house* symbolizes estrangement.

4842   *Judah said* symbolizes Jacob's descendants in general and those from Judah's line in particular. This can be seen from the symbolism of *Judah* in the first layer of meaning as the nation that came from Jacob and particularly the part that came through Judah, as also above in §4815.

The Word distinguishes between Judah and Israel, and on the narrative level, Judah means the tribe of Judah, while Israel means the ten tribes that split off from it. In a deeper, spiritual sense, though, Judah represents what is heavenly in the church, or goodness, and Israel represents what is spiritual in the church, or truth. In a negative sense, Judah represents evil in the church, and Israel represents falsity in the church. And they represent goodness, truth, evil, and falsity wherever these qualities existed, whether with the Judeans or the Israelites. The Word's inner, spiritual meaning is universal and does not make distinctions among tribes, as the outer, narrative meaning does. That is why Judah in the first layer of meaning symbolizes the entire nation from Jacob but the part that came through Judah in particular.

4843   *To Tamar, his daughter-in-law,* symbolizes a religion representing spiritual and heavenly qualities, which is called a *daughter-in-law* on account of the truth in it. This can be seen from the representation of *Tamar* as a religion representing spiritual and heavenly qualities (dealt with above at §4831) and from the symbolism of a *daughter-in-law* as the spiritual component of a religion, or truth. The reason a daughter-in-law has this meaning on an inner plane is that everyone and everything that had to do with marriage represented the kinds of things that are involved in the heavenly marriage; see above at §4837. Accordingly, it represented everything good and true, since goodness and truth are the partners in the heavenly marriage. That is why a husband in the Word symbolizes goodness, and a wife truth, and why sons and daughters symbolize the truth and goodness stemming from them. A daughter-in-law, because she is the wife of a son who is now a husband himself, symbolizes the truth known to a religion, united to goodness; and so on. The symbolism is not the same for people in a spiritual religion as it is for those in a heavenly religion, though. In a spiritual religion the husband is called a man and symbolizes truth, while the wife is called his woman and symbolizes goodness; see above at §4823.

[2] Passages in the Word that mention a daughter-in-law can show that in Scripture's inner meaning she symbolizes the truth in a religion, connected to its goodness, and therefore in a negative sense, the falsity in a religion, connected to its evil. In Hosea, for instance:

> On the mountain heads they sacrifice, and on the hills they burn incense, under oak and poplar and terebinth, because its shade is good. Therefore your daughters are whoring, and *your daughters-in-law* are committing adultery. Will I not bring punishment on your daughters for their whoring, and *on your daughters-in-law* for their adultery? (Hosea 4:13, 14)

This is talking about the worship of what is evil and false. Sacrificing on mountain heads symbolizes worship of evil, and burning incense on hills symbolizes worship of falsity. The whoring of the daughters symbolizes a life of evil, and the adultery of the daughters-in-law symbolizes false doctrine that leads to a life of evil. In the Word, adultery and whoredom symbolize the adulteration of goodness and the falsification of truth; see §§2466, 2729, 3399. The daughters-in-law in this passage, then, stand for a desire for falsity. [3] In Micah:

> The great are uttering the perversity of their soul, and they twist it. The good among them are like a thorn; the upright, like a pricker bush. *Son despises father; a daughter is rising up against her mother, daughter-in-law against her mother-in-law. A man's foes are those of his own household.* (Micah 7:3, 4, 6)

This is about the falsity growing out of evil that plagues a religion in its final days, when it is being devastated. In the first layer of meaning, it is about the falsity growing out of evil that plagued the Jewish religion. A daughter rising up against her mother symbolizes a desire for evil rising against truth. A daughter-in-law rising up against her mother-in-law symbolizes a desire for falsity rising against goodness.

[4] The situation is similar with us when we are undergoing times of trial, because at those times, evil battles against truth in us, and falsity battles against goodness. Spiritual trials are nothing but the stripping away of falsity and evil in us. The Lord therefore describes trials or spiritual battles in almost the same words in Matthew:

> Jesus said, "Do not suppose that I came to send peace onto the earth; I came not to send peace but a sword. For I came to pit *a person against that person's father*, and *a daughter against her mother*, and *a daughter-in-law against her mother-in-law*, and *people's foes will be those of their own household.*" (Matthew 10:34, 35, 36, 38)

In the prophet quoted just above, the equivalent words symbolized the devastation of the church, but here they symbolize the trials of people in the church, because trials are actually the devastation or stripping away of falsity and evil, as mentioned. As a result, both trials and devastation are symbolized and depicted by floods and deluges of water (§§705, 739, 756, 790). Here too, then, a daughter against her mother means a desire for evil opposed to truth, and a daughter-in-law against her mother-in-law means a desire for falsity opposed to goodness. Because the evil and falsity present with those of us who are being tested are inside us, or belong to us, they are called those of our own household, where the text says, "People's foes will be those of their own household."

It says the Lord came not to send peace onto the earth but a sword, when he really did come to give peace (John 14:27; 16:33), which shows that the passage is describing times of trial. A sword symbolizes truth engaged in battle, and in a negative sense, falsity engaged in battle (§§2799, 4499). A subsequent verse there reveals that trials are what are being described: "Whoever does not take up my cross and follow me is unworthy of me."

[5] Likewise in Luke:

> Do you think that I came to give peace on earth? No, I say to you, but division. For from now on there will be five in one house, divided three against two, and two against three. Father will be divided against son,

and son against father, mother against daughter, and daughter against mother, a *mother-in-law against her daughter-in-law,* and a *daughter-in-law against her mother-in-law.* (Luke 12:51, 52, 53)

This passage also bears out the idea that father, mother, son, daughter, daughter-in-law, and mother-in-law symbolize the kinds of things involved in the heavenly marriage—goodness and truth in their proper arrangement, and their opposites, too. The same holds true in Mark:

> Jesus said, "There are none who leave behind house or brothers or sisters or father or mother or wife or children or fields, for me and the gospel, without receiving hundreds of times as much—houses and brothers and sisters and mothers and children and fields at this time, with persecutions, and in the coming age eternal life." (Mark 10:29, 30)

Anyone who does not know the Word's inner meaning must believe that the house, brothers, sisters, father, mother, wife, children, and fields mean house, brothers, sisters, father, mother, wife, children, and fields. Instead, they are the kinds of things we have in us that are our own and that we have to leave behind. Spiritual and heavenly possessions of the Lord's are what we have to receive in their place, and we can receive them only through trials, which are meant by the persecutions. Anyone can see that we will not gain mothers by leaving our mother behind, nor will we gain brothers or sisters that way.

Stay a widow at your father's house symbolizes estrangement. This can be seen from Judah's intent in saying this, which was that she should go away and never come back. He did say she should stay there till Shelah his son grew up, but in actuality he was expecting not to give her to Shelah his son, because he said to himself, "Or he too might die like his brothers." The outcome also proves it, as verse 14 shows: "Tamar saw that Shelah had grown up and she had not been given to him as his woman." It follows, then, that these words mean that Judah was pushing her away. In an inner sense it means that the Jewish religion, represented by Judah, was estranging the religion represented by Tamar—a religion representative of spiritual and heavenly qualities (§§4811, 4831). They could not get along together, because Judaism was only a representation of a religion, not a representative religion (§§4307, 4500), since it acknowledged only what lay on the surface, not what lay inside.

[2] Furthermore, a *widow* symbolizes the truth a church knows without the goodness it possesses, because in a representative sense a wife symbolizes

4844

truth and a husband goodness (§§4823, 4843). A wife without a husband, then, is truth in the church without the goodness there. When such a woman is said to have stayed in her father's house, it means that the church's truth was pushed away and that it was not accepted in its own house. The Jewish nation could not accept the truth, because it was ruled not by goodness but by evil.

[3] Widows are mentioned many times in the Word, and readers who do not know the inner meaning cannot help thinking that a widow means a widow. In Scripture's inner meaning, though, a widow symbolizes religious truth without goodness. In other words, it symbolizes people who know truth and lack goodness but long to devote themselves to goodness and who consequently love being led by goodness—a husband being the goodness that would serve as a guide. Whether female or male, these are the ones who were meant in a positive sense by widows in the ancient church.

The people of the ancient church, you see, created many different categories for the neighbor toward whom they were to exercise charity. Some neighbors they called the poor; some the wretched and afflicted; some the jailed and imprisoned; some the blind and lame; some they called immigrants, orphans, and widows; and the characteristics of each group determined how they carried out their charitable deeds. Their doctrines taught them all this. The ancient church did not know any other doctrine.

Both the teaching and the writing of the people who lived in those times followed their doctrines, so when they mentioned widows, they actually meant people with truth but without goodness who nonetheless longed to be led by goodness.

[4] From this it is also evident that the teachings of the ancient church dealt with charity and one's neighbor. Their religious knowledge and scholarly knowledge consisted in knowing the symbolic meaning of outward acts and objects. It was a church representing the spiritual and heavenly realms, so the spiritual and heavenly qualities that were represented and symbolized were what they learned about through their doctrines and secular studies. By now, however, these doctrines and these secular facts have been obliterated so completely that no one knows they existed, and they have been replaced with teachings about faith. If these teachings are widowed and divorced from teachings about charity, they teach almost nothing. Doctrines about charity teach what goodness is, but doctrines about faith teach what truth is, and to teach truth without goodness is to walk blind. Goodness is what teaches and leads; truth is what is taught and

led. The difference between these two doctrines is as big as the difference between light and dark. If the dark is not relieved by light—if truth is not lit by goodness, or faith by love for one's neighbor—it is pure darkness.

This is why no one recognizes truth from insight or therefore from perception, only from teachings learned in youth and confirmed in adulthood. It is also why religions disagree so much, one saying that a thing is true, and another that it is false, and why they never come together.

[5] Places in the Word where widows are mentioned can show that in a positive sense they symbolize people with truth but without goodness who still long to be led by goodness. In David, for instance:

> . . . Jehovah who passes judgment for the *oppressed,* who gives bread to the *starving,* Jehovah who releases the *imprisoned,* Jehovah who opens [the eyes of] the *blind,* Jehovah who straightens up the *bowed,* Jehovah who loves the *fair-minded,* Jehovah who guards *immigrants;* the *orphan* and *widow* he sustains. (Psalms 146:7, 8, 9)

In an inner sense this passage deals with people who are being taught truth and led to goodness by the Lord, but some of them are called the oppressed, some the starving, some the imprisoned, the blind, the bowed, the immigrants, orphans, and widows, depending on their nature. No one can know what that nature is without the inner meaning. The doctrines of the ancient church taught what it was.

This passage like many others mentions the immigrant, orphan, and widow in the same breath. This is because an immigrant symbolizes people who want to learn religious truth (§§1463, 4444), an orphan symbolizes people with goodness and not truth who long to be led by truth to goodness, and a widow symbolizes people with truth and not goodness who long to be led by goodness to truth. These three are linked here and elsewhere in the Word because in an inner sense they constitute a single category. Taken together, they symbolize people who want to learn about and be led to goodness and truth. [6] In the same author:

> A father of *orphans* and judge of *widows* is God in his holy dwelling place. (Psalms 68:5)

Orphans stand for people who, like children, have an innocent goodness but not yet truth. The Lord is called their father because he leads them like a father, and he leads them by truth to goodness—specifically, to goodness in their lives, or a wise goodness. Widows stand for people who, like some adults, have truth but not yet goodness. The Lord is called their judge because he leads them, and he leads them by goodness to truth—specifically, to the truth that brings understanding. A judge means a leader.

Goodness without truth—an orphan—becomes a wise goodness through the learning of truth. Truth without goodness—a widow—becomes an understanding kind of truth through the living of a good life. [7] In Isaiah:

> Doom to those decreeing wicked decrees to turn the *poor* aside from judgment and to seize in judgment the *wretched* of my people, so that *widows* can be their spoil, and *orphans* they can plunder. (Isaiah 10:1, 2)

The poor, wretched, widows, and orphans do not mean those people but ones who are spiritually such. In the Jewish religion, as in the ancient church, everything represented something, so kindness to orphans and widows did too. When such kindness was being done, charity toward spiritual orphans and widows was represented in heaven. [8] In Jeremiah:

> Perform judgment and justice, and snatch *spoil* from the hand of the oppressor, and do not cheat *immigrant, orphan, and widow,* nor bully anyone, nor shed innocent blood in this place. (Jeremiah 22:3)

Again, the immigrant, orphan, and widow symbolize people in this condition spiritually. In the spiritual world, or heaven, no one knows what an immigrant, orphan, or widow is, because people who were so in the world are not so there. When we on earth read these words, then, angels perceive them according to their spiritual, inner meaning. [9] Likewise in Ezekiel:

> Here, now, the chieftains of Israel, each according to [the strength of] his arm, have been in you to shed blood; father and mother they have dishonored in you. With the *immigrant* they have acted oppressively in you; *orphan* and *widow* they have cheated in you. (Ezekiel 22:6, 7)

And in Malachi:

> I will come close to you for judgment and will be a speedy witness against sorcerers and against those swearing falsely and against those who oppress the *wage earner's* wage, the *widow,* and the *orphan,* and those turning the *immigrant* aside. Nor do they fear me. (Malachi 3:5)

Likewise in Moses:

> *Immigrants* you shall not bear down on, nor shall you oppress them; no *widow* or *orphan* shall you afflict. If you actually afflict them, and if they cry out at all to me, I will certainly hear their cry, and my anger

will blaze, and I will kill you with the sword, so that *your wives become widows,* and *your children orphans.* (Exodus 22:21, 22, 23, 24)

[10] Like all the other commandments, judgments, and statutes in the Jewish religion, this one was representative. It required people to act this way on the outside and in the process to represent a deeper kind of neighborly love, even though they had no such love—in other words, were not motivated by an inner desire. An inner approach would have been to teach truth willingly to the ignorant and lead them to goodness through truth, and to lead the knowledgeable to truth through goodness. In this way they would have done good to immigrant, orphan, and widow in a spiritual sense.

Still, to keep up the outward appearance for the sake of its representation, one of the curses delivered on Mount Ebal was a curse on turning aside rightful judgment on *immigrant, orphan,* and *widow* (Deuteronomy 27:19). Turning aside judgment on them means doing just the opposite—leading them to falsity and evil through education and life.

Depriving others of goodness and truth, and usurping it for oneself in order to obtain rank and wealth, was also among cursed behaviors, which is why the Lord said:

> Doom to you, scribes and Pharisees! Because *you consume widows' houses,* and do so with the excuse that you are praying copiously. Because of this, you will receive fuller judgment. (Matthew 23:14; Luke 20:47)

Consuming widows' houses stands for depriving people of the truth they long for and teaching them falsity.

[11] It was equally representative to assign what was left in fields, olive groves, and vineyards to the *immigrant, orphan,* and *widow* (Deuteronomy 24:19, 20, 21, 22). Likewise that when they finished tithing the tithes of their produce in the third year, they would give to *immigrant, orphan,* and *widow* so that these could eat in their gates and receive their fill (Deuteronomy 26:12, 13).

Since the Lord alone teaches us and leads us to goodness and truth, it says in Jeremiah:

> Leave your *orphans;* I myself will keep them alive, and *widows* will trust in me. (Jeremiah 49:10, 11)

And in Moses:

> Jehovah passes judgment for *orphan* and *widow* and loves *immigrants,* to give them bread and clothing. (Deuteronomy 10:18)

The bread stands for goodness that comes of love (§§2165, 2177, 3478, 3735, 3813, 4211, 4217, 4735). The clothing stands for truth that leads to faith (§§4545, 4763).

[12] When there was drought and famine in the land, Elijah was sent to Zarephath, to a *widow,* and begged her for a small cake. She was to first make one and give it to him and afterward make one for herself and her son, and then the jar of meal she had would not be used up and the flask of oil would not fail (1 Kings 17:1–15). This was representative, as was everything else said about Elijah and everything in the Word in general. Famine in the land caused by drought represented the devastation of truth in the church (§§1460, 3364). The widow of Zarephath represented people outside the church who long for truth. The cake she was to make first for Elijah represented the goodness belonging to love for the Lord (2177), whom from her tiny supply she was to love more than herself and her son. The jar of meal symbolizes truth developing out of goodness (2177), and the flask of oil symbolizes charity and love (886, 3728, 4582). Elijah represents the Word, which brings us these blessings (2762). [13] The same thing is also meant in an inner sense by the Lord's words in Luke:

> No prophets are accepted in their native land. In truth I say to you, there were *many widows* in Elijah's days in Israel, when the sky was closed for three years and six months, while there was great famine over the whole land, but to none of them was Elijah sent except to Zarephath of Sidon, to a *widow woman* (Luke 4:24, 25, 26),

that is, to people outside the church who long for truth. The widows within the devastated church to whom Elijah was not sent mean people lacking truth because they lack goodness. Where there is no goodness, there is no truth either, no matter how true the truth these people have appears on the surface. It is like a shell with no kernel. People with this kind of truth and people with falsity are symbolized by widows in a negative sense. [14] In Isaiah, for instance:

> Jehovah will cut head and tail, branch and reed off from Israel in a single day. Elders and those whose faces are honored are the head; and prophets—the teachers of a lie—are the tail. Therefore over [Israel's] youths the Lord will not rejoice, and on *its orphans* and *its widows* he will not have mercy. (Isaiah 9:14, 15, 17)

In Jeremiah:

> I will winnow them with a winnowing fan in the gates of the land; I will bereave them; I will destroy my people. They have not turned from

their ways. *Their widows have increased on me* more than the sand of the seas. As regards them, I will bring a young destroyer against a mother at noon. One who had given birth to seven will leave; she has breathed out her soul. Her sun set while it was still day. (Jeremiah 15:7, 8, 9)

In the same author:

Our inheritance has been turned over to strangers, our houses to foreigners. *Orphans* we have become—no father; our mothers are like *widows*. (Lamentations 5:2, 3)

[15] Since widows symbolized people lacking truth because they lack goodness, it was shameful to be called a widow, even in churches subscribing to falsity as a result of evil. In John, for example:

In her heart she said, "I am sitting as a queen and *am not a widow*, and I will not see mourning." Because of this, on a single day her plagues will come—death and mourning and famine—and she will be burned with fire. (Revelation 18:7, 8)

This is about Babylon. Likewise concerning Babylon in Isaiah:

Listen to this, pampered one—sitting securely, saying in her heart, "I am, and there is no other like me; *I will not sit as a widow*, nor will I know *bereavement*." But these two evils will come to you in an instant, on a single day: *bereavement* and *widowhood*. (Isaiah 47:8, 9)

[16] These passages now show what a widow means in the Word's inner sense. Since a widow represented and therefore symbolized the church's truth without its accompanying goodness (a wife symbolizing truth and a husband goodness), and since everything in the ancient churches represented something, a priest in those churches was forbidden to take a widow as his wife unless she was a priest's widow. Here is how Moses speaks of it:

The high priest shall take a wife in her virginity. A *widow* or divorced woman or fallen woman or prostitute—these he shall not take, but a virgin from among his peoples he shall take as a wife. (Leviticus 21:13, 14, 15)

And where Ezekiel talks about the new temple and new priesthood:

The priest Levites shall not take themselves a *widow* or a divorced woman as wives, but virgins from the seed of Israel's house. But the *widow* who was a *widow of a priest* they shall take. (Ezekiel 44:22)

The virgins whom they were to take as wives represented and therefore symbolized a desire for truth. A priest's widow represented and symbolized a desire for truth inspired by goodness, since a priest in a representative sense means the goodness belonging to the church. That is also why the *widows of a priest* who had no offspring were allowed to eat some of the offerings, or sacred items (Leviticus 22:12, 13).

[17] The people of the ancient church knew from their doctrines that this was the symbolism of a widow, because their doctrines taught about love and charity and contained an immense amount of knowledge that has now been entirely wiped out. From the doctrines they knew what kind of charity to perform—in other words, what they owed their neighbor—and they knew which ones were called widows, orphans, immigrants, and so on. Their religious knowledge and scholarly knowledge consisted in recognizing and learning what the rituals of their religion represented and symbolized. The better-educated among them knew what was represented by the features of the earth and the world, because they realized that the whole material world was a theater representing the heavenly kingdom (§§2758, 2989, 2999, 3483). Such knowledge lifted their minds to the heavenly realm, and their doctrines taught them how to live.

Eventually, though, the church turned aside from charity to faith and even isolated faith from charity, assigning faith the power to save without charity or charitable deeds. After that, sacred knowledge could no longer lift people's minds to the heavenly realm, nor could doctrine teach people how to live. In fact, by now hardly anyone believes in any life after death and hardly anyone knows what a heavenly quality is. People cannot even believe the Word has a spiritual meaning that is not visible in the literal text. Their minds are therefore closed.

4845   *Till Shelah my son grows up* means until the time should come. This can be seen from the meaning of *growing up* as reaching adulthood, and therefore until the time should come, and from the representation of *Shelah his son* as something idolatrous (discussed above in §§4825, 4826) and therefore as the Jewish religion, which was relatively idolatrous (§4825). The clause *till Shelah my son grows up,* then, means until the time when the Jewish religion would be able to welcome the inner dimension, or the spiritual and heavenly dimensions of the representative religion that Tamar stands for (§§4829, 4831, 4843).

4846   *For he said* symbolizes the thinking. This can be seen from the symbolism of *saying* in scriptural narratives as perceiving and also thinking (discussed at §§1791, 1815, 1819, 1822, 1898, 1919, 2080, 3395). In this case, then, *he said* means that Judah said or thought to himself that Tamar would not be given to Shelah his son as his woman. In an inner sense it means that the inner dimension of the representative religion would be kept at arm's length (§4844).

Or he too might die like his brothers symbolizes fear that it would die
out—that is, that the representation of a religion existing among Jacob's
descendants, and among those from Judah's line in particular, would die
out. This can be seen from the symbolism of *or else he might die* as fear
that it would die out.

A word about this idea, that the representation of a religion among Jacob's descendants would die out if the inner depths of a truly representative religion were connected with it: A representative religion like the one the ancients had should have been established among Jacob's posterity, but the people of that nation by nature wanted to worship and revere only superficialities. They had not the least interest in knowing about anything deeper, because they were immersed in the cravings of self-love and materialism and in resulting falsities. They had a stronger belief than the nations around them in a multitude of gods, but they considered Jehovah greater than the others because he could do greater miracles. So as soon as the miracles stopped, and even when they became frequent and familiar enough to lose all value, the people immediately turned to other gods, as the narrative and prophetic parts of the Word make quite plain. [2] Because that nation was like this, a representative religion like that of the ancients could not be established in it. Only a representation of a religion could be set up there, and the Lord provided for some level of communication with heaven through it. The evil can fill a representative role, because representation has to do with the quality represented, not the person representing it.

For the people of that nation, then, its worship was purely idolatrous (§4825), even though its representative objects and practices contained what was holy and divine. Nothing deep could be united with this idolatrous worship. If it had been—that is, if the people had acknowledged deeper things—they would have profaned what was holy. If a holy interior is combined with an idolatrous exterior, it becomes profane. That is why the deeper aspects were not revealed to that nation, which would have met its end if the deeper aspects *had* been revealed.

[3] The inability of that nation to accept and acknowledge deeper things, however openly such things might have been revealed to it, is plain to see from the same people today. These days they have heard of

4847

inner levels, because they live among Christians, but they still reject and even mock them. Even the ones who have been converted usually do just that in their hearts. These considerations show that a religion representing spiritual and heavenly qualities did not exist in that nation, only a representation of a religion, or the outer surface without the inner content, which is inherently idolatrous.

The same evidence also shows how mistaken those Christians are who believe that the Jewish nation will be converted in the church's final days and will then be more the chosen than Christians are. Even more mistaken are those who believe the Messiah, or the Lord, will then appear to Jews and lead them back to the land of Canaan by a great prophet, with great miracles. The people who fall into these errors are the ones who read scriptural prophecy and take Judah, Israel, and the land of Canaan to mean Judah, Israel, and the land of Canaan. They believe only the literal meaning of the Word and have no interest in any inner meaning.

4848   *And she stayed in her father's house* symbolizes estrangement. This can be seen from the discussion above at §4844 of the symbolism of *staying* a widow *in her father's house* as estrangement.

4849   Genesis 38:12, 13, 14. *And the days multiplied, and Shua's daughter, Judah's wife, died, and Judah was comforted; and he went up to the shearers of his flock, he and Hirah, his companion, the Adullamite, to Timnah. And it was told to Tamar, saying, "Look—your father-in-law is going up to Timnah to shear his flock." And she took the clothes of her widowhood off her and covered up in a veil and cloaked herself and sat in the gateway of the springs that are on the way to Timnah, because she saw that Shelah had grown up and she had not been given to him as his woman.*

The days multiplied symbolizes a change in state. *And Shua's daughter died* means in regard to the evil that rises out of falsity. *Judah's wife* symbolizes religiosity in the nation descended from Jacob, particularly through Judah. *And Judah was comforted* symbolizes rest. *And he went up to the shearers of his flock* symbolizes enough elevation to seek the church's best welfare. *He and Hirah, his companion, the Adullamite* means that [that nation] was still ruled by falsity. *To Timnah* symbolizes the state. *And it was told to Tamar, saying,* symbolizes some communication with a religion representing spiritual and heavenly qualities. *Look—your father-in-law is going up to Timnah to shear his flock* means that the Jewish religion wanted to seek its own welfare. *And she took the clothes of her widowhood off her* means pretending to have the truth that comes from goodness. *And covered up in a veil* symbolizes truth that was obscured. *And cloaked herself* means it was therefore unacknowledged. *And sat in the gateway of the springs that are on the way to Timnah* symbolizes something halfway between the church's truth and falsity. *Because she saw that Shelah had grown up and she had not been given to him as his woman* means seeing clearly that there was no other way to unite with the religiosity of Jacob's descendants, particularly those from Judah's line.

The days multiplied symbolizes a change in state. This can be seen from the symbolism of *days multiplying* as states changing. In an inner sense, a day or period of time means a state (§§23, 487, 488, 893, 2788, 3462, 3785), and multiplying means changing, when it is applied to days or time periods. What follows also makes it clear that a change of state is being symbolized. The word *multiply* is used because a change of state in regard to truth is involved, "multiply" being a word used for truth (§§43, 55, 913, 983, 2846, 2847).

4850

I keep mentioning states and changes in state, but few know what either is, so I need to define them. Neither time and the passage of time nor space and extension in space can be used to describe our inner depths, or our feelings and the thoughts they produce. They do not exist in time or in a place, even though they seem to do so, as far as our worldly senses can tell. Rather they exist in inner dimensions corresponding to time and place. These corresponding dimensions can only be called states; there is no other word for them.

It is called a change of state in our inner depths when we have a change of mind or heart, or a change in our feelings and the thoughts they produce, from sad to happy, from happy back to sad, from godless to godly or devout, and so on. These changes are called changes in state. They have to do with our feelings, and to the extent that our feelings control our thoughts, with our thoughts as well. Changes in the state of our thoughts lie within our feelings, as specific parts lie within a general whole, and are variations on our feelings, more or less.

And Shua's daughter died means in regard to the evil that rises out of falsity. This is established by the symbolism of *dying* as something's ceasing to be what it was (discussed in §494) and from that of *Shua's daughter* as evil rising out of falsity (discussed above in §§4818, 4819). The death of Shua's daughter after the days had multiplied, then, or after many days, symbolizes a change in state in regard to the evil that rises out of falsity, so that it was not the same as it had been before.

4851

Judah's wife symbolizes religiosity in the nation descended from Jacob, particularly through Judah, as the following shows: A *wife* symbolizes a

4852

religion, as discussed in §§252, 253, 409, 749, 770. Here it symbolizes a religiosity, though, because the topic is the Jewish nation, in which there was no religion, only the outer shell of a religion separated from its inner core (§§4281, 4288, 4289, 4307, 4433, 4500, 4680, 4825, 4844, 4847). Such a shell can only be called a religiosity. After all, the people of that nation could preserve a reverent veneer devoid of any inner reverence whatever (§4293). And *Judah* represents the nation descended from Jacob, particularly through Judah, as discussed above in §§4815, 4842.

4853   *And he went up to the shearers of his flock* symbolizes enough elevation to seek the church's best welfare, as the following shows: *Going up* symbolizes elevation from an outer to an inner level, as described in §§3084, 4539. A *shearer* symbolizes usefulness, as discussed in §4110, so it symbolizes wanting to help, or seeking what is useful. And a *flock* symbolizes the church, as discussed in §§343, 3767, 3768, 3772.

4854   *He and Hirah, his companion, the Adullamite* means that [that nation] was still ruled by falsity. This is established by the representation of *Hirah the Adullamite* as falsity (discussed above at §§4816, 4817). When it says Hirah was *his companion,* it therefore means that falsity was attached to [that nation]—in other words, that it was still ruled by falsity.

4855   *To Timnah* symbolizes the state—a state in which [that nation] was intent on the church's best welfare. This symbolism of *Timnah* is also evident from the part of Judges that says Samson went down to Timnah, where he took himself a woman from the daughters of the Philistines (Judges 14:1, 2, 3, 4, 7). There too Timnah symbolizes a state in which [that nation] looked out for the church's welfare. In a representative sense, the woman Samson took from among the daughters of the Philistines means truth from a source that was not good and therefore truth that was obscured, which Tamar represents in the current chapter. Philistines mean people who possess the doctrines of the faith but do not live according to them (§§1197, 1198, 3412, 3413). In addition, Timnah is one of the places named as an inheritance for the tribe of Dan (Joshua 19:43).

All names of places in the Word symbolize attributes and states; see §§1224, 1264, 1888, 3422, 4298, 4442.

4856   *And it was told to Tamar, saying,* symbolizes some communication with a religion representing spiritual and heavenly qualities, as the following shows: *Being told* symbolizes perception, as discussed in §3608, so it symbolizes communication, and in this case, *some* communication. And *Tamar* represents a religion that is representative of spiritual and heavenly qualities, as discussed in §§4829, 4831. [That nation] is said to have communicated with this religion when its state had changed, at which point it would be elevated enough to seek the church's best welfare, as discussed in §§4850, 4853.

Look—your father-in-law is going up to Timnah to shear his flock means **4857** that the Jewish religion wanted to seek its own welfare, as the following shows: Judah represents the church as it existed in the nation descended from Jacob, particularly in [the tribe of] Judah, as discussed at §§4815, 4842, 4852. Judah is being referred to as a *father-in-law* because the Jewish religion now had some communication with a religion representing the spiritual and heavenly planes, meant here by the daughter-in-law. *Going up* symbolizes a certain amount of elevation, as noted just above in §4853. *Shearing the flock* means seeking the church's welfare, as noted above at §4853. *Timnah* is the state in which this happens (§4855).

[2] One cannot possibly see from the literal meaning that this inner meaning is contained in the clause. The mind of a person reading it thinks about Judah, Timnah, and the shearing of the flock, not about spiritual concepts, which detach themselves from people, places, and the ways of the world. Angels, though, being surrounded by what is spiritual, perceive the words to have exactly the meaning given. When the literal sense passes over into the spiritual sense, anything having to do with people, places, and the world disappears and is replaced by what relates to the church, its state, and its ways.

[3] This claim seems unbelievable, but only because as long as we are living in the world, we think in terms of the physical and worldly phenomena there, not in terms of spiritual and heavenly phenomena. In addition, people who are immersed in bodily and earthly concerns do not even realize that anything spiritual or heavenly exists, let alone that it is distinct from worldly and physical entities. Yet it is as distinct as our spirit is from our body. A spiritual meaning is alive within the literal meaning as our spirit is alive within our body, and the spiritual meaning likewise survives when the literal meaning passes away. As a result, the inner meaning can be called the soul of the Word.

And she took the clothes of her widowhood off her means pretending to **4858** have the truth that comes from goodness. This can be seen from the symbolism of a *widow* as people who know truth and lack goodness but long to be led by goodness, as discussed at §4844. The *clothes* a widow wore represented this kind of truth, because clothes symbolize truth (§§2576, 4545, 4763). *Taking off* those clothes means shedding the representation of a widow—ceasing to represent truth devoid of goodness. Since Tamar covered herself with a veil, it also means pretending to have the truth that comes from goodness.

4859   *And covered up in a veil* symbolizes truth that was obscured, as can be seen from the symbolism of *covering* oneself or one's face with a *veil.* Doing so means hiding and therefore obscuring the truth that pretends to rise out of goodness (as just above in §4858) in order to unite with Judah.

A bride used to veil herself on first approaching her groom, as we read concerning Rebekah when she came to Isaac (Genesis 24:65). This symbolized apparent, seeming truth (see §3207), because a wife symbolized truth, and a husband symbolized goodness. Truth does not appear as it really is until it unites with its own proper goodness, so to represent this fact, a bride veiled herself as soon as she saw her husband. Tamar does so here because she considered Judah's son Shelah her husband, and seeing that she was not given to him, she viewed his father as taking Shelah's place in the performance of the levirate. That is why she veiled herself as a bride. She did not veil herself as a harlot—although Judah believed so, since prostitutes at the time were also in the habit of veiling their faces (as verse 15 shows). Judah viewed her as a harlot because the Jewish nation, which Judah is symbolizing, viewed the inner truth of a representative religion as nothing but a whore. For the same reason, Judah united with Tamar as a whore, though Tamar did not unite with *him* this way.

Because inner truth could not appear to that nation in any other form, Tamar's covering herself with a veil symbolizes truth that was obscured. Religious truth has been obscured from [the people of that nation], and this is represented by the fact that they still cover themselves with veils in their synagogues today.

[2] The same thing was also represented by Moses when the skin of his face glowed as he came down from Mount Sinai, in that he veiled himself whenever he spoke with the people (Exodus 34:28–end). Moses represented the part of the Word called the Law (see the preface to Genesis 18). As a consequence, the phrase the *Law and the Prophets* comes up several times (such as in Matthew 5:[17,] 18; 11:13; 22:36, 40), as does the phrase *Moses and the Prophets* (such as in Luke 16:29, 31; 24:27, 44). The glowing skin of his face represented the Word's inner plane—a face meaning what lies inside (§§358, 1999, 2434, 3527, 4066, 4796, 4797). The inner plane is spiritual, so heaven's light shines on it. Moses' veiling his face whenever he spoke with the people represented the way inner truth was screened off from them and obscured so that they would not be exposed to any light from it.

And cloaked herself means it was therefore unacknowledged. This can be seen from the meaning of *cloaking* something as hiding it and therefore as its not being acknowledged. See the discussion just above at §4859. **4860**

And sat in the gateway of the springs that are on the way to Timnah symbolizes something halfway between the church's truth and falsity. This can be seen from the symbolism of *springs* as truth that the church acquires from the Word. In a universal sense, a spring means the Word, as discussed in §§2702, 3096, 3424. *In the gateway* of them means in the entrance to them, and since the outer truth of the Word's literal meaning provides entrance, such truth is the gateway. Unless this truth is lit by inner truth, or by the contents of the inner meaning, it presents false ideas to people engrossed in evil. The gateway of the springs, then, symbolizes something halfway between the church's truth and falsity. *On the way to Timnah* means on the way to being useful to the church, since *Timnah* means a state in which the church's best welfare is considered (§§4855, 4857). **4861**

Because she saw that Shelah had grown up and she had not been given to him as his woman means seeing clearly that there was no other way to unite with the religiosity of Jacob's descendants, particularly those from Judah's line. This can be seen from the symbolism of *seeing* as having a clear sight (discussed in §§2150, 2325, 3764, 3863, 4403–4421). The reason it symbolizes a clear sight of the fact that there was no other way to unite with the religiosity of Jacob's descendants, particularly those from Judah's line, is that Judah symbolizes those descendants (§§4815, 4842, 4852). He therefore symbolizes the religiosity among them, with which [the representative religion] united, since it could not unite with Shelah. *Shelah* represents something idolatrous (§§4825, 4826, 4845), and the truth known to the representative religion (Tamar) could not unite with this. **4862**

Genesis 38:15, 16, 17, 18. *And Judah saw [her] and accounted her a prostitute because she had covered her face. And he turned aside to her on the way and said, "Grant, please, that I come to you"—because he did not know that she was his daughter-in-law; and she said, "What are you giving me, that you should come to me?" And he said, "I will send a kid of the goats from the flock," and she said, "If you give an earnest against your sending it." And he said, "What is the earnest that I shall give you?" and she said, "Your signet, your lanyard, and your staff that is in your hand"; and he gave them to her and came to her, and she conceived to him.* **4863**

Judah saw her symbolizes the religiosity of the Jewish nation and how it then viewed the inner depths of the representative religion. *And accounted her a prostitute* means as a mere lie. *Because she had covered her face* means that the inner depths were hidden from the people of that nation. *And he turned aside to her on the way* means that [that nation] became attached to it because it seemed false. *And said, "Grant, please, that I come to you,"* symbolizes a lust for close connection. *Because he did not know that she was his daughter-in-law* means that [that nation] did not recognize this as the truth of a representative religion. *And she said, "What are you giving me, that you should come to me?"* symbolizes an answering connection, on one condition. *And he said, "I will send a kid of the goats from the flock,"* symbolizes an emblem of the union. *And she said, "If you give me an earnest against your sending it,"* means that there would be an answering connection if there were certainty. *And he said, "What is the earnest that I shall give you?"* means that it was certain. *And she said, "Your signet,"* symbolizes a token of consent. *Your lanyard* means in the form of truth. *And your staff that is in your hand* means in the form of its power. *And he gave them to her* symbolizes resulting certainty. *And came to her* symbolizes union. *And she conceived to him* symbolizes resulting acceptance.

4864   *And Judah saw her* symbolizes the religiosity of the Jewish nation and how it then viewed the inner depths of the representative religion, as the following shows: *Seeing* means perceiving and understanding (discussed at §§2150, 2325, 2807, 3764, 3863) and therefore taking a certain view. Tamar, the *she* here, represents a religion that is representative of what is spiritual and heavenly (discussed at §§4829, 4831). In this case she represents the inner part of that religion, because the text is talking about the way the religious tradition of the Jewish nation viewed and received the inner dimension of that religion. Narrowly speaking, *Judah* represents the Jewish nation (discussed at §§4815, 4842), so he represents the religiosity of that nation. When the Word mentions a nation, in an inner sense it means some facet of that nation's religion. The inner meaning is not concerned at all with the historic events and tales of a nation, only with its character in the religious realm.

Judah saw her, then, clearly symbolizes the religious tradition of the Jewish nation and how it then viewed the inner depths of the representative religion.

4865   *And accounted her a prostitute* means as a mere lie. This can be seen from the symbolism of a *prostitute* as falsity (dealt with at §§2466, 2729, 3399). The meaning, then, is that the Jewish nation in its religiosity viewed the inner core of the church as a lie and nothing more.

The reason a prostitute means falsity is that marriage represents the heavenly marriage of goodness and truth. A husband represents goodness, and a wife truth, so sons represent truths, and daughters, types of goodness. Sons-in-law and daughters-in-law, fathers-in-law and mothers-in-law, and other relatives in their various degrees represent the kinds of things that are involved in the heavenly marriage. Adultery and prostitution, being its opposites, symbolize evil and falsity. They really are opposites, too. People who spend their lives in adultery and prostitution have no interest at all in what is good and true. This is because genuine marriage love descends from the heavenly marriage, which is the marriage of goodness and truth, but adultery and whoredom arise from the bond between evil and falsity, which comes from hell; see §§2727–2759.

[2] The Jewish nation past and present has considered the inner depths of the church to be simply a lie. That is what it meant that Judah accounted Tamar, his daughter-in-law, as nothing but a prostitute, and came together with her as such. The fact that the nation had origins like this represents the source and nature of its religiosity.

It is obvious that the people of that nation have considered the inner core of the church to be a harlot, that is, a lie. For example, if you tell them it is central to the church that the Messiah foretold of in scriptural prophecy and therefore awaited by them is the Lord, they reject it as utterly false. If you tell them it is central to the church that the Messiah's kingdom is not a worldly, temporal one but a heavenly, eternal one, they also pronounce it false. [3] If you tell them that the rituals of their religion represented the Messiah and his heavenly kingdom, they do not know what you are talking about. If you tell them that neighborly kindness and religious truth, in doctrine and in life, are central to the church, they look at it as pure falsity. Likewise for any other proposition. Even if you just propose that the church has an inner core, they laugh idiotically.

This is because they are wholly taken up with superficialities and in fact with the very lowest kinds of superficiality, which are harshly earthbound. More than anyone else they indulge in miserliness, which is totally earthly. People like this cannot possibly view the inner depths of the church in any other way, because they are farther removed from heavenly light than anyone else and are therefore more thickly surrounded by darkness.

Because she had covered her face means that the inner depths were hidden from the people of that nation. This is established by the representation of Tamar as a representative religion (discussed in §§4829, 4831), by the symbolism of *covering up* as being hidden, and from the symbolism of

4866

the *face* as the inner depths (discussed in §§358, 1999, 2434, 3527, 3573, 4066, 4326, 4796, 4797, 4798, 4799). *She had covered her face,* then, plainly means that the church's inner depths were hidden from them. For a discussion of this, see above at §§4859, 4865.

4867   *And he turned aside to her on the way* means that [that nation] became attached to it because it seemed false. This can be seen from the symbolism of a *way* as truth (discussed in §§627, 2333, 3123, 3142, 3477) and therefore in a negative sense as falsity. Here it symbolizes falsity because Judah viewed Tamar as a prostitute, and a prostitute symbolizes falsity (see just above at §4865). That is another reason the text says that he *turned aside* on the way, because the term *turn aside* is used in connection with falsity (§§4815, 4816).

4868   *And said, "Grant, please, that I come to you,"* symbolizes a lust for close connection. This can be seen from the symbolism of *coming to someone* or going in to her as uniting (discussed in §4820). Plainly this involves the kind of lust that seeks to unite with a prostitute, or in an inner sense with falsity. Again, the people of the Jewish nation, symbolized here by Judah (§§4815, 4842, 4864), have in the past and present viewed the inner truth of a representative religion simply as false (see above in §4865). The text is now speaking about the fact that they still formed a liaison with it, but as with a prostitute, not a wife—in other words, as with falsity, not truth. Connection with falsity, like connection with a whore, is characterized by lust.

[2] Everyone who believes only in the Word's outer or literal meaning and totally rejects its whole inner or spiritual meaning connects with inner truth as a whore. The main ones to do this are people who apply the Word's outer, literal meaning in a way that indulges their self-centered and worldly cravings—in other words, that bolsters their power and wealth. People who do this cannot possibly help regarding inner truth as a whore. If they unite with it, they do so out of the same lust they would feel in coupling with a prostitute. People belonging to the Jewish nation are especially prone to this, as are those meant in the Word by Babylon. However, the same is not true of people with an unsophisticated belief in the Word's literal meaning who nonetheless live according to the teachings of its inner meaning. That is, they live lives of love and charity and therefore of faith, because these constitute the inner meaning of the Word. Likewise for people who consequently teach the same values. The inner and outer meanings coincide in the two commandments to love the Lord above all and our neighbor as ourselves [Matthew 22:37, 39; Mark 12:30–31; Luke 10:27].

[3] Here are some examples illustrating the fact that the people of the Jewish nation view inner truth as a prostitute and connect with it, if at all, out of a lust like that for a liaison with a prostitute:

They might be told that the Word is holy—extremely holy—and that every tip of a letter in it is sacred. They acknowledge and connect with the idea, but only out of this type of lust. They believe that there is holiness in the literal meaning and not that a sense of holiness flows through it into people who read it with a passion for goodness and truth.

[4] They might be told that many of the figures named in the Word are to be revered as saints, including Abraham, Isaac, Jacob, Moses, Aaron, and David. They acknowledge and connect with the idea, but out of the same lust. They believe these people were chosen above others and were therefore holy and deserve to be worshiped as minor deities. The reality, though, is that all their holiness came from the fact that they represented the Lord. Representational holiness has no effect on the person doing the representing. Besides, everyone's life awaits him or her after death, without distinction.

[5] They might be told that some of the objects they had were holy—the ark, the Temple, the altar of burnt offering, the altar of incense, the bread on the table, the lampstand with its lamps, the eternal flame, the sacrifices, the incense, the oil, and Aaron's garments, particularly the breastplate, holding the Urim and Thummim. They acknowledge and connect with the idea, but out of a similar lust. They believe these items were intrinsically holy—the wood, stone, gold, silver, bread, fire—and deeply holy, because Jehovah was in them. That is, they believe that Jehovah's holiness, superimposed on these things, was actually in them. This is their inner truth, although it is relatively false. It is false because holiness exists only in what is good and true, which comes from the Lord and is present in love for him and for our neighbor and therefore in faith. So it exists only in living beings, which is to say, in people who receive these things from the Lord.

[6] They might be told that the Christian religion is one with the religion established among themselves, but that the former is the inner part of the religion, whereas the latter had been the outer part. They might be told, then, that when the religion set up among them sheds its superficial features and stands naked, Christianity appears. This they do not acknowledge except as a whore, or as false. Many of the ones who convert from Judaism to Christianity connect with this truth, but again out of the same type of lust.

The Word often refers to these attachments as acts of whoredom.

As for the people symbolized in the Word by Babylon, they take a similar view of the church's inner truth. Since they know inner truth, however, and acknowledge it in their youth but deny it in adulthood, the Word depicts [their attachments] as vile adulteries and unspeakable sexual transgressions, because they are acts of profanation.

4869 *Because he did not know that she was his daughter-in-law* means that [that nation] did not recognize this as the truth of a representative religion. This can be seen from the symbolism of a *daughter-in-law* as the truth in a religion, connected to its goodness (discussed at §4843). It is the truth of a representative religion that is being symbolized because Tamar, the daughter-in-law here, represents a religion that is representative of the spiritual and heavenly realms (§§4829, 4831).

On this topic, see what has been demonstrated above at §§4865, 4866, 4868.

4870 *And she said, "What are you giving me, that you should come to me?"* symbolizes an answering connection [on the part of the representative religion], on one condition. This can be seen from the symbolism of *coming to me* as a close connection (discussed at §§4820, 4868). It is evident without explanation that the connection was an answering one, with a condition.

4871 *And he said, "I will send a kid of the goats from the flock,"* symbolizes an emblem of the union. This can be seen from the symbolism of a *kid of the goats* as the innocence of a person's outer, earthly self (discussed in §3519). Since it means innocence, it is an emblem of marriage love, or of union. After all, true marriage love consists in innocence (see §2736).

As a result, it was customary for men in ancient times to send a goats' kid ahead when they went in to their wives for the first time. This is clear from details of Samson's story in Judges:

> It happened days afterward, in the days of the wheat harvest, *that Samson visited his wife with a goats' kid.* Because he said, "*I will go in to my wife,* into her room." (Judges 15:1)

Likewise in the current verse, but since Tamar was not going to accept the promised goats' kid, she demanded an earnest.

I call it an emblem of union, not of marriage, because on Judah's part the connection was like a liaison with a prostitute.

4872 *And she said, "If you give me an earnest against your sending it,"* means that there would be an answering connection if there were certainty. This can be seen from Tamar's words above, "What are you giving me, that you should come to me?" which mean an answering connection, on one condition (§4870). The current sentence means that there would be an answering connection if there were certainty, because an earnest was intended to guarantee delivery on a promise.

What is the earnest that I shall give you? means that it was certain. This can be seen from the symbolism of an *earnest* as a source of certainty (mentioned just above in §4872). What follows soon—the giving of the earnest—shows that it was certain [§4877].

4873

And she said, "Your signet," symbolizes a token of consent. This can be seen from the symbolism of a *signet* as a token of consent. The reason a signet betokens consent is that it was used in ancient times for confirming decrees. Strictly speaking, then, it symbolizes the actual confirmation, and proof that a thing was so.

4874

Note that Tamar demanded Judah's signet, lanyard, and staff as an earnest that he would send her a goats' kid, which she ended up not taking. This involves a secret that cannot possibly be known without the inner meaning. The secret is that the goats' kid symbolized a truly marriagelike bond and consequently a deep one—anything that is genuine is also deep—which was out of the question on Judah's part. So Tamar did not take the goats' kid, as a later part of the story shows, but instead appropriated something superficial that would be united to the inner depths of the religion that she symbolizes. The religion's outer dimension is symbolized by the signet, lanyard, and staff—the signet symbolizing consent itself; the lanyard, outer truth; and the staff, the power of that truth. The same objects are also emblems of union for the outer, earthly self.

[2] The union of inner truth with something superficial, or with the religiosity of the Jewish nation, is represented by Tamar's coming together with Judah as a daughter-in-law with her father-in-law under the pretext of the levirate. The union of the Jewish nation's religiosity with the inner core of the church is represented by Judah's coming together with Tamar as a prostitute. The two kinds of union work exactly the same way. What they are like, though, is not easy to explain intelligibly. That nature stands out plain to see before angels and good spirits, because it is presented to them in heaven's light, in which the Word's secrets lie open as clear as day. The situation is quite different in the world's light, which shines on people on earth.

Let me say just a little about this. The representative practices established among Jacob's descendants were not exactly like those of the ancient church. The majority of their practices resembled those of the religion established by Eber, which was called the Hebrew church. In this church there were many new forms of worship unknown to the ancient church, such as burnt offerings, sacrifices, and so on. The inner core of the church did not connect with these representative practices as directly as it did with those of the ancient church. The way the inner core of the church connected with such practices in the Jewish nation, and the way such practices connected with the inner core, is described in the inner sense by Tamar's union with Judah as a daughter-in-law with her father-in-law under the pretext of the levirate, and by Judah's union with Tamar as a prostitute.

Concerning the Hebrew church, see §§1238, 1241, 1327, 1343, 3031, 4516, 4517. For the idea that the sacrifices performed in this church did not exist in the ancient church, see §§923, 1128, 1343, 2180, 2818.

4875   *Your lanyard* means in the form of truth, that is, a token of consent in the form of truth. This can be seen from the symbolism of a *lanyard,* [or strap,] as truth. The reason a strap means truth is that it belongs in the category of clothing. Clothes in general symbolize truth because truth clothes goodness in the same way garments clothe the flesh (§§297, 2132, 2576, 4545, 4763). Among the ancients, therefore, every article of clothing symbolized some specific, particular sort of truth. A tunic symbolized one thing, a royal robe another, a coat another, headgear like a miter or turban another, leggings such as breeches or stockings another, and so on. A lanyard symbolized the outermost or lowliest type of truth. It was made of twisted threads, which symbolize the defining forms of this truth.

A strap symbolizes the same kind of truth [elsewhere] in Moses:

> Every open vessel on which there is no cover *strap* is unclean (Numbers 19:15),

which meant that nothing should be ill defined; what is ill defined is "open." This truth is the outermost kind of truth, which gives inner truth definition and a foundation to rest on.

4876   *And your staff that is in your hand* means in the form of its power—the power of that truth. This can be seen from the symbolism of a *staff* as power (discussed below) and from that of a *hand* as power too (discussed in §§878, 3091, 3387, 3563). The text says *that is in your hand* because this clause symbolizes the power of that truth—namely, the very lowliest truth, characteristic of the Jewish nation's religiosity, meant here by Judah. For power being predicated of truth, see §§3091, 3563.

The Word frequently mentions staffs, [or rods,] and it is surprising that hardly anyone today knows they represent something in the spiritual world. For instance, there is meaning to the fact that Moses was ordered to lift his staff whenever miracles were happening, and that when he did, they happened.

Non-Jewish nations also knew about this, as shown by their folktales, in which magic-workers are depicted with staffs, [or wands]. The reason a staff symbolizes power is that it provides support. It supports the hand and arm and through them the whole body. As a result a staff takes on the symbolism of the part it directly supports, which is the hand and arm. In the Word, both the hand and the arm symbolize the power of truth. The ends of the chapters will show that the hand and arm of the universal human also correspond to this power [§§4931–4937].

[2] The representation of a staff as power is clear from what is mentioned about Moses, as I said. He was ordered to take up the *staff* with which he would perform miracles, and he took *God's staff* in his hand (Exodus 4:17, 20). The water that was struck *with the staff* in Egypt turned to blood (Exodus 7:15, 19). *When the staff was stretched out* over the rivers, frogs appeared (Exodus 8:5–15). When the dust was struck *by the staff*, it became lice (Exodus 8:16–20). *When the staff was stretched out toward the sky*, hail fell (Exodus 9:23). *When the staff was stretched out over the land*, locusts appeared (Exodus 10:3–21). Since a hand is the main symbol of power, and a staff is just a tool, miracles also happened when his *hand was stretched out* (Exodus 10:12, 13). *When his hand was lifted toward the sky*, darkness fell over the land of Egypt (Exodus 10:21, 22). And *when his hand was stretched out* over the Suph Sea, an east wind turned the sea into dry land; and again *when his hand was stretched out*, the water returned (Exodus 14:21, 26, 27).

[3] Furthermore, when the rock of Horeb was struck *by the staff*, water gushed out (Exodus 17:5, 6; Numbers 20:7, 8, 9, 10). When Joshua fought against Amalek,

> Moses said to Joshua, "Choose men for us, and go out, fight with Amalek; tomorrow I myself will stand on the head of the hill, and *God's staff* will be *in my hand.*" And it happened when Moses lifted *his hand* that Israel prevailed, and when he lowered *his hand* that Amalek prevailed. (Exodus 17:9, 11, 12)

This evidence shows plainly that a staff, like a hand, represented power, and in the highest sense, the Lord's divine omnipotence. It also makes several other points clear: that in those days the outward aspects of religion consisted of representative acts and objects; that the inner core, or spiritual and heavenly qualities as they exist in heaven, corresponded to the outward features; and that this correspondence gave them their efficacy. Finally, it shows how absurd it is to believe there was any power actually infused into the staff or Moses' hand.

[4] The meaning of a staff in a spiritual sense as power is also evident from many passages in the Prophets. In Isaiah, for example:

> Look: the Lord Jehovah Sabaoth is taking away out of Jerusalem *staff* and *stave*—the whole *staff of bread* and the whole *staff of water.* (Isaiah 3:1)

A staff of bread stands for support and power lent by goodness that embodies love; a staff of water, for support and power lent by the truth that leads to faith. For the meaning of bread as goodness associated with love, see §§276, 680, 2165, 2177, 3464, 3478, 3735, 3813, 4211, 4217, 4735. For the meaning of water as the truth associated with faith, see §§28, 680, 739, 2702, 3058, 3424. A staff of bread is also mentioned in Ezekiel 4:16; 5:16; 14:13; Psalms 105:16. [5] Again in Isaiah:

> The Lord Jehovih Sabaoth has said: "My people, resident in Zion, do not be afraid of Assyria, *who will strike you with a rod* and *lift a staff over you* on the way to Egypt." Jehovah will stir a whip up against him (as in the blow dealt to Midian at the rock of Oreb), and *[Assyria's] staff will hang over the sea,* [the staff] that he will lift on the way to Egypt. (Isaiah 10:24, 26)

In this passage the staff stands for the power of skewed reasoning and secular knowledge, as they exist in people who reason against religious truth on the basis of secular learning, either twisting this truth or undercutting it. This behavior is symbolized by the rod Assyria would strike with and the staff he would lift on the way to Egypt. For the meaning of Assyria as skewed reasoning, see §1186. For that of Egypt as secular knowledge, §§1164, 1165, 1186, 1462. [6] Again in Zechariah:

> The pride of Assyria will be thrown down, and the *staff of Egypt* will withdraw. (Zechariah 10:11)

In Isaiah:

> You relied on a *staff of crushed reed*—on Egypt—which, when one leans on it, goes into one's hand and pierces it. (Isaiah 36:6)

Egypt stands for secular knowledge, as above. The power it has in spiritual matters is the staff of crushed reed. The hand it goes into and pierces means the power of the Word. In the same author:

> Jehovah has broken the *staff of the dishonest, the rod of rulers.* (Isaiah 14:5)

The staff and rod obviously stand for power. [7] In Jeremiah:

> Grieve, everyone in the environs of Moab! Say, "How the *strong staff, the beautiful staff* has been broken!" (Jeremiah 48:17)

A strong staff stands for the power of goodness, and a beautiful staff for the power of truth. [8] In Hosea:

> My people ask questions of their wood, and *their staff* answers them, because a spirit of whoredom has led them astray. (Hosea 4:12)

Asking questions of wood stands for consulting with evil. "Their staff answers" means that the result is falsity, which obtains its power from the evil that these people justify. A spirit of whoredom stands for a life of falsity based on evil. In David:

> Even when I walk in the valley of shadow I will not be afraid of evil, because you are with me; *your rod* and *your staff* comfort me. (Psalms 23:4)

"Your rod and your staff" stand for divine truth and goodness, which have power. In the same author:

> The *staff* of wickedness will not rest on the lot of the upright. (Psalms 125:3)

[9] In the same author:

> You will crush them with an *iron rod;* like the vessels of a potter will you scatter them. (Psalms 2:9)

The iron rod stands for the power that spiritual truth has on the earthly plane. All earthly truth that contains spiritual truth has power. Iron means earthly truth (§§425, 426). Likewise in John:

> To those who conquer and preserve my work right to the end I will give authority over the nations, to *shepherd them with an iron rod,* as if clay pots were being crushed. (Revelation 2:26, 27; and also Revelation 12:5; 19:15)

[10] Because a staff represented the power of truth—that is, the power goodness has through truth—monarchs had scepters, and scepters were shaped like short staffs. Monarchs represent the Lord's truth, and the essence of royalty is divine truth (§§1672, 1728, 2015, 2069, 3670, 4581). A scepter means the power monarchs have not through their high office but through truth, which must reign supreme, and not through any other truth than the kind that develops out of goodness. So first and foremost a scepter means divine truth, and among Christians it means the Lord, the source of all divine truth.

4877   *And he gave them to her* symbolizes resulting certainty. This can be seen from the symbolism of the earnest that Tamar sought, and that was *given* to her, as certainty (discussed above at §§4872, 4873).

4878   *And came to her* symbolizes union. This is established by the symbolism of *coming to someone* or going in to her as union (also discussed above at §§4820, 4868, 4870).

4879   *And she conceived to him* symbolizes resulting acceptance. This is established by the symbolism of *conceiving* as acceptance (discussed at §§3860, 3868, 3919). For the nature of that acceptance, see §4874 above.

4880   Genesis 38:19, 20, 21, 22, 23. *And she rose and went and took her veil off her and put on the clothes of her widowhood. And Judah sent a kid of the goats in the hand of his companion, the Adullamite, to receive the earnest from the hand of the woman, and he did not find her. And he asked the men of that place, saying, "Where is that harlot at the springs along the way?" and they said, "There wasn't a harlot there." And he went back to Judah and said, "I didn't find her, and in addition the men of the place said, 'There wasn't a harlot there.'" And Judah said, "Let her take it for herself, [though] we might be held in contempt. Look, I sent the kid but you did not find her."*

She rose symbolizes elevation. *And went* symbolizes living a life. *And took her veil off her* means that this happened to the obscurity. *And put on the clothes of her widowhood* symbolizes understanding. *And Judah sent a kid of the goats* symbolizes an emblem of marriage. *In the hand of his companion, the Adullamite,* means in the form of falsity. *To receive the earnest from the hand of the woman* means to replace the superficial emblems. *And he did not find her* means because there was nothing marriagelike on his part. *And he asked the men of that place, saying,* means that truth was consulted. *Where is that harlot?* means, was it a lie? *At the springs along the way* means that looked like the truth. *And they said* symbolizes a perception yielded by truth. *There wasn't a harlot there* means that it was not a lie. *And he went back to Judah* symbolizes reflection. *And said, "I didn't find her,"* means that falsity cannot discover this. *And in addition the men of the place said, "There wasn't a harlot there,"* symbolizes a perception, yielded by truth, that it was not a lie. *And Judah said, "Let her take it for herself,"* means it was all the same to him. *[Though] we might be held in contempt* means even though this stigmatized them. *Look, I sent the kid* means it was enough that the emblem existed. *But you did not find her* means if there was no marriage.

And she rose symbolizes elevation. This can be seen from the discussion in §§2401, 2785, 2912, 2927, 3171, 4103 of the symbolism of *rising,* which involves some kind of elevation. The elevation symbolized by rising is from an obscure state into a clearer one, spiritually speaking. An example is an elevation from ignorance to understanding, since this raises a person from a state lit by the world's light to one lit by heaven's.

4881

And went symbolizes living a life. This can be seen from the discussion in §§3335, 3690 of the symbolism of *going* as living a life.

4882

Admittedly, the idea that "going" in an inner sense means living seems rather far-fetched, or distant from our usual way of thinking. This is because we inhabit space and time, from which we have formed the ideas composing our thoughts, such as our idea of going, advancing, traveling, journeying, moving. These cover space and take time, so space and time permeate our idea of them, with the result that we have difficulty grasping that they mean states of life. However, when we put aside or shed our image of them, the spiritual phenomenon being symbolized springs forth. In the spiritual world, or heaven, no hint of space or time goes into the inhabitants' thinking, but something having to do with a state of life instead (§§1274, 1382, 2625, 2788, 2837, 3356, 3404, 3827, 4814). Spirits and angels do feel as though they are advancing and moving from place to place, exactly as people on earth feel it, but changes in their state of life are what produce the impression. It is like the appearance that we live on our own—an appearance that is just as strong for them as it is for us—when in reality life is not inherent in us but comes from the Lord's divinity, the source of all life.

These appearances as they exist with angels are called real appearances, because they appear as they really are. [2] Sometimes I have talked with spirits about these appearances. The ones who lack goodness and therefore truth do not want to hear that they only appear to live on their own; they like the idea that they truly do live on their own. They have been shown by personal experience that life is not inherent in them and that progress from place to place is a change and progression in the condition of their life, but I have also said this to them: The fully convincing appearance that the life they have originates in themselves can satisfy them; they could not gain any greater benefit if it actually were the case. But it is even better for them to know what the real situation is, because then they have the truth, and if they have the truth, they also have heaven's light—heaven's light being the truth itself that comes from the Lord's divinity. With the benefit of heaven's light they would not claim goodness as their own, and evil would not cling to them either. Angels possess this truth not only by knowledge but also by perception.

[3] The following experience shows that time and space in the spiritual world are states of life and that all life comes from the Lord: Spirits and angels each see those who are good on their right and those who are evil on their left, no matter what direction they turn. If they face east, that is where the good and the evil appear to them; the same if they face west, and if they face south or north too. This is true for every spirit or angel individually. If there are two of them, say, and one looks east while the other looks west, they both still see the good on their right and the evil on their left. It looks the same way to distant observers too, even if they stand behind the ones they are observing. The plain conclusion is that all life comes from the Lord, or that the Lord is within everyone's life. The Lord appears in the spiritual world as the sun, on his right being the good, or the sheep, and on his left the evil, or the goats. It is the same for everyone else too, since the Lord is the whole of life, as I said.

This notion cannot help baffling people, because as long as they are in the world they take their thinking from worldly cues and consequently from space and time. In the spiritual world, though, as noted above, ideas do not start with space and time but with the state of a person's feelings and consequent thoughts. It is because of this that extents of space and periods of time in the Word symbolize states.

4883 *And took her veil off her* means that this happened to the obscurity—that is, it was dispelled. This can be seen from the symbolism of covering oneself in a veil as obscuring the truth (discussed above at §4859). *Taking a veil off,* then, means dispelling the obscurity.

4884 *And put on the clothes of her widowhood* symbolizes understanding. This can be seen from the symbolism of a *widow* as people who have truth and not goodness but long to be led by goodness (discussed above at §4844) and from the symbolism of *clothes* as truth (discussed at §§297, 2576, 4545, 4763). Taken together, the two symbolize understanding, because truth is precisely what creates understanding. People who learn about truth from goodness have understanding. Truth based on goodness brings their intellectual mind into heaven's light, and heaven's light constitutes understanding, because it consists in divine truth born of divine goodness.

Another reason *putting on the clothes of her widowhood* symbolizes understanding is that a widow in a positive sense symbolizes someone who knows truth and longs to be led by goodness to the truth that brings understanding (as also shown above in §4844) and therefore to understanding itself.

[2] A brief explanation is needed to show how this works: The truth we know is not an understanding kind of truth until we are led by goodness. Once we are led by goodness, it becomes an understanding kind of truth for the first time. Truth does not possess life on its own; it only receives life from goodness, and truth receives life from goodness when we live according to it. When we do, truth injects itself into our will, from our will into our actions, and therefore into our whole self. The truth we only know or grasp stays outside our will and accordingly outside our life (since our will is our life). When we will the truth, though, it moves to the threshold of our life, and when we act on the truth willingly, it pervades our entire being. When we repeatedly act on the truth, it comes back to mind not only out of habit but also out of a liking for it and therefore out of free choice.

Consider, if you will, whether we can have anything instilled into us that we do not act on voluntarily. If we think about something without putting it into act—especially if we think about it without any *desire* to act—it lies entirely outside us and blows away like straw scattered by a puff of wind. In the other world too it scatters away. From this you can see what faith is without good deeds.

This discussion now clarifies what the truth that brings understanding is. It is truth originating in goodness. Truth is ascribed to the intellect, and goodness to the will; or to put the same thing another way, truth has to do with theology, and goodness with life.

And Judah sent a kid of the goats symbolizes an emblem of marriage. **4885** This can be seen from the symbolism of a *kid of the goats* as an emblem of marriage love, or proof of union (discussed above at §4871).

In the hand of his companion, the Adullamite, means in the form of **4886** falsity. This can be seen from the representation of Hirah the *Adullamite,* Judah's *companion,* as falsity (discussed in §§4817, 4854).

To receive the earnest from the hand of the woman means to replace the **4887** superficial emblems. This can be seen from the symbolism of the signet, lanyard, and staff, which were the *earnest,* as proof of union for the superficial, earthly self and therefore as superficial emblems (discussed at §4874).

4888   *And he did not find her* means because there was nothing marriagelike on his part—that is, on the part of Judah. He went in to Tamar not as a wife but as a prostitute, so she did not want the goats' kid, which symbolized an emblem of marriage (§4885). Moreover, not even on Tamar's part was there anything genuinely marriagelike, because [for her the connection] was like that of a daughter-in-law with her father-in-law under the pretext of the levirate. These things are symbolized by *he did not find her.*

4889   *And he asked the men of that place* means that truth was consulted. This can be seen from the symbolism of *asking* as consulting, and from that of the *men* as truth (discussed at §§265, 749, 1007, 3134, 3309 at the beginning). The *men of that place* means truth concerning this state of affairs, a *place* meaning a state (§§2625, 2837, 3356, 3387).

4890   *Where is that harlot?* means, was it a lie? This can be seen from the symbolism of a *harlot* or prostitute as falsity (discussed at §4865).

4891   *At the springs along the way* means that looked like the truth. This can be seen from the symbolism of *springs* as truth known to the church (discussed at §§2702, 3096, 3424, 4861). The text says *along the way* because a way is mentioned in connection with truth and in a negative sense with falsity (§§627, 2333, 3123, 3142). Since the question being asked is, "Where is that harlot at the springs along the way?" it means, was it a lie that looked like the truth?

4892   *And they said* symbolizes a perception yielded by truth. This can be seen from the symbolism of *saying* in the Word's narratives as perceiving (discussed at §§1791, 1815, 1819, 1822, 1898, 1919, 2080, 2619, 2862, 3509). The perception is one yielded by truth because the men of the place "said," and the men of the place mean truth (see just above at §4889).

4893   *There wasn't a harlot there* means that it was not a lie. This can be seen from the symbolism of a *harlot,* or prostitute, as falsity, as above in §4890.

The thread of meaning running through this text—the text for which the symbolism of the words has so far been explained—is partly visible from the remarks above at §§4865, 4868, 4874. Beyond this it cannot be grasped, except by one who knows the nature of the union between the inner and outer truth of the Jewish religion, on the part of both the inner truth represented by Tamar and the outer truth represented by Judah. This is an area of ignorance for most people, so to explain it further would be to cast it into shadow, not into any clear idea in the intellect. Our intellect, which is our inner eye, has its light and its shadow. Anything that does not match ideas with which we are already familiar lands in the shadow. However, all these details and their running thread, along with countless other details we cannot begin to grasp, in an angel's intellect enter with clarity into the light—which shows how much more understanding an angel has and what it is like in comparison with ours.

And he went back to Judah symbolizes reflection, as the following shows: Judah's Adullamite companion symbolizes falsity (§§4817, 4854, 4886), and when falsity is said to *go back* and report what had happened, as Judah's companion did here, it simply means recalling the situation to mind and reflecting on it.

4894

And said, "I didn't find her," means that falsity cannot discover this, as the following shows: *I didn't find* means not having discovered. And since it is said by the Adullamite, who symbolizes falsity, as above in §4894, it follows that *he said, "I didn't find her,"* means that falsity could not—in other words, cannot—discover this.

4895

And in addition the men of the place said, "There wasn't a harlot there," symbolizes a perception, yielded by truth, that it was not a lie. This can be seen from just above at §§4892, 4893, where the same words occur.

4896

And Judah said, "Let her take it for herself," means it was all the same to him. This can be seen from the emotion in the words, which is irritation and a resulting indifference.

4897

[Though] we might be held in contempt means even if this stigmatized them. This can be seen from the symbolism of *being held in contempt* as a stigma.

4898

Look, I sent the kid means it was enough that the emblem existed. This can be seen from the symbolism of a goats' *kid* as an emblem of marriage love, or of union (discussed at §4871). Here it is merely an emblem, because the kid was not accepted, for the reason (given above [§4888]) that there was no bond of marriage. Because this was the reason, *you did not find her* means if there was no marriage. This attitude also results from the indifference mentioned in §4897.

4899

I decline to explain these ideas further, for the reason discussed above at §4893—that they would land in the shadowy corners of the intellect, and what lands in the shadows also lands in disbelief. Take the idea that there must be a marriage—a marriage between truth and goodness—if there is to be a church. Take also the idea that there must be an inner core within the outer shell and that without these two there is no religion. The inner meaning here is talking about the nature of these elements in the Jewish religion. It says that in respect to that nation there was not an inner core within the outer shell, but that in respect to the statutes and laws themselves, without reference to the nation, there was.

[2] Who today does not believe the church existed with the Jewish nation? In fact, who does not believe that this nation was chosen and loved above all others? The main reason for the belief is the number and importance of the miracles performed among the people of that nation, the number of prophets sent to them, and the presence of the Word among them. Yet that nation did not have a bit of the church in it, because it had no neighborly love. Its people had absolutely no idea what real love for their neighbor was and did not believe in the Lord. They knew he was going to come, but [supposedly] for the purpose of raising them above everyone else in the whole world. Because this did not happen, they flatly rejected him. They did not want to know anything about his heavenly kingdom. All of this, so core to the church, they failed to acknowledge even in their theology, let alone in their lives. The only conclusion that can be drawn is that not a bit of the church existed in that nation.

[3] It is one thing for the church to exist *with* a nation, and another for it to exist *in* a nation. For example, the Christian church exists *with* people who possess the Word and preach about the Lord from doctrine. Not a bit of the church exists *in* them, though, unless they participate in the marriage of goodness and truth, that is, unless they engage in charity for their neighbor and in faith as a result, and therefore unless the inner core of the church lies within the outer shell. People who engage only in an outward display detached from any inward content do not have the church in them. People devoted to a faith detached from charity also do not have the church in them. People who acknowledge the Lord from doctrine and not from life also do not have the church in them. Obviously, then, it is one thing for the church to exist with a nation, and another for it to exist in a nation. [4] The inner meaning of this chapter is about the church with and in the Jewish nation. What it was like with that nation is depicted by Tamar's union with Judah under the pretext of the levirate. What it was like in that nation is depicted by Judah's union with Tamar as a prostitute.

I decline to lay the matter out in any greater detail, however, for the reason given above; as I said, it would land in the shadowy corners of the intellect. The shadows filling the intellect on this subject can be seen from the fact that hardly anyone today knows what the church's core is. Charity for our neighbor present in our will and from our will in our deeds, and a resulting faith present in our perceptions—who knows that this is the church's core? The fact is not known, and more importantly, it is denied by those who claim that faith without charitable deeds saves us. As a result, how can shadow be prevented from swallowing up the message of this chapter's inner meaning on the union of the church's inner core and outer shell, with and in the Jewish nation?

Anyone who does not see that charity is the core and is therefore essential to the church stands far from the first step on the way to understanding these things. Such a person consequently stands far from the countless indescribable experiences of heaven, where that which relates to love for the Lord and love for one's neighbor is the whole of life and therefore the whole of wisdom and understanding.

Genesis 38:24, 25, 26. *And it happened in about three months that it was told to Judah, saying, "Tamar your daughter-in-law whored, and here, now, she is also pregnant from her whoredoms," and Judah said, "Bring her out and let her be burned." She was brought out, and she sent to her father-in-law, saying, "By the man to whom these belong I am pregnant." And she said, "Recognize, please, whose the signet and the lanyard and the staff are." And Judah recognized [them] and said, "She is more justified than I, because I did not give her to Shelah my son." And he did not know her ever again.* **4900**

It happened in about three months symbolizes a new state. *That it was told to Judah* symbolizes communication. *Saying, "Tamar your daughter-in-law whored,"* symbolizes a perception at this point that it was false that any marriage existed between them. *And here, now, she is also pregnant from her whoredoms* means or that their connection could produce any fruit. *And Judah said* symbolizes the sentence passed by the religiosity that the Jewish nation practiced. *Bring her out and let her be burned* means that it was to be eradicated. *She was brought out* means that this was nearly carried out. *And she sent to her father-in-law* symbolizes an implication. *Saying, "By the man to whom these belong I am pregnant,"* means that something like this was present in the religiosity of that nation. *And she said, "Recognize, please, whose the signet and the lanyard and the staff are,"* means that this was known from the proofs. *And Judah recognized [them]* means that because it was his he affirmed this. *And said, "She is more justified than I,"* means that the outer part had no bond with the inner part, but that the inner part did have a bond with the outer. *Because I did not give her to Shelah my son* means since that was what the outer part was like. *And he did not know her ever again* means that there was no further connection.

It happened in about three months symbolizes a new state. This is established by the symbolism of *three* as something complete and therefore as the last and the first, or as an end and beginning (discussed at §§1825, **4901**

2788, 4495), and from that of a *month* as a state (discussed at §3814). States are symbolized on an inner level by all periods of time, such as an hour, day, week, month, year, or century; by the times of those periods, such as midday, evening, night, and morning (times of day), and summer, fall, winter, and spring (times of year); and by times of life, such as childhood, youth, early adulthood, full adulthood, and old age. All these and more symbolize states. For the definition of a state, see §4850.

[2] Times symbolize states because time does not exist in the other life. Spirits' and angels' lives do seem to develop as if over time, but they themselves do not think in terms of time, the way we in the world do. Instead, they think in terms of the states in their life, without any concept of time. They think this way because developments in their life are not divided into stages of maturity, since they do not age. There are no days or years there, because the sun, which is the Lord, always rises and never sets. That is why no notion of time enters their thoughts, only the notions of state and development of state. They take their way of thinking from things that exist and emerge before their senses.

[3] These statements must seem mind-boggling, but only because every last idea in our mind has some element of time and space attached to it. Such is the source of our memory and recall and of our lower thinking, which is made up of ideas described as concrete. But this memory from which concrete ideas arise goes to sleep in the other life. The inhabitants there make use of a deeper kind of memory and the ideas it produces. The thoughts emerging from this memory do not have time and space attached to them but rather states and their development. That is also why they correspond and, because they correspond, why periods of time in the Word symbolize states.

We have an outer memory, suited to us while we inhabit our body, and an inner memory, suited to our spirit; see §§2469–2494.

[4] *In about three months* symbolizes a new state because months, which are one way of dividing up time in the world, symbolize states, and three symbolizes the last and the first, or an end and beginning, as noted above. In the spiritual world there is constant development of states from one to the next, so the last part or end of every state holds a first step or beginning. Accordingly, it holds continuity. "In about three months," then, symbolizes a new state.

The case is the same in the church, which is the spiritual world, or the Lord's kingdom, on earth. The end of religion with one nation is always the start of it with another. It is because the last continues into the first in this way that the Lord is several times called the First and the Last, as in Isaiah 41:4; 44:6; Revelation 21:6; 22:13. In a secondary sense this symbolizes something perpetual, and in the highest sense, something eternal.

That it was told to Judah symbolizes communication, which can be seen from the discussion above in §4856 of the symbolism of *being told* as communication.

§4902

Saying, "Tamar your daughter-in-law whored," symbolizes a perception at this point that it was false that any marriage existed between them, as the following shows: *Saying* in the Word's narratives symbolizes a perception (discussed above at §4892). *Whoring* symbolizes falsity (discussed at §§2466, 2729, 3399, 4865). *Tamar* represents the inner core of a representative religion (also discussed above, at §4864). And a *daughter-in-law* symbolizes the truth known to a religion (discussed at §§4843, 4869). *Saying, "Tamar your daughter-in-law whored,"* then, symbolizes a perception at this point that it was false that any marriage existed between them.

§4903

How this fits into the context may be seen above at §§4864, 4865, 4866. To be specific, the Jewish nation in its religiosity viewed the inner values of the church simply as a whore, and the preaching of those values and a life according to them simply as whoredom. People who focus only on what is superficial and lack what is deep take no other view of the church's inner core. They call truth false and falsity true. This is because no one can see from the outside alone whether a thing is false or true, only from deep inside. It must be the inner eye that judges the evidence of the outer eye, and in order to judge its own evidence, the inner eye absolutely must have the use of heaven's light. It does not have the use of that light except in a person who possesses faith in the Lord and reads the Word in that faith.

[2] The concern of the Jewish nation for what was superficial, its lack of inner depth, and its consequent belief in truth as false and falsity as true is plain to see from the doctrines and life of its people. It is plain from their doctrines in that they were allowed to hate their enemy. It is plain from their life in that they did hate anyone who was not of their persuasion. In fact, they believed they were pleasing and serving Jehovah when they tortured and abused the people of the surrounding nations, butchering them and then exposing their bodies for wild animals and birds to devour, sawing them up alive, hacking them up with iron threshing boards and axes, and sending them through a brick furnace (2 Samuel 12:31). It was even in line with their teachings to inflict almost the same kinds of torture on a companion who had been declared a foe for some reason.

These considerations make it clear enough that there was no depth in their religiosity. If anyone back then had told them that such behavior violated the core of religion, they would have called it a lie.

The Lord's teaching in Matthew 5:21–48 also shows that they focused exclusively on superficialities, had absolutely no idea what the inner dimension was, and lived contrary to that dimension.

4904 *Here, now, she is also pregnant from her whoredoms* means or that their connection could produce any fruit, as the following shows: Expecting, or *being pregnant,* means producing something. Seed symbolizes religious truth, and conception symbolizes the acceptance of it, so expecting or being pregnant means producing. And *whoredom* symbolizes falsity— falsity from the religious tradition of the Jewish nation, as above in §4903. Clearly, then, "Saying, 'Tamar your daughter-in-law whored; here, now, she is also pregnant from her whoredoms,'" symbolizes a perception that it was false that any marriage existed between them or that their connection could produce any fruit.

When the church is said to produce fruit, it means that goodness is produced through truth. Goodness is produced when truth passes through the intellect into the will and from the will into act. To repeat, seed means religious truth, and conception means acceptance. Acceptance occurs when truth in our intellect passes over into goodness in our will, or when the truth that composes faith passes over into the goodness that constitutes charity. When this goodness exists in our will, it is in its womb, and that is when it is first produced. When we commit to active goodness, or when we produce something good from our will and therefore from pleasure and freedom, it leaves the womb, or is born. Rebirth, or regeneration, means the same thing. From this you can see what is symbolized on a spiritual level by pregnancy.

The symbolism in this case is the opposite, though—that *nothing* good could be produced, because the nation under discussion here subscribed to falsity rather than truth, since it lacked any inner dimension of religion.

[2] The idea of being reborn, or regenerated, or becoming a person of depth, was entirely unknown to that nation, so they viewed the concept as a whore. This can be seen from Nicodemus, who was a ruler of the Jews (John 3:1–13). Consider that he said, "How can we be born when we are old? Can we enter our mother's womb a second time?" (John 3:4).

People recognize that the Lord revealed the deeper levels of his kingdom and the church, but the ancients knew about those inner levels too.

They knew that we have to be reborn in order to enter life; that we then discard our old self, or self-love and materialism with their cravings; that we put on a new self, or love for our neighbor and God; that those who have been reborn have heaven inside them; and other deep concepts. All of this was familiar to the people of the ancient church, but they were led to the knowledge by the outward means of representations, which were completely lost to memory among the people of the Jewish nation. The Lord accordingly taught the concepts, but he did away with the representations, because most of them looked forward to him. The image vanishes when the manifestation itself appears. [3] As a consequence he instituted a new church, which would not be led to inner knowledge by representations, as the earlier church had been, but would learn the concepts without representations. The Lord commanded only a couple of outward practices to replace them: baptism and the Holy Supper. Baptism was to remind us about rebirth, and the Holy Supper was to remind us about the Lord, his love for the whole human race, and the love we reflect back to him.

The point of these remarks is to show that the inner depths of the church that the Lord taught about were known to the ancients but were entirely forgotten among the people of the Jewish nation—so much so that they viewed it all simply as false.

And Judah said symbolizes the sentence passed by the religiosity that the Jewish nation practiced. This can be seen from the representation of *Judah* as the religiosity of the Jewish nation (discussed at §4864). What follows next shows that the phrase refers to a sentence it passed. **4905**

Bring her out and let her be burned means that it was to be eradicated— the inner core of the church, represented by Tamar. This can be seen from the symbolism of *bringing her out* and *burning* as eradicating. *Bringing out* has to do with truth, and *burning* has to do with goodness, which were to be eradicated. **4906**

The association of "burning" with the annihilation of goodness can be seen from many Scripture passages. It arises from the fact that fire and flame in a spiritual sense mean goodness, and their warmth means a desire for goodness. In a negative sense, fire and flame mean evil, and their heat means a desire for evil (§§1297, 1861, 2446). [2] What is more, goodness actually is spiritual fire, giving off spiritual heat that brings things to life, and evil is a fire and heat that consumes things.

Anyone who considers and reflects can easily see that a loving goodness is spiritual fire and that the desires connected with such goodness are spiritual warmth. If you ponder the source of the fire and warmth that keep people alive, you will find they come from love. For one thing, as soon as love dies, we become cold, and the more love we feel, the warmer we grow. If our vitality did not originate in fire, we could not possibly receive life. Among the evil, though, this spiritual, life-giving fire or warmth becomes a scorching, consuming blaze, because that is what it is converted to in them.

Even with animals devoid of reason, spiritual warmth flows in and sparks life, but the nature of this life depends on its reception by the organic forms in them. From it they have innate knowledge and drives, as is seen in bees and all the rest.

4907   *She was brought out* means that this was nearly carried out. In other words, it was nearly eradicated. This can be seen from the symbolism of being *brought out* and burned as being eradicated (discussed just above in §4906). Tamar's being brought out to be burned, then, means that the eradication was nearly carried out.

4908   *And she sent to her father-in-law* symbolizes an implication—an implication that he had impregnated her. This can be seen from the story line, which leads to such a meaning.

4909   *Saying, "By the man to whom these belong I am pregnant,"* means that something like this was present in the religiosity of that nation. This is established by the representation of Judah, the *man,* as the religiosity of the Jewish nation (discussed at §§4864, 4905) and from the symbolism of expecting, or *being pregnant,* as being produced (discussed at §4904). Here it means being present in, though, because what is produced—that is, what is conceived—is present within.

The fruit produced is the first effect, and because it is instrumental, it is called a means and leads to a further effect, as delineated above in §4904.

What lay inside the religiosity of that nation can be seen from the discussion above at §4899 and from the discussion that follows.

4910   *And she said, "Recognize, please, whose the signet and the lanyard and the staff are,"* means that this was known from the proofs. This can be seen from the symbolism of the *signet, lanyard, and staff* as emblems of union for the outer, earthly self (mentioned in §§4874, 4887).

4911   *And Judah recognized [them]* means that because it was his he affirmed this. This can be seen from the symbolism of *recognizing* as affirming, and affirming because he recognized from the emblems that it was his.

This sentence depicts the character of that nation's people. They reject the inner [truth] of the church as a lie, but when they hear it implied that such [truth] belongs to them, they accept it and agree. People given to that most sordid of passions, greed, and to self-love, as these people are, cannot lift their mind's eye to see that truth comes from anywhere but themselves. When it is credited to them, therefore, they affirm it.

For example, if you tell them the Word is intrinsically divine and contains secrets of heaven, secrets so deep that only angels can understand them, they affirm it as true. They affirm it because they consider the Word theirs, since it was addressed to them, exists among them, and talks about them in its literal text. But if you reveal the actual secrets to them—in other words, the spiritual truth—they reject them.

[2] If you tell them the rituals of their religion were all inherently sacred, they affirm it as true, because they consider the rituals theirs. But if you say that the holiness was in the rituals and not in them, the people, they deny it.

If you tell them the religion of Judah was heavenly and the religion of Israel was spiritual, and if you define "heavenly" and "spiritual," they affirm this too. But if you say those religions are called heavenly and spiritual because everything about them represented something heavenly or spiritual, and that representation has to do with the attributes represented, not with people, they deny it.

If you tell them Moses' staff had power from Jehovah and therefore divine power, they agree and call it true. But if you tell them the power was not in the staff, only in the divine command, they deny it and call it false.

[3] If you tell them the bronze snake set up by Moses healed the people bitten by snakes and was consequently miraculous, they agree. But if you say it was not healing or miraculous on its own, only from the Lord, whom it represented, they deny it and call it false. (Compare what is reported and said about the snake in Numbers 21:7, 8, 9; 2 Kings 18:4; John 3:14, 15.)

Likewise for any other truth.

Such is the attitude symbolized by Judah's acknowledgment. Such was also the attitude—on the part of the nation symbolized by him—that united with the inner core of the church as represented by Tamar. Because it was like this, Judah did not go in to her as a brother-in-law to a wife but as a sexually immoral person to a prostitute.

And said, "She is more justified than I," means that the outer part had no bond with the inner part, but that the inner part did have a bond with the outer. This can be seen from the description above in §4899 of religion as it existed with and in the Jewish nation. To be explicit, religion existed *with* that nation, or an inner core was united to the outer shell, but no religion existed *in* it; its outer shell was not united to the inner core. For the church to exist *in* a nation, the bond must be reciprocal.

4913   *Because I did not give her to Shelah my son* means since that was what the outer part was like. This can be seen from previous explanations: Tamar could not be given to Shelah, Judah's son, because this kind of union would be like that of a wife with a husband according to the law of the levirate, whereas the religiosity of the Jewish nation, which is what was being represented, was not capable of this. In reality the union was like that of a father-in-law with his daughter-in-law as a prostitute.

4914   *And he did not know her ever again* means that there was no further connection. This can be seen from the symbolism of *knowing* as forming a connection, and from that of *he did not ever again,* which means no further. So it means that there was no further connection with the inner dimension of religion (Tamar representing that dimension).

For the same reason, Judah also had no more children.

4915   Genesis 38:27, 28, 29, 30. *And it happened in the time when she gave birth that here, there were twins in her womb! And it happened when she gave birth that [one of them] put out his hand, and the midwife took and tied double-dyed [scarlet thread] on his hand, saying, "This one came out first." And it happened as he took back his hand that here, his brother came out! And she said, "Why have you breached yourself a breach?" and called his name Perez. And afterward his brother came out, on whose hand was the double-dyed [scarlet thread], and they called his name Zerah.*

It happened in the time symbolizes the next state. *When she gave birth* symbolizes acknowledgment on the part of inner truth. *That here, there were twins in her womb* means that both go to make up the church. *And it happened when she gave birth* symbolizes producing fruit. *That [one of them] put out his hand* symbolizes power. *And the midwife took* symbolizes the earthly level. *And tied double-dyed [scarlet thread] on his hand* means that it marked that; *double-dyed [scarlet thread]* means goodness. *Saying, "This one came out first,"* means that it had priority. *And it happened as he took back his hand* means that it hid its power. *That here, his brother came out* symbolizes truth-from-goodness. *And she said, "Why have you breached yourself a breach?"* symbolizes its apparent separation from goodness. *And called his name Perez* symbolizes its nature. *And afterward his brother came out* means that goodness actually comes first. *On whose hand was the double-dyed [scarlet thread]* symbolizes an acknowledgment that it does. *And they called his name Zerah* symbolizes its nature.

It happened in the time symbolizes the next state. This can be seen from the symbolism of a *time* as a state (discussed in §§1274, 1382, 2625, 2788, 2837, 3254, 3356, 3827, 4882, 4901). *It happened in the time* clearly means the next state, since what happened now follows. In addition, see §4814.

§4916

When she gave birth symbolizes acknowledgment on the part of inner truth. This can be seen from the symbolism of *giving birth* as acknowledging in faith and deed (discussed in §§3905, 3915, 3919) and from the representation of Tamar—*her*—as the inner core of a representative religion and therefore as inner truth.

§4917

That here, there were twins in her womb means that both go to make up the church. This can be seen from the symbolism of *twins* as both—both goodness and truth (discussed at §3299)—and from that of a *womb* as the place where goodness and truth lie after conception and consequently where that which composes the church exists. In a positive sense a womb symbolizes the inmost core of marriage love, where innocence resides, because the womb in the universal human corresponds to marriage love. Marriage love traces its origin to the love of goodness and truth, which is love for the heavenly marriage. This marriage is heaven itself, or the Lord's kingdom, and the Lord's kingdom on earth is the church, so a womb also symbolizes the church. The church exists where goodness and truth are married.

§4918

This is why the initial opening of a womb means the resulting theologies of various religions (§3856) and a capacity for accepting the truth and goodness in a religion (§3967). It is why leaving the womb means being reborn, or regenerated (§4904)—that is, becoming an individual church, since anyone who is reborn or regenerates becomes a church.

[2] Since leaving the womb symbolizes rebirth and therefore the church, the Word refers to the Lord as the one who forms people from the womb and draws them from the womb. People who have been reborn and have become a church are described as being carried in the womb. In Isaiah, for instance:

> This is what Jehovah has said, your maker, the *one who formed you from the womb* (he helps you). (Isaiah 44:2)

In the same author:

> This is what Jehovah has said, your Redeemer and the *one who formed you from the womb*. (Isaiah 44:24)

In the same author:

> Jehovah has said—*who formed me from the womb into his servant,* to bring Jacob back to him, and for Israel to be gathered to him. (Isaiah 49:5)

In David:

> Jehovah, *who drew me from the womb.* (Psalms 22:9)

In Isaiah:

> Listen to me, house of Jacob, and all you survivors of the house of Israel, *carried from the womb* and borne from the uterus. (Isaiah 46:3)

In David:

> The godless are estranged *from the womb* and go astray *from the belly* with lying words. (Psalms 58:3)

Being estranged from the womb means from the goodness that belongs to the church. Going astray from the belly means from the truth. In Hosea:

> The pains of a woman in labor will come on him. He is an unwise child, because when the time comes *he does not present himself in the womb, which is for children.* (Hosea 13:13)

Not presenting oneself in the womb, which is for children, means not in the truth-based goodness that belongs to the church. [3] In the same author:

> Like a bird their glory will fly away, *abandoning delivery, abandoning the womb,* and *abandoning conception.* (Hosea 9:11)

This stands for the total annihilation of truth in the church—"abandoning delivery," for the annihilation of fully born truth; "abandoning the womb," of gestating truth; and "abandoning conception," of embryonic truth. In Isaiah:

> I knew you would commit base treachery, and you will be called [by the name] of *transgressor from the womb.* (Isaiah 48:8)

This means that the religion was like this from its beginning. In John:

> A great sign was seen in heaven: a woman enveloped in the sun, and the moon under her feet, and on her head a crown of twelve stars. *Being*

pregnant, though, she shouted out laboring and wracked with pain to give birth. (Revelation 12:1, 2)

The woman means the church (§§252, 253, 255). The sun enveloping her means the goodness that comes from love (30–38, 1529, 1530, 2441, 2495, 4060, 4696). The moon under her feet means the truth taught by faith (30–38, 1529, 1530, 2120, 2495, 4696). The stars mean knowledge of goodness and truth (2495, 2849, 4697). There are twelve of them because twelve means everything and therefore everything having to do with faith (577, 2089, 2129 at the end, 2130 at the end, 3272, 3858, 3913). Being pregnant means that religious truth had been conceived of. Laboring and being wracked with pain to give birth means that it was accepted with difficulty.

And it happened when she gave birth symbolizes producing fruit. This **4919** can be seen from the symbolism of *giving birth* as acknowledging in faith and deed (discussed at §§3905, 3915, 3919). What we acknowledge in faith and deed we produce as fruit, so giving birth also symbolizes producing fruit—the fruit of goodness and truth, which go to make up the church.

That [one of them] put out his hand symbolizes power, which can be **4920** seen from the discussion in §§878, 3387 of the symbolism of a *hand* as power.

And the midwife took symbolizes the earthly level, which can be seen **4921** from the discussion in §4588 of the symbolism of a *midwife* as the earthly level. How the situation stands with this will be seen in what follows.

A midwife means something different in the spiritual world than in the physical world, since there is no birth process there and consequently no practice of midwifery. When we on earth read the current clause, then, the angels who are with us obviously perceive something else—something spiritual—instead of a midwife. Since ideas of spiritual birth dominate their thoughts, they take a midwife to be the entity that helps in spiritual delivery and catches what is born. That entity is the earthly level, as you may see demonstrated earlier at §4588.

And tied double-dyed [scarlet thread] on his hand means that it marked **4922** that power; and *double-dyed [scarlet thread]* means goodness. This can be seen from the symbolism of *tying something on a hand* as marking power, a *hand* meaning power (§4920), and from that of *double-dyed [thread]* as goodness, and in fact spiritual goodness. The reason double-dyed [thread] means spiritual goodness is that its color is scarlet, and when the color scarlet appears in the other world it symbolizes spiritual goodness, which is goodness born of charity for one's neighbor. All colors visible in the other world symbolize something good or true, because they derive from heaven's light, which in its essence is wisdom and understanding radiated by the Lord's divinity. The variegations or modifications of that light are therefore varieties and modifications, if you will, of wisdom and understanding, and accordingly of goodness and truth. On the point that the light in heaven comes from the divine wisdom and understanding of the Lord, who appears as the sun there, see §§1053, 1521–1533, 1619–1632, 2776, 3138, 3167, 3190, 3195, 3222, 3223, 3225, 3337, 3339, 3340, 3485, 3636, 3643, 3862, 3993, 4180, 4214, 4302, 4405, 4408, 4413, 4415, 4523–4533. On the point that colors come from this light and that they are variegations and modifications of it, and therefore of understanding and wisdom, see §§1042, 1043, 1053, 1624, 3993, 4530, 4677, 4742.

[2] The meaning of double-dyed [scarlet thread] as spiritual goodness is evident from places in the Word that mention it, as, for instance, in Jeremiah:

> If therefore you are devastated, what will you do? *Though you dress in double-dyed [scarlet]* and adorn yourself with adornment of gold, in vain will you beautify yourself; your lovers will abhor you. (Jeremiah 4:30)

This is about Judah. Dressing in double-dyed [scarlet] stands for spiritual goodness; adorning oneself with adornment of gold stands for heavenly goodness. In 2 Samuel:

> David lamented over Saul and over Jonathan and titled [the lamentation] "To teach the children of Judah the bow": "Daughters of Israel, weep over Saul, *who clothed you in double-dyed [scarlet]* and other delights and put an ornament of gold on your garment." (2 Samuel 1:17, 18, 24)

Teaching the bow means teaching a theology of love and charity, this theology being what a bow symbolizes. Clothing someone in double-dyed [scarlet] stands once again for spiritual goodness, and putting an ornament of gold on someone's garment, for heavenly goodness.

[3] Since this was the symbolism of double-dyed [scarlet thread], the people were also commanded to use double-dyed scarlet [thread] on the curtains for the dwelling place [of the tabernacle], the veil, the curtain for the doorway of the tent, the curtain at the gate of the courtyard, the table of [the bread of] presence when they set out on a journey, and Aaron's holy garments, such as the ephod, breastplate of judgment, and fringes

for the robe of the ephod. They were to use it on the curtains for the dwelling place:

> For the dwelling place you shall make ten curtains—interwoven byssus and blue-violet and red-violet and *double-dyed scarlet.* (Exodus 26:1)

On the veil:

> You shall make a veil of blue-violet and red-violet and double-dyed scarlet and interwoven byssus. (Exodus 26:31)

On the curtain for the doorway of the tent:

> You shall make a curtain for the doorway of the tent out of blue-violet and red-violet and double-dyed scarlet and interwoven byssus. (Exodus 26:36)

[4] On the curtain for the gate of the courtyard:

> For the gate of the courtyard you shall make a curtain out of blue-violet and red-violet and *double-dyed scarlet* and interwoven byssus, the work of an embroiderer. (Exodus 27:16)

On the table of [the bread of] presence when they set out:

> When the camp sets out, they shall spread over the table [of the bread] of presence a cloth of *double-dyed scarlet* and cover it with a covering of badger hide. (Numbers 4:8)

On the ephod:

> You shall make the ephod out of gold, blue-violet and red-violet and *double-dyed scarlet,* interwoven byssus, the work of an artisan. [Likewise on the belt.] (Exodus 28:5, 6, 8)

On the breastplate of judgment:

> You shall make a breastplate of judgment, with the work of an artisan, like the work of the ephod, out of gold, blue-violet and red-violet and *double-dyed scarlet* and interwoven byssus. (Exodus 28:15)

On the fringes of the robe of the ephod:

> Pomegranates of blue-violet and red-violet and *double-dyed scarlet.* (Exodus 28:33)

[5] The meeting tent with the ark represented heaven, so the colors ordered were ones that symbolized the heavenly and spiritual attributes of heaven in their proper hierarchy. Blue-violet and red-violet symbolized heavenly goodness and truth. Double-dyed scarlet and interwoven byssus symbolized spiritual goodness and truth. Anyone who believes in the holiness of the Word can see that every detail means something. Those who believe that the Word is holy because it was sent down from the Lord through heaven can see that heavenly and spiritual qualities of his kingdom were meant.

The same is true of the use of cedar wood, *scarlet cloth,* and hyssop to cure leprosy (Leviticus 14:4, 6, 52). The same with the addition of cedar wood and hyssop and *double-dyed crimson [thread]* to the fire when a red cow was burned to make the water for removing [sin] (Numbers 19:6).

[6] The same colors are used in John to depict the profanation of goodness and truth:

> I saw a woman, sitting on a *scarlet* beast, full of the names of blasphemy. And it had seven heads and ten horns. The woman was dressed in red-violet and *scarlet* and was gilded with gold and precious stone and pearls, having a golden cup in her hand, full of abominations and the uncleanness of whoredoms. (Revelation 17:3, 4)

At a later point:

> Alas, alas, you great city, who were dressed in fine linen and red-violet and *scarlet* [and were] gilded with gold and precious stone and pearls! (Revelation 18:16)

This is about Babylon, which symbolizes the profanation of what is good (§§1182, 1283, 1295, 1304, 1306, 1307, 1308, 1321, 1322, 1326), and in this case the profanation of both goodness and truth that is typical of Babylon. In the Old Testament prophets, Babylon means the profanation of goodness, and Chaldea, the profanation of truth.

[7] In a negative sense, scarlet symbolizes the evil that opposes spiritual goodness, as in Isaiah:

> Even if your sins are like *scarlet,* they will grow as white as snow; even if they are as red as crimson, they will be like wool. (Isaiah 1:18)

Scarlet symbolizes this type of evil because in a positive sense, blood, which is also red, symbolizes spiritual goodness, or charity for one's neighbor, and in a negative sense, violence inflicted on charity.

Saying, "This one came out first," means that it had priority. This can
be seen from the symbolism of *coming out first* or being firstborn as priority and supremacy (discussed at §3325).

This verse and the rest of the chapter are about birthrights. Anyone
unfamiliar with the Word's inner meaning might suppose the passage is
talking only about birthrights and therefore about the privileges a firstborn
won under the law. However, anyone who knows a little of the inner meaning can see plainly enough that something loftier also lies hidden here. For
one thing there is the event itself, in which one of the babies put his hand
out and took it back, and then the other one came out. For another, they
were named for this maneuver, and the midwife tied double-dyed [scarlet
thread] on the hand of the first baby. For yet another, in strikingly similar circumstances, Esau and Jacob clashed in the womb, and when Esau
emerged first, Jacob was holding his heel (Genesis 25:[22,] 23, 24, 26). In
addition, when Jacob blessed Joseph's two sons, he put his right hand on
the younger and his left on the older (Genesis 48:17, 18, 19).

[2] Jews and some Christians do in fact believe that these stories and
the rest of the Word contain a hidden dimension, which they describe
as mystical. Their belief is due to a reverence for the Word stamped on
them ever since they were children. If you ask what the mystical element
is, though, they do not know. You might argue that since the mystical
dimension of the Word is divine, it has to be the kind that exists in heaven
among the angels. No other mystical sense is possible in the Word. If
there were another, it would be the stuff of fantasy or of magic or of
idolatry. You might also point out that this mystical element in heaven
among the angels is actually the element described as spiritual and heavenly. It has to do exclusively with the Lord, his kingdom, and the church,
and consequently with goodness and truth. If they knew what goodness
and truth were—that is, what love and faith were—they could also know
this mystical sense. If you say such things to them, though, hardly any of
them believe it. In fact, people in the church today are afflicted with such
ignorance that what I have said about the heavenly and spiritual planes is
nearly incomprehensible to them.

But even so, the Lord in his divine mercy has granted me the opportunity to live simultaneously as a spirit in heaven and as a person on earth
and therefore to talk with angels for many years now without interrup-
tion. As a result I cannot avoid revealing these so-called mystical elements
of the Word—in other words, its deeper levels, which are the spiritual
and heavenly levels of the Lord's kingdom.

The next few sections will explain what the story of Tamar's two sons embraces in its inner meaning.

4924   *And it happened as he took back his hand* means that it hid its power. This is established by the symbolism of a *hand* as power (discussed at §§878, 3387, 4920). *Taking it back* means hiding the power.

4925   *That here, his brother came out* symbolizes truth-from-goodness. This is established by the symbolism of a *brother* as something related by [shared] goodness (discussed at §§3815, 4267), and therefore as truth-from-goodness. Truth-from-goodness is the truth that comes of goodness, or the faith that comes of neighborly love.

The inner meaning here is about birth order in people being reborn, or regenerated by the Lord, so it is about birth order in the church. Since earliest times people have disputed which is firstborn, the goodness urged by neighborly love, or the truth taught by faith. While we are being reborn and becoming an individual church, goodness is invisible. It hides in our inner self and reveals itself only in a sort of desire that is not openly accessible to the awareness of our outer, earthly self until we have been reborn. Truth does reveal itself, though, because it enters through the senses and lodges in the memory belonging to our outer, earthly self. Because of this, many have fallen into the error that truth is firstborn, and eventually even into the error that truth is the essential part of religion. In fact, they see truth, which is called faith, as being so essential that it can save us without the goodness that rises out of neighborly love.

[2] This one mistake has led to numerous others, which have infected not only their theology but also their life, including these misconceptions: No matter how we live, as long as we believe, we are saved. Even the most criminal people go to heaven if they just claim to accept certain tenets of faith at the moment of death. Anyone can go to heaven out of pure grace, no matter how she or he has lived. And because such people have this kind of theology, they eventually lose any notion of what neighborly love is and any concern about it. In the end they do not believe it exists or therefore that heaven and hell exist. The reason for this deterioration is that faith without charity, or truth without goodness, teaches nothing. The further it shrinks from goodness, the more foolish we become. Goodness is what the Lord acts on and through to give us understanding and wisdom, and lofty insight, and the sense of whether a thing is so or not so.

[3] These comments show what the case is with the birth order: goodness actually has the birthright, and truth only apparently does. That is what the birth of Tamar's two sons depicts in its inner meaning. The

double-dyed [scarlet thread] that the midwife tied on one baby's hand symbolizes goodness (as was shown in §4922). Coming out first symbolizes priority (§4923). Taking back his hand means that goodness hid its power (as mentioned just above). "His brother came out" symbolizes truth. "You breached yourself a breach" symbolizes the apparent separation of truth from goodness. "Afterward his brother came out" means that goodness actually comes first. And "on whose hand was the double-dyed [scarlet thread]" symbolizes an acknowledgment that it does. We do not acknowledge that goodness comes first until after we have been reborn, because then we act on goodness and look at truth and its quality from the standpoint of goodness.

[4] These are the contents of the inner meaning, which teaches how matters stand with goodness and truth in a person who is being born anew. It teaches that goodness actually comes first but truth apparently does, and that goodness does not appear in first place while we are being reborn but is clearly seen as first once we have been reborn. However, there is no need to pursue this further, since it has already been explained. See the explanations at §§3324, 3325, 3494, 3539, 3548, 3556, 3563, 3570, 3576, 3603, 3701, 4243, 4245, 4247, 4337. For the idea that since ancient times people have debated whether the birthright belongs to goodness or truth, to neighborly love or faith, see §2435.

[5] The firstborn in the highest sense is the Lord and is therefore love for him and charity for our neighbor. For this reason a law was laid down in the representative religion that firstborns were Jehovah's, as recorded in Moses:

> Consecrate to me *every firstborn, that which opens the womb* among the children of Israel; among human and among animal, let them be mine! (Exodus 13:2)

> You shall hand *everything that opens the womb* over to Jehovah; and *every offspring of an animal that opens [the womb],* however many males you have, will be Jehovah's. (Exodus 13:12)

> *Everything that opens the womb* is mine, so in regard to every head of your livestock, you shall give me the male that *opens [the womb], of ox and of flock member.* (Exodus 34:19)

> *Everything that opens the womb* among all flesh that they bring to Jehovah, of humans and of animals, shall be yours, but still you absolutely shall redeem *every firstborn of a person.* (Numbers 18:15)

I—look—I have taken the Levites from the midst of the children of Israel in place of *every firstborn, those who open the womb* from among the children of Israel, so that the Levites may be mine. (Numbers 3:12)

[6] Since whatever "opens the womb" is the firstborn, wherever these passages mention a firstborn they also speak of that which opens the womb, so that goodness will be what is symbolized. The fact that goodness is being symbolized becomes clear from the inner meaning of all the details, especially the statements here concerning Tamar's sons. Zerah opened the womb with his hand, and he represents goodness, as can also be seen from the double-dyed [scarlet thread] placed on his hand (discussed at §4922). Moreover a womb, which is described as being opened, means a place for goodness and truth and consequently for the church (see §4918). To open it means to make it possible for truth to be born.

[7] The Lord is the only firstborn, because he is goodness itself, and all truth comes from his goodness. This is also the reason Jacob was allowed to buy the birthright from his brother Esau, so that he could represent the Lord even though he was not a firstborn. And since this was not enough, he was given the name Israel, which would enable him to represent truth-based goodness. In a representative sense, Israel means the goodness that comes through truth (§§3654, 4286, 4598).

4926 *And she said, "Why have you breached yourself a breach?"* symbolizes its apparent separation from goodness. This can be seen from the symbolism of a *breach* as intruding on truth and distorting it by separating it from goodness (discussed below). This *breaching a breach* plainly means tearing the double-dyed [scarlet thread] off the baby's hand and therefore detaching what is good (double-dyed [scarlet thread] symbolizing goodness, §4922). The separation was merely apparent because that is how the situation looked to the midwife; this was not the baby with the double-dyed [scarlet thread] but his brother, who represents truth. See the explanation just above at §4925, which shows that goodness is actually the firstborn, and truth only apparently so.

The case can be illustrated further by the functions and limbs of the human body. It looks as though the limbs and organs come first, and their functions, second. We look at the organs and limbs with our eyes and come to know them before we see and know their functions. Nevertheless, the limbs and organs come after their functions because they rise out of the functions and are consequently formed to meet those functions. In fact, the function itself shapes them and adapts them to itself. If

it did not, we could not possibly have a body in which absolutely everything aims so harmoniously at unity.

It is the same with goodness and truth. Truth appears to be first, but
goodness *is* first. Goodness forms truth and adapts truth to itself. Viewed
in itself, then, truth is nothing but goodness in a form, or a form embodying goodness. Truth also relates to goodness as the organs and fibers in
the body relate to function. Goodness viewed in itself is nothing but
usefulness.

[2] Other places in the Word also show that a breach symbolizes intruding on truth and distorting it by separating it from goodness. In David, for
instance:

> Our barns are full, supplying us from meal to meal. Our flocks number
> thousands, and ten thousand in our streets; our oxen are laden. *There is
> no breach.* (Psalms 144:13, 14)

This describes the ancient church as it was in its youth. The meals with
which the barns were full stand for spiritual food, or truth and goodness.
The flocks and oxen stand for inner and outer goodness. "There is no
breach" means that truth had not been infringed on or ruptured by being
separated from goodness. [3] In Amos:

> I will raise up David's fallen tent, and *wall up their breaches,* and its
> wreckage I will restore; I will rebuild it as in the days of old. (Amos 9:11)

The subject here is a religion engaged in goodness. David's fallen tent
means goodness that embodies love and charity, received from the Lord.
For the meaning of a tent as this kind of goodness, see §§414, 1102, 2145,
2152, 3312, 4128, 4391, 4599; and for the meaning of David as the Lord, see
§1888. Walling up the breaches stands for correcting falsities introduced
through the separation of truth from goodness. Rebuilding as in the days
of old means as in the church's state in ancient times. The Word refers to
that state and those times as the days of old and of generation after generation. [4] In Isaiah:

> He rebuilds from you the age-old wastelands, the foundations of gen-
> eration after generation, and let the name given to you be "*the one who
> repairs the breach,*" "the one who brings back the paths to dwell by."
> (Isaiah 58:12)

This is about a religion that considers neighborly love and the way we live
to be essential. Repairing the breach again stands for correcting falsities

that have crept in through the separation of goodness from truth, which is the source of all falsity. Bringing back the paths to dwell by stands for bringing back truth characterized by goodness. Paths, or ways, mean truth (§§627, 2333), and dwelling is spoken of in relation to what is good (§§2268, 2451, 2712, 3613). [5] In the same author:

> You have seen the *breaches in David's city,* that there are *many,* and you collected the water of the lower pool. (Isaiah 22:9)

The breaches in David's city stand for false doctrines. The water of the lower pool stands for traditions through which [the scribes and Pharisees] intruded on the truth in the Word (Matthew 15:1–6; Mark 7:1–14). In Ezekiel:

> *You have not gone up into the breaches* or built a wall for the house of Israel in order to stand fast in war on the day of Jehovah. (Ezekiel 13:5)

In the same author:

> I sought from them a man walling up a wall and *standing in the breach* before me for the sake of the land, to prevent me from destroying it— but did not find one. (Ezekiel 22:30)

Standing in the breach stands for defending and standing guard to prevent falsity from breaking in. In David:

> Jehovah said he would destroy the people unless Moses, his chosen, *stood in the breach before* him. (Psalms 106:23)

Standing in the breach stands once again for preventing falsity from breaking in. Moses is the Word (preface to Genesis 18 and §4859 at the end). [6] In Amos:

> They will haul your posterity out with fishing hooks. Through the *breaches you will go out,* each straight in front of you, and cast down the palace. (Amos 4:2, 3)

Going out through the breaches stands for going out through falsities produced by skewed logic. The palace means the Word and therefore doctrinal truth rising out of goodness.

Since breaches symbolize falsity that results when goodness is detached from truth, shoring up and repairing breaches in the house of Jehovah also has the same symbolism on a representative level in 2 Kings 12:5, 7, 8, 12; 22:5.

In 2 Samuel:

> David grieved that Jehovah had *caused a rupture* in Uzzah. So he called that place *Perez*-uzzah. (2 Samuel 6:8)

This is about Uzzah, who died because he touched the ark. The ark represented heaven and in the highest sense the Lord and therefore divine goodness. Uzzah represented something assistant and therefore truth, since truth assists goodness. Their separation is symbolized by the rupture, [or breach,] in Uzzah.

And called his name Perez symbolizes its nature—the nature of truth's apparent separation from goodness. This is established by the symbolism of *calling a name* as the quality of something (discussed in §§144, 145, 1754, 1896, 2009, 2724, 3006, 3421). *Perez* is the nature itself, because in the original language, Perez means a breach.   **4927**

And afterward his brother came out means that goodness actually comes first. This can be seen from the representation of Zerah, the *brother,* as goodness. After all, he was the one who opened the womb, so he was the firstborn and the one with the double-dyed [scarlet thread] on his hand. For this meaning goodness, see §4925.   **4928**

The reason *afterward his brother came out* means that goodness is actually first is that goodness does not appear while we are being reborn. It hides in our inner self and merely flows into truth in the form of a desire, depending on how closely truth unites with it. Once truth unites with goodness, which happens when we have been reborn, goodness shows itself. We then act on the basis of goodness and regard truth from the standpoint of goodness, since we are now more interested in life than in theology.

On whose hand was the double-dyed [scarlet thread] symbolizes an acknowledgment that goodness does come first. This can be seen from the fact that Zerah was now recognized by the *double-dyed [scarlet thread] on his hand;* it was acknowledged that goodness was what had opened the womb, or that goodness was the firstborn.   **4929**

The midwife's tying double-dyed [scarlet thread] on the baby's hand means that she marked which was the firstborn, so acknowledgment is what is symbolized here.

And they called his name Zerah symbolizes its nature. This can be seen from the symbolism of *calling a name* as the quality of something (as above at §4927).   **4930**

The nature symbolized by Zerah is the nature of the subject the text has dealt with so far in its inner meaning—specifically, the idea that goodness is actually the firstborn, and truth apparently so. The quality itself has count-less facets, facets that cannot be seen in the world's light but in heaven's and therefore only by angels. If you could see the quality of only one aspect, as it appears to angels, you would be dumbfounded and confess that you never would have believed it, that what you know is almost nothing by comparison.

In the original language, Zerah means a rising and applies to the sun and the first appearance of its light. Zerah was named for the sun-rise because goodness resembles dawn in a person who is being reborn. [That is when] goodness first rises and sheds light, which illuminates [truth] in the person's earthly self, so that it can be seen, acknowledged, and eventually believed. If this light did not shine from goodness inside us, we could never see truth to the point of acknowledging and believ-ing it. Instead, we would see it either as mere talk to appease common-ers or as falsity.

Correspondence with the Universal Human (Continued): Correspondence of the Hands, Arms, Feet, and Lower Torso

4931 IT has already been shown that the whole of heaven resembles a single human being, with all a human's organs, limbs, and viscera, and it resembles a human because it reflects the Lord. The Lord is the all-in-all of heaven—so much so that in its proper sense "heaven" means divine goodness and divine truth from the Lord. As a result, heaven is divided into as many regions, so to speak, as there are viscera, organs, and limbs in a human; and the regions correspond to them. If the human being did not correspond with heaven in this way and through heaven with the Lord, we would not survive a single moment.

The interconnection among all these parts is maintained through spir-itual inflow.

[2] All the regions are grouped into two kingdoms, a heavenly one and a spiritual one. The heavenly kingdom is the kingdom of the heart in the

universal human, and the spiritual kingdom is the kingdom of the lungs. In the human being likewise the heart and the lungs rule all the parts.

The two kingdoms are united in a miraculous manner. What is more, the bond between them is represented in the union of heart and lungs in the human being, and in the joint activity of both throughout the limbs and organs.

[3] When we are embryos, still in the womb, we are under the dominion of the heart, but when we struggle out of the womb, we immediately enter the kingdom of the lungs. If we allow ourselves to be led by faith's truth to love's goodness, we return from the kingdom of the lungs into that of the heart in the universal human, since by doing so we go back into the womb and are reborn. Then the two kingdoms unite in us, but only by switching places. At first the heart's kingdom is under the command of the lungs in us; that is, at first religious truth dominates in us, but afterward, charitable goodness does.

To see that the heart corresponds with a loving goodness, and lungs with faith's truth, see §§3635, 3883–3896.

[Spirits and angels] in the universal human who correspond to the hands, arms, and shoulders are the ones with power, which they receive through religious truth that springs from goodness. People devoted to this kind of truth have the Lord's power, because they attribute all power to him and none to themselves. The more they disclaim any personal power, not just with their mouth but in their heart, the greater the power they have. That is why angels are called powers and authorities [Romans 8:38; Ephesians 3:10; 1 Peter 3:22].   **4932**

Hands, arms, and shoulders correspond to power in the universal human because the strengths and powers of the whole body and all its organs relate to them. It is through the arms and hands that the body exerts its strength and power.   **4933**

That is why hands, arms, and shoulders in the Word symbolize power. To see that hands do, consult §§878, 3387. The fact that arms do can be seen from many places, such as the following:

Be an *arm* every morning. (Isaiah 33:2)

The Lord Jehovih comes in might, and *his arm* will rule for him. (Isaiah 40:10)

They work it with *their strong arm.* (Isaiah 44:12)

My arms will judge peoples. (Isaiah 51:5)

Put on strength, *arm of Jehovah!* (Isaiah 51:9)

I looked around, and no one was helping; therefore *my arm* achieved salvation for me. (Isaiah 63:5)

A curse on those who trust in humankind and use flesh as *their arm.* (Jeremiah 17:5)

I made the earth, the human, and the animal by my great power and by *my outstretched arm.* (Jeremiah 27:5; 32:17)

The horn of Moab has been cut off and his *arm* broken. (Jeremiah 48:25)

I am breaking the *arms* of Egypt's monarch; on the other hand I will strengthen the *arms* of Babylon's monarch. (Ezekiel 30:22, 24, 25)

Jehovah, break the *arm* of the scoundrel. (Psalms 10:15)

According to the greatness of *your arm,* let the children of death survive. (Psalms 79:11)

They were led out of Egypt by a mighty *hand* and an *outstretched arm.* (Deuteronomy 7:19; 11:2, 3; 26:8; Jeremiah 32:21; Psalms 136:12)

From this it can also be seen that a *right hand* in the Word symbolizes a higher form of power, and that sitting on *Jehovah's right* symbolizes omnipotence (Matthew 26:63, 64; Luke 22:69; Mark 14:61, 62; 16:19).

4934 I saw a bare arm, flexed forward, so powerful and terrifying that I not only shuddered but felt as though it could pulverize my innermost parts. It was unstoppable. I have seen the arm twice and in the process was allowed to learn that arms symbolize strength and hands symbolize power. I also felt heat radiating from the arm.

4935 This bare arm is presented to view in various positions, each of which inspires a different kind of dread. In the position I just described, it generates incredible fear, because it looks able to shatter bone and marrow instantly. Even people who were not timid during bodily life are reduced to abject terror by the arm.

4936 Several times I saw people with staffs and was told they were sorcerers. They are situated a long way out in front and to the right, deep in caves. The more dangerous their magic had been, the deeper they are hidden away. They see themselves with staffs and fantasize new kinds of staffs for themselves, which they believe they can use for performing miracles. They imagine there is power in the actual staffs, because staffs support one's hand and arm, or (by correspondence) one's strength and power.

From this I could see why the ancients described sorcerers as having staffs. Ancient people outside the church inherited this symbol from the ancient, representative church, in which staffs, like hands, symbolized power; see §4876. Because they symbolized power, Moses was commanded to stretch out either his staff or his hand when miracles were to be done (Exodus 4:17, 20; 8:5–15, 16–20; 9:23; 10:3–21; 14:21, 26, 27; 17:5, 6, 11, 12; Numbers 20:7–10).

Hellish spirits too sometimes create the illusion of a shoulder and use it for repelling [hostile] forces, which are actually unable to pass by it. However, this works only for spirits subject to the illusion, who know that a shoulder in the spiritual world corresponds to omnipotence. A shoulder also symbolizes omnipotence in the Word, as the following places show: 4937

> You shattered the yoke of their burden and the *rod on their shoulder.* (Isaiah 9:4)

> With side and *shoulder* you push, and with your horns you strike. (Ezekiel 34:21)

> You will split *every shoulder* of theirs. (Ezekiel 29:6, 7)

> . . . so that they may serve Jehovah with a *single shoulder.* (Zephaniah 3:9)

> A child has been born for us, and sovereignty will be on *his shoulder.* (Isaiah 9:6)

> I will put the key of David's house on *his shoulder.* (Isaiah 22:22)

[Spirits and angels] in the universal human who correspond to the feet, soles, and heels are those with an earthly character. Consequently feet in the Word symbolize the earthly dimension (§§2162, 3147, 3761, 3986, 4280); the soles symbolize the lower reaches of the earthly level; and the heels, the lowest of all. 4938

What is heavenly in the universal human makes up its head, what is spiritual makes up its body, and what is earthly makes up its feet. The three also progress in that order. In addition, heavenly qualities, which are the highest, rest on spiritual ones, which are in the middle, and spiritual qualities rest on earthly ones, which come last.

Once when I went up into heaven, it looked to me as though my head was there and my body was beneath it but my feet were still lower. The experience gave me a conception of how the higher and lower parts 4939 of a human being correspond to those of the universal human and how one flows into the other. The heavenly element, which is a loving goodness and comes first in order, acts on the spiritual element, which is truth resulting from that goodness, and which comes second. Last it acts on the earthly element, which comes third. This clarifies the idea that the earthly realm is like feet supporting the higher realms.

The material world is what everything in the spiritual world and in heaven rests on. That is why the whole material world is a theater representing the Lord's kingdom and why every object in it has a representation (§§2758, 3483). It is also why a spiritual inflow preserving the sequence of levels keeps the physical world in existence, and why the world could not survive even a moment without it.

4940   When I was surrounded with a pillar of angels a second time and sent down to some areas underground, I was allowed to sense in a palpable way that the inhabitants of the underground region corresponded to the soles of the feet. Those areas are in fact located under the soles of the feet. I actually talked with the inhabitants there. They are the kind whose pleasures were earthly rather than spiritual.

Concerning the underground realm, see §4728.

4941   The same regions also contain spirits who had ascribed everything to nature and little to the Divine. I talked to them there, and when we conversed about divine providence, they ascribed everything to nature. Still, when they have been held there for a while, the ones who had lived a good, moral life gradually throw off such principles and adopt true ones.

4942   While I was there, I heard it hinted in one room that there were some spirits on the other side of the wall who wanted to break in. The spirits in the room were terrified of them, believing they were robbers. I was told that this fear was fostered in the spirits there in order to make them wary of evil, because fear is corrective for some people.

4943   In the underground region, under the soles of the feet, there are also spirits who had taken credit for their good deeds and acts. Many of them appear to themselves to be cutting wood. The place they occupy is rather cold, and they feel that their hard work warms them up. I actually spoke with them and was given the opportunity to ask whether they did not want to leave that place. They said they had not worked hard enough yet to deserve it. When they finish that stage, though, they are released.

These spirits have an earthly orientation, because the desire to earn salvation is not spiritual. Furthermore, they consider themselves better than others, and some of them even despise others. If they do not receive more joy in the next life than anyone else, they feel angry at the Lord. As a result, it sometimes looks as though something of the Lord lies under the wood as they cut it up. This is due to their resentment.

However, since they lived a godly life, and since they behaved as they did out of ignorance that had a measure of innocence in it, angels are sent to them from time to time to console them. Occasionally something resembling a sheep appears to them, too, coming down from above on their left, and when they see it they likewise take comfort.

Some who come from the Christian part of the world had lived a good, moral life and treated their neighbor somewhat charitably but took little interest in spiritual matters. Most of them are sent to the realm under the soles of the feet. They are kept there until they strip themselves of the earthly values they had adopted and take on spiritual and heavenly qualities so far as they can, depending on how they had lived. After they have taken these on, they are lifted up from there to heavenly communities. At times I have seen them as they emerge and observed how happy it makes them to come into heavenly light.   **4944**

How the places under the feet are situated in relation to each other I have not yet learned. There is a large number of them, and they are very different from each other. Taken together they are called the underground realm.   **4945**

There are those who had absorbed the idea in their bodily life that we should not bother with the concerns of our inner self or therefore with spiritual matters but only with the concerns of our outer self, or earthly matters. Their reason was that deeper matters disturb the pleasures of their life and make them unpleasant.   **4946**

They acted on my left knee and a little above my knee in front, and also on the sole of my right foot.

I talked with them where they lived. They said they had thought during physical life that only what existed outwardly was alive. They did not understand what inner depths were. They knew about earthly phenomena, then, but not what the spiritual dimension was. "By thinking that way, you have shut off countless influences from the spiritual world that could have affected you if you had acknowledged an inner realm and let it into your thoughts," I was allowed to tell them.

"Every idea that goes into your thinking has myriads of components," I continued. "To a human being—especially one whose mind remains on the earthly level—they appear only as a single, uncomplicated unit, but in reality there are unlimited elements flowing in from the spiritual world. In a spiritual person, they create a higher insight that enables the person to see and perceive whether a thing is true or untrue."

They were dubious about this and were therefore given a demonstration by direct experience. A single idea was represented to them, and they saw it as an uncomplicated whole and accordingly as a vague dot. (It is easy to create a representation like this in heaven's light.) When the idea was unfolded, and their inner eyes opened, it was as though a universal path to the Lord lay exposed to view. I said that it is the same with every idea of goodness and truth; each is an image of all heaven, because it comes from the Lord, who is the totality of heaven, or the very entity that is called heaven.

4947   Under the soles of the feet are also found those who had lived a life of worldly indulgence during their time in the body, enjoying what the world has to offer. They loved living sumptuously, but only at the urge of a craving that was superficial, an appetite belonging to the body, not at the urge of a craving deep within, an appetite belonging to the mind. They were not conceited and did not consider themselves better than others, even though they were of high rank on the social scale. In living as they did, they acted on mere physical impulse. As a consequence, they had not rejected what the church teaches, let alone proved to themselves that it was untrue. In their hearts they accepted the doctrines, saying, "People who study the Word see it this way."

In some people like this, the inner depths are open toward heaven and are gradually sown with heavenly qualities, such as fair-mindedness, integrity, religious devotion, neighborly love, and mercy. Afterward they are taken up into heaven.

4948   People who centered all their inner thoughts and energies during physical life on self-centered and materialistic goals have shut themselves off from any path to heaven or any inflow from there. Love for oneself and one's worldly advantages opposes heavenly love.

Of these people, the ones who lived a life of sensual pleasure, or of luxury united with profound deceit, are located under the sole of the right foot. They are way down deep there and are consequently below the underground realm, where the hell of such beings exists. Their houses contain nothing but garbage, which they seem to themselves to be carrying, since garbage corresponds to such a life. The air there stinks of different kinds of filth, depending on the general and particular type of life they lived.

Many of the world's most famous people spend their existence there.

The number of people who make their home under the soles of the **4949**
feet is rather large, and I have sometimes spoken with them. I once saw
some of them trying to work their way up from there and was allowed to
feel the effort of their climb, all the way up to the level of the knees; but
then they fell back down. That is how it is represented to the senses when
spirits want to leave their own homes for something higher up, just as
these wanted to reach the dwellings of spirits in the area of the knees and
thighs. I was told they are the types who look on others with contempt,
which is why they want to burst out, not only up through the lower leg to
the thigh but even over the head if possible. They always fall back down
again, though.

They possess a certain kind of stupidity, because arrogance like this
extinguishes and smothers the light of heaven. So it snuffs out all understanding. The aura that surrounds them consequently looks like thick
sediment.

Under the left foot and a little farther left are the types who attrib- **4950**
uted everything to nature but admitted there was an entity in the universe that was the source of everything in nature. I probed to see whether
they believed in any universal entity or supreme deity that had created
everything, but when they shared their thinking with me, I perceived that
what they believed in was an inanimate something-or-other devoid of
life. From this I could see that they did not acknowledge a creator of the
universe but nature. They also said they could not form any notion of a
living deity.

There is a hell deep under the heel and slightly farther back, and **4951**
the intervening space looks empty. In this hell are the most malevolent
spirits. They secretly probe others' minds for a means of hurting them,
and secretly plot to destroy them. That had been the highest pleasure of
their life. I have often observed them. They spew their poisonous malice
at spirits in the world of spirits and use various ploys to stir up trouble
among them. Their malevolence is profound. In their hell they appear
to be dressed in cloaks and sometimes in other clothes. Often they are
punished and then sink deeper, where they are blanketed in a kind of
fog, which is the cloud of malice wafting off them. Sometimes an almost
murderous uproar is heard rising from that great depth.

These spirits can bring others to tears and can also strike fear into
them. It is a trick they learned during their life in the body by consort-
ing with the uneducated and the unwell in order to get money from
them. They would reduce these people to tears in order to stir their

pity. If they could not get what they wanted this way, they would intimidate them.

Most of them are the kind that had used this method to plunder numerous households for the benefit of their monasteries.

I have also observed some spirits at a medium distance, but they appear to themselves to be sitting in a kind of room, consulting. They are malicious as well, but not to the same degree.

4952   Some of those who attribute everything to nature said they did not know what they were to believe. The reason they did not know is that the life we live and the thoughts we think on the basis of premises we have confirmed determines what kind of lot awaits each of us.

"It is enough for you to believe that God is the one who governs everything, and that there is a life after death," I responded, "and especially to live like a human rather than a beast. That means living a life of love for the Lord and charity for your neighbor, which is to say a life of truth and goodness rather than one opposing truth and goodness."

"That *is* how we lived," they retorted.

"You looked as though you did, on the outside," I said. "But if the law hadn't stood in the way, you would have been more savage than wild animals in attacking the life and wealth of anyone you could."

"We don't know what charity for our neighbor means, or what the inner realm is," they said.

"You *couldn't* know," I answered, "because self-love and materialism and superficial concerns monopolized all your thinking and all your intentions."

4953   There will be more on this at the end of the next chapter [§§5050–5062].

Genesis 39

[Matthew 25:34–36]

THE Lord's description in Matthew 25:31, 32, 33 of a judgment on the **4954** good and the evil was explained in the material at the head of the previous chapter; see §§4807–4810. Now comes an explanation of the words that follow next in that passage:

> Then the King will say to those on his right, "Come, you who are blessed by my Father! Take possession of the kingdom prepared for you from the foundation of the world. For I was hungry and you gave me something to eat. I was thirsty and you gave me a drink. I was a foreigner and you gathered me in; naked and you put a robe around me. I was sick and you visited me. I was in jail and you came to me." (Matthew 25:34, 35, 36)

What these words embrace in their inner meaning will become clear **4955** below. First the reader needs to know that the actions listed here are the essence of neighborly love, laid out in order. This cannot be seen by anyone who does not know the Word's inner meaning—that is, anyone who is unaware what it means to give the hungry something to eat, give a drink to the thirsty, gather in foreigners, dress the naked, visit the sick, and come to those in jail. People who think about it only in literal terms gather that the passage refers to superficially good deeds and that it holds no additional, secret meaning. In reality, though, every word holds a secret, and a divine secret at that, since it comes from the Lord.

People do not understand the secret these days, however, because there are no modern doctrines teaching neighborly love. After people detached charity from faith, such teachings died out. Doctrines concerning faith were accepted and invented to replace them, and these do not teach in any way what neighborly love is or what one's neighbor is.

[2] The doctrines of the ancients taught all the major and minor types of neighborly love and identified the neighbor toward whom that love was to be exercised. They showed how one person is a neighbor on a different

level and in a different respect than another person, so they showed how to exercise charity differently in one case than in another. They also divided the neighbor into categories, to which they gave names, calling some the poor, needy, wretched, and afflicted, some the blind, lame, and maimed, some orphans and widows, some the hungry, thirsty, foreign, naked, sick, and imprisoned, and so on. From this they knew what their duty was toward this one, that one, and the other.

As noted, though, these doctrines died out, and with them, an understanding of the Word. It all died out so completely that everyone today thinks the poor, widowed, and orphaned in the Word mean just that. Everyone thinks this as well in regard to the hungry, thirsty, foreign, naked, sick, and imprisoned. Yet these categories actually serve to show what charity is like in its essence and what the exercise of charity needs to be like in its practice.

4956   The essence of charity for our neighbor is a desire for what is good and true and the acknowledgment that we ourselves consist of evil and falsity. In fact, our real neighbor is goodness and truth itself. To be moved by these is to possess charity. Evil and falsity are opposed to our neighbor, and people with charity turn their back on them. If we have charity for our neighbor, then, we are drawn to goodness and truth, because they come from the Lord, and we reject evil and falsity because they come from ourselves. When we do so, we feel humble because we acknowledge what we are really like, and when we feel humble, we are in a state that is receptive to goodness and truth from the Lord.

These are the facts about charity that are involved in the inner meaning of the Lord's statement here: "I was hungry and you gave me something to eat, I was thirsty and you gave me a drink, I was a foreigner and you gathered me in, naked and you put a robe around me, I was sick and you visited me, I was in jail and you came to me."

[2] No one can see that this is what the words involve except from the inner meaning. The ancients with their doctrines about charity knew it, but today it seems so far-fetched that people will be surprised to hear that such concepts are present there. It is exactly how the angels who are with us understand those words, though. They take the hungry to be people who long for goodness with genuine desire. They take the thirsty to be people who long for truth with genuine desire. They take foreigners to be people who want to be taught, the naked to be people who acknowledge they have nothing good or true in them, the sick to be people who acknowledge they have nothing but evil in them, and prisoners,

or people in jail, to be those who acknowledge they have nothing but
falsity in them.

If all of this is condensed into a single meaning, the passage has the
symbolism given just above.

These remarks show that there was something divine in everything
the Lord said, even if it looks otherwise to people completely absorbed by
worldly and especially by bodily concerns. To them it appears as though
anyone could have said the kind of things he said. In fact, people engrossed
in what is bodily are bound to say there is less grace and therefore less
weight in this or any other saying of the Lord's than in the oratory and
sermons of speakers in the present age, with their learned, eloquent style.
In truth, though, the speeches and sermons of these people are like mere
chaff and stubble compared to the kernel inside it.

Being *hungry* means longing for goodness with genuine desire because
in an inner sense bread means good done out of love and charity, and
food in general means what is good (§§2165, 2177, 3478, 4211, 4217, 4735).
Being *thirsty* means longing for truth with genuine desire because wine
and water mean the truth that leads to faith (wine, §§1071, 1798; water,
§2702). For a *foreigner* meaning someone who wants to be taught, see
§§1463, 4444. The meaning of the *naked* as those who acknowledge they
have nothing good or true in them, of the *sick* as those focused on evil,
and of *prisoners* or *those in jail* as people focused on falsity can be seen
from numerous Scripture passages mentioning them.

The reason the Lord describes himself as suffering in these ways is
that he is present in people as they go through such things. That is
also why he says, "Truly, I say to you: so far as you did it for one of
these least consequential brothers and sisters of mine, you did it for me"
(verses 40, 45).

Genesis 39

1. And Joseph was taken down to Egypt, and Potiphar, Pharaoh's chamberlain, the chief of the bodyguards, an Egyptian man, bought him from
the hand of the Ishmaelites who had taken him down there.

2. And Jehovah was with Joseph, and he was a prosperous man, and he was in the household of his master, the Egyptian.

3. And his master saw that Jehovah was with him, and everything that he was doing Jehovah was making prosperous in his hand.

4. And Joseph found favor in his eyes and waited on him, and he set him in charge over his household, and whatever was his he gave into [Joseph's] hand.

5. And it happened from the time he set him in charge in his household and over everything that was his that Jehovah blessed the household of the Egyptian on account of Joseph. And Jehovah's blessing was on everything that was his in the house and in the field.

6. And he left everything that was his in Joseph's hand and had no knowledge of anything with him except the bread that he was eating. And Joseph was beautiful in form and beautiful in appearance.

7. And it happened after these words that the wife of his master lifted her eyes to Joseph and said, "Lie with me!"

8. And he refused and said to the wife of his master, "Look, my master doesn't know what is in the household with me, and everything that is his he has given into my hand.

9. He is not greater in this household than I and has not held anything back from me except yourself, in that you are his wife. And how can I do this great evil, and sin against God?"

10. And it happened as she spoke to Joseph day by day that he did not listen to her, to lie with her, to be with her.

11. And it happened that on a certain day he came to the house to do his work, and no man of the men of the household was there in the house.

12. And she grabbed him by his garment, saying, "Lie with me!" And he left his garment in her hand and fled and went outside.

13. And it happened, as she saw that he had left his garment in her hand and fled outside,

14. that she shouted out to the men of her household and said to them, saying, "See? He has brought us a Hebrew man to mock us. He came to me to lie with me, and I shouted in a loud voice.

15. And it happened as he heard it, because I raised my voice and shouted, that he left his garment with me and fled and went outside."

16. And she set his garment aside with her until his master's coming to his house.

17. And she spoke to him according to these words, saying, "There came to me the Hebrew slave whom you brought to us to mock me.

18. And it happened, as I raised my voice and shouted, that he left his garment with me and fled outside."

19. And it happened, as his master heard the words of his wife which she spoke to him, saying, "According to these words your slave did to me," that his anger burned.

20. And Joseph's master took him and put him into the prison house, the place where the monarch's prisoners were imprisoned, and he was there in the prison house.

21. And Jehovah was with Joseph and extended mercy to him and gave him favor in the eyes of the prison house chief.

22. And the prison house chief gave into Joseph's hand all the prisoners who were in the prison house; and everything that they were doing there, he was the doer.

23. The prison house chief was not looking at anything whatever in [Joseph's] hand, for the reason that Jehovah was with [Joseph], and what he was doing, Jehovah was making prosperous.

Summary

THE inner meaning here deals with the Lord and the way he made his inner self divine. Jacob was his outer self, the preceding topic of discussion. Joseph is his inner self, the topic here and in what follows. **4960**

Because this was accomplished according to the divine plan, the chapter depicts that plan. It also depicts spiritual crisis, which is the means of union. **4961**

Inner Meaning

GENESIS 39:1. *And Joseph was taken down to Egypt, and Potiphar, Pharaoh's chamberlain, the chief of the bodyguards, an Egyptian man, bought him from the hand of the Ishmaelites who had taken him down there.* **4962**

And Joseph symbolizes spiritual heavenliness drawing on rationality. *Was taken down to Egypt* means to religious learning. *And Potiphar, Pharaoh's chamberlain, bought him* means that it had a place among items of inner knowledge. *The chief of the bodyguards* means that were of primary importance in interpretation. *An Egyptian man* symbolizes earthly truth. *From the hand of the Ishmaelites* means from simple goodness. *Who had taken him down there* means from this goodness to that knowledge.

4963   *And Joseph* symbolizes spiritual heavenliness drawing on rationality. This can be seen from the discussion in §4286 of the representation of *Joseph* as a heavenly-spiritual person who draws on rationality. Since the current text is talking about the Lord, then, Joseph represents the Lord's inner self.

Every person born has an outer and an inner self. Our outer self is the one visible to the eye, the one that enables us to interact with other people and to carry out the business of the earthly world. Our inner self is the one not visible to the eye, the one that enables us to interact with spirits and angels and to carry out the business of the spiritual world. We each have an inner and an outer plane—an inner and an outer self—so that heaven can unite with the world through us. Heaven flows into our outer self through our inner, which allows heaven to perceive what is in the world, and which allows our outer self in the world to perceive what is in heaven. That is how we were created to be.

[2] The Lord's human side also had an outer and an inner part, because he chose to be born like any other person. Jacob, later Israel, represented the Lord's outer part, or outer self, but Joseph represents his inner self. This inner self is what is being called the heavenly-spiritual self drawing on the rational side. In other words, the Lord's inner level, which was human, is being called spiritual heavenliness drawing on rationality. The inner meaning of this chapter and the remaining ones that tell about Joseph deal with this level and its glorification.

Earlier, at §§4286, 4585, 4592, 4594, I explained what spiritual heavenliness drawing on rationality is—that it is higher than the spiritual heavenliness drawing on earthliness represented by Israel.

[3] The Lord really was born like any other person. However, it is recognized that when human beings are born, we inherit something from our father and something from our mother—our inmost core from our father, and the outer levels that envelop this core from our mother. Both our father's gift and our mother's are tainted with inherited evil, but it was different for the Lord. What he received from his mother contained a heredity like anyone else's, but what he received from his Father, who was Jehovah, was divine. As a result, his inner self was not like that of any

other person, because his inmost core was Jehovah. This part in between is what is being called spiritual heavenliness drawing on rationality.

More will be said on the subject in what follows, though, by the Lord's divine mercy [§4971].

Was taken down to Egypt means to religious learning. This is estab-   **4964** lished by the symbolism of *Egypt* as knowledge, or learning in general (discussed at §§1164, 1165, 1186, 1462). However, I have not yet explained what kind of knowledge it is that Egypt properly symbolizes.

The ancient church had doctrines on one hand and knowledge they had acquired on the other. Their doctrines had to do with love for the Lord and charity for their neighbor. Their knowledge had to do with the correspondence between the physical and spiritual worlds and with the representation of spiritual and heavenly attributes in physical and earthly objects. These were things known to the people of the ancient church.

[2] Egypt was among the regions and countries where the ancient church existed (§§1238, 2385), but because the people there mostly handed down items of knowledge, Egypt symbolizes knowledge in general. That is also why the prophetic parts of the Word so often speak of Egypt. When they do, this is the kind of knowledge specifically meant by it. Indeed such knowledge provided the origin of Egyptian magic. Egyptians knew what the objects of the physical world corresponded to in the spiritual world, and after the ancient church had died out among them, they misused the knowledge for magic.

This was the knowledge they possessed, then—information teaching about correspondence and about representation and symbolism. Such knowledge supported the doctrinal teachings of their religion, particularly in helping them understand what their Word said. (The Word of the ancient church had prophetic and narrative parts, which were similar to our Word; see §2686.) As a consequence, *he was taken down to Egypt* means to religious learning.

[3] Since Joseph represents the Lord, and the text says that Joseph was taken down to Egypt, the meaning is that when the Lord was glorifying his inner self, or making it divine, he was first trained in religious learning. From items of knowledge and through them he progressed deeper and deeper until he reached divine knowledge. This he did because it pleased him to follow the same pattern in glorifying himself, or making himself divine, as he follows in regenerating us, or making us spiritual (§§3138, 3212, 3296, 3490, 4402). The pattern proceeds step by step from the outer level, which consists in knowledge and religious truth, to the

inner depths, which have to do with charity for one's neighbor and love for the Lord.

This shows what the following words in Hosea symbolize:

> When Israel was a boy, then I loved him, and *out of Egypt I called my child.* (Hosea 11:1)

For confirmation that this is about the Lord, see Matthew 2:15.

4965 *And Potiphar, Pharaoh's chamberlain, bought him* means that [spiritual heavenliness] had a place among items of inner knowledge. This can be seen from the discussion in §4789 of the symbolism of *Pharaoh's chamberlain* as inner knowledge. *Buying* means that [the Lord] claimed it as his own (§§4397, 4487).

Items of inner knowledge are those that come comparatively close to being spiritual, and they consist in the application of knowledge to heavenly subjects. This is the kind of knowledge the inner self sees, when the outer self sees only its outward form.

4966 *The chief of the bodyguards* means that were of primary importance in interpretation. This can be seen from the discussion in §4790 of the symbolism of a *chief of the bodyguards* as something of primary importance in interpretation. What is of primary importance in interpretation is whatever helps the most in interpreting the Word and therefore in understanding doctrines from the Word concerning love for the Lord and charity for our neighbor.

It is important to realize that the knowledge of the ancients was completely different from today's. As was said above [§4964], what the ancients knew focused on the correspondence of objects in the physical world with qualities in the spiritual world. The people of old were entirely unacquainted with the knowledge that is now called philosophy, such as Aristotelian science and so on. You can even tell this from the books of the ancients, most of which were written using images that symbolized and represented the inner realm and corresponded to it. From many possible examples, take just these:

[2] They set Helicon on a mountain, and by it they meant heaven. They set Parnassus on a hill below Helicon, and by it they meant knowledge. They said that a flying horse, which they called Pegasus, used its hoof to strike a spring open there. They referred to the arts and sciences as maidens, and so on. From correspondences and representations they knew that a mountain was heaven; a hill was heaven as it exists lower down,

among people on earth; a horse was the intellect; the wings it flew with were spiritual qualities; a hoof was something earthly; a spring was the ability to understand; the three young women called the Graces were desires for goodness; and the young women named for Helicon and Parnassus were desires for truth.

Likewise they said that the sun had horses, whose food they referred to as ambrosia, and whose drink they referred to as nectar. They knew that the sun symbolized heavenly love, horses symbolized contents of the intellect springing from that love, food symbolized what is heavenly, and drink symbolized what is spiritual.

[3] From the ancients we inherit the tradition that when monarchs are being crowned they must sit on a silver throne and be wrapped in a crimson robe and anointed with oil; they must carry a crown on their head and a scepter, sword, and keys in their hands; they must ride in royal splendor on a white horse shod with silver and afterward be waited on at table by the nobles of the kingdom; besides much else. The ancients knew that a monarch represented divine truth stemming from divine goodness, from which they knew what was meant by a silver throne, crimson robe, anointing oil, crown, scepter, sword, keys, white horse, silver horseshoes, and being waited on by nobles. Who today knows any of these meanings, or where to find the knowledge that explains them? People call such things emblems, because they know nothing at all about correspondence and representation.

These remarks show what the ancients' learning was like. Clearly it led them to a knowledge of the spiritual and heavenly dimensions, though nowadays people hardly even know that those dimensions exist.

[4] The discipline that has replaced that of the ancients and that is properly called philosophy is more likely to draw the mind *away* from such knowledge. This is because it can also be used to prove falsity. Even when used to prove truth, modern methods cloud the mind, because for the most part they consist merely in empty terms used for reinforcement. Few understand the terms; and those few argue over them.

Such considerations show how far the human race has departed from the learning of the ancients, which led to wisdom.

People outside the church inherited this kind of learning from the ancient church, whose outward worship consisted in representations and symbols, and whose inward worship consisted in the qualities represented and symbolized.

This is the learning that Egypt symbolizes in a positive sense.

4967 *An Egyptian man* symbolizes earthly truth. This can be seen from the symbolism of a *man* as truth (discussed in §3134) and from that of *Egypt* as learning in general (discussed just above in §§4964, 4966). Since Egypt means learning, it also means the earthly level. Everything we know is earthly, because it belongs to our earthly self—even what we know about spiritual and heavenly things. This is because we see those things on the earthly level and from an earthly viewpoint. If we do not see something from an earthly standpoint, we do not grasp it.

However, the higher planes appear one way to a regenerate person, who is called spiritual, and another way to a person who is not regenerate but just plain earthly. In a regenerate person, knowledge is illuminated by heaven's light. In an unregenerate person it is illuminated not by heaven's light but by a light flowing in through spirits immersed in falsity and evil. This light does derive from heaven's light, but in such spirits it fades to an evening or nighttime dimness. Spirits like this and therefore people like this have the vision of an owl, sharp by night and dull by day. That is, they see falsity clearly and truth dimly, so they see what belongs to the world clearly and what belongs to heaven dimly if at all.

This discussion shows that genuine knowledge is earthly truth, since all genuine knowledge of the kind symbolized in a positive sense by Egypt is earthly truth.

4968 *From the hand of the Ishmaelites* means from simple goodness. This can be seen from the representation of the *Ishmaelites* as people with simple goodness (discussed at §§3263, 4747), and in this case, then, as earthly truth growing out of simple goodness.

Genesis 37:36 says that the *Midianites* sold Joseph into Egypt, to Potiphar, Pharaoh's chamberlain, the chief of the bodyguards. The current verse, though, says that Potiphar, Pharaoh's chamberlain, the chief of the bodyguards, bought him from the hand of the *Ishmaelites* who had taken him down there. The text speaks this way because of the inner meaning. Genesis 37 was about disowning divine truth, which is done not by people with simple goodness but by people with simple truth, who are represented by the Midianites; see §4788. The current chapter is about acquiring knowledge, or laying claim to it, and about earthly truth that grows out of simple goodness. The Ishmaelites are therefore said to be the ones selling it, because they represent people with simple goodness. Plainly, then, the text says what it does for the sake of the inner meaning.

Moreover, the story does not contradict itself. It says that the Midianites drew Joseph out of the pit and consequently that he was handed over by them to the Ishmaelites who took him down into Egypt. Because the Midianites turned him over to Ishmaelites headed for Egypt, then, they sold him into Egypt.

Who had taken him down there means from this goodness to that knowledge. This can be seen from the representation of the Ishmaelites *who had taken him down* as people with simple goodness (discussed just above in §4968) and from the symbolism of *there*, Egypt, as learning in general (discussed just above in §§4964, 4966).

4969

The text says *down* because it is talking about knowledge, which is external. The Word speaks of "going down" from inner levels to outer but of "going up" from outer levels to inner; see §§3084, 4539.

Genesis 39:2, 3, 4, 5, 6. *And Jehovah was with Joseph, and he was a prosperous man, and he was in the household of his master, the Egyptian. And his master saw that Jehovah was with him, and everything that he was doing Jehovah was making prosperous in his hand. And Joseph found favor in his eyes and waited on him, and he set him in charge over his household, and whatever was his he gave into [Joseph's] hand. And it happened from the time he set him in charge in his household and over everything that was his that Jehovah blessed the household of the Egyptian on account of Joseph. And Jehovah's blessing was on everything that was his in the house and in the field. And he left everything that was his in Joseph's hand and had no knowledge of anything with him except the bread that he was eating. And Joseph was beautiful in form and beautiful in appearance.*

4970

And Jehovah was with Joseph means that there was divinity within spiritual heavenliness. *And he was a prosperous man* means that everything was provided. *And he was in the household of his master, the Egyptian,* means for being introduced into earthly goodness. *And his master saw that Jehovah was with him* symbolizes a perception by earthly goodness that divinity lay within. *And everything that he was doing Jehovah was making prosperous in his hand* means that it all resulted from divine providence. *And Joseph found favor in his eyes* means that this was agreeable. *And waited on him* means that knowledge was adopted by the goodness associated with it. *And he set him in charge over his household* means that goodness adapted to it. *And whatever was his he gave into [Joseph's] hand* means that everything belonging to that kind of goodness was under its authority, so to speak. *And it happened from the time he set him in charge in his household and over everything that was his* symbolizes the second stage after goodness had adapted to it, and everything belonging to goodness had been put under its authority, so to speak. *That Jehovah blessed the household of the Egyptian on account of Joseph* means that it now received an earthly heavenliness from the Divine. *And Jehovah's blessing* symbolizes growth. *Was on everything that was his in the house and in the field* means in life and in theology. *And he left everything that was his in Joseph's hand* means that it seemed as though everything was under its authority. *And had no knowledge of anything with him except the bread that he was eating* means that goodness was therefore adopted. *And Joseph was beautiful in form* symbolizes the well-lived life that results. *And beautiful in appearance* symbolizes the religious truth that results.

4971   *And Jehovah was with Joseph* means that there was divinity within spiritual heavenliness. This is established by the representation of *Joseph* as spiritual heavenliness drawing on rationality (discussed above at §4963). Since the current subject is the Lord, and in this case the inner self of his human side, *Jehovah was with him* means that there was divinity within. Divinity lay within his humanity, because he was conceived by Jehovah.

In the case of angels, though, divinity is present *with* them, not *in* them, because they are merely forms that receive divinity from the Lord.

4972   *And he was a prosperous man* means that everything was provided. This can be seen from the symbolism of *prospering,* when applied to the Lord, as being provided. In other words, he was enriched with everything good.

4973   *And he was in the household of his master, the Egyptian,* means for being introduced into earthly goodness. This can be seen from the symbolism of a *master,* [or lord,] as goodness (discussed below) and from that of an *Egyptian* as learning in general and therefore the earthly plane (discussed in §4967). *Being in the household* means being introduced [into goodness] because a house means a mind containing goodness (§3538), and in this instance, the earthly mind. Besides, a house is mentioned in connection with goodness (§§3652, 3720).

Human beings have an earthly mind and a rational mind. Our earthly mind is in our outer self, and our rational mind is in our inner self. Items of knowledge are the earthly mind's truth, and they are said to be in their own household in the earthly mind when they unite with goodness there. Goodness and truth together constitute a single household, as a husband and wife do.

However, the goodness and truth being discussed here are deep, because they correspond to spiritual heavenliness drawing on rationality, as represented by Joseph. Deep, corresponding truth on the earthly level is truth put to use. Deep goodness on that level is useful activity itself.

[2] The Word uses the term *lord* all the time. People unaware of the inner sense assume it has the same meaning it does when people use it in everyday speech, but Scripture uses the term only when dealing with goodness. The same is true of the name *Jehovah.* Where Scripture deals with truth, on the other hand, it uses the words *God* and *king.* That is why the word *lord* symbolizes goodness. The following passages as well demonstrate this. In Moses:

> Jehovah your God is God of the gods and *Lord of the lords.* (Deuteronomy 10:17)

In David:

> Acclaim Jehovah; acclaim the God of the gods; acclaim the *Lord of the lords!* (Psalms 136:1, 2, 3)

Jehovah, or the Lord, is being called God of the gods for the divine truth that radiates from him, and he is being called Lord of the lords for the divine goodness that is in him. [3] Likewise in John:

> The Lamb will defeat them, because he is *Lord of Lords* and King of Kings. (Revelation 17:14)

And in the same author:

> The one sitting on the white horse has a name written on his garment and on his thigh: King of Kings and Lord of Lords. (Revelation 19:16)

Every detail shows that the Lord is being called King of Kings because of his divine truth, and Lord of Lords because of his divine goodness. The written name means his quality (§§144, 145, 1754, 1896, 2009, 2724, 3006). The garment on which it was written means religious truth (§§1073, 2576, 4545, 4763). The thigh on which the Lord's quality was also written means a loving goodness (§§3021, 4277, 4280, 4575). This too shows that the Lord is called King of Kings for his divine truth, and Lord of Lords for his divine goodness. On the point that the Lord is called a king because of his divine truth, see §§2015, 2069, 3009, 3670, 4581.

[4] These considerations also make clear what is meant by "the Lord's Christ" in Luke:

> Simeon received an answer from the Holy Spirit that he would not see death until he saw the *Lord's Christ.* (Luke 2:26)

The Lord's Christ means divine truth from divine goodness. The Christ is the same as the Messiah, and the Messiah is the anointed, or king (§§3008, 3009). In this verse, the Lord means Jehovah. The New Testament Word never mentions Jehovah but substitutes "the Lord" and "God"; see §2921. In Luke, for instance:

> Jesus said, "How can they say the Christ is the child of David, when David himself says in the Book of Psalms, 'The *Lord* said to *my Lord:* "Sit on my right"'"? (Luke 20:41, 42)

In David the statement appears this way:

> *Jehovah* said to *my Lord,* "Sit at my right." (Psalms 110:1)

Clearly David's Jehovah is being called the Lord by the Gospel writer. "The Lord" stands for the divine goodness of his divine humanity. Sitting on the right symbolizes omnipotence (§§3387, 4592, 4933 at the end).

[5] When the Lord was in the world, he was divine truth, but after he was glorified—after he made his human side divine—he became divine goodness, from which divine truth has radiated ever since. That is why the disciples did not call him Teacher after his resurrection as they had before, but Lord, as is plain in John 21:7, 12, 15, 16, 17, 20, and in the rest of the Gospels.

The divine truth that the Lord was when he was in the world and that has radiated from him (or from his divine goodness) ever since is also called "the Angel of the Covenant." The phrase is used by Malachi:

> Suddenly to his Temple will come the *Lord,* whom you are seeking, and the *Angel of the Covenant,* whom you desire. (Malachi 3:1)

[6] Because "the Lord" means divine goodness, and a king divine truth, lordly power refers to divine goodness and kingship to divine truth in passages that say the Lord has both. For the same reason, the Lord is called the Lord of the Nations and King of the Peoples, since nations symbolize those devoted to goodness, and peoples symbolize those devoted to truth (§§1259, 1260, 1849, 3581).

[7] Goodness is called a master in relation to a slave and is called a father in relation to a child, as in Malachi:

> Children will honor their father, and *slaves their master.* Because if I am father, where is my honor? If I am *master,* where is the fear of me? (Malachi 1:6)

And in David:

> As a *slave* was *Joseph* sold; Jehovah's speech tested him. The *king* sent
> and released him; the *ruler of the nations* freed him. He made him *mas-*
> *ter of his household* and *ruler* over all his possessions. (Psalms 105:17, 19,
> 20, 21)

Joseph means the Lord, as every word of the passage shows. "Master"
means the divine goodness of his divine humanity.

And his master saw that Jehovah was with him symbolizes a perception by earthly goodness that divinity lay within, as the following shows:
Seeing symbolizes understanding and perceiving, as discussed in §§2150,
3764, 4339, 4567, 4723. A *master* symbolizes goodness, as discussed just
above in §4973, and in this case earthly goodness, since an Egyptian is the
master. The presence of divinity within is symbolized by the clause *that*
Jehovah was with him, as above in §4971.

4974

And everything that he was doing Jehovah was making prosperous in
his hand means that it all resulted from divine providence. This is established by the symbolism of *prospering* as being provided (discussed above
at §4972), as a result of which *Jehovah was making prosperous in his hand*
means divine providence.

4975

[2] *And Joseph found favor in his eyes* means that this was agreeable—
agreeable to the earthly goodness symbolized by Joseph's master. This can
be seen from the symbolism of *finding favor in someone's eyes* as being
agreeable. The text says *in his eyes* because favor is an attribute of the
intellect, and the intellect is symbolized by the eyes (§§2701, 3820, 4526).

And waited on him means that knowledge was adopted by the goodness associated with it. This can be seen from the meaning of *waiting on*
people as serving them by supplying what they need. Here it symbolizes being adopted, because the passage is talking about earthly goodness,
which needs to adopt the knowledge supplied to it. In addition, "waiting
on" is a term used in connection with knowledge. In the Word, a person
who waits on or serves another symbolizes knowledge, or earthly truth,
because this is subordinate to goodness as its master.

4976

The relationship between knowledge and pleasure in the earthly self—
that is, between earthly truth and the goodness associated with it—is exactly
like the relationship of water to bread, or drink to food. Water or other
drink causes bread and food to dissolve and be absorbed into the blood,
circulating to all parts of the body and nourishing them. Without water
or some kind of drink, bread or food does not break all the way down or

travel around doing its work. [2] The case is the same for the relationship between knowledge and pleasure, or truth and goodness. As a result, goodness hungers and longs for truth, wanting truth to fill its function by ministering to what is good and serving it.

Furthermore, these pairs correspond to each other. It is not earthly but spiritual food and drink that nourish people in the other life. Spiritual food is goodness, and spiritual drink is truth. Where the Word mentions bread or food, then, the angels take it to mean spiritual bread or food, which is good that is done out of love and charity. Where it mentions water or drink, they take it to mean spiritual water or drink, which is religious truth.

From this you can see what religious truth is without charitable goodness. You can also see how effective at nourishing the inner self that truth is without this goodness; it works no better than water or drink alone without bread and food. Obviously a body would starve to death on such a diet.

4977   *And he set him in charge over his household* means that goodness adapted to it, as the following shows: The *master* who set him in charge symbolizes goodness, as discussed above in §4973. And *setting him in charge over his household* means adapting to it—to knowledge, or earthly truth. The validity of this interpretation can be seen from the next clause, which says that whatever was his he gave into [Joseph's] hand, meaning that everything belonging to this kind of goodness was under the authority of earthly truth, so to speak. Goodness is the master, and truth waits on it. When the text says the master set an underling in charge, or goodness set truth in charge, the inner meaning is not that goodness surrendered control to truth but that goodness adapted. On the inner level, things are perceived as they really are, but on a literal level, they are presented according to appearances. Goodness always has the controlling power, but it adapts in order to unite truth to itself.

When we focus on truth, as we do until we have been reborn, we know hardly anything of goodness. Truth flows in along an external or sensory route, but goodness along an internal route. We are aware of whatever enters along an external route, but until we have been reborn we are not aware of what enters along an internal route. Therefore, unless a kind of control were given to truth in the earlier stage, which is to say, unless goodness adapted in this way, it would never be able to adopt truth as its own.

This idea is the same as one demonstrated many times before: that truth seems to come first or to be master when we are in the process of rebirth, but goodness is clearly seen as first and as master when we reach the end of the process. On this subject, see §§3539, 3548, 3556, 3563, 3570, 3576, 3603, 3701, 4925, 4926, 4928, 4930.

And whatever was his he gave into [Joseph's] hand means that every-   **4978**
thing belonging to that kind of goodness was under its authority, so to speak. This can be seen from the symbolism of a *hand* as power (discussed at §§878, 3091, 3387, 3563, 4931–4937). *Giving something into his hand,* then, means putting it under the authority of knowledge, but since this only appears to happen, this reads "under its authority, *so to speak.*" On the point that this happens only apparently, or so to speak, see §4977 directly above.

And it happened from the time he set him in charge in his household and   **4979**
over everything that was his symbolizes the second stage after goodness had adapted to it, and everything belonging to it had been put under its authority, so to speak. This can be seen from the following: *It happened,* which is said many times in the Word, has a meaning that involves tran-sition and accordingly a second stage. The same is true below in verses 7, 10, 11, 13, 15, 18, 19. *From the time he set him in charge in his household* means after goodness had adapted to knowledge, as discussed above in §4977. And *over everything that was his* means and everything belonging to it had been put under its authority, so to speak, as also discussed above, in §4978.

That Jehovah blessed the household of the Egyptian on account of Joseph   **4980**
means that it now received an earthly heavenliness from the Divine, as the following shows: Being *blessed* means being enriched with heavenly and spiritual goodness. The fact that it came from the Divine is sym-bolized by *Jehovah blessed.* And the *household of the Egyptian* symbolizes goodness in the earthly mind, as above in §4973. It follows that *Jehovah blessed the household of the Egyptian* means that [goodness in the earthly mind] now received an earthly heavenliness from the Divine.

Earthly heavenliness is goodness on the earthly level that corresponds to goodness on the rational level—in other words, to spiritual heavenli-ness drawing on rationality, which is *Joseph* (§4963).

[2] Heavenliness, like spirituality, is attributed to both the rational and the earthly planes. That is, it is attributed to the inner self (the rational self) and the outer self (the earthly self). Spirituality in its essence is divine

truth that radiates from the Lord, and heavenliness is divine goodness within that divine truth. When divine truth containing divine goodness is received by the rational plane, or the inner self, it is called a spiritual element on the rational plane, and when it is received by the earthly plane, or the outer self, it is called a spiritual element on the earthly plane. Likewise, when divine goodness within divine truth is received by the rational plane, or the inner self, it is called a heavenly element on the rational plane, and when it is received by the earthly plane, or the outer self, it is called a heavenly element on the earthly plane.

A human being receives each of the two from the Lord, both by indirect inflow through angels and spirits and by direct inflow. When the Lord was in the world, though, he received it from himself, because the Divine was in him.

4981   *And Jehovah's blessing* symbolizes growth, as can be seen from the following symbolism of *Jehovah's blessing:* In a genuine sense, Jehovah's blessing symbolizes love for the Lord and charity for one's neighbor. People who receive these gifts are referred to as being blessed by Jehovah, because they then receive the gift of heaven and eternal salvation. Jehovah's blessing in an outward sense, as it relates to our state in the world, means being content in God. So it means being content with the state of our status and wealth, no matter whether we are among the distinguished and rich or the less distinguished and poor. If we are content in God, we view status and wealth as a means to being useful. When we contemplate them alongside eternal life, we account them as nothing, and eternal life as essential.

[2] Because Jehovah's or the Lord's blessing involves all this in a genuine sense, a blessing holds numerous benefits within it. Consequently, it symbolizes different resulting effects, such as enrichment with spiritual and heavenly goodness (§§981, 1731), fruitfulness resulting from a desire for truth (2846), rearrangement in divine order (3017), being gifted with a loving goodness and united with the Lord (3406, 3504, 3514, 3530, 3584), and joy (4216). The specific symbolism can be seen from the context before and after. The symbolism here of Jehovah's blessing as growth in goodness and truth, or in life and theology, is evident from what follows, which says that Jehovah's blessing was on both house and field. A house symbolizes goodness in a person's life, while a field symbolizes truth in a person's theology. Growth in these things is plainly what *Jehovah's blessing* symbolizes here.

4982   *Was on everything that was his in the house and in the field* means in life and in theology, as the following shows: A *house* symbolizes goodness, as discussed in §§2048, 2233, 2559, 3128, 3652, 3720. Since it symbolizes goodness, it also symbolizes life, because all goodness is a matter of life. And a *field* symbolizes the church's truth, as discussed in §§368, 3508, 3766, 4440, 4443. Since it symbolizes the church's truth it also symbolizes theology, because all truth is a matter of theology.

Several other passages in the Word also speak of house and field, and in those that are about heavenly people, the house symbolizes heavenly goodness, and the field, spiritual goodness. Heavenly goodness is goodness that comes of love for the Lord, and spiritual goodness is goodness that comes of love for one's neighbor. In passages that are about spiritual people, though, the house symbolizes what is heavenly in them, or the goodness that comes of charity for one's neighbor, and the field symbolizes what is spiritual in them, or the truth taught by faith. Both sets are symbolized in Matthew:

> Those on the roof of the *house* should not go down to take anything *in their house*. And those in the *field* should not turn back behind to take their garment. (Matthew 24:17, 18)

See §3652.

And he left everything that was his in Joseph's hand means that it seemed as though everything was under the authority [of knowledge]. This can be seen from the explanation above in §4978, where almost the same words occur, and from the remarks in §4977.

4983

And had no knowledge of anything with him except the bread that he was eating means that goodness was therefore adopted. This is established by the symbolism of *bread* as goodness (discussed at §§276, 680, 3478, 3735, 4211, 4217, 4735) and from that of *eating* as being adopted (discussed at §§3168, 3513 at the end, 3596, 3832, 4745). *He had no knowledge of anything with him except the bread* means that nothing but goodness was accepted.

4984

You might think that when goodness adopts truth, what it adopts is truth itself—religious truth—but what it really adopts is the goodness belonging to that truth. Truth that is not useful does edge close to goodness but is not welcomed into it. Any useful purpose to which truth is put is actually goodness belonging to that truth. Truth that has no purpose is separate from goodness, but some of it is kept and some of it is rejected. The kind that is kept is the kind that introduces us directly or indirectly to goodness, and it actually is useful. The kind that is rejected is the kind that neither leads to goodness nor applies to it.

Everything useful starts with doctrinal truth. As this truth develops, it turns into goodness, and it does so when we act according to it. The act itself gives truth this character. All action descends from the will, and the will itself turns what used to be truth into goodness.

Clearly, then, truth in the will is no longer the truth belonging to faith but is goodness belonging to faith. Faith's truth does not make anyone happy, only the goodness belonging to faith does. This goodness has an effect on the very center of our life, which is our will, and gives us deep pleasure, or a sense of being blessed. In the other world, it gives us the happiness that is called heavenly joy.

4985   *And Joseph was beautiful in form* symbolizes the well-lived life that results. *And beautiful in appearance* symbolizes the religious truth that results. This can be seen from the symbolism of *beautiful in form and beautiful in appearance.* Form here means the essence of a thing, and appearance means what emerges from it. Since goodness is essence itself, and truth is what emerges from it, *beautiful in form* symbolizes a well-lived life, and *beautiful in appearance* symbolizes religious truth. Goodness in life is our very being, because it belongs to our will, and the truth of our faith is what emerges from it, because this belongs to our intellect. Anything that belongs to the intellect emerges from the will. The being of our life consists in willing, and the emergence of our life consists in understanding. Our intellect is simply our will unfolded and given shape so that its nature can appear and be seen.

[2] This shows that the beauty of our inner self comes from goodness in our will by way of truth in our faith. Religious truth makes the beauty visible in our outward form, but goodness in our will supplies the beauty and shapes it.

That is why the angels of heaven have indescribable beauty. They are love or charity in a form, so to speak, so when they appear in their beauty, it affects our inmost reaches. The loving goodness they receive from the Lord gleams out through the truth of their faith and touches us deeply.

This shows what is symbolized on an inner level by *beautiful in form and beautiful in appearance,* as also in §3821.

4986   Genesis 39:7, 8, 9. *And it happened after these words that the wife of his master lifted her eyes to Joseph and said, "Lie with me!" And he refused and said to the wife of his master, "Look, my master doesn't know what is in the household with me, and everything that is his he has given into my hand. He is not greater in this household than I and has not held anything back from* *me except yourself, in that you are his wife. And how can I do this great evil, and sin against God?"*

And it happened after these words symbolizes a third stage. *That the wife of his master lifted her eyes to Joseph* symbolizes nonspiritual earthly truth that was connected to earthly goodness, and what it perceived. *And said, "Lie with me!"* means that it craved union. *And he refused* symbolizes aversion. *And said to the wife of his master* symbolizes a perception about that truth. *Look, my master doesn't know what is in the household with me* means that earthly goodness did not even seek to be appropriated. *And everything that is his he has given into my hand* means that everything was under the authority of [spiritual-earthly goodness]. *He is not greater in this household than I* means that earthly goodness was first in time, not in state. *And has not held anything back from me except yourself* symbolizes a prohibition against uniting with the truth belonging to that goodness. *In that you are his wife* means because it was not to unite with any other goodness. *And how can I do this great evil, and sin against God?* means that the result would be a rift rather than union.

And it happened after these words symbolizes a third stage, as the following shows. *It happened* has a meaning that involves transition, as above in §4979, so in this verse it symbolizes a third stage. And *after these words* means after those events had taken place.

The original language does not separate one series from another by punctuation, as other languages do, but appears continuous from beginning to end. The contents of the inner meaning are continuous too, and flow from one state of affairs to another. When one phase ends and is replaced by another, though, and the new state is an important one, this is indicated by "it happened." A less significant change of state is marked by "and." That is why these expressions come up so often.

This third stage now being dealt with is deeper than the one before it.

That the wife of his master lifted her eyes to Joseph symbolizes nonspiritual earthly truth that was connected to earthly goodness, and what it perceived, as the following shows: A *wife* symbolizes truth connected to goodness, as discussed at §§1468, 2517, 3236, 4510, 4823. Here it symbolizes nonspiritual earthly truth that is connected to earthly goodness, because the topic of discussion is this goodness and that truth. The *master* is this goodness, to which truth is united (§4973). And *lifting one's eyes* symbolizes thought, focus, and perception, as discussed at §§2789, 2829, 3198, 3202, 4339.

[2] This *wife* symbolizes earthly truth, but not earthly truth that is spiritual, and her husband, the *master*, symbolizes earthly goodness, but not earthly goodness that is spiritual. As a consequence, I need to define earthly goodness and truth that are not spiritual, and earthly goodness and truth that are spiritual.

The goodness in us has two sources. One is our heredity and therefore something that originates outside us. The other is teachings about faith and charity, and for non-Christians, their religious tradition. Goodness and truth from the first source is earthly goodness that is not spiritual. Goodness from the latter source is earthly goodness that is spiritual. From the same source comes truth, because every kind of goodness has its own truth connected to it.

[3] Earthly goodness from the first source (heredity, which originates outside us) has a strong resemblance to earthly goodness from the second source (teachings about faith and charity, or a religious tradition), but only in its outward form. On the inside it is entirely different. Earthly goodness from the first origin can be compared to the goodness existing in tame animals. Earthly goodness from the second origin is distinctive to people who act from reason and who therefore know how to spread kindness in different ways, depending on the purpose. They learn this from teachings about justice and fairness, and on a higher level, from teachings about faith and charity. In many instances the lessons are also confirmed by the power of reason that truly rational people possess.

[4] People who do good from the first origin are moved blindly, almost instinctively, to exercise charity, but people who do good from the second origin are moved by an inner obligation and have their eyes open, so to speak.

In short, people who do good from the first origin do not act with any conscientious awareness of justice and fairness, let alone of spiritual truth and goodness, but people who do good from the second origin do act from conscience. See earlier discussions of the subject at §§3040, 3470, 3471, 3518 and the discussion below at §4992.

The situation in all this cannot be explained intelligibly, because people who are not spiritual, or who have not been reborn, see goodness in terms of its outward form. That is because they do not know what charity is or what their neighbor is. The reason they do not know is that there are no doctrinal teachings about charity.

The distinctions are very clear in heaven's light and therefore to spiritual people, or those who have been reborn, because they see by heaven's light.

And said, "Lie with me!" means that it craved union. This can be seen from the symbolism of *lying with me* as union between the spiritual-earthly goodness that Joseph now stands for and the nonspiritual earthly truth that his master's wife stands for—an illicit union.

The Word depicts the union of goodness with truth and of truth with goodness as a marriage (see §§2727–2759, 3132, 3665, 4434, 4837), so it depicts illicit unions as sexual transgressions. That is why the union of non-spiritual earthly truth with spiritual-earthly goodness is depicted by this desire in the wife of Joseph's master to lie with Joseph. No inner bond exists between them, only a superficial tie that looks like union but is merely a distant connection. That is why she grabbed him by his garment and why he left his garment in her hand. The garment on an inner level symbolizes a superficial factor that creates the seeming union of what is actually a distant connection, as will be seen below at verses 12, 13 [§§5006–5010].

[2] As long as we train our mind or thoughts on the story, we cannot see that these concepts are symbolized, because then all we think about is Joseph, Potiphar's wife, and how Joseph fled, leaving his garment behind. If we trained our mind or thoughts instead on the *symbolism* of Joseph, Potiphar's wife, and the garment, we would be able to tell that the passage is actually talking about an illicit spiritual liaison. And we can train our mind or thoughts on the symbolism if only we believe that the divinity of scriptural narrative is due not just to the story but to something spiritual and divine in the story. If we believed this, we would see that the spiritual, divine component has to do with goodness and truth in the church and in the Lord's kingdom, and on the highest plane, with the Lord himself.

When people who are going to be taken up to heaven enter the other world (which happens right after death), they have to learn that they keep no memory of the Scripture stories. They do not even know anything about Joseph, or about Abraham, Isaac, and Jacob, only about the spiritual and divine lessons they learned from the Word and applied to their lives. These are the concepts that lie inside the Word and are called its inner meaning.

And he refused symbolizes aversion. This can be seen from the symbolism of *refusing* as aversion—aversion to that union. Someone who refuses something so strongly as to flee outside has aversion for it.

4991   *And said to the wife of his master* symbolizes a perception about that truth. This can be seen from the symbolism of *saying* in the Word's narratives as perceiving (dealt with many times before) and from that of the *wife of his master* as nonspiritual earthly truth linked with earthly goodness (discussed above at §4988).

4992   *Look, [my] master doesn't know what is in the household with me* means that earthly goodness did not even seek to be appropriated. This can be seen from the symbolism of his *master* as earthly goodness (discussed at §4973) and from that of *not knowing what is in the household with me* as not seeking to be appropriated.

No one can see that this is the meaning except from the series of ideas in the inner meaning. The current subject is a third stage, in which spiritual heavenliness existed on the earthly level. At that stage, earthly goodness and truth that are spiritual are separated from earthly goodness and truth that are not spiritual. *Not knowing what is in the household,* then, means that there is no desire to be appropriated.

Because these concepts are secrets, though, the only way to throw light on them is to use examples. By way of illustration, then: For a husband to sleep with his wife solely out of lust is earthly and not spiritual. For a husband to sleep with his wife out of married love, on the other hand, is spiritual-earthly. If he afterward sleeps with her out of lust alone, he feels he has transgressed, as if he had done something obscene. He no longer wants to appropriate that [earthly goodness].

For another example: To help a friend no matter what the person's character, as long as he or she is a friend, is earthly, not spiritual. To help a friend for the sake of what is good in the person, and particularly to view the goodness itself as the friend we are helping, is spiritual-earthly. When we reach this stage, we know we are transgressing if we help a friend who is evil, because we are hurting others through that friend. At this point, we are loath to appropriate earthly goodness that is not spiritual—the goodness we previously engaged in.

And so on.

4993   *And everything that is his he has given into my hand* means that everything was under the authority of [spiritual-earthly goodness]. This can be seen from the remarks above at §4978, where the same words occur, although there is a difference. The text there is about a second stage for spiritual heavenliness on the earthly plane, when earthly goodness adapted to truth and adopted it (§§4976, 4977). At that stage, goodness actually had the controlling power but truth seemed to, which is why the meaning of the clause there was that everything belonging to that goodness was under the authority of truth, so to speak. The text here, though, is about a third stage for spiritual heavenliness, when it became spiritual on the earthly level. At this stage there is no adoption, so the meaning of the clause is that everything was under the authority of [spiritual-earthly goodness].

He is not greater in this household than I means that earthly goodness was first in time, not in state. This can be seen from the symbolism of *not being greater in the household than I* as equality between the two powers, both being first. The context of the inner meaning makes it plain that nonspiritual earthly goodness is first in time, and that spiritual-earthly goodness is first in state, and the illustrations above at §4992 make the same thing clear.

Being first in state means being superior in quality. **4994**

And has not held anything back from me except yourself symbolizes a prohibition against uniting with the truth belonging to that goodness, as the following shows. *To have held something back from him* symbolizes a prohibition on it. The wife—who was the one being held back, meant here by *yourself*—symbolizes nonspiritual earthly truth, as discussed in §4988. **4995**

In that you are his wife means because it was not to unite with any other goodness. This is established by the symbolism of a *wife* as truth connected to its goodness (discussed at §§1468, 2517, 3236, 4510, 4823), and in this case, nonspiritual earthly truth connected with nonspiritual earthly goodness (as above in §4988). **4996**

And how can I do this great evil, and sin against God? means that the result would be a rift rather than union. This can be seen from the symbolism of *evil* and *sin* as a rift rather than union, specifically when spiritual-earthly goodness unites with nonspiritual earthly truth. The two are unlike and unequal and pull apart from each other. **4997**

This is referred to as doing evil and sinning against God because evil and sin viewed in themselves are actually a rift with goodness. In fact, evil consists in disconnection. This is clear from goodness, which is the same as union. All goodness has to do with love for the Lord and love for our neighbor. The goodness that comes from love for the Lord unites us to the Lord and therefore to everything good that comes from him. The goodness that comes from love for our neighbor unites us with heaven and its communities. In the process it also unites us to the Lord, because properly speaking, heaven is the Lord, since he is the all-in-all there.

[2] It is the opposite with evil. Evil has to do with love for ourselves and love for worldly advantages. The evil of self-love disconnects us not

only from the Lord but also from heaven. We love no one but ourselves, and we love others only so far as we see them in ourselves, or so far as they merge with us. We make ourselves the center of everyone's attention, always diverting attention away from others and especially from the Lord. When lots of people in a single community behave this way, all of them are inevitably at odds. Each member inwardly views the next as an enemy. They hate anyone who works against them in any way, and take pleasure in such a person's ruin. The evil of love for worldly advantages is no different. This evil covets the wealth and possessions of others and wants to own everything that belongs to another. This too results in hostility and hatred, though to a lesser degree.

If you want to know what evil is and therefore what sin is, all you need to do is work at learning what self-love and love for worldly advantages are. If you want to know what goodness is, all you need to do is work at learning what love for the Lord and love for your neighbor are. From this you will know what is evil and consequently what is false, and you will know what is good and consequently what is true.

4998 Genesis 39:10, 11, 12, 13, 14, 15. *And it happened as she spoke to Joseph day by day that he did not listen to her, to lie with her, to be with her. And it happened that on a certain day he came to the house to do his work, and no man of the men of the household was there in the house. And she grabbed him by his garment, saying, "Lie with me!" And he left his garment in her hand and fled and went outside. And it happened, as she saw that he had left his garment in her hand and fled outside, that she shouted out to the men of her household and said to them, saying, "See? He has brought us a Hebrew man to mock us. He came to me to lie with me, and I shouted in a loud voice. And it happened as he heard it, because I raised my voice and shouted, that he left his garment with me and fled and went outside."*

And it happened symbolizes a fourth stage. *As she spoke to Joseph day by day* symbolizes thinking about the subject. *That he did not listen to her, to lie with her,* symbolizes aversion to being united. *To be with her* means so as not to become one. *And it happened that on a certain day* symbolizes a fifth stage. *He came to the house to do his work* means while at work uniting with spiritual goodness on the earthly level. *And no man of the men of the household was there in the house* means without anyone's help. *And she grabbed him by his garment* means that nonspiritual truth clung to the outermost plane of spiritual truth. *Saying, "Lie with me!"* means for the sake of union. *And he left his garment in her hand* symbolizes the snatching away of this outermost truth. *And fled and went outside* means that this left him without truth for self-defense. *And it happened, as she saw* symbolizes a perception about the matter. *That he had left his garment in her hand and fled outside* means about the separation of outermost truth. *That she shouted out to the men of the household* symbolizes falsity. *And said to them, saying,* symbolizes an urgent plea. *See? He has brought us a Hebrew man* symbolizes a slave. *To mock us* means that it would rebel. *He came to me to lie with me* means that it wanted to unite. *And I shouted in a loud voice* symbolizes aversion. *And it happened as he heard it* means when it was perceived. *Because I raised my voice and shouted* means that the aversion was extreme. *That he left his garment with me* symbolizes evidence that it had come close. *And fled and went outside* means that it had detached anyway.

And it happened symbolizes a fourth stage. This can be seen from the remarks above at §§4979, 4987. **4999**

As she spoke to Joseph day by day symbolizes thinking about the subject. This can be seen from the symbolism of *speaking* as thinking (discussed at §§2271, 2287, 2619), namely, about Joseph and so about the subject being dealt with under the figure of Joseph. *Day by day,* or every day, means intensely. **5000**

The reason speaking means thinking, in an inner sense, is that thought is inner speech, and when we are thinking, we are talking to ourselves. The literal story expresses inner processes in terms of the outer ones corresponding to them.

That he did not listen to her, to lie with her, symbolizes aversion to being united, as the following shows: *Not listening* means not heeding, or not obeying, as discussed at §§2542, 3869. Here it symbolizes aversion, because Joseph refused to heed—so much so that he fled, leaving his garment behind. And *lying with her* symbolizes illicit union, as discussed at §4989. **5001**

To be with her means so as not to become one. This can be seen from the symbolism of *being with someone* as being joined more closely, or becoming one. **5002**

The reason *being* means becoming one is that the actual being of a thing consists of goodness, and all goodness is a matter of love, which is spiritual union or oneness.

In the highest sense, the Lord is called "Being," which is to say, Jehovah, because he is the source of all the goodness embraced by love, or by spiritual union.

Heaven forms a single whole through the love it receives from the Lord, through the love it returns after receiving it, and through mutual love. As a result, heaven is called a marriage, which enables it to *be*. This would hold true for the church as well if love and charity were its central being.

Where there is no union or oneness, then, there is no being. Unless there were a force that reduced a thing to oneness, or united it into one, it would dissolve and disappear.

[2] Sometimes it is everyone for her- or himself in the public sphere, and no one is looking out for anyone else, except as a matter of self-benefit. If under these circumstances there were no laws to unite people—no threat of losing wealth, position, reputation, or one's life—society would be obliterated. So the central being of such a culture is likewise union or oneness, but only on the outside. In regard to its inner depths, it has no being. In the other life, people like this are kept in hell, where outward restraints, and threats in particular, again hold them captive. Whenever the restraints are loosened, each inhabitant rushes to hurt the other and wants nothing more than to annihilate the other.

Not so in heaven, where an inner bond is created by love for the Lord and by the mutual love that results. When outward restraints loosen there, the inhabitants develop an even tighter bond with each other. Since this drives them closer to the divine being that comes from the Lord, they are inwardly under the power of their desires. This means that they are in freedom, and consequently that they have blessedness, happiness, and joy.

5003 *And it happened that on a certain day* symbolizes a fifth stage. This can be seen from the symbolism of *it happened* as involving transition, as above in §§4979, 4987, 4999, and therefore as a new stage—in this case, a fifth one.

5004 *He came to the house to do his work* means while at work uniting with spiritual goodness on the earthly level. This can be seen from the fact that such a union is what the chapter is talking about, under the figure of Joseph. When it says *he came to the house to do his work,* then, it symbolizes work on that union.

5005 *And no man of the men of the household was there in the house* means without anyone's help. This can be seen from the sense of the clause, which is that Joseph was alone. Since the inner meaning uses the figure of Joseph to tell how the Lord glorified his inner humanity, or made it divine, the clause means that he did so without anyone's help.

To see that the Lord made his humanity divine by his own power, without anyone's help, consider that he was conceived by Jehovah and therefore had divinity inside him as his own possession. For this reason, when he was in the world, making the humanity in himself divine, he did so from his divine side—in other words, from himself.

His self-reliance is depicted this way in Isaiah:

> Who is this who comes from Edom, spattered in his clothes, from Bozrah; this one who is honorable in his apparel, *marching in the abundance of his strength?* "The winepress I have *trodden alone,* and from among the *peoples not a man was with me.* I looked around, but *no one was helping,* and I was astounded, but *no one was supporting me.* Therefore *my arm achieved salvation for me."* (Isaiah 63:1, 3, 5)

And elsewhere in the same prophet:

> *He saw that there was no man* and was dumbfounded, so to speak, that no one was interceding. Therefore *his arm achieved salvation for him,* and his righteousness supported him. So he put righteousness on like a coat of armor and a helmet of salvation on his head. (Isaiah 59:16, 17)

On the point that the Lord made the humanity in himself divine by his own power, see §§1616, 1749, 1755, 1812, 1813, 1921, 1928, 1999, 2025, 2026, 2083, 2500, 2523, 2776, 3043, 3141, [3381,] 3382, 3637, 4287.

And she grabbed him by his garment means that nonspiritual truth clung to the outermost plane of spiritual truth, as the following shows: Potiphar's wife, the subject of the clause, represents nonspiritual earthly truth, as discussed in §4988. *Grabbing* in this case means clinging. And a *garment* symbolizes truth, as discussed in §§1073, 2576, 4545, 4763. Here it symbolizes the outermost plane of the spiritual truth that belongs to Joseph in this state, since he currently stands for spiritual-earthly goodness (§§4988, 4992). The truth belonging to this goodness is what nonspiritual earthly truth wanted to unite with, as context in the inner meaning makes plain.

[2] What does it mean to say that nonspiritual earthly truth wanted to unite with spiritual-earthly truth? What does it involve? This is a secret nowadays, especially because few care or want to know what spiritual and nonspiritual truth are. People are so uninterested that they can barely stand to hear the word "spiritual" spoken. Simply say it out loud and immediately a kind of darkness creeps over them along with depression, they become nauseated, and the idea is rejected. The fact that this happens was even demonstrated for me. Once, when my mind was on spiritual matters, spirits from the Christian world were present, and they were sent back to the state that had been theirs in the world. Just the thought

5006

of spiritual goodness and truth depressed them. Not only that, it gripped them with such loathing and disgust that they said they felt the same way they had in the world when they were about to vomit. I was allowed to tell them that this came from their emotional preoccupation with earthly, bodily, and worldly concerns. When these are all we care about, anything having to do with heaven turns our stomach. Maybe they went to church to hear the Word preached, I said, but it was not because they yearned to know all about heaven; it was due to some other desire they had developed as little children. This experience clarified for me the nature of the modern Christian world.

[3] The general reason for this distaste is that the Christian religion currently preaches faith alone and not charity. It preaches doctrine and not life. When a religion does not preach life, people do not develop any desire for goodness, and when they have no desire for goodness, they have no desire for truth. That is why it violates most people's highest pleasure to hear anything more about heavenly matters than what they have known since they were children.

[4] However, the fact of the matter is that we are in this world to learn heavenly behavior by practicing it here. Our life in the world is barely like a moment compared to our life after death, which is eternal. There are not many who believe they will live on after death, though, which is another reason they view information about heaven as worthless. Yet I can assert that the instant we die we find ourselves in the other life, where we continue in every way the life we had in the world and where our nature remains the same as it had been in the world. I can assert this because I know it. I have talked with almost everyone I knew during physical life after each has left that life. Doing so has allowed me to learn by personal experience what kind of future awaits us all, and that future is one that matches our life. But the type of people I am describing do not even believe this.

Just below [§5008] I will explain what it means and what it involves to say that nonspiritual earthly truth wanted to unite with spiritual-earthly truth—the symbolic meaning of *she grabbed Joseph by his garment.*

5007 *Saying, "Lie with me!"* means for the sake of union. This can be seen from the symbolism of *lying [with someone]* as union (dealt with above at §§4989, 5001). Here it means for the sake of union, or in order to unite.

5008 *And he left his garment in her hand* symbolizes the snatching away of this outermost truth, as the following shows: *Leaving something in her hand* symbolizes leaving it in her power, a hand meaning power (§§878, 3091, 3387, 3563, 4931–4937). Since she had grabbed his garment, the word currently symbolizes a snatching away. And the *garment* symbolizes outer-most truth, as noted above at §5006.

Unless the matter is illustrated by examples, no one can understand the idea that nonspiritual earthly truth wanted to unite with spiritual-earthly truth, which repudiated the connection and therefore left outermost truth behind, or allowed it to be snatched away. First, though, see what non-spiritual earthly truth and spiritual-earthly truth are (§§4988, 4992), and that on the outermost level there is a distant connection but no union.

[2] To repeat, the idea needs to be illustrated by examples. The first: It is a nonspiritual earthly truth within the church that we are to do good to the poor, the widowed, and the orphaned, and that doing good to them is the charity commanded in the Word. Nonspiritual truth, or rather people governed by nonspiritual truth, take the poor, widowed, and orphaned to mean the people literally called that. Spiritual-earthly truth, or rather people governed by that truth, agree, but they put the literal interpreta-tion of paupers, widows, and orphans last. They say to themselves that not all those who call themselves poor are paupers. The ranks of the poor include some who live wicked lives, not fearing God or humankind, who would readily commit any outrage if fear did not hinder them. In addi-tion, by "the poor" the Word means spiritual paupers—people who know and sincerely admit that they have no truth or goodness on their own but receive all of it free, as a gift. Likewise for widows and orphans, with dif-ferences in regard to their state. This example shows that doing good to those who are called poor, widowed, and orphaned is the outermost plane of truth for people committed to spiritual-earthly truth and is like a gar-ment clothing something deeper. It also shows that this outermost plane of truth coincides with truth as viewed by people committed to non-spiritual earthly truth, although there is no union between them, only a distant connection.

[3] Take as another example the obligation to help one's neighbor. Individuals subscribing to spiritual-earthly truth consider everyone their neighbor, but each in a different respect and to a different degree. They say to themselves that people devoted to what is good are the neighbor they should help above all others. People wallowing in evil are also their neigh-bor, but such people are helped when the law punishes them, because punishment changes them for the better. Punishment also prevents them from hurting good people by setting a bad example. Individuals in the church who subscribe to nonspiritual earthly truth also call everyone their neighbor but deny differences in respect and degree. Consequently, if they

practice earthly kindness, they help everyone who stirs their pity, without distinction. They usually help the evil more than the good, because the evil in their malevolence know how to arouse pity. This example also shows that outermost truth brings together those who adopt nonspiritual earthly truth and those who adopt spiritual-earthly truth, but that there is still no union there, only a distant connection. The one group has a different picture and a different understanding of their neighbor and of charity for that neighbor than the other group.

[4] As another example, people who adopt spiritual-earthly truth say broadly that the poor and wretched will inherit the kingdom of heaven, but for them it is a superficial truth. They conceal inside it the idea that the poor and the wretched are those who are spiritually such. They are the ones to whom the Word means to assign the kingdom of heaven. People in the church who adopt nonspiritual earthly truth, on the other hand, say that only those who have been reduced to poverty in the world, live in misery, and bear greater afflictions than anyone else are able to inherit the kingdom of heaven. They also describe wealth, position, and worldly joys as so many distractions leading us away from heaven. This example too reveals the identity and character of the outermost truth the two groups agree on but shows that there is no union between them, only a distant connection.

[5] As another example, people intent on spiritual-earthly truth take it as true on the outermost plane that objects the Word describes as sacred were sacred. This includes the ark with its appeasement cover, along with the lampstand, incense, bread, and all the rest; it includes the altar; it includes the Temple; and it includes Aaron's garments, the "garments of holiness," especially the ephod with the breastplate containing the Urim and Thummim. Nonetheless, their concept of this outermost truth is that these items were neither holy in themselves nor infused with holiness but were holy as representations. That is, they were holy because they represented spiritual and heavenly qualities of the Lord's kingdom, and on the highest level, the Lord himself. People intent on nonspiritual earthly truth also call these objects sacred, but intrinsically sacred, because they are infused with holiness. Plainly the two views agree, then, but do not unite. This truth takes a different shape in a spiritual person than in a merely earthly one because it comes from a different way of thinking.

[6] As yet another example, to a spiritual person it is outwardly true that all divine truth can be confirmed by the Word's literal sense and by the rational or intellectual proofs of the enlightened. An earthly person also acknowledges this broad, outermost truth but believes in all simplicity that anything capable of being confirmed by the Word is true, especially if

he or she has personally come up with the confirmation. On this the two come together, then—that anything divinely true can be confirmed; but one party sees this broad truth differently than the other. People who are merely earthly consider divine truth to be whatever they have confirmed to their own satisfaction or what they have heard others confirm. They do not realize that falsity can be proved as surely as truth, and that once it is proved, it looks completely true. In fact, falsity is more amenable to proof than real truth, because the illusions of the senses add their support and present the idea in worldly light separated from heaven's light.

[7] This makes it clear that outermost spiritual truth as seen by an earthly person is like a garment. When the garment is snatched away, [the two kinds of truth] do not harmonize at all, and consequently the spiritual person no longer has any means of self-defense against the earthly person. That is the symbolic meaning of "Joseph fled and went outside, leaving his garment." A merely earthly person does not acknowledge inner [truth], so when outer [truth] is removed or snatched away, the two immediately move apart.

Furthermore, everything spiritual people use to confirm outermost truth is called falsity by earthly people, because earthly people cannot see whether the confirmation is valid. Using earthly light to look at objects of spiritual light is impossible; it goes against the ordained plan. But using spiritual light to look at objects of earthly light is according to the plan.

And fled and went outside means that he had no truth for self-defense. This can be seen from the symbolism of *fleeing and going outside,* after Joseph had left his garment behind, as achieving separation, or the loss of any common ground. Since a garment means outermost truth, then, the symbolism is that he had no truth for self-defense. See the explanation just above at the end of §5008.   **5009**

And it happened, as she saw symbolizes a perception about the matter. This can be seen from the symbolism of *seeing* as perception (discussed at §§2150, 3764, 4567, 4723). "About the matter" means about the separation that caused outermost truth not to be acknowledged anymore, symbolized by *he left his garment in her hand and fled outside.* This is evident from the discussion above at §§5008 and 5009.   **5010**

That she shouted out to the men of the household symbolizes falsity. This can be seen from the discussion in §2240 of the symbolism of a shout as falsity, so that to *shout* relates to falsity. *Men of the household* in a positive sense are the true ideas that come of goodness, but in a negative sense, the false notions that come of evil. What Potiphar's wife says to the men   **5011** of the household now and to her husband later is untrue, as her words themselves show.

Earthly truth, which is Potiphar's wife here, cannot help saying what is false, or the opposite of truth, after the wrenching away of outermost spiritual truth, which on its outer surface appears to be a means of union. See above at the end of §5008.

5012   *And said to them, saying,* symbolizes an urgent plea. This can be seen from the symbolism in this case of *saying* as a plea. In an inner sense, saying means perception (§§2862, 3395, 3509) and communication (§§3060, 4131). The text says that Potiphar's wife shouted, and then that she *said, saying,* so in this instance it means a forceful communication—in other words, an urgent plea to be heard.

5013   *See? He has brought us a Hebrew man* symbolizes a slave. This can be seen from the symbolism of a *Hebrew man,* a term associated with servitude, as discussed in §1703. It is also clear from what follows, since Joseph is called a Hebrew slave, and also simply a slave: "There came to me the *Hebrew slave* whom you brought to us" (verse 17); and "According to these words *your slave* did to me" (verse 19).

The main reason a Hebrew man means a slave here is this: People immersed in earthly truth and goodness that are not spiritual (whom Potiphar and his wife represent) regard spiritual truth and goodness (which Joseph represents) simply as a slave. Their lives and theology are upside down. In them the earthly level is master, and the spiritual level is slave, but the proper arrangement is for the spiritual level to be master, and the earthly level, slave. What is spiritual is prior, more inward, higher, and closer to divinity, while what is earthly is secondary, more outward, lower, and farther from divinity. As a consequence, what is spiritual in a person and in the church is compared to heaven and is called heaven; and what is earthly is compared to earth and is called earth. As a further consequence, spiritual people, or people in whom the spiritual plane is master, appear in heaven's light in the other world with their head up toward the Lord and their feet down toward hell. Earthly people, or people in whom the earthly plane is master, appear in heaven's light with their feet up and their head down—although they appear differently in their own light, which is a false light springing from the cravings and resulting delusions in which they indulge (§§1528, 3340, 4214, 4418, 4531, 4532).

Earthly people's view that spiritual attributes are slaves was represented by the Egyptians' view of the Hebrews as nothing but slaves. Egyptians represented people with earthly learning and therefore represented earthly people, but the Hebrews represented people in the church and therefore people who were comparatively spiritual. Egyptians considered the Hebrews as contemptible as slaves and in fact so contemptible that it would have been abhorrent to them to eat with the Hebrews (Genesis 43:32). The sacrifices of the Hebrews were also abhorrent to them (Exodus 8:26).

To mock us means that it would rebel. This can be seen from the context itself in its inner meaning and from the symbolism of *mocking* (when the word is spit out forcefully) as rebelling. **5014**

He came to me to lie with me means that spiritual-earthly truth wanted to unite. This can be seen from the symbolism here of *coming* as wanting, since one who comes with some purpose wants something, and from the symbolism of *lying with* as uniting (dealt with above at §§4989, 5001, 5007). **5015**

And I shouted in a loud voice symbolizes aversion. This can be seen from the symbolism of a shout as lying words (discussed at §5011). *Shouting,* then, involves the same thing. Since Potiphar's wife shouted to the men of the household for help, the lie was that [nonspiritual earthly truth] resisted [spiritual-earthly truth] and even felt aversion for it, since the text says she shouted *in a loud voice.* **5016**

And it happened as he heard it means when it was perceived. This is established by the symbolism of *hearing* as obeying and as perceiving. For the idea that it symbolizes obedience, see §§2542, 3869. The fact that it symbolizes perception as well is evident just from the function of the ear and therefore from the nature of hearing. The ear's function is to receive another's words and relay them to the overall seat of sensation, which can then perceive what the speaker is thinking. That is why hearing means perceiving. Its nature, as a consequence, is to take the words expressing one person's thoughts and transfer them into a second person's thoughts, from there into the person's will, and from there into action. That is why hearing means obeying. These two tasks are assigned to the sense of hearing. Various languages distinguish between them by using *hear* for "perceive," and *listen to* or *heed* for "obey." These two tasks are assigned to hearing because we have no other way to convey what we are thinking and what we want, or to use reason in persuading and convincing another to do and obey what we want. **5017**

These remarks illustrate the circular path of communication, from the will into the thought and then into speech, and from speech by way of another's ear into that other's thought and will.

A result is that spirits and angels corresponding to the ear or the sense of hearing in the universal human are embodiments not only of perception but also of obedience. For their embodying obedience, see §§4652–4660.

Because they embody obedience, they also embody perception, since the one involves the other.

5018 *I raised my voice and shouted* means that the aversion was extreme. This is established by the symbolism of *shouting* in a loud voice as aversion (mentioned above in §5016). *Raising one's voice and shouting*, then, means extreme aversion.

5019 *That he left his garment with me* symbolizes evidence that it had come close. This can be seen from the discussion in §5008 of the symbolism of *leaving a garment* as snatching away outermost truth. Here, though, it means evidence because the garment in the hand of Potiphar's wife, which she displayed—that is, the outermost truth used as proof that [spiritual-earthly truth] wanted to unite—was evidence that it had come close.

This meaning does seem rather far-fetched but is nonetheless the one contained in her words. See below at §5028.

5020 *And fled and went outside* means that it had detached anyway. This is established by the symbolism of *fleeing and going outside* as detaching, [or separating,] as above in §5009.

These, then, are the lies Potiphar's wife told the men of the household about Joseph. In an inner sense, they are the lies that nonspiritual earthly truth tells about spiritual-earthly truth, or that a person who is earthly and not spiritual tells about a spiritual-earthly person. See §§4988, 4992, 5008.

5021 Genesis 39:16, 17, 18. *And she set his garment aside with her until his master's coming to his house. And she spoke to him according to these words, saying, "There came to me the Hebrew slave whom you brought to us to mock me. And it happened, as I raised my voice and shouted, that he left his garment with me and fled outside."*

And she set his garment aside with her symbolizes holding on to outermost truth. *Until his master's coming to his house* means in order to communicate with earthly goodness. *And she spoke to him according to these words* symbolizes the telling of a lie. *Saying, "There came to me the Hebrew slave whom you brought to us,"* symbolizes that slave. *To mock me* means that it would rebel. *And it happened, as I raised my voice and shouted* means when extreme aversion was felt. *That he left his garment with me* symbolizes evidence. *And fled outside* means that it then detached.

5022 *And she set his garment aside with her* symbolizes holding on to outermost truth. This can be seen from the symbolism of *setting something aside with one* as holding on to it, and from that of a *garment* as outermost truth (discussed above at §§5006, 5008). Once this truth is snatched away, a spiritual person no longer has any means of self-defense against people who are purely earthly (§§5008 at the end, 5009) and therefore comes to harm. You see, no matter what the spiritual person says at that point, purely earthly people say they do not understand. They also deny the validity of what they are hearing. At the mere word "inner" or "spiritual" they either laugh derisively or call it mystical. Any connection between the two parties then breaks off. The connection broken, the spiritual person suffers harshly at the hands of the purely earthly. This is represented by Joseph's being thrown into the prison house when Potiphar's wife presented the garment to her husband as evidence.

Until his master's coming to his house means in order to communicate with earthly goodness. This can be seen from the symbolism of the *master* as nonspiritual earthly goodness (discussed at §§4973, 4988). A *house* in an inner sense means the earthly mind, which resembles a house, as the rational mind also does. The husband there is goodness; the wife is truth; the daughters and sons are desires for what is good and true, and also goodness and truth born from the kind represented by their parents; the female and male slaves are sensual pleasures and factual knowledge that serve to provide confirmation. *Until his master's coming to his house,* then, means until earthly goodness comes to its dwelling place, which is also home to the truth united with it. In this case, though, it is home to falsity, which persuades goodness that it (falsity) is true. Nonspiritual earthly goodness is easily convinced that falsity is true, and truth false.

§5023

The text says *his master* because nonspiritual earthliness considers spirituality its slave (§5013).

[2] The following passages show that a person's earthly and rational minds are called a house. In Luke:

> When an unclean spirit leaves a person, it roams dry places seeking a resting place, and if it does not find one, it says, "*Let me go back to my house* that I left"; and if, coming, it finds it swept and decorated, it then goes and takes seven other spirits worse than itself and, entering, they settle there. (Luke 11:24, 25, 26)

The house stands for the earthly mind, which is called a house empty and swept when it contains none of the goodness and truth that are husband and wife, none of the desires for goodness and truth that are daughters and sons, and none of the confirmations that are female and male slaves. We ourselves are a house because our rational and earthly minds make us human. Without these things—goodness and truth, a desire for them, and support for the desire—we are not human beings but brute animals. [3] Again in the same author a house means the human mind:

> Every kingdom divided against itself is devastated, and *house falls upon house*. (Luke 11:17)

And in Mark:

> If a kingdom is divided against itself, that kingdom cannot stand. Also, if a *house* is divided against itself, *that house* cannot stand. No one can plunder the belongings of a strong person, *having entered that person's house*, without first overcoming the strong person; and then one may plunder that person's *house*. (Mark 3:24, 25, 27)

The kingdom symbolizes truth (§§1672, 2547, 4691), and the house symbolizes goodness (§§2233, 3720, 4982). This is more properly the symbolism of a house. [4] In Luke:

> If the householder knew at what hour the thief was to come, he would certainly be watchful and *not allow his house to be broken into*. (Luke 12:39)

In the same author:

> From now on there will be five *in one house*, three against two, and two against three. Father will be divided against son, and son against father; mother against daughter, and daughter against mother. (Luke 12:52, 53)

The subject here is spiritual battles that people in the church will undergo once the Word's spiritual depths have been disclosed. The house stands for an individual or the individual's mind. The father, mother, son, and daughter mean different types of goodness and truth along with desires for them. In a negative sense they mean different types of evil and falsity along with desires for them, which are the causes of the battles and are one's adversaries in battle.

[5] The Lord commanded his disciples in Luke:

> Into *whatever house* you enter, first say, "*Peace to this house*," and if a child of peace really is there, your peace will rest on it. But if not, it will return upon you. But *stay in the same house; eat* and drink what they have; *do not pass from house to house*. (Luke 10:5, 6, 7)

This represented the idea that they should stay with genuine goodness—the goodness associated with love for the Lord and charity for their neighbor—and not pass over to another kind.

For more on the idea that we and our minds are a house, see §§3538, 4973.

And she spoke to him according to these words symbolizes the telling of a lie. This can be seen from what follows, since what she said to her husband was untrue.

5024

Saying, "There came to me the Hebrew slave whom you brought to us," symbolizes that slave. This can be seen from the discussion above at §5013. "That slave" means the spiritual truth and goodness that Joseph currently stands for, which nonspiritual earthliness sees as a slave.

5025

For example, spiritual truth and goodness ask us to take satisfaction not in high position or in superiority over others but in serving our country, society at large, and our community in particular. What they ask of us, then, is to take pleasure in the use to which high position can be put. People who are merely earthly have no idea what this kind of pleasure is and deny it exists, although hypocrisy can lead them to say similar things. They make a master out of the self-seeking type of pleasure in high office, and they make a slave out of pleasure in high office for the sake of society on the large and small scales. In everything they do, they have an eye on self-interest and make society secondary to themselves, promoting society's interest only when it promotes their own.

[2] For another example, take the assertion that usefulness and purpose make a thing spiritual or nonspiritual. To adopt the common good, the church, or the kingdom of God as one's aim and purpose is spiritual. To adopt oneself and one's cronies as an aim and purpose that outweighs the prior purpose is not spiritual. Earthly people can actually acknowledge this assertion with their lips, but not with their heart—with their lips because their intellect has received instruction, but not with their heart because their intellect has been destroyed through greed. As a result, they make a master out of aims and purposes focusing on themselves, and a slave out of aims and purposes focusing on the common good, the church, and the kingdom of God. In their hearts they even ask, "How can anyone be any other way?"

[3] In short, earthly people absolutely despise and reject anything they see as separate from themselves, and they value and welcome anything they see as closely connected to themselves. They do not know and do not wish to know that it is spiritual to feel a connection with anyone devoted to goodness, whether that person is unknown or known to us, and to feel disconnected from anyone devoted to evil, whether that person is known or unknown to us, because we then unite with the inhabitants of heaven and disconnect from the inhabitants of hell. Since earthly people are not

open to spiritual inflow, though, they sense no pleasure in this attitude. Consequently, they view it as utterly vile, menial, and practically worthless by comparison with the pleasure they do feel, as it flows in through their physical senses and the cravings of self-love and materialism. This pleasure is dead, because it comes from hell, but the pleasure produced by spiritual inflow is alive and living, because it comes through heaven from the Lord.

5026 *To mock me* means that it would rebel. This can be seen from the symbolism of *mocking* as rebelling, as above in §5014.

5027 *And it happened, as I raised my voice and shouted* means when extreme aversion was felt. This can be seen from the symbolism of *raising one's voice and shouting* as extreme aversion, as also above in §5018.

5028 *That he left his garment with me* symbolizes evidence. This can be seen from the symbolism of *leaving his garment with her* as evidence that [spiritual-earthly truth] had come close (dealt with at §5019). On an inner level, a garment symbolizes truth, and to leave a garment means to snatch away outermost truth (§5008). The reason it symbolizes evidence of a near approach in this case is that outermost truth, when left behind, or snatched away, provides an earthly person with evidence against a spiritual one.

Outermost truth appears to create a bond between a spiritual and an earthly person but does not really do so; see §5008. When the spiritual person explains outermost truth, the incompatibility comes to light. Take the examples laid out above in §5008 as illustration: [2] A spiritual person is just as likely as an earthly person to say that we should do good to the poor, widowed, and orphaned. However, the spiritual person does not believe in doing good to paupers, widows, and orphans who are evil and who call themselves poor, widowed, and orphaned when they are actually rich, using the terms themselves to deceive. This consideration leads the spiritual person to conclude that by the poor, widowed, and orphaned the Word means people who are spiritually so. On the other hand, the earthly person believes in doing good to those who are called poor, widowed, and orphaned, considers them alone to be the ones the Word is referring to, and does not care whether they are evil or good. What it is to be spiritually so, the earthly person does not know and does not want to know. The outermost truth that we are to do good to paupers, widows, and orphans, then, looks the same to both parties but plainly differs when it is explained. Once the difference arises and causes a rift, the earthly person uses it as evidence that the spiritual person had made advances. In other words, the earthly person lies about the spiritual one, who no longer has any means of self-defense. This clarifies why and how a garment also symbolizes evidence.

[3] As another example, a spiritual person is just as likely as an earthly person to say that we are to help our neighbor and to say that everyone is our neighbor. However, the spiritual person believes that one person is our neighbor in a different respect and to a different degree than another. Spiritual people also believe that to help the evil just because they call themselves a neighbor is to hurt their true neighbor. Earthly people unite with spiritual ones on the outermost truth that we are to help our neighbor and on the truth that everyone is our neighbor, but they consider anyone who treats them with favoritism to be their neighbor, not caring whether that person is good or evil. This example too shows that the two sides apparently unite on outermost truth but that there is no real bond, and that as soon as it is explained, a rift opens. Outermost truth then serves the earthly person as evidence against the spiritual person that the latter was "mocking."

The same holds true for all the other examples.

And fled outside means that it then detached. This can be seen from the symbolism of *fleeing outside* as detaching (as above in §5020) and therefore as a lack of truth for self-defense (as in §5009).

5029

Genesis 39:19, 20. *And it happened, as his master heard the words of his wife which she spoke to him, saying, "According to these words your slave did to me," that his anger burned. And Joseph's master took him and put him into the prison house, the place where the monarch's prisoners were imprisoned, and he was there in the prison house.*

5030

And it happened symbolizes a new stage. *As his master heard the words of his wife which she spoke to him* symbolizes the communication of falsity that looked like truth. *Saying, "According to these words your slave did to me,"* symbolizes proof. *That his anger burned* symbolizes an aversion for spiritual truth. *And Joseph's master took him* symbolizes being tested by the earthly level. *And put him into the prison house* means in respect to lies attacking what is good. *The place in which the monarch's prisoners were imprisoned* symbolizes the state in which there are people who succumb to falsity. *And he was there in the prison house* symbolizes how long the trials lasted.

And it happened symbolizes a new stage. This can be seen from the symbolism of *it happened,* which involves transition, or a new stage (discussed at §§4979, 4987, 4999). Here it is a state of spiritual-earthly goodness, a

5031

state represented by Joseph after the outermost layer of truth had been snatched away from him and therefore after there was no longer any union with nonspiritual earthly truth and goodness.

5032   *As his master heard the words of his wife which she spoke to him* symbolizes the communication of falsity that looked like truth, as the following shows: *Hearing the words* symbolizes communication, since hearing means perceiving (§5017) and therefore being communicated. A *wife* symbolizes nonspiritual earthly truth, as mentioned earlier [§4988], but in this case, falsity. The lying words themselves are symbolized by *which she spoke to him,* as above in §5024. The falsity is communicated to nonspiritual earthly goodness, symbolized by *his master,* as above in §5023. The fact that the falsity looked like truth to him is evident from what follows.

[2] The message here concerns how easily nonspiritual earthly goodness is persuaded—so easily that it sees falsity as absolutely true.

For the identity and nature of nonspiritual earthly goodness, or of people with that kind of goodness, see above at §§4988, 4992, 5008, 5013, 5028. To be specific, they are the ones who are mild and upright by heredity, or for reasons originating outside them. They do good by nature and not at the call of religion. To do good by nature and to do good at the call of religion are two entirely different things. In the world we cannot distinguish between them, because we do not know what lies inside, but in the other life the difference is obvious, because one's inner depths are clear to see. One's thoughts and one's intentions and aims reveal themselves there and lie open as plain as day.

[3] As a result I was able to learn what people with nonspiritual goodness and people with spiritual goodness are like. People with nonspiritual earthly goodness allow anyone to persuade them. The evil have an easy time doing so, because evil spirits and demons are in their element or in the highest pleasure of their life when they are able to infiltrate anyone's appetites. Once they have entered, they entice the person into every kind of evil, because they then convince the person that falsity is true. It is easy for them to do so with people given to nonspiritual earthly goodness. With people intent on spiritual goodness they cannot manage it, because these recognize evil and falsity from something inside. The reason people with spiritual goodness recognize it is that when they lived in the world they accepted the rules laid down by doctrine and steeped their inner self in those rules, with the result that heaven can have an effect on their inner self. When people with nonspiritual earthly goodness lived in the world, they did not accept any rules laid down by doctrine or steep their

inner self in those rules, so they have no platform on which heaven can operate. Whatever comes into them from heaven flows on through, and when it reaches their earthly self it is not accepted, because the wicked—the Devil's gang—instantly steal it and smother it, deflect it, or corrupt it.

[4] People who have a merely earthly goodness therefore suffer hardship in the other life. Sometimes they complain a great deal about being placed among hellish spirits, even though (according to themselves) they had behaved as well as anyone. However, the situation is explained to them this way: Their good behavior was exactly like that of a tame, witless animal. They did not care about the goodness and truth that belong to religion and accordingly have no reservoir of goodness and truth in their inner self, so angels cannot protect them. In addition, they did a great deal of evil under the pretense of goodness.

Saying, "According to these words your slave did to me," symbolizes proof. This can be seen from the strength of [Potiphar's] belief that his wife was telling the truth, so that to him the thing had been proved. The wife who persuaded him means nonspiritual earthly truth, but in this case, falsity. For the idea that nonspiritual earthly goodness readily allows falsity to persuade it, see just above at §5032.

People realize that falsity can be proved convincingly enough to look exactly like truth. It is evident from every heresy and from every tenet of every heresy, which appears true to people who adopt the heresy, because of the proofs, but is false. The same is evident from people without any religion who provide themselves with sure proof against religious thinking. They even reach the point where they see it as true that religion exists only for the masses, on whom it acts as a restraint. They see it as true that the material world is the all-in-all, and that divinity is so remote that it hardly amounts to anything. They see it as true that a person's death is no different from the death of an animal. On these points and other points like them, people with nonspiritual earthly goodness let themselves be persuaded and convinced more easily than anybody else. They have no mirror, so to speak, on the inside, only one on the outside, in which illusions look real.

That his anger burned symbolizes an aversion for spiritual truth. This can be seen from the symbolism of *anger* as a departure from charitable goodness (discussed in §357) and therefore as aversion—here, an aversion for spiritual truth, because that is the subject.

The reason *anger* means aversion is that during times when we feel angry at someone, we avert our mind from that person. Anger emerges or is roused when someone or something opposes some bond of love that ties us to an individual or to anything else. When the bond is broken, we blaze up with anger, as if we had lost some of our life's core pleasure and therefore some of our life itself. The grief turns to pain, and the pain to anger.

5035   *And Joseph's master took him* symbolizes being tested by the earthly level. This can be seen from what immediately follows, since it deals with Joseph's being sent to the prison house, which on an inner level depicts the testing of spiritual goodness on the earthly level. Since these ideas are wrapped up in the clause *Joseph's master took him,* they are also symbolized by it.

Trials are of two kinds, one regarding truth and the other regarding goodness. Spirits try us in regard to truth, but demons try us in regard to goodness.

In the other life, what distinguishes spirits from demons is that spirits act on the intellect and therefore on matters of faith, while demons act on the will and therefore on matters of love. Spirits make themselves visible and reveal themselves by talking, but demons make themselves invisible and do not reveal themselves except by their influence on our longings and cravings. In the other world they are separate. Evil, hellish spirits appear out in front and on both sides, beneath the underground realm. Evil, hellish demons appear under the rear end and behind the back, deep under the earth there. Again, evil spirits try us in regard to truth, and evil demons, in regard to goodness.

The next few verses are about trials, but trials inflicted by evil spirits and therefore trials involving lies that attack what is good. These trials are milder than those inflicted by evil demons and arise earlier on.

5036   *And put him into the prison house* means in respect to lies attacking what is good. This can be seen from the symbolism of *being put into the prison house* and held prisoner there as being subjected to trials involving lies that attack what is good (discussed below). First I need to say something about times of trial.

Hardly anyone in the Christian world today knows where trials come from. People who undergo trial believe it is simply anguish that worms its way into us from the evils inside us, first causing us disquiet, then anxiety, then torture. They have no idea it is brought about by evil spirits present with us. The reason they have no idea is that they do not believe they are in communion with spirits while living in the world. They hardly even believe they have any spirit with them. The reality, though, is that in our inner depths we are always in the company of spirits and angels.

[2] Times of trial occur when we are actively regenerating (no one can be reborn without undergoing trial), and they are brought about by the evil spirits around us. At such times we are brought into the state of evil that is ours, or rather the state of evil characterizing the part of us that is most our own. When we enter this state, evil, hellish spirits surround us. When they notice that angels are guarding us from inside, they stir up the distorted thoughts we have had and the wrongs we have done, but the angels defend us from within. This fight is what we perceive as a trial, but so dimly that we can hardly tell it is not simple anxiety. We humans—especially those of us who disbelieve in spiritual inflow—live in a totally obscure state. We sense scarcely a thousandth of the issues over which the evil spirits and angels are fighting. Yet we and our eternal salvation are the whole point, and we provide the resources. What is inside us supplies both the ammunition with which the combatants fight and the issues over which they fight.

I have been allowed to know for certain that this is how the case stands. I have heard the fighting, perceived the inflow, and seen the spirits and angels. I have also spoken with them about the fight during and after it.

[3] To repeat, the primary time for trials to occur is when we are becoming spiritual, because we then understand doctrinal truth in spiritual terms. Often we are unaware that we do, but the angels with us see something spiritual in our earthly preoccupations, because our inner levels then lie open to heaven. That is why we end up among angels after life in the world, if we have been reborn, and there we see and perceive a spiritual dimension that previously seemed earthly to us. If we are this kind of person, angels can defend us when evil spirits attack us during our crises, because they then have a platform on which they can operate. They act on what is spiritual in us, and through what is spiritual on what is earthly.

[4] Consequently, when outermost truth has been snatched away and we therefore have no means of defending ourselves against earthly people (as discussed in §§5006, 5008, 5009, 5022, 5028), we come into spiritual crisis and find ourselves accused by evil spirits, all of whom are purely earthly. One of their main charges is that we lie about what is good. They will say, for instance, "You used to think and say that we should do good to our neighbor, and you proved it with your deeds. But now by 'neighbor' you mean only people with goodness and truth, not people with evil and falsity who cannot be reformed. You do not want to help the evil anymore. If you *are* going to help them, you want them punished, for their

own improvement and in order to head off any harm from your neighbor. That means," they charge, "that you have thought and spoken falsely; your thoughts are at odds with your words."

[5] For another instance, when we become spiritual we no longer consider it reverent and devout to give to monasteries or even to well-endowed churches. Before becoming spiritual we did have the thought that it was reverent and devout, so the evil spirits accuse us of falsity. They stir up all the thoughts we previously held about this holy, pious practice, and all the times we acted on the thought. The same in countless other cases—these examples are only illustrations.

Most of all, the evil spirits infiltrate and stir up the feelings we used to have, as well as anything false or evil we thought or did. In this way they cause us worry and often doubt, even to the point of despair.

[6] This, then, is the source of spiritual distress and of the torture called pangs of conscience. These look to us as though they are inside us, because of the way they flow in and are communicated. People who know and believe these things can be compared to those who see themselves in a mirror and realize that what appears in the mirror (or on the other side of it) is not themselves but only their reflection. People who do not know or believe it can be compared to people who see themselves in a mirror and imagine that they themselves rather than their reflection are what appears there.

5037   Here is why *being put into the prison house* and held prisoner there means being subjected to trials involving lies that attack what is good. *Prison house* is the term for every place just under the sole of the foot and thereabouts where people being devastated are held. These are people with false assumptions who have lived an evil life on the basis of that falsity but nonetheless have had good intentions. They cannot go to heaven until they have rid themselves of their false assumptions, along with the pleasure they took in a life based on those assumptions. The people there are subjected to trials, because false premises and pleasures rooted in a life based on them cannot be removed by any other means.

The place where these people are, or rather the state in which they are, is symbolized in general by a prison house, and the specific locations, by pits. On the process of devastation in the other life, see §§698, 699, 1106–1113, 2699, 2701–2704.

People undergoing devastation are called prisoners—not that they are bound by any chains, but that they have no freedom in regard to their previous thoughts and the resulting emotions. [2] They are the ones the

Word means when it talks about prisoners, or people in jail, as other passages in the Word make plain. In Isaiah, for example:

> I will give you as a pact with the people, as a light for the nations, to open blind eyes, *to lead the prisoner out from prison,* those sitting in darkness out of the *jailhouse.* (Isaiah 42:6, 7)

This is about the Lord and his Coming. Opening blind eyes and leading the prisoner out from prison and those sitting in darkness out of the jailhouse stand for people who lack knowledge of goodness and truth but long to have that knowledge and to become steeped in it. "Prison" is expressed by another word in the original language here, though. [3] In the same author:

> All the youths are hidden *in prison houses;* they have become plunder, and there is none rescuing *and none saying, "Bring them out!"* (Isaiah 42:22)

The youths in an inner sense mean religious truth, which is said to be hidden in prison houses and to become plunder when it is no longer acknowledged. In the same author:

> It will happen on that day that Jehovah will punish the army of the heights on high, and the monarchs of the ground down on the ground, and *the prisoners in the pit will be gathered* and will be shut up *in jail.* After a multitude of days they will be visited. (Isaiah 24:21, 22)

The prisoner in the pit stands for people being devastated, or tested. [4] In the same author:

> What will you do on the day of visitation and devastation, [which] comes from far away? To whom will you flee for help? Those who have not bowed down will fall *under the prisoner* and under the slain. (Isaiah 10:3, 4)

"Under the prisoner" stands for hell, which is under the places where people are devastated. The slain stand for people who have snuffed out religious truth in themselves by their false assumptions, but to a lesser extent than the victims of stabbing discussed at §4503. [5] In Zechariah:

> He will speak peace to the nations, and his rule will be from sea to sea, and from the river to the ends of the earth. And as for you, by the blood of your pact *I will let the prisoners out of a pit* in which there is no

water. Return to the stronghold, *you prisoners with something to hope for.* (Zechariah 9:10, 11, 12)

Letting prisoners out of the pit stands for letting out people who are being devastated and who are being tried. The locations of people being devastated are called pits; see §§4728, 4744. In David:

Jehovah listens to the needy, and *his prisoners he does not despise.* (Psalms 69:33)

In the same author:

Let the *prisoner's groan* come before you. (Psalms 79:11)

In the same author:

Jehovah looked back from the heavens to the earth to hear the *prisoner's groan,* to open up for the children of death. (Psalms 102:19, 20)

The prisoners stand for people who are being devastated and who are being tried. In Isaiah:

In a time of good pleasure I answered you, and on the day of salvation I heard you; I also guarded you and gave you as a pact with the people, to restore the earth, to apportion devastated inheritances, *to say to prisoners, "Go on out!"* and to those in darkness, "Show yourselves!" On paths they will graze, and on all the slopes will be good pasture. And *they will not be hungry and not be thirsty.* (Isaiah 49:8, 9, 10)

[6] In the same author:

The spirit of the Lord Jehovah is on me; Jehovah has anointed me. To bring good news to the *poor* he has sent me, and to bind up the broken at heart; to declare freedom to *captives* and to *prisoners,* to *one whose eyes are bound;* to proclaim a year of good pleasure for Jehovah. (Isaiah 61:1, 2)

In David:

. . . Jehovah who passes judgment for the oppressed, who *gives bread to the hungry,* Jehovah who *releases prisoners,* Jehovah who opens [the eyes of] the *blind,* Jehovah who straightens up the bowed, Jehovah who loves the fair-minded, Jehovah who guards *foreigners;* the *orphan* and *widow* he sustains. (Psalms 146:7, 8, 9)

The prisoners stand for people subjected to devastation and to trials because of falsities. These passages also show who is meant in Matthew by the prisoners, or people in jail, and who by the hungry, the thirsty, and foreigners:

> Then the King will say to those on his right, "I was *hungry* and you gave me something to eat. I was *thirsty* and you gave me a drink. I was a *foreigner* and you gathered me in; naked and you put a robe around me; sick and you visited me. *I was* in *jail* and you came to me." (Matthew 25:34, 35, 36)

To read about them, see the beginning of this chapter, §§4954, 4955, 4956, 4957, 4958.

The place in which the monarch's prisoners were imprisoned symbolizes **5038** the state in which there are people who succumb to falsity, as the following shows: A *place* symbolizes a state, as discussed in §§2625, 2837, 3356, 3387, 4321, 4882. The *monarch's prisoners* symbolize people who succumb to falsity, and since they succumb to falsity, they undergo devastation. The ones who are regenerating in the world undergo trials, because to be tried spiritually is to have one's falsity devastated and one's truth strengthened. Such people are called the monarch's prisoners because a monarch in an inner sense means truth (§§1672, 1728, 2015, 2069, 3009, 3670, 4575, 4581, 4789, 4966). A monarch's prisoners are therefore people stuck in falsity.

The places where the monarch's prisoners were held were also called pits, which is why Joseph said, "I was stolen from the land of the Hebrews, and even here I have not done anything that they should put me *in the pit*" (Genesis 40:15). Concerning a pit as a place of devastation, see §§4728, 4744.

And he was there in the prison house symbolizes how long the trials **5039** lasted. This can be seen from the symbolism of a *prison house* as devastation and as trials (discussed just above at §§5036, 5037), and from that of *being in one* as staying there a while and consequently as the length of time.

Genesis 39:21, 22, 23. *And Jehovah was with Joseph and extended mercy* **5040** *to him and gave him favor in the eyes of the prison house chief. And the prison house chief gave into Joseph's hand all the prisoners who were in the prison house; and everything that they were doing there, he was the doer. The prison house chief was not looking at anything whatever in [Joseph's] hand, for the reason that Jehovah was with [Joseph], and what he was doing, Jehovah was making prosperous.*

And Jehovah was with Joseph means that divinity was in him. *And extended mercy to him* symbolizes divine love in every move. *And gave him favor in the eyes of the prison house chief* symbolizes being buoyed up in his trials as a result. *And the prison house chief* symbolizes truth that governs in a state of trial. *Gave into Joseph's hand all the prisoners who were in the prison house* means from the Lord, over all falsity. *And everything that they were doing there, he was the doer* symbolizes absolute power. *The prison house chief was not looking at anything whatever in [Joseph's] hand* means that he controlled truth. *For the reason that Jehovah was with [Joseph]* means from the divinity inside him. *And what he was doing, Jehovah was making prosperous* means that divine providence is from him.

5041   *And Jehovah was with Joseph* means that divinity was in him—in the Lord, whom *Joseph* in the highest sense represents—and in this case, that it was in him during his times of trial, which are the current theme. Divinity itself is Jehovah, and his presence in the Lord is symbolized by *Jehovah was with Joseph.* Since the literal story is about Joseph, the phrasing is *with* him, but in the inner meaning, which treats of the Lord, it means *in* him.

Anyone in the church can see that Jehovah was in the Lord, because he was conceived by Jehovah. That is why he calls Jehovah his father so many times.

Our very being, and therefore the inmost core of our life, comes from our father. The clothing of it, or our outer levels, comes from our mother. The Lord's being and therefore the inmost core of his life was accordingly divine, because it was Jehovah himself. The clothing or outer levels constituted the humanity he took from his mother by birth. This humanity by its very nature was capable of being tested, polluted as it was with evil inherited from his mother. Because his inmost core was divine, though, he was able by his own power to throw off this evil inherited from his mother. He did so gradually, by undergoing trials, and eventually by undergoing his final trial on the cross. At that point he fully glorified his humanity, or made it divine.

This shows what is meant by the statement that divinity was in him.

5042   *And extended mercy to him* symbolizes divine love in every move. This is established by the symbolism of *mercy* on the highest level as divine love (discussed in §§1735, 3063, 3073, 3120, 3875). God's very being is love, taking "love" in its highest sense, which is completely incomprehensible to humankind. It is from love through truth that everything comes into existence and remains in existence, whether it has life or not.

This divine love flowed from being itself through the inmost core of life in the Lord into every move he made with the humanity he received from his mother. It focused all his efforts on the goals of those efforts and all the goals on the ultimate goal of saving the human race. From the divinity itself within him the Lord saw his human nature for what it was—namely, immersed in evil by heredity. That is why the text says that Jehovah extended mercy to him and why this clause in its highest sense means divine love in every move. Divine mercy is nothing but divine love for people established, as we are, in misery (§§1049, 3063, 3875)—in other words, people being tested. Such people suffer misery and are the main ones meant in the Word by the wretched.

And gave him favor in the eyes of the prison house chief symbolizes being buoyed up in his trials as a result, as the following shows: *Giving favor* means buoying up, because to give favor in times of trial is to comfort and buoy up with hope. A *chief* symbolizes truth of primary importance, as discussed in the next section. And a *prison house* symbolizes the devastation of falsity and therefore times of trial, as noted above in §§5038, 5039.

§5043

And the prison house chief symbolizes truth that governs in a state of trial. This can be seen from the symbolism of a *chief* as truth of primary importance and therefore as a governing truth (discussed below), and from that of a *prison house* as the devastation of falsity and therefore as trial (noted above at §§5038, 5039, 5043).

§5044

First I need to define truth that governs in a state of trial. Truth from the Lord flows into all who are undergoing spiritual trials, and rules and governs their thoughts. It lifts them up whenever they fall into doubt or even despair.

This governing truth is the kind and type of truth that we have learned from the Word or from doctrine and have strengthened in ourselves. We do recall other kinds of truth as well at such times, but they do not exert control over our inner depths. Sometimes this governing truth is invisible to our intellect, but it hovers secretly in the dark and governs us nonetheless. This is because the Lord's divine power flows into it, focusing the inner reaches of our mind on it. If it comes out into the open during our trials, then, we take comfort from it and feel buoyed up.

[2] It is not this truth itself but our desire for it through which the Lord governs us in our times of crisis. The Divine does not flow into anything but what we desire. Truth sown and rooted in our inner dimensions is sown and rooted by desire. Absolutely nothing takes root without desire. Truth sown and rooted through a desire for truth lasts, and the desire brings it back to mind. When it does, such truth brings forward the desire connected with it, and this desire is our response.

That being the case with people undergoing trials, we are never allowed into spiritual crisis until we reach adulthood and have steeped ourselves to this extent in some type of truth through which we can be governed. If not, we succumb, and then our situation grows worse than ever.

These remarks show what is meant by truth governing in a state of trial, as symbolized by the prison house chief.

[3] A *chief,* [or prince,] symbolizes an important truth because on an inner level a monarch symbolizes truth itself (§§1672, 1728, 2015, 2069, 3009, 3670, 4575, 4581, 4789, 4966). Chiefs, being underlings of the monarch, consequently symbolize the main forms of that truth. For this symbolism of chiefs, see §§1482, 2089. Those sections do not do much to illustrate the point with other passages from the Word, though, so let me quote some of them here. In Isaiah:

> A child has been born for us, a son has been given to us, *on whose shoulder will be principality,* . . . *the Prince of Peace,* increasing *principality* and peace; there will not be an end. (Isaiah 9:6, 7)

This is about the Lord. The principality on his shoulder is all the divine truth in the heavens that comes from him. The heavens are divided into principalities according to the truth-from-goodness in them, which is why angels are called principalities. Peace is a state of bliss in the heavens intimately affecting what is good and true there (§3780). As a result, the Lord is called the Prince of Peace and is said to increase principality and peace without end. [4] In the same author:

> Stupid are the *chieftains of Zoan,* the sages, advisors of Pharaoh. How can you say to Pharaoh, "I am the offspring of sages, *the offspring of the monarchs of old"?* The *chieftains of Zoan* have become fools; the *chieftains of Noph* have been deceived. And they led Egypt—the cornerstone of the tribes—astray. (Isaiah 19:11, 13)

This is about Egypt, which symbolizes the church's knowledge (§4749) and therefore earthly truth, on the outermost level of the divine design. That is why Egypt is called the cornerstone of the tribes, since tribes mean all facets of truth taken together (§§3858, 3862, 3926, 3939, 4060). However, in this passage Egypt means knowledge that perverts the truth known to the church, and consequently it means falsified truth on the outermost level of the design. This kind of truth is meant by the chieftains of Zoan and the chieftains of Noph. Egypt calls itself the offspring of the monarchs of old because the knowledge it possessed came from the truth known to the ancient church. Monarchs symbolize truth itself, as shown above, and the monarchs of old symbolize the truth known to the ancient church. [5] In the same author:

> Assyria thinks what is not right, and his heart contemplates what is not right, for his heart is to destroy, and to cut off not a few nations, for he says, *"Aren't my chieftains monarchs?"* (Isaiah 10:7, 8)

Assyria stands for skewed reasoning about divine truth, which gives rise to falsity. So it stands for a perverted power of reason (§1186). "He says, 'Aren't my chieftains monarchs?'" symbolizes this falsified truth—which is to say falsity—that springs from twisted reasoning and looks like real truth.

As long as we are preoccupied with the literal, narrative meaning, we cannot see and therefore cannot believe that Assyria means twisted reasoning, and that chieftains who are monarchs mean the main falsities that are believed to be truth itself. Still less can we see or believe it if we doubt there is anything holier and more universal in divine Scripture than is visible in the literal text. The reality is that in the Word, in an inner sense, Assyria actually means the power of reason and the use of that power, monarchs mean truth itself, and chiefs mean the main forms of truth. What is more, no one in heaven knows what Assyria is, and angels will have nothing to do with the idea of a monarch or prince. When they perceive the idea in us, they transfer it to the Lord and perceive what radiates from him and belongs to him in heaven—in other words, divine truth stemming from his divine goodness. [6] In the same author:

> Assyria will fall by a sword that is not a man's, and a sword that is not a human's will devour him; his rock will also pass away for fright, and by a banner *his chieftains* will be unnerved. (Isaiah 31:8, 9)

This too is about Egypt, which means the church's knowledge perverted. Using knowledge for twisted reasoning about divine truths, which perverts and falsifies them, is Assyria. Those truths, once perverted and falsified, are the chieftains. The sword by which Assyria will fall means falsity fighting truth and devastating it (§§2799, 4499). In the same author:

> For you, Pharaoh's strength will turn to shame, and trust in Egypt's shadow to disgrace, since *his chieftains* were *in Zoan*. (Isaiah 30:3, 4)

Chieftains in Zoan stand for falsified truth and consequently for falsity, as above. [7] In the same author:

> Spoonbill and harrier will possess it, and owl and raven will live in it. He will stretch over it a line measuring the void and plummets measuring

its devastation. Let its nobles, who are not there, call it a kingdom, and *all its chieftains will be nothing.* (Isaiah 34:11, 12)

The spoonbill, harrier, owl, and raven stand for types of falsity that come into being when the divine truth in the Word is regarded as worthless. The ruination and devastation of truth is symbolized by the line measuring the void and plummets measuring its devastation. The falsities that such people take as their main truths are symbolized by the chieftains. In the same author:

I will render the *holy princes* profane, and give Jacob over to extermination, and Israel to insults. (Isaiah 43:28)

Rendering the holy princes profane stands for doing so to sacred truth. The eradication of truth from both the outer and the inner parts of the church is symbolized by giving Jacob over to extermination and Israel to insults. Jacob is the outer part of the church, and Israel the inner part; see §4286. [8] In Jeremiah:

Through the gates of this city will enter *monarchs* and *chieftains,* sitting on David's throne, riding in a chariot and on horses, *they* and their *chieftains.* (Jeremiah 17:25)

People who take the Word in its narrative sense cannot see that this verse conceals anything more profound or holy than the fact that monarchs and chieftains will enter through the gates of the city in a chariot and on horses. From this they gather that the longevity of the kingdom is being symbolized. However, one who knows the inner-level symbolism of the city, monarchs, chieftains, David's throne, and riding in a chariot and on horses sees something more profound and holy there. The city, Jerusalem, symbolizes the Lord's spiritual kingdom (§§2117, 3654); the monarchs, divine truth, as shown above; the chieftains, the main forms of truth; David's throne, the Lord's heaven (1888); riding in a chariot and on horses, a spiritual power of intellect in the church (2760, 2761, 3217). [9] In the same author:

O sword against the Chaldeans and against the inhabitants of Babylon and against *its chieftains* and against its sages! O sword against liars! O sword against its horses and against its chariots! (Jeremiah 50:35, 36, 37)

A sword stands for truth that is battling falsity, and for falsity that is battling truth and devastating it (§§2799, 4499). The Chaldeans stand for people who profane what is true, and the inhabitants of Babylon for people who profane what is good (§§1182, 1283, 1295, 1304, 1307, 1308, 1321, 1322, 1326, 1327 at the end). Chieftains stand for falsities that these people consider to be important truths. Horses stand for the church's power of intellect, and chariots for its doctrine. The devastation of these is symbolized by a sword against horses and against chariots. [10] In the same author:

> How the Lord in his anger overclouds the daughter of Zion! The Lord has swallowed it up; he has not spared any dwellings in Jacob. In his wrath he has destroyed the strongholds of Judah's daughter; he threw them down to the earth. He defiled the kingdom *and its chieftains*. The gates have sunk into the earth, and he has smashed their bars; the *monarch and chieftains* live among the nations. (Lamentations 2:1, 2, 9)

The daughter of Zion and Judah stands for a heavenly religion, and in this case, a heavenly religion destroyed. The kingdom stands for doctrinal truth in that religion (§§2547, 4691). The monarch stands for truth itself; the chieftains for important forms of it. [11] In the same author:

> Our hides have been blackened like a kettle because of tempests of famine. They have raped women in Zion; young women in the cities of Judah. *Chieftains have been hung by their hands.* (Lamentations 5:10, 11, 12)

"Chieftains hung by their hands" stands for the profanation of truth, since hanging represented the damnability of profanation. This representation was also the basis for the command that when the people whored after the Baal of Peor and revered the gods of [the Moabites], *the chieftains were to be hanged* before the sun (Numbers 25:1, 2, 3, 4). To whore after the Baal of Peor and revere the gods of [the Moabites] was to profane their own worship. In Ezekiel:

> The *monarch* will mourn and the *chieftain* will be clothed in shock, and the hands of the people of the land will be terrified; I will deal with them for their way. (Ezekiel 7:27)

Again the monarch stands for truth in general, and the chieftain for the main examples of it. [12] In the same author:

> The *chieftain* who is in their midst will be borne on their shoulder in the dark and go out; through the wall they will dig to take him out through it. His face he will veil so that he himself will not see the land with his eye. (Ezekiel 12:12)

The chieftain does not mean a chieftain, obviously, but truth known to the church. When the text says this truth will be borne on their shoulder in the dark, the meaning is that it is shunted off among falsities as force-fully as possible—darkness meaning falsity. The veiling of the chieftain's face means that truth is utterly invisible. "So that he will not see the land with his eye" means that there is no religion, the land meaning the church; see §§662, 1066, 1068, 1262, 1413, 1607, 1733, 1850, 2117, 2118 at the end, 2928, 3355, 4447, 4535. In Hosea:

> For many days the children of Israel will sit: *no monarch* and *no chieftain* and no sacrifice and no pillar and no ephod and no teraphim. (Hosea 3:4)

[13] And in David:

> All glorious is the *king's daughter* within [the palace], and her clothing is made of gold braid; in embroidery she will be brought to the *king.* In place of your forebears will be your children; *you will make them chief-tains in the whole earth.* (Psalms 45:13, 14, 16)

The king's daughter means the Lord's spiritual kingdom. His kingdom is called spiritual because of his divine truth, which is depicted here by the clothing of gold braid and embroidery. The children are the truths in that kingdom, which come from the Lord's divinity and will be chieftains, or foremost in importance.

Where Ezekiel speaks of the chieftain and his possession in the new Jerusalem and new land (Ezekiel 44:3; 45:7, 8, 17; 46:8, 10, 12, 16, 18; 48:21), the chieftain in a general way symbolizes truth from the Lord's divine being. The new Jerusalem, the new temple, and the new land mean the Lord's kingdom in the heavens and on earth, which is depicted through representations here, as it also is elsewhere in the Word.

5045   *Gave into Joseph's hand all the prisoners who were in the prison house* means from the Lord, over all falsity—that is, truth governing in a state of trial—as the following shows: *Giving into Joseph's hand* means putting into his power, a *hand* symbolizing power (§5008). The meaning is, then, that it was from the Lord, since anything resulting from his power and authority comes from him. *Joseph* in an inner sense means the Lord, as shown many times before. And the *prisoners in the prison house* symbol-ize falsity, as discussed above in §§5037, 5038. "The prison house chief gave into Joseph's hand all the prisoners who were in the prison house" therefore symbolizes truth from the Lord governing over all the falsity in a state of trial. That is, the truth through which he controlled the falsity in a state of trial came from himself.

The text from here to the end of the chapter has to do with the Lord in its inner meaning. It says that in a state of trial he used his own power to control—in other words, conquer—the hells, which were awash in evil and falsity, and which were constantly flooding the human race with their evil and falsity.

On the point that the Lord overcame and subdued the hells by his own power and in this way glorified the humanity in himself, or made it divine, see §§1616, 1749, 1755, 1813, 1904, 1914, 1921, 1935, 2025, 2026, 2083, 2159, 2574, 2786, 2795, 3036, [3381,] 3382, 4075, 4287, 5005. This can be seen from many Scripture passages, including this one from John:

> I lay my soul down so that I can take it back; no one takes it from me,
> but I lay it down by myself. I have the power to lay it down, and I have
> the power to take it back. (John 10:17, 18)

The Lord's suffering on the cross was the final of his trials, through which he fully glorified the humanity in himself, or made it divine, as is shown by many passages in the Word, including John 13:31, 32; 17:1, 5; Luke 24:26.

And everything that they were doing there, he was the doer symbolizes **5046** absolute power, as is self-evident. After all, these words imply that everything was from the Lord and consequently that he had absolute power to act or not act.

The prison house chief was not looking at anything whatever in [Joseph's] **5047** *hand* means that he controlled truth, as the following shows: The *prison house chief* symbolizes truth governing in a state of trial, as discussed above at §5044. And *not looking at anything in his hand* means that it came from him and therefore from absolute power, as above in §§5045, 5046.

For the reason that Jehovah was with [Joseph] means from the divinity **5048** inside him, as the remarks above in §5041 show.

And what he was doing, Jehovah was making prosperous means that **5049** divine providence is from him. This can be seen from the symbolism of *making something prosperous* as providence (mentioned at §§4972, 4975). The divinity of the providence is meant by *Jehovah,* and the fact that it comes from him, by *he was doing.*

The reason *making something prosperous* in the highest sense means providence is that everything visible on the outermost level of the earthly world that is prosperous has its origin in the Lord's divine providence. Elsewhere, with the Lord's divine mercy, I will demonstrate from experiences in the spiritual world that this is so and that everything involving what we call luck has the same origin [§§6493–6494].

Correspondence with the Universal Human (Continued): Correspondence of the Lower Torso and the Reproductive Organs

5050 AT the end of the previous chapter, §§4931–4953, I showed from experience who belongs to the area of the hands, arms, and feet in the universal human, or heaven. Now I need to identify the communities in heaven, or in the universal human, to which the lower torso and the associated organs (called the reproductive organs) correspond.

To address the subject generally, the lower torso and the associated organs correspond to real marriage love and consequently to communities where [angels] who have that love exist. The inhabitants of those communities are more heavenly and live a life of greater pleasure and peace than any others.

5051 Once, in a peaceful dream, I saw several trees in a wooden planter. One of them was tall, another was shorter, and two were small. The shorter tree gave me intense delight. During the dream my mind was filled with a wonderful calm that I cannot describe.

After waking up, I talked with the spirits who had brought me the dream. They were angelic spirits (see §§1977, 1979), and they told me that what I had seen symbolized marriage love. The tall tree symbolized a husband, the shorter tree a wife, and the two small trees, children. They also said that the wonderful calm filling my mind showed the nature of the pleasant peace felt by inhabitants of the other world who had lived lives of genuine marriage love.

They added that this is the character of [spirits] belonging to the area of the thighs just above the knees, and that [spirits] whose state is even more pleasant belong to the genital area.

I was also shown that communication takes place through the lower legs with the soles and heels of the feet. The existence of this communication can also be seen from the large nerve in the thigh that branches out not only through the groin to the reproductive organs—the organs of marriage love—but also through the lower legs to the soles and heels of the feet.

At the same time it was disclosed what the Word meant by the hip joint and the thigh tendon that Jacob dislocated when wrestling with the angel (Genesis 32:25, 31, 32, discussed in §§4280, 4281, 4314, 4315, 4316, 4317).

[2] Next I saw a big dog, like the one the earliest authors call Cerberus. It had a terrifying maw. I was told that a dog like this symbolizes protection against our overstepping the bounds between heavenly marriage love and a love of adultery, which is hellish. Heavenly marriage love exists when we live content in the Lord with our spouse, whom we tenderly love, and with our children. In the world this brings us deep satisfaction, and in the other life heavenly joy. When we pass from this love to its opposite and view the joy it contains as heavenly, even though it is hellish, such a dog appears and acts as a guard to prevent opposite pleasures from communicating back and forth.

The inmost heaven is the one through which the Lord instills marriage love. The inhabitants there live in greater peace than any others. Peace in the heavens resembles springtime in the world, which gladdens everything. It is the origin of true heavenliness. **5052**

The angels in the inmost heaven are the very wisest, and innocence makes them look to others like little children. Not only that, they love children far more than even the children's fathers and mothers do.

They are present with a baby in the womb, and through them the Lord makes sure the fetus is nourished and develops. So they are in charge of those who are pregnant.

Each and every reproductive member and organ in both sexes has a heavenly community to which it corresponds. These communities are distinct from the others, just as the genital area of the human body is perfectly distinct and separate from the other parts. **5053**

The reason these communities are heavenly is that marriage love is fundamental to all love (§§686, 2733, 2737, 2738). It has a more excellent function and therefore provides more exquisite pleasure than any other kind of love. Marriage, you see, is the breeding ground of the whole human race and of the Lord's heavenly kingdom (since heaven comes from the human race).

People who loved babies tenderly, such as adoring mothers, are located in the region of the uterus and of the organs surrounding it—specifically, **5054** of the cervix and ovaries. The inhabitants there have an incredibly sweet, wonderful life and more heavenly joy than others.

5055   I was not allowed to learn the identity and nature of the communities relating to the individual genital organs, though, because they are too deep to be comprehended by anyone in a lower realm. These communities also relate to hidden functions of the organs, which are far from being understood. The providential reason they are hidden is that such things, which are absolutely heavenly in themselves, would otherwise be damaged by the foul thoughts associated with lust, whoredom, and adultery. For many people, these thoughts are aroused simply by the mention of those organs.

As a consequence, let me talk about some less central phenomena that I did see.

5056   Once a spirit from another planet was with me. (Spirits from other planets will be discussed elsewhere, by the Lord's divine mercy.) He begged me desperately to intercede for him so that he could go to heaven. He said he was unaware of having done wrong, aside from criticizing the inhabitants of that planet. (There are spirits who rebuke and castigate anyone who does not live right, and they will also be discussed in the treatment of the spirits of other planets [§§7801–7810].) He added that after criticizing them he would instruct them. His voice cracked as he spoke. He was able to elicit pity, but all I could answer him was, "I cannot help you. That is for the Lord alone to do, and if you are worthy, you have reason to hope." Then he was sent back to join some upright spirits from his planet, but they said he could not mix with them because he was not like them.

Still, in his intense longing he demanded to be let into heaven, so he was sent to a community of good and decent spirits from our planet, but they also said he could not be with them. Seen in heaven's light, his color was black, but *he* said he was brown rather than black.

[2] I was told that spirits who are later accepted among the ones making up the province of the seminal vesicles are like this at first. The seminal vesicles collect the seed and the fluid to go with it and combine the two. The combination prepares the seed for ejaculation into the cervix, where it separates, and in this way serves to bring about conception. The substance of the seed contains an energy and what you might call a yearning to perform its function and accordingly to rid itself of the fluid that clothes it.

A similar trait appeared in that spirit, who came back to me now in shabby clothes, saying he longed intensely to go to heaven and could now tell he was a good candidate. I was allowed to suggest that it might be a

sign he would soon be accepted. Some angels then told him to get rid of
his clothes. In his eagerness he took them off so fast that hardly anything
could be quicker. This represented the nature of the longings in inhabitants of the area to which the seminal vesicles correspond.

I saw a mortar and standing next to it a man with an iron tool who
fantasized that he was pounding people in the mortar, hurting them in
ghastly ways. The man had tremendous pleasure doing it. The pleasure
itself was communicated to me so that I could learn its nature and strength
in people like this. It was a hellish pleasure.

Angels told me that this kind of delight reigned supreme in Jacob's
descendants, who enjoyed nothing more than torturing non-Jews, exposing
their dead bodies for wild animals and birds to devour, hacking them up
alive with saws and axes, sending them through a brick furnace (2 Samuel
12:31), and dashing children in pieces and tossing them aside. This behavior
was never commanded, and never tolerated except in types whose thigh
tendon was dislocated (§5051).

Spirits like this live under the right heel, where adulterers with a mean
streak are located.

[2] It is amazing, then, that anyone could possibly believe this nation
was chosen above others. That is why many people harden themselves
in the view that the way we live makes no difference, that we are chosen
and consequently accepted into heaven on pure mercy, no matter how we
have lived. However, anyone of sound reason can see that such a way of
thinking goes against the Divine. The Divine is mercy itself, so if heaven
resulted from pure mercy, regardless of a person's life, absolutely everyone
would be welcomed in. Sending anyone down to hell to be tormented
there when such a person could be taken to heaven would be ruthless, not
merciful; and to choose one individual over another would be injustice,
not justice.

[3] Therefore when people have adopted and hardened themselves
in the belief that some have been chosen and the rest have not, and that
entrance into heaven is based on mercy alone, no matter how a person has
lived, they are told—and I have heard and seen this several times—that
the Lord never denies heaven to anyone. If they want, they can learn this
from experience. They are taken up to a certain community in heaven
whose inhabitants lived lives marked by a desire for goodness—in other
words, by neighborly love. When the subjects of the experiment arrive,
though, being evil, they start to suffer distress and inner torment, because
the life there is opposed to them. When heavenly light appears, it makes
them look like devils, almost devoid of human shape. Some have their

faces drawn back, some look like a set of teeth, and some look monstrous in other ways. So they cringe at themselves and throw themselves head-long into hell—the deeper the better, as far as they are concerned.

5058   There was also one man of fairly high rank in the world, who had been known to me at the time. I had not known what he was like inside, but in the next world, after several upheavals in the state of his life, it became clear that he was a swindler.

Having stayed a little while among other deceivers in the next world and having suffered difficulties there, he wanted to separate from them. I heard him saying he wanted to go to heaven. He too had believed that get-ting in was simply a matter of mercy, but I told him that if he went there, he would not be able to stay long. I said he would be in as much pain as people in the world who are in the throes of death, but he still insisted. He too was admitted into a community of the good and simplehearted, who were out in front, above the head. On arriving, he acted according to the life within him by starting to deal treacherously and deceitfully. After one short hour, the kind, simplehearted inhabitants began to com-plain that he was taking away their perception of goodness and truth and therefore their pleasure, destroying their state. Then some light from an inner heaven was let in, and by that light the man was seen as a devil, the top of his nose hideously gashed. He himself started to undergo inward torture, and upon this sensation, he hurled himself into hell.

To be chosen and received, then, is clearly not a result of mercy. No, it is the way we live that makes heaven. A life of goodness and belief in the truth, and everything that goes with them, are granted out of mercy to those who accept mercy in the world. They are the ones received out of mercy, and they are the ones referred to as the chosen (§§3755 at the end, 3900).

5059   When I was approached by [spirits] who had lived in violation of marriage love—that is, in adultery—they filled my groin with pain; and the larger the part adultery had played in their lives, the worse the pain. This inflow also showed me that the area of the lower torso corresponds to marriage love.

Their hell is in fact beneath and behind that area, under the but-tocks. There they spend their lives in filth and excrement, which delight them, because in the spiritual world such muck corresponds to adulter-ous pleasures.

However, all this will be addressed where the hells are discussed in general and specific, the Lord in his divine mercy willing.

Likewise I was able to tell who corresponds to the testicles from [spirits] devoted to violating marriage love who inflict pain on the testicles. **5060** When communities [in the other world] operate, they act on those areas and parts of the body to which they correspond. The inflow from heavenly communities is soft, sweet, and agreeable. The inflow from hellish communities in opposition to them is harsh and painful. Their inflow is not noticed, though, except by people whose inner reaches have opened up and who therefore have been given perceptible communication with the spiritual world.

[The spirits] devoted to violating marriage love who inflict pain on the testicles are those that use love, friendship, and professional duties as a cover for treachery. When they came to me, they wanted to talk with me privately, being extremely fearful of bystanders. That is what they had been like during their physical life, and since they were such then, they are also such in the next life. Our life always follows us.

[2] There blew up from the area around Gehenna a kind of invisible gust. It was a troop of these spirits. Later, although there were many spirits in the troop, it appeared to me as only a single individual, bound with straps that he nonetheless removed, as it seemed to him. This meant that they wanted to remove all obstacles. (That is how one's thoughts and mental efforts appear represented in the world of spirits, and when they appear, the symbolism is immediately understood.)

Afterward it seemed to me as if there came out of his body a small, snow-white being who walked up to me. This represented a thought and intention they had, that they wanted to clothe themselves in a state of innocence so that no one could suspect them of such a thing.

When he reached me, he moved down toward my hips and seemed to wrap himself around them both, which represented their desire to present themselves as possessing chaste marriage love. Then he spiraled around my feet, which represented their desire to worm their way in through the kinds of things in the physical realm that give pleasure. Finally this one small individual became almost invisible, which represented their wish to lie perfectly hidden.

[3] Angels told me that this kind of infiltration is typical of those who scheme against marriage love. They are the people who, when they were in the world, ingratiated themselves in order to commit adultery with other men's wives. They speak chastely and sanely about marriage love, compliment the children, and praise the husband in every way so as to be considered a chaste, unoffending friend, when they are really adulterous frauds.

I was also shown what they are like, as a result. At the end of the events above, the little snow-white man became visible and appeared dark, in fact very black, and extremely ugly too. He was thrown into his hell, which was actually deep under the middle section of the lower torso. There the inhabitants live in revoltingly disgusting surroundings and are among the robbers who relate to general involuntary sensation, as discussed at §4327.

I then talked with such spirits as well, and they were amazed that anyone should have a conscience over adultery, that anyone might choose in conscience not to lie with another man's wife, even when given permission. When I spoke with them about conscience, they denied that anyone has one.

I was told that most of them come from the Christian world and rarely do any come from other parts.

5061   In place of a postscript, let me add this note. There were some spirits who were hidden away for a long time, shut up in their own hell unable to escape. Occasionally I stopped to wonder who they were. One evening they were released, and I then heard them make a muttering sound that was quite agitated and lasted quite a while. Once they were given the opportunity, I heard them lampooning me and sensed their effort and wish to come up and destroy me. I asked the angels why. They said the spirits had hated me when they were alive, even though I had done absolutely nothing to hurt them, and I was taught that when spirits like this simply perceive the aura of one they hated, they seek that person's ruin. But they were sent back into their hell.

This made it plain to me that people who hated each other in the world come together in the other life and attempt to hurt each other over and over—which I was allowed to learn from many other examples as well. After all, hatred is opposed to love and charity. It is spiritual aversion and antipathy. So in the other world, as soon as these people sense the aura of someone they hated they go into a kind of fury.

This shows what is involved in the Lord's statement in Matthew 5:22, 23, 24, 25, 26.

5062   More is said about correspondence with the universal human at the end of the next chapter [§§5171–5190].

Genesis 40

[Matthew 25:37–46]

THE previous chapter, Genesis 39, began with an explanation of the Lord's words in Matthew 25:34, 35, 36 about a judgment on the good and the evil. Next comes the following: **5063**

> Then the righteous will answer him, saying, "Lord, when did we see you hungry and feed you? Or thirsty and give you a drink? But when did we see you as a foreigner and gather you in? Or naked and clothe you? But when did we see you sick or in jail and come to you?" But answering, the King will say to them, "Truly, I say to you: so far as you did it for one of these least consequential brothers and sisters of mine, you did it for me." Then he will also say to those on the left, "Go away from me, you cursed ones, into eternal fire prepared for the Devil and the Devil's angels! For I was hungry and you did not give me something to eat; I was thirsty and you did not give me a drink; I was a foreigner and you did not gather me in; naked, and you did not clothe me; sick and in jail, and you did not visit me." Then these also will answer him, saying, "Lord, when did we see you hungry or thirsty or a foreigner or naked or sick or in jail and not tend to you?" Then he will answer them, saying, "Truly, I say to you: so far as you did not do it for one of these least consequential, you also did not do it for me." And these will go away into eternal punishment, but the righteous into eternal life. (Matthew 25:37–46)

The material at the head of the previous chapter, §§4954–4959, explained what is symbolized on an inner level by giving the hungry something to eat, giving a drink to the thirsty, gathering in a foreigner, clothing the naked, and visiting the sick and imprisoned. That is, the essential nature of neighborly love is what these words embrace and depict. The hungry, thirsty, and foreign symbolize a desire for goodness and truth, and the naked, sick, **5064** and imprisoned symbolize an acknowledgment of what we really are; see §§4956, 4958.

5065   Since the same words are repeated three times in this selection and, as just mentioned, have been explained before, there is no need to expound their inner-level symbolism individually or go over each word again. Here I will limit myself to telling the symbolism of the answer given by those who were on the right and by those who were on the left, that they had not seen the Lord hungry, thirsty, a foreigner, naked, sick, or in prison, and then the symbolism of the king, of a righteous person and eternal life, and of a cursed person and eternal fire.

5066   The answer of those on the right—"Lord, when did we see you hungry and feed you? Or thirsty and give you a drink? When did we see you as a foreigner and gather you in? Or naked and clothe you? When did we see you sick or in jail and come to you?"—means that if they had seen the Lord himself, they would all have performed those duties. However, they would have done their duty not from love for him but from fear, because he was going to be judge of the universe. They would have acted not for his sake but for their own and therefore not with inner motivation, from the heart, but for shallow motives, as a mere gesture. Their attitude is like that of people seeing a monarch whose favor they want to earn, in hopes of becoming important and rich, and whom they therefore treat with deference.

The situation is the same when people engage in outwardly reverent worship in which they "see" the Lord and humble themselves to him, believing they will receive eternal life as a result, even though they have no love for their neighbor and do good to no one except for their own sake or for themselves alone. They are like subjects who make an outward show of approaching their monarch most reverently but sneer at royal commands because in their heart they despise the sovereign.

This and more of the same is what is symbolized by the answer of those on the right. Since the actions of the evil are similar on the outside, those on the left answered almost the same way.

5067   The Lord does not care about the outer surface, then, but about the inner core, and we testify to our inner core not only by our worship but also by our love for our neighbor and by putting that love into practice. Consequently the Lord answered, "Truly, I say to you: so far as you did it for one of these least consequential brothers and sisters of mine, you did it for me." The people the Lord is calling his brothers and sisters are the ones who dedicate themselves to active, charitable goodness. He is present with them, because he is in the goodness itself. They are also the people properly meant by "one's neighbor." Not even in them does the Lord make himself visible, since they are relatively inferior, but they make themselves visible to the Lord as people who worship him from deep within.

The Lord calls himself a king ("When the Son of Humankind comes in his glory, he will sit on a glorious throne. Then the King will say to them . . ." [Matthew 25:31, 34]) because the Lord's royal aspect is divine truth, by which and according to which judgment is passed. **5068**

However, the good are judged by and according to divine truth in one way, and the evil in another. The good have accepted divine truth, so they are judged by goodness and therefore by mercy. The evil have not accepted divine truth, so they are judged by truth and therefore not by mercy. Mercy is something they have rejected, and as a result they consistently reject it in the other life.

To accept divine truth is not only to believe but also to act on that belief. In other words, it is to put matters of doctrine into practice so that they become matters of life.

That is why the Lord calls himself a king.

For the Lord's royal aspect being divine truth, see §§1728, 2015 at the end, 3009, 3670, 4581, 4966.

The description of those on the right as righteous ("The *righteous* will answer him, saying, . . . And the *righteous* will go into eternal life") means that they are governed by the Lord's righteousness. Everyone given to neighborly kindness is called righteous—not that the righteous create this quality in themselves. No, it is created in them by the Lord, whose righteousness becomes their own. **5069**

If we believe that we make ourselves righteous, or that we have become so upright that we no longer have any evil, we are among the unrighteous rather than the righteous. We attribute goodness to ourselves and grow self-righteous over it, and people who do this can never worship the Lord with true humility.

That is why the people the Word calls righteous and holy are the ones who realize and acknowledge that all goodness comes from the Lord and all evil from themselves—or rather from hell in themselves.

The eternal life given to the righteous is life flowing from goodness. Goodness contains life because goodness comes from the Lord, who is life itself. Life from the Lord holds wisdom and understanding, because to accept goodness from the Lord and to therefore will what is good is **5070** the mark of wisdom, while to accept truth from the Lord and therefore believe truth is the mark of understanding. People who have this wisdom and understanding have life, and since this kind of life brings happiness with it, "life" also symbolizes eternal happiness.

Something opposite is given to people immersed in evil. They do seem to have life, especially in their own eyes, but it is the kind of life that the Word refers to as death and that really is spiritual death, because they have no wisdom about goodness and no understanding of truth. Anyone who gives some thought to it can see this. If goodness and the truth resulting from it contain life, evil and the falsity resulting from it cannot possess life. Evil and its falsity oppose life and snuff it out, so they do not possess any life except the kind possessed by lunatics.

5071   Those on the left are described as cursed, and their punishment is called eternal fire. ("Then he will also say to those on the left, 'Go away from me, you *cursed ones,* into *eternal fire* prepared for the Devil and the Devil's angels!' . . . And these will go away into *eternal punishment.'*) This is because they turned away from goodness and truth toward evil and falsity. In the Word's inner meaning, being cursed means turning away (§§245, 379, 1423, 3530, 3584).

The eternal fire they depart into is not physical fire and is not the torments of conscience but is a craving for evil. Our cravings are spiritual fires that consume us during bodily life and torment us in the other life. These fires drive hell's inhabitants to torture each other in horrendous ways.

[2] It stands to reason that eternal fire is not physical fire. It is not the torments of conscience because people who are awash in evil never have any conscience, and people who had no conscience during bodily life cannot have any in the other life either. Eternal fire consists in cravings because all the fire of life comes from what a person loves. Heavenly fire comes from a love for what is good and true; hellish fire, from a love for what is evil and false. To say the same thing another way, heavenly fire comes from love for the Lord and love for one's neighbor, and hellish fire comes from love for oneself and love of worldly advantages.

Anyone who pays attention can see that this is the source of all the fire or warmth inside us. That is why love is called spiritual warmth and why love is precisely what is meant by fire and warmth in the Word (§§934 at the end, 1297, 1527, 1528, 1861, 2446, 4906).

The fire of life in the evil is such that when their cravings intensify, they have a fire within that burns with a raging desire to cause others pain. The fire of life in the good is such that when they rise to a new level of desire, they also have a kind of fire within, but one that gives them a love and zeal to help others.

Genesis 40

1. And it happened after these words that the cupbearer of Egypt's king and the baker sinned against their master, Egypt's king.

2. And Pharaoh was enraged over his two court attendants—over the chief of the cupbearers and over the chief of the bakers.

3. And he put them into the jail of the house of the chief of the body-guards, at the prison house, the place where Joseph was a prisoner.

4. And the chief of the bodyguards set Joseph in charge of them, and he waited on them, and for days they were in jail.

5. And the two of them dreamed a dream, each his own dream, in one night, each according to the interpretation of his dream—the cupbearer and the baker, who belonged to Egypt's king, who were prisoners in the prison house.

6. And Joseph came to them in the morning and looked at them, and here, they were troubled.

7. And he questioned Pharaoh's court attendants who were with him in the jail of his master's house, saying, "Why are your faces ill today?"

8. And they said to him, "A dream we have dreamed, and there is no interpreter for it." And Joseph said to them, "Don't interpretations belong to God? Tell me, please."

9. And the chief of the cupbearers told his dream to Joseph, and he said to him, "[I was] in my dream, and look: a grapevine before me!

10. And on the vine three shoots, and it seemed to be sprouting; its flower came up, and its clusters ripened into grapes.

11. And Pharaoh's cup was in my hand, and I took the grapes and squeezed them into Pharaoh's cup, and I put the cup on Pharaoh's palm."

12. And Joseph said to him, "This is its interpretation: The three shoots are three days.

13. In another three days Pharaoh will lift your head and return you to your position, and you will put Pharaoh's cup into his hand according to your former custom when you were his cupbearer.

14. But remember me within yourself when it is well with you, and may you please show mercy on me and remind Pharaoh of me and bring me out of this house.

15. Because I was treacherously stolen from the land of the Hebrews, and even here I have not done anything that they should put me in the pit."

16. And the chief of the bakers saw that he had given a good interpretation, and he said to Joseph, "I too was in my dream and look: three baskets with holes in them on my head!

17. And in the top basket, some of every food of Pharaoh's, the work of a baker, and birds eating it from the basket on my head."

18. And Joseph answered and said, "This is its interpretation: The three baskets are three days.

19. In another three days Pharaoh will lift your head off you and hang you on wood, and birds will eat your flesh off you."

20. And it happened on the third day, the day on which Pharaoh had been born, that he made a banquet for all his servants and lifted the head of the chief of the cupbearers and the head of the chief of the bakers in the midst of his servants.

21. And he returned the chief of the cupbearers to his position as cupbearer, and he put the cup on Pharaoh's palm.

22. And the chief of the bakers he hanged, as Joseph had interpreted to them.

23. And the chief of the cupbearers did not remember Joseph, and forgot him.

Summary

5072 THE inner meaning of this chapter continues to talk about a state of trial—trial being the means by which even the bodily level is brought into correspondence. Strictly speaking, the bodily level consists in sense impressions, which are of two kinds. Some come under the control of the mind's intellectual side, and some come under the volitional side. Those under the intellectual side are represented by the cupbearer of Egypt's king, and those under the volitional side, by the baker. We keep the first kind of sense impressions for a while, but the second kind is discarded, and this is represented by the fact that the cupbearer returned to his position, while the baker was hanged.

The rest will become clear from the running thread of the inner meaning.

Inner Meaning

G ENESIS 40:1, 2, 3, 4. *And it happened after these words that the cup-* **5073**
bearer of Egypt's king and the baker sinned against their master, Egypt's king. And Pharaoh was enraged over his two court attendants—over the chief of the cupbearers and over the chief of the bakers. And he put them into the jail of the house of the chief of the bodyguards, at the prison house, the place where Joseph was a prisoner. And the chief of the bodyguards set Joseph in charge of them, and he waited on them, and for days they were in jail.

And it happened symbolizes a new stage and what follows. *After these words* means after what comes before. *They sinned* symbolizes disorder. *The cupbearer of Egypt's king* means in the parts of the body under the control of the intellectual side. *And the baker* means in the parts of the body under the control of the volitional side. *Against their master, Egypt's king* means that they opposed the new state of the earthly self. *And Pharaoh was enraged* means that the new earthly self turned away. *Over his two court attendants* means from physical sensations of both kinds. *Over the chief of the cupbearers and over the chief of the bakers* means from sensations subordinate to the intellectual side and to the volitional side in general. *And he put them into the jail* symbolizes rejection. *Of the house of the chief of the bodyguards* means by [facts] of primary importance in interpretation. *At the prison house* means among false ideas. *The place where Joseph was a prisoner* symbolizes the current state of heavenliness on the earthly plane in regard to [the outer senses]. *And the chief of the bodyguards set Joseph in charge of them* means that the heavenly part of the earthly plane taught [the outer senses], using the main [facts] needed for interpretation. *And he waited on them* means that it gave instruction. *And for days they were in jail* means that they stayed a long time in a state of rejection.

And it happened symbolizes a new stage and what follows. This can be **5074**
seen from the fact that in the Word, *it happened* involves a new stage (see

§§4979, 4999). In the original language it takes the place of a division between one sequence of events and the next (§4987), which is why "it happened" also symbolizes what follows.

5075   *After those words* means after what comes before. This can be seen from the fact that *words* in the original language also mean "things." *After those words,* then, means after those things, or after what comes before.

Words in the original language also mean "things" because on an inner level they symbolize doctrinal truth. That is why all divine truth as a whole is called the Word, and in its highest sense the Word means the Lord himself, the source of all divine truth (§1288). Nothing that exists in the universe is anything—nothing is a "thing"—unless it springs from divine goodness through divine truth, and for this reason *words* in the Hebrew language also mean "things."

It is clear in John that nothing in the universe is anything, nothing is a thing, unless it springs from divine goodness through divine truth, that is, through the Word:

> In the beginning there was the *Word,* and *the Word was with God,* and the *Word* was God. Everything was made by him, and nothing that was made was made without him. (John 1:1, 3)

[2] Terms or expressions mostly trace the origin of their inner symbolism to the inner self, which interacts with spirits and angels. In every one of us, the spirit, or the actual person that survives the body's death, lives in community with angels and spirits, even though our outer self is unaware of it. Because our inner self lives in community with angels and spirits, along with them it also has access to the universal language and therefore to the origins of words. That is why many terms are assigned a symbolism that to outward appearances seems inconsistent with the term but inwardly matches it, as in the current case, in which words symbolize things. The same is true in many other instances: the intellect is called the inner eye, and light is attributed to it; being aware and obeying is referred to as listening and hearing; sensing something is referred to as catching a whiff of it; and so on.

5076   *They sinned* symbolizes disorder. This can be seen from the symbolism of *sinning* as going against divine order. Anything that goes against divine order is a sin. Divine order itself is divine truth derived from divine goodness. The people who are in that order are all those devoted to truth as a result of goodness, or to faith as a result of neighborly love (since truth belongs to faith, and goodness is a matter of neighborly love). The people

who go against divine order are those who are not devoted to truth resulting from goodness and are therefore devoted to truth resulting from evil
or to falsity resulting from evil. Sin means nothing else.

The ones who sinned were the cupbearer and the baker, and the meaning is that outer and inner sensation were in disorder, so that they did not
agree, or correspond.

The cupbearer of Egypt's king means in the parts of the body under
the control of the intellectual side. This can be seen from the symbolism
of a *cupbearer* as outer, bodily sensation that is subordinate or subject to
the inner self's intellectual side (discussed below) and from that of *Egypt's
king* as the earthly self (discussed below at §5079).

Because the discussion that follows concerns the cupbearer and the
baker, who symbolize the outer, bodily senses, something first needs to be
said about these senses.

There are five outer, bodily senses, which are sight, hearing, smell,
taste, and touch. People know this, and they also know that these senses
constitute all the life in the body. Without these senses the body is not
at all alive, so it dies and becomes a corpse when deprived of them. This
means that our actual physical part exists simply to receive sensation and
consequently to receive the life yielded by sensation. What is primary is
our capacity for sensation, and its instrument is our body. Without the
primary element, to which it is adapted, the instrument cannot even be
called the kind of physical body we carry around while alive in the world.
Only the instrument together with its primary attribute, when the two
form a single whole, can be called the body. This, then, is the nature of
the bodily level.

[2] Our outer senses all relate to our inner senses. They were given to
us and placed in our body to serve our inner self while we are in the
world, and to be subject to the senses of our inner self. So when our outer
senses start to take control of our inner senses, it is all over for us. We
then consider our inner senses mere underlings, which serve to justify
what the outer senses tyrannically demand. When our outer senses achieve
this state, they are in disorder, as described above in §5076.

[3] Again, our outer senses relate to our inner senses, and in general to
our intellect and our will. Some of our outer senses are therefore under
the command and control of our intellectual part and some under our
volitional part. The main sense under the control of our intellectual part
is sight. Hearing comes primarily under our intellectual part and sec-
ondarily under our will part. Smell is subject to both, and taste even

more so, but touch comes under the will part. A great deal of evidence can show that the outer senses are under the control of these faculties and can show *how* they come under that control, but broadening the explanation to include it would take too long. The material at the end of the preceding chapters on the correspondence of those senses gives some clue [§§4318–4331, 4403–4421, 4523–4534, 4622–4634, 4652–4660, 4791–4806].

[4] It is also important to know that all truth, which is associated with faith, belongs to the intellectual side, and goodness, which is associated with love and charity, to the volitional side. The intellectual side, then, is the part that believes in, acknowledges, knows, and sees truth and also goodness, but the volitional side is the part that is moved by goodness and loves it. Goodness is what moves us and what we love. How does the intellectual side flow into the will side, though, when truth turns into goodness? And how does the will side flow into the intellectual side when it puts this truth-turned-goodness into practice? The question requires still deeper investigation and will be addressed in various later sections, by the Lord's divine mercy.

[5] The cupbearer means the senses subject or subordinate to the intellectual side of the inner self because everything used as a drink, everything people imbibe—wine, milk, water—relates to truth, which is on the intellectual side, and therefore relates to the intellectual side itself. Since the outer, bodily senses are the servants that supply truth, the cupbearer symbolizes these senses, or this function of the senses. Serving a drink and taking a drink in general have to do with truth, which belongs to the intellectual side; see §§3069, 3071, 3168, 3772, 4017, 4018. Wine in particular means truth that comes of goodness, or faith that comes of charity (§§1071, 1798). Water means truth (§§680, 2702, 3058, 3424, 4976).

All this now shows what a cupbearer means.

5078 *And the baker* means in the parts of the body under the control of the volitional side. This can be seen from the symbolism of a *baker* as the outer or bodily senses under the command and control of the inner self's volitional side. The baker has this symbolism because everything used for food, everything people eat—bread, food in general, and all "the work of a baker"—is mentioned in connection with goodness and therefore relates to the volitional side. All goodness is on the volitional side, just as all truth is on the intellectual side, as noted directly above in §5077. Bread means what is heavenly, or goodness; see §§1798, 2165, 2177, 3478, 3735, 3813, 4211, 4217, 4735, 4976.

[2] The reason the outer senses of both kinds are discussed in the inner meaning here and in the rest of the chapter is that the previous chapter was about the way the Lord glorified the inner reaches of his earthly part, or made them divine. The current chapter, then, is about the way the Lord glorified the outer level of his earthly part, or made it divine. This outer level of the earthly part is what is properly called the bodily level, or the senses of both kinds, together with the organs that support them. The senses and their organs together constitute what is called the body; see above at §5077.

The Lord made the actual bodily part in himself divine, and this includes both his senses and the organs that support them. That is why he rose from the grave with his body and said to his disciples after his resurrection, "Look at my hands and my feet, that I am he; feel me and see. Because a spirit does not have flesh and bones as you see me having" (Luke 24:39).

[3] Most people in the church today believe that everyone will rise again on the last day, clothed in a body. This opinion is so universal that hardly anyone believes differently on the basis of doctrine. The opinion has taken hold because people limited to the earthly plane think the body alone is what lives. Unless they believed the body would return to life all over again, they would totally deny there is a resurrection.

The real case, though, is that we rise again right after death. We then see ourselves clothed in a body just as in the world, with the same kind of face and the same kind of limbs, arms, hands, legs, chest, belly, and genitals. In fact, when we see and touch ourselves, we say we are just as much a person as we were in the world.

Still, it is not the outer shell we carried around in the world that sees and touches but an inner dimension. This inner dimension constitutes the actual human element in us that is alive. Previously it had an outer shell around itself, or around all its parts, enabling it to live in the world and to act and function in a suitable manner there. [4] Now the earthly body is no longer any use to us. We are in another world, with new duties and new strengths and powers to which the body we have there is adapted. This body sees with its own eyes—not the eyes we had in the world but the eyes we have there, or the eyes of our inner self. It was from these eyes through the physical eyes that our spiritual body had formerly looked at worldly and earthly objects. Our spiritual body also feels, not with the hands or sense of touch we enjoyed in this world but with the ones we enjoy there, our spiritual sense of touch being the source of the ability we had to feel things in the world. All our senses there are keener and fuller, because they are the senses of an inner self freed from the outer self. The state of the inner plane is more perfect because it gives the outer plane the capacity for sensation; but when it operates on the outer plane, as it does in the world, the sensation is blunted and dimmed. Moreover, the inner plane is what senses the inner plane, and the outer plane, the outer. That is why people can see each other after death and live together in community, depending on their inner qualities. In order to assure myself of this, I have actually been allowed to touch spirits and discuss the subject many times with them; see §§322, 1630, 4622.

[5] People after death—who are then called spirits or (if they lived a good life) angels—are astonished at those in the church who believe that they will not see eternal life until the last day, when the world ends, and that they will then be reclothed in their discarded dust. Yet people in the church know they rise again right after death. After someone dies, who does not say that the person's soul or spirit is in either heaven or hell? Do parents not say that their dead children are in heaven? Do we not comfort sick people and even prisoners condemned to death with the thought that they will soon arrive in the other world? And that is precisely the belief held by people in the throes of death who have prepared themselves. In fact, the same belief prompts many to claim for themselves the authority to release souls from places of damnation, admit them into heaven, and say mass for them.

Who does not know that the Lord said to the robber, "Today you will be with me in paradise" (Luke 23:43)? Concerning the rich man and Lazarus, he said the first was taken over into hell and the second into heaven by angels (Luke 16:22, 23). And of course in regard to the resurrection he taught that he was not the God of the dead but of the living (Luke 20:38). [6] People know this, and they think and speak this way when they think and speak from their spirit, but when they think and speak from doctrine, they say something entirely different, which is that they will not rise again until the last day. However, the last day comes for each of us when we die, and that, as many people also say, is when we face our judgment. (For what being wrapped in one's skin and seeing God from one's flesh means in Job 19:25, 26, see §3540 at the end.)

These remarks have been made to show that people never rise again with the body that enveloped them in the world. Only the Lord did so, and that is because when he was in the world he glorified his body, or made it divine.

Against their master, Egypt's king means that they opposed the new **5079** state of the earthly self. That is, the outer, physical senses symbolized by the cupbearer and baker opposed it. This can be seen from the symbolism of *Egypt's king* as learning in general (discussed at §§1164, 1165, 1186, 1462, 4749, 4964, 4966). Egypt's king has the same symbolism as Egypt, because a monarch is the head of a nation. The same holds true in other passages referring to or naming the monarch of some nation (§4789). Because Egypt's king symbolizes learning in general, he also symbolizes the earthly self, since all knowledge is the truth of the earthly self (§4967). Real goodness in the earthly self is symbolized here by the *master* (§4973).

A new state of the earthly self is being symbolized because the previous chapter dealt with the inner reaches of the earthly level and the fact that they turned into something new. In the highest sense, which is about the Lord, it dealt with the fact that they were glorified. Now the theme is the outer reaches of the earthly self, which had to be brought into agreement or correspondence with the inner reaches. These inner reaches of the earthly self, now new—in other words, the new state of this earthly self—is what the *master, Egypt's king,* symbolizes. The outer reaches, not reduced to order and therefore opposed to order, are what the cupbearer and baker symbolize.

[2] The earthly self has inner attributes and outer ones. The inner attributes of the earthly self are knowledge and the desire for it, while the outer attributes are sense impressions of both kinds (discussed above at §5077). The outer attributes of the earthly self we leave behind when we die, but the inner attributes of the earthly self we take with us to the other world, where they serve as a foundation for spiritual and heavenly attributes.

When we die, we lose nothing but flesh and bones. We keep the memory of everything we did, said, and thought, and we keep all our earthly desires and cravings. As a consequence, we keep all the inner contents of our earthly level. The superficial contents we have no need for—we do not look at anything in the world, or hear anything in the world, or smell, taste, or touch anything in the world, only things in the other life. What exists in the other life does mostly seem the same as what exists in the world, but it is not the same. Things in the other world contain a living quality not possessed by things belonging strictly to the physical world. Absolutely everything in the other world emerges into lasting existence from a sun that is the Lord, so it all has something living in it. Absolutely everything in the physical world, though, emerges into lasting existence from a sun made of elemental fire, so it has nothing living in it. Any vitality that physical things seem to have comes exclusively from the spiritual world, or rather from the Lord through the spiritual world.

5080   *And Pharaoh was enraged* means that the new earthly self turned away. This can be seen from the representation of *Pharaoh,* Egypt's king, as the new earthly self, or the new state of the earthly self (mentioned just above at §5079), and from the symbolism of being *enraged* or angry as feeling aversion (discussed at §5034). The meaning is, then, that the inner earthly level, which had changed into something new, turned away from the outer earthly level, or from the physical senses, since the outer part did not correspond with the inner part.

5081   *Over his two court attendants* means (that it turned away) from physical sensations of both kinds. This can be seen from the symbolism of the *court attendants,* the cupbearer and the baker, as sensations of both kinds (discussed above at §§5077, 5078). The bodily senses—sight, hearing, smell, taste, and touch—are like royal attendants in relation to the inner self, which is master and monarch. They wait on the inner self in order to supply it with experiential proof from the visible world and from human society, which enables the inner self to gain understanding and wisdom.

A human is not born with any knowledge, let alone understanding and wisdom, but only with the ability to receive and absorb knowledge, understanding, and wisdom. This happens by two routes, an inner one and an outer one. The Divine flows in by the inner route, the world by the outer route, and the two meet inside us. After that, the more we allow ourselves to be enlightened by the Divine, the more we come into wisdom.

The inflow that comes by the outer route comes through the physical senses, but it does not flow in on its own. Rather it is summoned by the inner self, to serve as a foundation for heavenly and spiritual qualities flowing in from the Divine along the inner route.

This shows that the physical senses are like court attendants. More generally, anything superficial is an attendant in relation to something deeper. The entire earthly self is nothing but an attendant in relation to the spiritual self.

[2] In the original language this term means an attendant, courtier, chamberlain, or eunuch. On an inner level it symbolizes goodness and

truth in the earthly self, and that is the symbolism here. More narrowly it symbolizes goodness in the earthly self, as in Isaiah:

> It is not to be said by the child of a foreigner who clings to Jehovah, saying, "Jehovah utterly removes me from among his people." And the *eunuch* is not to say, "Look: I am dry wood." Because this is what Jehovah has said to the *eunuchs* "who keep my Sabbaths and choose what I delight in, and are holding to my compact: I will give them, in my house and within my walls, a place and a name better than sons and daughters; an eternal name I will give them, which will not be cut off." (Isaiah 56:3, 4, 5)

The eunuch stands for goodness in the earthly self, and the child of a foreigner for truth in the earthly self. The Lord's church has an outer part and an inner part, and the people in the outer part of the church are limited to the earthly level, while those in the inner part are spiritual. The earthly-level ones who possess goodness are the eunuchs, and the ones who possess truth are the children of a foreigner. It is not possible for people to be truly spiritual or deep except in the church. As a result, the children of a foreigner also symbolize people outside the church, or non-Christians, who nonetheless possess truth harmonizing with their religious tradition (§§2049, 2593, 2599, 2600, 2602, 2603, 2861, 2863, 3263), while eunuchs symbolize those possessing goodness.

Over the chief of the cupbearers and over the chief of the bakers means **5082** from sensations subordinate to the intellectual side and to the volitional side in general, as the following shows: A *cupbearer* symbolizes the senses subject and subordinate to the intellectual side, as discussed above at §5077. A *baker* symbolizes the senses subject and subordinate to the volitional side, as also discussed above, at §5078. And a *chief* symbolizes what is primary, as discussed at §§1482, 2089, 5044. In this case it means in general, because what is primary is also general, since it reigns supreme in everything else. Particulars lead back to primary elements as their general categories, so as to form a unified whole and prevent contradictions from coming about.

And he put them into the jail symbolizes rejection. This can be seen **5083** from the symbolism of *putting into jail* as rejection, since one who is put in jail is rejected.

Of the house of the chief of the bodyguards means by [knowledge] of pri- **5084** mary importance in interpretation. This can be seen from the discussion in §§4790, 4966 of the symbolism of the *chief of the bodyguards* as [knowledge] that is of primary importance in interpretation. The symbolism here, then, is that sense impressions of both kinds were rejected by the main [knowledge] used for interpretation—that is, [knowledge] regarding the Word's inner meaning. Sense impressions are said to be rejected when they put no stock in this kind of thing. The senses are misleading, as is the sensory evidence that enters directly into our thinking. Any fallacy taking hold of our minds comes from the senses. It is because of the senses that few believe in the truths that belong to faith and also that our earthly self opposes our spiritual self, or our outer self opposes our inner.

Consequently, if our earthly, outer self starts to dominate our spiritual, inner self, we stop believing in the tenets of faith. Our delusions cast those tenets into the shadow, and our cravings smother them.

[2] Not many people know what sensory delusions are. Not many believe that those delusions throw such deep shadow over rational ideas and especially over the spiritual concepts of faith, to the point of extinguishing them, particularly in a person who also indulges the cravings of self-love and materialism. Let me illustrate the matter with some examples, then. First I will show what sensory delusions are when they involve just the earthly level, or the material world. Then I will deal with sensory delusions in spiritual affairs.

1. One purely physical delusion of the senses, or a delusion involving nature, is the belief that the sun travels around our planet once a day, as does the sky with all its stars. You can say it is impossible and therefore unbelievable that such an immense ocean of fire as the sun should revolve [around the earth] once a day—and not only the sun but also countless stars, without changing their position relative to each other. You can add that the wandering stars show us that the earth goes through the daily and yearly motions of rotation and revolution. After all, these wanderers are also planets (some of them even have orbiting moons), and it has been observed that they go through the same daily and yearly motions as our planet. Nevertheless, among many people the sensory delusion prevails that the situation is exactly as the eye sees it.

[3] 2. It is purely a physical delusion of the senses, or a delusion involving nature, that there is only one atmosphere, which simply grows purer from layer to layer, and that where it ends there is a vacuum. Our outer senses, if we consult them alone, cannot comprehend the situation any other way.

3. It is a purely physical delusion of the senses that from the moment of creation seeds were imprinted with the characteristic of growing into trees and flowers and reproducing, and that this is how everything comes into being and lasts. You can tell people who believe this that nothing can last unless it is constantly coming into being, according to the law that continued existence is constant emergence. You can say that anything lacking connection with something prior to itself collapses into nothingness. Nevertheless, these ideas are incomprehensible to the bodily senses and to thinking based on them. It is also incomprehensible to them that everything continues in existence as it came into existence, through an inflow from the spiritual world, or rather through an inflow from the Divine coming by way of the spiritual world.

[4] 4. A purely physical delusion of the senses that results is the idea that there are simple substances, which are monads and atoms. If something lies deep within the outer senses, an earthly-level person believes it is either a simple substance or nonexistent.

5. It is a purely physical delusion of the senses that everything is part of nature and produced by nature, and that something incomprehensible does indeed exist at a purer or deeper level of nature. If you say, though, that within or above nature lies a spiritual and heavenly realm, the idea is rejected. People believe that if something does not belong to nature it is nothing.

6. It is a delusion of the senses that only the body is alive and that its life ends when we die. The senses absolutely do not grasp that there is an inner self inside each part of the outer self, or that the inner self exists in the spiritual world that lies behind nature. As a result, they do not believe we will live on after death unless we are reclothed in a body (§§5078, 5079), because they do not grasp the concept.

[5] 7. A resulting delusion of the senses is the idea that we can no more live on after death than animals, since animals too have a type of life that resembles human life in many ways, humans merely being more perfect animals. The senses—or rather people who base their thoughts and conclusions on the senses—do not grasp that we are higher than animals in this respect. We have a higher kind of life because we can think not only about the causes of things but also about the Divine. We can unite with the Divine through faith and love, accept an inflow from the Divine, and make it our own. Therefore, since we possess an ability to reciprocate, we possess a capacity for receiving something that animals cannot possibly receive.

[6] 8. A resulting delusion is the idea that the actual living part in us, called the soul, is only a bit of thin air or fire that vanishes when we die, and that it dwells in our heart or brain or some other part of us, from which it controls the body like a machine. The senses do not comprehend that we have an inner self in every part of our outer self, that our eye does not see on its own and our ear does not hear on its own but that both operate under the power of the inner self.

9. It is a delusion of the senses that neither light nor warmth can radiate from anywhere but the sun or physical fire. The senses do not comprehend that there is a light that contains intelligence, or a warmth that contains heavenly love, or that all angels enjoy this light and warmth.

10. It is a delusion of the senses when we think that we live on our own, or that life is infused into us. That is the only way the senses can view the situation. They absolutely do not grasp that only the Divine has life on its own, so that the Divine is the only life force, and living things in the world are just forms for receiving life; see §§1954, 2706, 2886–2889, 2893, 3001, 3318, 3337, 3338, 3484, 3742, 3743, 4151, 4249, 4318, 4319, 4320, 4417, 4523, 4524, 4882.

[7] 11. Sensory-minded people in their delusion believe that adultery is fine. They decide on the basis of their senses that marriage exists merely to provide for the orderly raising of children. As long as this arrangement is not destroyed, they think, it does not matter who produces the children. They also believe that the marital urge is like any other lust except for being allowable, which means that it would not be disorderly to marry more than one wife if the Christian world did not prohibit it on the basis of Sacred Scripture. You can tell them that there is a correspondence between the heavenly marriage and marriage on earth, that we have no capacity for marriage unless we commit ourselves to spiritual truth and goodness, that a real marriage cannot exist between a husband and many wives, and that marriage is therefore inherently sacred; but people tethered to their senses reject all this as worthless.

[8] 12. It is a delusion of the senses that the Lord's kingdom, or heaven, resembles an earthly kingdom in that joy and happiness there consists in one person's having more importance and consequently greater glory than another. The senses have no idea what it means to say that the least is the greatest, or that the last is first. If you tell people with this delusion that for heaven and its angels, joy consists in serving others by helping them, without any thought of earning credit or being repaid, it strikes them as depressing.

13. It is a delusion of the senses that good deeds earn credit and that being kind to another person for one's own benefit is a good deed.

14. It is also a delusion of the senses that we are saved by faith alone, that faith can exist in people who lack love for their neighbor, and that our faith (not our life) awaits us after death.

The case is similar with many other questions. Accordingly, when our senses are in charge within us, we see nothing with a rational mind that is enlightened by the Lord. We live in thick darkness, and we then believe that every conclusion to which our senses lead is a rational one.

At the prison house means among false ideas. This can be seen from the symbolism of a *prison house* as the stripping away of falsity and therefore as falsity itself (see §§4958, 5037, 5038). **5085**

The place where Joseph was a prisoner symbolizes the current state of heavenliness on the earthly plane in regard to [the outer senses], as the following shows: A *place* symbolizes a state, as discussed at §§2625, 2837, 3356, 3387, 4321, 4882. *Joseph* represents spiritual heavenliness growing out of rationality, as discussed at §§4286, 4585, 4592, 4594, 4963. At this point he represents what was heavenly on the earthly plane, since [the Lord] was now focusing on the earthly plane, the source of spiritual trials (§§5035, 5039). And a *prisoner* symbolizes a state of trial, as discussed at §5037. The previous chapter talked about a state of trial experienced by spiritual heavenliness on the earthly plane, in regard to attributes of the inner earthly dimension [§§5035–5049]. The current chapter has regard to attributes of the outer earthly dimension. **5086**

And the chief of the bodyguards set Joseph in charge of them means that the heavenly part of the earthly plane taught [the outer senses], using the main [knowledge] needed for interpretation, as the following shows: The *chief of the bodyguards* symbolizes [knowledge] of primary importance in interpretation, as discussed at §§4790, 4966, 5084. *Joseph* represents heavenliness on the earthly plane, as mentioned just above at §5086. And being *set in charge* in this case means teaching. One who is set in charge of something that has been rejected, in order to examine or reform it, is doing the job of teaching. **5087**

And he waited on them means that it gave instruction. This can be seen from the symbolism of *waiting on someone* as giving instruction. **5088**

In this case, waiting on the courtiers does not mean doing so as a servant, which is evident from the fact that Joseph was set in charge of them. As a result it means supplying them with what they could use. Since the subject is the outer, sensory part of a new earthly dimension, being set in charge means teaching, and waiting on someone means instructing. Being set in charge is connected with goodness, which is a matter of life, and waiting on someone is connected with truth, which is a matter of doctrine (§4976).

5089   *And for days they were in jail* means that they stayed a long time in a state of rejection. This is established by the symbolism of *days* as a state (discussed in §§23, 487, 488, 493, 893, 2788, 3462, 3785, 4850). *For days,* then, means for a long time in that state—a state of rejection, rejection being symbolized by *jail* (§5083).

I cannot go into greater detail in explaining the individual contents of the inner meaning, because they are not the kind of concepts that worldly phenomena can give us an idea of. They have to do, for instance, with the spiritual-heavenly self and its state on the earthly plane, both when the inner earthly plane is turning into something new, and when it has finished turning and the outer earthly plane is rejected. Heavenly phenomena do give us an idea of these concepts and others like them, though. Such an idea by its very nature is incompatible with any idea formed from worldly phenomena, except in people who can withdraw from their senses when they are thinking. [2] Unless we can lift our minds above our senses and see them as being below us, we can never develop the wisdom to perceive any inner content in the Word, let alone the kinds of things that belong to heaven, separately from those that belong to the world. The senses swallow up anything heavenly and smother it.

This is the reason that people who cannot rise above their senses and who have energetically pursued knowledge rarely have any grasp of heavenly subjects. They have flooded their thoughts with worldly subjects, or with the terms and distinctions belonging to worldly subjects. So they have immersed themselves in their senses and can no longer be lifted out of them to achieve a loftier view. Their thoughts can no longer range freely across the entire field of their memory, choosing what agrees, rejecting what clashes, and applying anything relevant. As I said, their thinking is always confined by and immersed in terms and therefore in sensory information, so that it cannot look very far around.

That is why scholars have less faith than the uneducated and in fact less wisdom in heavenly matters. The uneducated can rise above terms and learning and consequently above the senses to consider a question, but the educated cannot. They view it *from* terms and learning, because their mind is engrossed in them and is therefore held captive in a kind of jail or prison.

Genesis 40:5, 6, 7, 8. *And the two of them dreamed a dream, each his* **5090** *own dream, in one night, each according to the interpretation of his dream— the cupbearer and the baker, who belonged to Egypt's king, who were prisoners in the prison house. And Joseph came to them in the morning and looked at them, and here, they were troubled. And he questioned Pharaoh's court attendants who were with him in the jail of his master's house, saying, "Why are your faces ill today?" And they said to him, "A dream we have dreamed, and there is no interpreter for it." And Joseph said to them, "Don't interpretations belong to God? Tell me, please."*

And the two of them dreamed a dream symbolizes foresight about them. *Each his own dream, in one night,* means about the outcome, which was obscure to them. *Each according to the interpretation of his dream* means [the outcome] that they contained in themselves. *The cupbearer and the baker* means about sense impressions of both kinds. *Who belonged to Egypt's king* means which were subordinate to the inner part of the earthly level. *Who were prisoners in the prison house* means which were among falsities. *And Joseph came to them in the morning* symbolizes what was clearly revealed to earthly heavenliness. *And looked at them* symbolizes a perception. *And here, they were troubled* means that they were in a state of gloom. *And he questioned Pharaoh's court attendants* symbolizes those sense impressions. *Who were with him in the jail of his master's house* means which had been rejected. *Saying, "Why are your faces ill today?"* means, what emotion caused the gloom? *And they said to him* symbolizes a perception about [the senses]. *A dream we have dreamed* symbolizes a prediction. *And there is no interpreter for it* means that no one knows what they contain. *And Joseph said to them* symbolizes earthly heavenliness. *Don't interpretations belong to God?* means that they contained a divine quality. *Tell me, please* means that it would be known.

And the two of them dreamed a dream symbolizes foresight about them. **5091** This can be seen from the discussion in §3698 of the symbolism of a *dream* as foresight. The *two of them* means both kinds of sense impressions, as symbolized by the cupbearer and the baker. They are what the dreams were about, as is plain from what follows.

A *dream* in the highest sense means foresight because dreams that flow in directly through heaven from the Lord foretell the future. This includes Joseph's dreams, the dreams of the cupbearer and the baker, Pharaoh's dream, Nebuchadnezzar's dream, and all prophetic dreams in general. The future that dreams foretell comes straight out of the Lord's divine foresight.

This also shows that absolutely everything is foreseen.

5092   *Each his own dream, in one night,* means about the outcome, which was obscure to them, as the following shows: A *dream* symbolizes foresight and therefore a prediction, and because it symbolizes a prediction, it also symbolizes the outcome, since that is what a prediction is about. And *night* symbolizes obscurity. In a spiritual sense, night symbolizes a state of shadow brought on by falsity that grows out of evil (§§1712, 2353), so it also symbolizes obscurity, or mental darkness.

The dark of night in the world is a physical darkness, but the dark of night in the other life is a spiritual darkness. Physical darkness results from the absence of the world's sun and the consequent withdrawal of its light, but spiritual darkness results from the absence of heaven's sun (the Lord) and the consequent withdrawal of its light (the power of understanding). Heavenly light is withdrawn not because heaven's sun sets the way earth's sun does, but because people or spirits subscribe to the falsity that evil produces, remove themselves, and bring on their own darkness.

By itself, the idea of night and its darkness in both meanings shows how the spiritual meaning relates to the earthly meaning of the same thing.

[2] In addition, there are three kinds of spiritual obscurity. One results from the falsity that comes of evil. A second results from ignorance of the truth. A third characterizes superficial levels, relative to inner depths, and therefore characterizes the outer self's sensory information relative to the inner self's rational ideas. Still, all three kinds result from a failure to receive heaven's light, or understanding and wisdom from the Lord. This light is always streaming in, but the falsity that comes of evil rejects or smothers or perverts it; ignorance of the truth takes in only a little of it; and the senses of our outer self weaken it because they generalize it.

5093   *Each according to the interpretation of his dream* symbolizes the outcome that they contained in themselves. This can be seen from the symbolism of the *interpretation of a dream* as an unfolding of the outcome and accordingly a knowledge of it, and therefore as the outcome that [the senses] contained in themselves. A *dream* means the outcome; see just above at §5092.

5094   *The cupbearer and the baker* means about sense impressions of both kinds. This can be seen from the symbolism of the *cupbearer* as the senses under the control of the mind's intellectual side (discussed at §5077) and from that of the *baker* as the senses under the volitional side (discussed at §5078). They were rejected by the inner earthly level, as mentioned above at §§5083, 5089.

Please be aware, though, that the actual sensations of sight, hearing, smell, taste, and touch were not rejected, because the body lives on them. What were rejected were viewpoints or thoughts based on them, and feelings and cravings inspired by them.

Objects enter our outer or earthly memory on one side from the world through these senses and on the other side through rational concepts. In this outer memory they divide. The objects that entered through rational concepts place themselves on the inside, but those that entered through the senses place themselves on the outside. This makes the earthly plane twofold, inner and outer, as was also mentioned earlier [§§5078, 5079]. [2] The inner earthly level is what Pharaoh, Egypt's king, represents, and the outer earthly level is what the cupbearer and the baker represent.

The nature of the difference between the two can be seen from their viewpoints, or from their thoughts and resulting conclusions. When people think and draw conclusions with their inner earthly level, then the more they have absorbed through their rational side, the more rational they are. When people think and draw conclusions with their outer earthly level, then the more they have absorbed through their senses, the more sense-oriented they are. These are called sense-oriented people, and the others are called rational earthly people.

When we die, we take our whole earthly level with us, and whatever form it took in us in the world, that is the form it keeps. The more we soaked up from our rational mind, the more rational we are, and the more we soaked up from our senses, the more sense-oriented we are. The difference is this: The more that our earthly plane absorbed and adopted from our rational mind, the more it tends to look down on the sense impressions of its own outer part and exert control over them, despising and rejecting the delusions they lead to. But the more that our earthly plane absorbed and adopted from our physical senses, the more it tends to look down on rational ideas, despising and rejecting them.

[3] For example, rational earthly people can understand that we do not live on our own but depend on an inflow of life through heaven from the Lord. Sense-oriented people cannot understand this, because they say that they clearly feel and sense the presence of life in themselves and that it is useless to argue against the senses.

For another example, rational earthly people understand that there is a heaven and a hell, but sense-oriented people deny it, because they do not grasp that a purer world exists than the one they see with their eyes. Rational earthly people understand that there are spirits and angels and that they are invisible, but sense-oriented people do not understand it, thinking that anything they cannot see and touch is nonexistent.

[4] For yet another example, rational earthly people understand that looking toward goals and foreseeing and arranging for the means to an ultimate goal requires an intelligent being. When they consider the way the material world is organized, they see that it is a complex of means, which tells them that an intelligent Supreme Being arranged it all. Still, they do not see what the ultimate goal is unless they become spiritual. Sense-oriented people, though, do not understand that anything can exist apart from the material world, so they do not understand that there is some Being that is above it. They do not grasp what it is to understand, be wise, look toward goals, and arrange the means, unless such activity is called a function of the material world. When it is called a function of the material world, they view it the way a machine maker views an automaton.

These brief remarks show what is meant by the inner and outer earthly levels. They also show what is meant by the idea that what was rejected was not sensation—not what belongs to sight, hearing, smell, taste, and touch in the body—but conclusions about the inner realm based on sensation.

5095   *Who belonged to Egypt's king* means which were subordinate to the inner part of the earthly level. This can be seen from the representation in the current chapter of Pharaoh, *Egypt's king,* as a new state for the earthly level (discussed at §§5079, 5080) and consequently as the inner earthly level, since this is what turned into something new. For a definition of the inner and outer earthly levels, see just above at §5094.

I should quickly explain what the inner meaning of the Word is like in its narrative and prophetic parts. Where the narrative level mentions a number of people—in this case, Joseph, Pharaoh, the chief of the bodyguards, the cupbearer, and the baker—on an inner level they certainly symbolize various attributes, but only within a single individual. The reason is that names symbolize qualities. For instance, Joseph represents the Lord in respect to spiritual heavenliness, both as it draws on rationality and as it exists on the earthly plane. Pharaoh represents the new state of the Lord's earthly plane, or his inner earthly level. The cupbearer and the baker represent what belonged to the outer earthly level in the Lord. That is what the inner meaning is like. [2] The same holds true in other places, such as those mentioning Abraham, Isaac, and Jacob. On the literal level they are three people, but in the highest sense all three represent the

Lord. Abraham represents his divinity itself, Isaac represents the level of his divine intellect, and Jacob represents the level of his divine earthliness.

The same holds true in the Prophets, too, where the message sometimes consists purely of names, whether they are names of people, kingdoms, or cities. Yet taken together they portray and depict a single entity in the inner meaning.

Anyone who does not know this can easily be carried off by the literal meaning into thinking that there are various things there, which breaks up the idea of a single entity.

Who were prisoners in the prison house means which were among falsities. This can be seen from the symbolism of being a *prisoner in the prison house* as being among falsities (discussed in §§4958, 5037, 5038, 5085). **5096**

People who succumb to falsity and especially to evil are said to be prisoners and in prison, not because they are actually chained but because they do not have freedom. Anyone who lacks freedom is inwardly imprisoned. After all, people who have proved a false idea to themselves no longer have any freedom to choose or accept the truth. Those who have proved it repeatedly do not even have the freedom to see truth, let alone acknowledge and believe it. They are convinced that falsity is true, and truth false. Conviction by its very nature removes all freedom of thinking otherwise and therefore keeps one's very thoughts fettered in a kind of prison.

This has become clear to me from much experience among individuals in the other world who had become convinced of a false idea through self-persuasion. By nature, they never allow truth in. They deflect it or push it away, more or less harshly according to the strength of their conviction, especially if the falsity grows out of evil, or if evil is what convinces them.

They are the people meant in the Lord's parable in Matthew:

Some seeds fell on the hard path, and birds came and ate them. (Matthew 13:4)

The seeds mean divine truth. The hard stone means conviction. The birds mean false assumptions.

People of this type do not even know they are bound or in prison, because they feel drawn to their falsity and love it on account of the evil from which it grew. As a consequence, they consider themselves free, because anything marked by desire or love seems free.

[2] People who have not hardened themselves in falsity—that is, have not persuaded themselves of it—readily let the truth in, see it, choose it,

feel drawn to it, and from then on look down on falsity. They also see the shackles binding a person who is persuaded of falsity. They possess such great freedom that their thoughts and insights can traverse all of heaven, so to speak, reaching out to limitless truth. But the only people who can enjoy this freedom are the ones with goodness. Goodness puts them in heaven, and goodness in heaven makes truth visible.

5097 *And Joseph came to them in the morning* symbolizes what was clearly revealed to spiritual heavenliness. This is established by the representation of *Joseph* as spiritual heavenliness (discussed at §§4286, 4592, 4963) and by the symbolism of *morning* as an enlightened state (discussed at §3458) and therefore as something clearly revealed.

The reason *morning* has this symbolism is that times of day, like seasons of the year, symbolize various states, in keeping with various levels of heavenly light. Changes in heaven's light are not like daily and yearly changes in light on the earth but are variations in understanding and love. Heaven's light is actually divine understanding from the Lord, which also provides light for the eye. The warmth that goes with that light is the Lord's divine love, which is also a palpable warmth. Heaven's light gives us our intellectual ability, and heaven's warmth gives us our vital heat and our will for goodness.

In heaven, morning is a state of enlightenment regarding questions of goodness and truth. This state comes into being when we acknowledge, and particularly when we perceive, that goodness is good and truth true. Perception is inner revelation, so morning symbolizes what is revealed. Since what was formerly obscure then becomes clear, morning also symbolizes clarity.

[2] Besides, morning in the highest sense symbolizes the Lord himself, because he is the sun from which all light in heaven radiates, and he is always rising, so it is constantly morning with him. He is also rising always in anyone who accepts the truth that leads to faith and the goodness that comes from love, but he sets in anyone who does not accept them. It is not that heaven's sun sets, because (to repeat) it is always rising. Rather, those who do not accept truth and goodness make the sun set in themselves.

The situation can to some degree be compared with phases of the world's sun relative to the earth's inhabitants. The world's sun also does not set, because it always stays where it is and is always shining from that place. It seems to set, though, because the earth rotates on its axis once a day. When it does, it removes the inhabitants from the sight of the sun; see §5084, point 1. Not even the [earthly] sunset is in the sun, then, but in the removal of the earth's inhabitants from the sun's light. This comparison provides illustration, and since everything in the physical world represents something about the Lord's kingdom, it also provides instruction. It shows that when there is a loss of heaven's light, or of understanding and wisdom, the reason is not that the Lord as the radiant sun of understanding and wisdom is setting in anyone but that the inhabitants of his kingdom are removing themselves. That is, they are allowing themselves to be led by hell, and hell removes them from the light.

And looked at them symbolizes a perception. This can be seen from the symbolism of *looking at* as understanding and perceiving (discussed at §§2150, 3764, 4567, 4723). **5098**

And here, they were troubled means that they were in a state of gloom, as is self-explanatory. **5099**

And he questioned Pharaoh's court attendants symbolizes those sense impressions. This is established by the symbolism of *Pharaoh's court attendants* as sensations of both kinds, the kind under the control of the intellectual side, and the kind under the control of the volitional side (discussed above at §5081). **5100**

Who were with him in the jail of his master means which had been rejected. This is established by the symbolism of being put in jail and therefore of *being in jail* as being at the stage of rejection (also discussed above, at §5083). **5101**

Saying, "Why are your faces ill today?" means, what emotion caused the gloom? This can be seen from the symbolism of *faces* as inner depths (discussed in §§358, 1999, 2434, 3527, 4066, 4796, 4797) and consequently as emotions. Emotions are our inner depths and give rise to our thoughts, which also exist inside us. Since emotions go to make up love, they also go to make up our life. **5102**

It is recognized that in people with innocence, the face visibly displays emotion, and because it displays their emotions it also displays their thoughts in a general way, thought being the form of emotion. Considered in itself, then, the face is simply an image representing what lies inside. That is exactly how all faces look to angels, because angels do not see human faces in their material form but in their spiritual form. That is, they see human faces in the form that our feelings and resulting thoughts present. Even in people on earth, emotions are what make the real face. This can be seen from the fact that a face stripped of emotion is nothing but a piece of dead flesh. Feelings give the face life and make it attractive.

The gloominess of the emotion—or the question of what emotion caused it—is symbolized by Joseph's saying, "Why are your faces ill today?"

5103   *And they said to him* symbolizes a perception about [the senses]. This can be seen from the symbolism of *saying* in Scripture narrative as a perception (mentioned many times before).

5104   *A dream we have dreamed* symbolizes a prediction. This can be seen from the symbolism of a *dream* as foresight and therefore as a prediction (discussed above at §5091).

5105   *And there is no interpreter for it* means that no one knows what they contain. This can be seen from the symbolism of *interpretation* as an unfolding of the contents (dealt with above at §5093) and therefore of what [the senses] contain.

5106   *And Joseph said to them* symbolizes earthly heavenliness. This can be seen from the representation mentioned above in §5086 of *Joseph* as earthly heavenliness.

5107   *Don't interpretations belong to God?* means that they contained a divine quality. This can be seen from the symbolism of an *interpretation* when applied to dreams as their content—a meaning given just above in §5105. The divine quality is symbolized by *God.*

5108   *Tell me, please,* means that it would be known. This can be seen from the meaning of *tell me, please,* which implies that it would be known. What follows also shows that he knew.

5109   Genesis 40:9, 10, 11, 12, 13. *And the chief of the cupbearers told his dream to Joseph, and he said to him, "[I was] in my dream, and look: a grapevine before me! And on the vine three shoots, and it seemed to be sprouting; its flower came up, and its clusters ripened into grapes. And Pharaoh's cup was in my hand, and I took the grapes and squeezed them into Pharaoh's cup, and I put the cup on Pharaoh's palm." And Joseph said to him, "This is its interpretation: The three shoots are three days. In another three days Pharaoh will lift your head and return you to your position, and you will put Pharaoh's cup into his hand according to your former custom when you were his cupbearer."*

And the chief of the cupbearers told his dream to Joseph means that spiritual heavenliness could tell what the outcome would be for sensations subject to the intellectual side, which had so far been rejected. *And he said to him* symbolizes a revelation yielded by perception. *[I was] in my dream* symbolizes a prediction. *And look: a grapevine before me!* symbolizes the intellect. *And on the vine three shoots* symbolizes outgrowths, right to the last of them. *And it seemed to be sprouting* symbolizes an inflow that would lead to rebirth. *Its flower came up* symbolizes a state close to rebirth. *And its clusters ripened into grapes* symbolizes the union of spiritual truth and heavenly goodness. *And Pharaoh's cup was in my hand* symbolizes the inflow of the inner earthly plane into the outer, and the start of its acceptance. *And I took the grapes and squeezed them into Pharaoh's cup* symbolizes a reciprocal inflow into the goodness from a spiritual origin there. *And I put the cup on Pharaoh's palm* symbolizes adoption by the inner earthly plane. *And Joseph said to him, "This is its interpretation,"* symbolizes revelation gleaned from a perception by heavenliness on the earthly plane, showing what [the senses subject to the intellectual side] contained. *The three shoots are three days* symbolizes continuing developments, right to the last of them. *In another three days* symbolizes something new at that point. *Pharaoh will lift your head* symbolizes what would be provided and therefore decided. *And return you to your position* means that sensations subject to the intellectual side would be reduced to order, so as to come last. *And you will put Pharaoh's cup into his hand* means where they could serve the inner earthly plane. *According to your former custom* means in keeping with the laws of order. *When you were his cupbearer* means as sensations of that kind are used to doing.

And the chief of the cupbearers told his dream to Joseph means that spiritual heavenliness could tell what the outcome would be for sensations subject to the intellectual side, which had so far been rejected, as the following shows: *Joseph* represents spiritual heavenliness, as discussed at §§4286, 4585, 4592, 4594, 4963. A *dream* symbolizes foresight and therefore the outcome, as noted above at §§5091, 5092, 5104, so it symbolizes an outcome foreseen or perceived. And the *chief of the cupbearers* symbolizes the senses subject to the intellectual side, in general, as discussed at §§5077, 5082. Their rejection is meant by his being in jail (§§5083, 5101). These remarks show that this is the inner meaning of the clause. In addition, what follows makes it plain that Joseph, who represents spiritual heavenliness, could tell what the outcome would be.

[2] I speak of spiritual heavenliness, and by it I mean the Lord. It is legitimate to speak of him in abstract terms too, since he is heavenliness itself and spirituality itself, or goodness itself and truth itself. Admittedly, we cannot conceive of these qualities in isolation from a person, because something earthly is attached to them in all our thinking, but we can still consider the fact that everything in the Lord is divine. We can consider that the Divine transcends all thought and is totally incomprehensible,

5110

even to angels. So if we then take away the part that is comprehensible, what remains is reality and presence itself, which is heavenliness and spirituality itself, or goodness and truth itself.

[3] However, we are made in such a way that we cannot form any idea whatever of abstractions unless we add some earthly quality taken in from the world through our senses. Without this perspective, our thoughts in effect fall into a vast gulf and evaporate. There is a danger, though, that any idea of divinity will be completely submerged in concrete physical thinking in us and die. Even people in whom the concept survives are apt to pollute it with their unclean thoughts, and along with it, every heavenly and spiritual quality from the Lord. To prevent this, therefore, it pleased Jehovah to reveal himself as he actually is and as he appears in heaven: as a divine human being. Everything in heaven aims at the human form (see the explanations at the chapter ends showing that everything in a person corresponds with the universal human, which is heaven). This divine being, or this manifestation of Jehovah in heaven, is the Lord from eternity. The Lord reclaimed it when he glorified his humanity, or made it divine. This is obvious from the form in which he appeared before Peter, James, and John when he was transfigured (Matthew 17:1, 2) and from the form in which he occasionally appeared to the prophets.

The result is that everyone can now think of the Divine itself as a human, which brings to mind the Lord, in whom all divinity exists and in whom the trinity is complete. In him, after all, divinity itself is the Father, the same divinity in heaven is the Son, and the divine influence radiating from it is the Holy Spirit. Clearly, then, these three are one, as the Lord teaches.

5111   *And he said to him* symbolizes a revelation yielded by perception. This can be seen from the symbolism of *saying* in scriptural narrative as a perception (discussed at §§1791, 1815, 1819, 1822, 1898, 1919, 2080, 2619, 2862, 3395, 3509) and therefore as a revelation too. Revelation is inward perception and results from perception.

5112   *[I was] in my dream* symbolizes a prediction. This can be seen from the symbolism of a *dream* as foresight and accordingly as a prediction (discussed above in §§5091, 5092, 5104).

5113   *And look: a grapevine before me!* symbolizes the intellect. This can be seen from the symbolism of a *grapevine* as the intellect in a spiritual religion (discussed below).

A cupbearer symbolizes the senses subject to the intellectual side, and the theme here is the intellect's inflow into the senses subordinate to it.

Consequently, the grapevine in the dream appeared with shoots, flower, clusters, and grapes, depicting that inflow and the rebirth of those senses.

Regarding the intellect in a spiritual religion, it should be known that where the Word deals with a spiritual religion, it frequently deals with that religion's intellect as well. This is because in a person belonging to a spiritual religion, the intellectual side is reborn and becomes an individual church.

[2] You see, there are two overall types of religion, a heavenly one and a spiritual one. A heavenly type of religion exists among people whose volitional side can be reborn or become a church, whereas a spiritual type of religion exists among people whose intellectual side alone can be reborn, as just mentioned. The earliest church, which came before the Flood, was heavenly, because the people in it had a perfection to their will part. The ancient church, which came after the Flood, was spiritual, because the people in it had a perfection not to their will part but to their intellectual part. This, then, explains why it is that where the Word deals with a spiritual religion, it deals in part with that religion's intellect as well. On this subject, see §§640, 641, 765, 863, 875, 895, 927, 928, 1023, 1043, 1044, 1555, 2124, 2256, 2669, 4328, 4493.

The fact that the intellectual part is reborn in people belonging to a spiritual religion can also be seen from this: People in a spiritual religion do not receive any perception of truth from goodness as the people of the heavenly church did. First they have to work at learning religious truth and steep their mind in it, and then truth enables them to recognize what is good. Once they learn to recognize it, they can think about it, then apply their will to it, and finally act on it. At that point the Lord forms a new will in their intellectual part, and through this new will he raises the spiritual person to heaven. Evil remains in that individual's own will, but it is eventually isolated in a miraculous way, through a higher power that withholds the person from evil and anchors him or her in goodness.

[3] People in the heavenly church, on the other hand, were reborn in respect to their will part by being steeped in charitable goodness from the time they were small. Having acquired a perception of this goodness, they were led to a perception of love for the Lord. As a result, all religious truth presented itself in their intellect as in a mirror. Their intellect and will made an absolutely undivided mind, because they perceived in their intellect whatever inhabited their will. This constituted the perfection of the first human, who symbolizes the heavenly church.

[4] The meaning of a grapevine as intellect in a spiritual religion can be seen from many other passages in the Word. In Jeremiah, for instance:

> Why should you go to Egypt to drink the waters of the Sihor, or why should you go to Assyria to drink the waters of the river? Yet I had *planted you as a choice grapevine through and through,* the seed of truth. How then could you turn *into the degenerate branches of a foreign grapevine* before my eyes? (Jeremiah 2:18, 21)

This is about Israel, which symbolizes a spiritual religion (§§3654, 4286). Egypt and the waters of the Sihor stand for knowledge that twists the truth (§§1164, 1165, 1186, 1462). Assyria and the waters of the River stand for arguing from these facts against a good life and religious truth (§§119, 1186). The choice grapevine stands for people in a spiritual religion, who are called a vine on account of their intellect. The degenerate branches of a foreign grapevine stand for people in a religion that has been corrupted. [5] In Ezekiel:

> A riddle and parable about the house of Israel: A large eagle took some of the seed of the land and put it in a field suitable for sowing. It sprouted and became a *luxuriant grapevine,* low in height, so that *its branches* turned to face [the eagle] and its roots were under [the eagle]. So it became a *vine* that made *branches* and sent *shoots* out to the eagle. *This vine* applied its roots and sent *its branches* out to [the eagle] in a good field, near many waters. It had been planted to produce a branch so that it would become a *majestic grapevine.* (Ezekiel 17:2, 3, 5, 6, 7, 8)

The eagle stands for rationality (§3901), and the seed of the land for truth in the church (§§1025, 1447, 1610, 1940, 2848, 3038, 3310, 3373). The seed became a luxuriant grapevine and a majestic grapevine, and this means that it became a spiritual church. This church is called a grapevine because it yields wine, which symbolizes spiritual goodness or neighborly kindness leading to religious truth, planted in the intellectual side of the mind. [6] In the same author:

> Your mother was like a *grapevine* that resembled you, planted next to the water; she became fruitful and full of branches because of the many waters. Therefore she had strong rods as rulers' scepters. And her stature raised itself above the tangled branches so that she appeared in her height with an abundance of branches. (Ezekiel 19:10, 11)

This too is about Israel, the symbol of a spiritual religion, which is being compared to a grapevine for the same reason mentioned just above. The passage depicts the offshoots from such a religion, down to the very last ones in the earthly self—in other words, to facts gleaned with the senses—these being the tangled branches (§2831). [7] In Hosea:

> I will be like dew to *Israel;* its branches will spread, and its honor will be like an olive tree's, and it will have a scent like Lebanon's. Those living in its shade will return, they will bring the grain to life, and they will blossom like a *grapevine;* its memory will be like the *wine of Lebanon.* Ephraim, what do I care anymore about idols? (Hosea 14:5, 6, 7, 8)

Israel here stands for a spiritual religion. Its blossoming is compared to a grapevine and its memory to the wine of Lebanon on account of the faith-inspired goodness planted in its intellect. Ephraim is the intellect of a spiritual religion (§3969). [8] In Zechariah:

> The remnant of the people will be the seed of peace; *the grapevine will yield its fruit,* and the earth will yield produce, and the heavens will yield their dew. (Zechariah 8:11, 12)

The remnant of the people stands for truth the Lord stores up inside us (§§468, 530, 560, 561, 660, 798, 1050, 1738, 1906, 2284). The seed of peace stands for the goodness there, and the grapevine for the intellect. [9] In Malachi:

> I will harangue the demolishing pest for you, so that it does not spoil the fruit of the earth for you, *and the grapevine in the field will not be bereft for you.* (Malachi 3:11, 12)

The grapevine stands for the intellect. It is said not to be bereft when the intellect is not deprived of religious truth and goodness. When the intellect contains falsity and consequent evil, on the other hand, it is called an empty grapevine. In Hosea:

> *Israel is an empty grapevine;* they make the fruit resemble themselves. (Hosea 10:1)

[10] In Moses:

> He will tie his young donkey *to the grapevine,* and his jenny's foal *to the choice vine,* after he washes his clothing *in wine,* and his robe in the *blood of grapes.* (Genesis 49:11)

This is the prophecy of Jacob, who by then was Israel, concerning his twelve sons—here, concerning Judah, who represents the Lord (§3881). The grapevine stands for the intellect of a spiritual religion, and the choice vine for the intellect of a heavenly religion. [11] In David:

> Jehovah, a *grapevine* you have caused to set out *from Egypt;* you have driven away the nations and planted *it.* You have cleared out before *it* and rooted *its* roots so that *it* fills the land; mountains are covered with *its* shade, and the cedars of God with *its* branches. You have sent *its* *shoots* all the way out to the sea, and to the Euphrates *its tendrils.* A boar from the forest tramples *it,* and the wild animal of the fields feeds on *it.* (Psalms 80:8, 9, 10, 11, 13)

The grapevine from Egypt in the highest sense stands for the Lord, and the glorification of his human side is depicted through this grapevine and its offshoots. The same vine in an inner sense means a spiritual religion and the people belonging to it such as they are when the Lord has remade or regenerated their intellect and will. The boar in the forest means falsity, and the wild animal of the fields means evil, which destroy the church and faith in the Lord. [12] In John:

> The angel sent his sickle into the earth and *harvested the grapevine of the* *earth* and threw it into the great winepress of God's anger. The winepress was trodden outside the city, and blood issued from the winepress all the way to the horses' bridles. (Revelation 14:19, 20)

Harvesting the grapevine of the earth stands for destroying the church's intellect, because the church's intellect is what a grapevine symbolizes. The passage also says that blood issued from the winepress all the way to the horses' bridles, horses symbolizing intellectual matters (§§2761, 2762, 3217). In Isaiah:

> It will happen on that day that every place that *holds a thousand grape-* *vines* going for a thousand pieces of silver will become a bramble and a brier patch. (Isaiah 7:23)

In the same author:

> The residents of the land will be destroyed by fire, and the humanity left behind will be sparse; the new wine will mourn, and *the grapevine* *will droop.* (Isaiah 24:6, 7)

In the same author:

> They beat their breasts because of the fields of *unmixed wine,* because
> of the *fruitful grapevine;* on my people's land, the thorn, the brier comes
> up. (Isaiah 32:12, 13, 14)

The topic in these passages is the devastation of a spiritual religion in regard
to the goodness and truth advocated by faith and therefore in regard to
the intellect. After all, the intellectual part of the mind is where faith's
truth and goodness reside in the people of a spiritual religion, as noted
above. Anyone can see that the vine here does not mean a vine, and the
land does not mean the land, but that they mean something having to do
with religion.

[13] A grapevine in its true sense symbolizes goodness in the intellect, and a fig tree symbolizes goodness on the earthly level. To put it
another way, a grapevine symbolizes goodness in the inner self, and a fig
tree goodness in the outer self. As a consequence, many of the places in
the Word that mention a grapevine also mention a fig tree, including the
following examples. In Jeremiah:

> I will utterly consume them; *there are no grapes on the grapevine and no
> figs on the fig tree,* and the leaf drifts down. (Jeremiah 8:13)

In the same author:

> I will bring onto you a nation from far away, house of Israel, which will
> eat *your grapevine* and *your fig tree.* (Jeremiah 5:15, 17)

In Hosea:

> I will devastate *her grapevine* and *her fig tree.* (Hosea 2:12)

In Joel:

> A nation has come up over the land; it has reduced *my grapevine* to a
> ruin and *my fig tree* to scum. It has stripped *them* bare and discarded
> them; *their branches* have turned white. The *grapevine* has dried up, and
> the *fig tree* droops. (Joel 1:6, 7, 12)

In the same author:

> Do not be afraid, animals of my fields; because the living-places of the
> desert have become grassy. Because the tree makes its fruit, and the *fig
> tree* and *grapevine* will yield their strength. (Joel 2:22, 23)

In David:

> He has struck *their grapevine* and *their fig tree* and shattered the tree within their border. (Psalms 105:33)

In Habakkuk:

> The *fig tree* will not bloom, nor will there be produce *on the grapevines*. (Habakkuk 3:17)

In Micah:

> From Zion will issue instruction, and Jehovah's Word from Jerusalem. They will sit, each *under their own grapevine* and *under their own fig tree*, and none frightening them. (Micah 4:2, 4)

In Zechariah:

> On that day you will shout, a man to his companion, *under the grapevine* and *under the fig tree*. (Zechariah 3:10)

In 1 Kings:

> In the time of Solomon there was peace on all sides round about, and Judah and Israel lived in security, *each under their own grapevine* and *under their own fig tree*. (1 Kings 4:24, 25)

For a fig tree meaning goodness in the earthly, outer self, see §217.

[14] A grapevine means a new intellect, or an intellect regenerated through the goodness that comes of truth and the truth that comes of goodness, as can be seen from the Lord's words to his disciples after he had established the Holy Supper. In Matthew:

> I say to you that from now on I will not drink *any of this produce of the grapevine* until that day when I drink it new with you in my Father's kingdom. (Matthew 26:29)

The produce of the grapevine symbolizes the goodness that comes of truth and the truth that comes of goodness, through which the intellect is remade or a person becomes spiritual. Drinking symbolizes the adoption of this goodness and truth. (On the point that drinking means adopting something and has to do with truth, see §3168.) We do not fully adopt them until the other life, which is symbolized by "until that day when I drink it new with you in my Father's kingdom." Obviously, the produce of the vine does not mean new or aged wine but something heavenly in the Lord's kingdom.

[15] Because the intellect of a spiritual person is remade and regenerated through truth that comes only from the Lord, the Lord compares himself to a grapevine. When people are grafted onto the truth coming from him and consequently grafted onto him, he compares them to branches, and he compares the goodness that results to fruit. The passage is in John:

> I am the true grapevine, and my Father is the vinedresser. Every branch in me not bearing fruit he removes; but every one bearing fruit he will prune so that it will bear more fruit. Remain in me; I will also remain in you. Just as a branch cannot bear fruit on its own, if it does not remain on the vine, so you cannot either, if you do not remain in me. I am the grapevine; you are the branches. Those who remain in me and in whom I remain bear much fruit; because without me you cannot do anything. This is my commandment: that you love one another as I have loved you. (John 15:1, 2, 3, 4, 5, 12)

[16] Because a grapevine symbolizes the Lord as divine truth on the highest level and therefore symbolizes the people of a spiritual religion on an inner level, a vineyard symbolizes a spiritual religion itself (§§1069, 3220).

[17] A Nazirite represented a heavenly person, and heavenly people are regenerated by a loving goodness rather than by religious truth—the means of rebirth for spiritual people. So it is the will rather than the intellect that is reborn in them (see what is said about this above). That is why a Nazirite was forbidden to eat anything that came out of the grapevine and therefore to drink wine (Numbers 6:3, 4; Judges 13:14). This too shows that a grapevine symbolizes the intellect in a spiritual person, as has been demonstrated. (For the representation of a Nazirite as a heavenly person, see §3301.) Clearly, then, one can never know why everything that came out of the grapevine was forbidden to a Nazirite, and so on, without knowing what a grapevine symbolizes in its proper sense. One also needs to know that there is a heavenly type of religion and a spiritual type and that people in a heavenly religion are reborn in a different way than people in a spiritual religion. The former are regenerated through seed planted in their will part; the latter, through seed planted in their intellectual part.

Such are the secrets hidden in the Word's inner meaning.

5114   *And on the vine three shoots* symbolizes outgrowths, right to the last of them, as the following shows: A *vine* symbolizes the intellect, as discussed just above in §5113. *Three* symbolizes completion and continuing developments, right to the end, as discussed in §§2788, 4495. And *shoots* symbolize outgrowths. Considering that a vine means the intellect, shoots are simply its outgrowths, and since three symbolizes continuing developments right to the end, or from first to last, the three shoots symbolize outgrowths from the intellect, down to the last level, which is the sensory level. The first level in order is the intellectual one, and the last is the sensory one.

The intellect in general is the eye of the inner self, which sees by the light of heaven shining from the Lord, and everything it sees is spiritual and heavenly. The senses in general, though, belong to the outer self, and in this case [the pertinent sense is] the sense of sight, since it corresponds to and is under the control of the intellect. This sense sees by the light of the world shining from the sun, and everything it sees is worldly, physical, and earthbound.

[2] In the human being, there are outgrowths from the intellect (which heaven's light shines on) that reach as far as the senses (which the world's light shines on). If these outgrowths did not exist, the senses would not have any human life. Our senses have life not because we see by worldly light, which contains no life, but because we see by heavenly light, which does contain life. When heavenly light falls on the impressions left in us by worldly light, it brings them to life and enables us to see objects with our intellect—in other words, to look at them in a human way. Knowledge grows out of what we have seen and heard in the world—what has entered through our senses—and from this knowledge we gain, first, understanding and wisdom, and through these, civil, moral, and spiritual life.

[3] To be more specific about the outgrowths in a person, they are not something that can be explained quickly. There are several levels (like steps on a ladder) between the intellect and the senses, but no one can begin to understand them without knowing something about them and the fact that the different levels are utterly distinct from each other. In fact, they are so distinct that the inner levels can emerge into lasting existence without the outer levels, although the outer levels cannot do so without the inner. For instance, our spirit can exist without our body and its matter, and does exist without them when separated from the body by death. Our spirit is on an inner plane and our body on an outer one.

The same thing happens with our spirit after death, if we are among the blessed. We are on the lowest level there when we are in the first heaven, on an inner level when we are in the second, and on the inmost level when we are in the third. When we are in the third heaven, we are actually in the others too, but these other levels are unconscious in us, in almost the same way that our body is unconscious during sleep. The difference is that in heaven our inner levels are wide awake among the angels. There are as many distinctly different levels in us, then, as there are heavens, except for the last level, which is the body with its senses.

[4] This shows to some extent how matters stand with outgrowths from first to last, or from the intellect to the senses.

The life force in us, which comes from the Lord's divinity, passes through these levels from the inmost to the outermost and produces outgrowths at every level, becoming more and more comprehensive until the outermost level, where it is all-encompassing. The outgrowths on the lower levels are merely conglomerations or rather syntheses of the particulars and minute details on the higher levels in order, overlaid with the more refined and then the cruder substances of the physical world, which can serve as containers. When these containers dissolve, the particulars and minute details belonging to inner levels that were synthesized in them return to the next higher level. We have a connection with the Divine, and our deepest core is capable of receiving what is divine—not just of receiving it but even of making it our own by acknowledging it and feeling desire for it and therefore by reciprocating. Because of this, we are grafted to the Divine and as a consequence can never die. We abide in what is eternal and infinite not only because the Divine flows into us but also because we accept that inflow.

[5] This shows how ignorant and weak the thinking is that puts us on the same footing with mindless animals and does not believe we will live on after death any more than they do. People who think this way do not weigh the fact that mindless animals do not receive what is divine, do not reciprocate and make it their own by acknowledging and feeling desire for it, and are not united with it. This being the condition of animals, the forms they have for receiving life cannot help dissolving. What flows into animals passes through their organic forms and on into the world, where it comes to a halt and vanishes. It never makes a return.

And it seemed to be sprouting symbolizes an inflow that would lead to rebirth. This can be seen from the symbolism of *sprouting*—putting

5115

out leaves so that there will eventually be flowers—as the start of rebirth. It symbolizes an inflow because when we are being reborn, spiritual life flows into us in the same way life carried by warmth from the sun flows into a sprouting tree.

The Word often draws a comparison between every human born and members of the plant kingdom, especially trees. This is because the whole plant kingdom, like the animal kingdom, represents characteristics of a human being and therefore attributes of the Lord's kingdom. After all, a human is heaven on its smallest scale (as can be seen from explanations of the correspondence between an individual and the universal human, or heaven, at the ends of the chapters). That is also why the ancients called a person a microcosm. They would have called a person a miniature heaven as well if they had known more about the state of heaven. On the point that the whole material world is a theater representing the Lord's kingdom, see §§2758, 3483, 4939.

[2] But it is particularly a person being born anew—one being regenerated by the Lord—who is called a heaven. We are then being planted with divine goodness and truth from the Lord and consequently with heaven, because when we are being reborn, we start from a seed, just as a tree does. A seed in the Word accordingly symbolizes truth that develops out of goodness. From there, just like a tree, we put out leaves, flowers, and finally fruit. First we produce the effects of understanding, symbolized in the Word by leaves; then the effects of wisdom, symbolized by flowers; and finally matters of life, or a loving, charitable goodness put into act, symbolized in the Word by fruit.

Such is the representational similarity that exists between a fruit tree and a person being reborn. In fact, we can learn from the tree about the way regeneration works, as long as we first know something about spiritual goodness and truth.

Plainly, then, the grapevine in the cupbearer's dream represents and depicts the whole process by which the senses that are subordinate to our intellect are reborn. The process is portrayed first by the three shoots, then by the sprouting, the flowering, and the ripening of the clusters into grapes, and finally by the cupbearer's squeezing the grapes into Pharaoh's cup and giving it to him.

[3] What is more, representation is always involved in the images of dreams that flow in through heaven from the Lord. People who do not know what one object or another in the physical world represents therefore cannot help believing that the images are simply the kinds of metaphors

we use in everyday speech, and this is even more true of people who have no idea that anything has a representation. They are metaphors, it is true, but of a kind that has a correspondence. As a result the images actually appear in the world of spirits when angels in an inner heaven are talking about the spiritual and heavenly attributes of the Lord's kingdom. For information on dreams, see §§1122, 1975, 1977, 1979, 1980, 1981.

And its flower came up symbolizes a state close to rebirth. This can be seen from the symbolism of a *flower*, which buds on the tree before the fruit, as the state before rebirth. As noted just above in §5115, the sprouting and fruiting of a tree represents human regeneration. Its turning green with leaves represents a first stage, its blossoming a second, or the stage directly preceding rebirth, and its fruiting a third stage, which is the actual state of a person reborn. That is why leaves symbolize matters of understanding, or the true ideas of faith (§885), which form the beginning of rebirth or regeneration. Flowers symbolize matters of wisdom, or good that is done out of faith, because these come right before rebirth or regeneration. Fruit symbolizes matters of life, or deeds of neighborly love, since these come next and constitute the actual state of a person reborn.

[2] The occurrence of these features in the plant kingdom is due to an inflow from the spiritual world. People who attribute everything to nature and nothing to the Divine cannot possibly believe so, but people who attribute everything to the Divine and nothing to nature are given the ability to see that every detail is due to that inflow. Not only that, they see that it all has a correspondence, and that because it has a correspondence, it has a representation. Finally, they are given the ability to see that the whole material world is a theater representing the Lord's kingdom. Divinity is in every part—so much so that there is a representation of eternity and infinity there as well. There is a representation of eternity because plants propagate to eternity, and there is one of infinity because seed multiplies to infinity. These tendencies could never come out in the various members of the plant kingdom unless the Divine was constantly flowing in. The inflow leads to a tendency, the tendency to a force, and the force to an effect.

[3] A person who ascribes everything to nature says that these attributes were infused into fruits and seeds at the beginning of creation and that the force then infused into them afterward leads them spontaneously into such activities. People like this do not consider, though, that continued existence is constant emergence, or what is the same, that

5116

propagation is constant creation. They also do not consider that an effect extends from its cause, and that when the cause stops, the effect stops. So without a constant inflow from the cause, every effect dies instantly. Again, they do not consider that anything disconnected from the first entity of all and consequently from the Divine subsides immediately into nothingness. What is prior has to maintain a constant presence in what is subsequent, if what is subsequent is to exist.

[4] People who ascribe everything to nature and so little to the Divine that it may as well be nothing could consider these points. If they did, they too would be able to acknowledge that absolutely everything in the physical world represents the kinds of things that exist in the spiritual world and consequently in the Lord's kingdom, where the Lord's divinity is represented directly. That is why I have said that the spiritual world flows into this world, although I mean that the Lord's divinity flows in through the spiritual world.

The reason people whose attention is on the earthly plane do not consider these points is that they do not want to acknowledge them. They are taken up with earthly and bodily considerations and therefore with a life of self-love and materialism, so their approach to anything involving the spiritual world, or heaven, is completely upside down. To see these points upside down is impossible, because lower planes then seem higher, and higher planes seem lower. As a result, when such people are seen in heaven's light in the other world, they appear with their head down and their feet up.

[5] When they look at flowers on a tree or any other plant, who among them considers that the vegetation is more or less rejoicing in the fact that it is now producing fruit or seeds? They can see that the flower comes first and continues to bloom until it has the rudiments of fruit or seed in its embrace, which allows it to transfer its sap to the fruit or seed. If such people knew anything about human rebirth or regeneration—or rather if they wanted to know—the similarity would lead them to see in the flowers a representation of our state before rebirth. They would see that we then blossom in a similar way with the goodness that belongs to understanding and wisdom. That is, we rejoice and turn beautiful inside, because we are then making an effort to plant the seeds of that goodness in our life, or to produce fruit. Such people are also incapable of seeing that this is then our state. The nature of the inner gladness and beauty being represented is entirely unknown to people who indulge only in the joys of materialism and the pleasures of self-love. Such joys and pleasures make the other

kind look joyless and unpleasant to them—so much so that they loathe them, and since they loathe them, reject them as something worthless or nonexistent. Consequently they deny them, denying also that the spiritual or heavenly dimension is anything.

This is the source of the insanity of our times, which is believed to be wisdom.

And its clusters ripened into grapes symbolizes the union of spiritual truth and heavenly goodness, as the following shows: *Ripening* means proceeding with rebirth or regeneration to the point where truth unites with goodness, so it symbolizes union. *Clusters* symbolize the truth that comes of spiritual goodness, and *grapes* symbolize the goodness that comes of heavenly truth, both of them on the sensory plane represented by the cupbearer. The union of these two on the sensory plane resembles the ripening of clusters into grapes. During rebirth or regeneration, all truth has an inclination to unite with goodness. Until they unite, truth does not receive life, so it does not produce fruit. This is represented in the ripening of fruit. Unripe fruit—the clusters, here—represents a state in which truth still predominates, but ripe fruit—the grapes—represents a state in which goodness has dominance. The dominance of goodness is also represented by the flavor and sweetness we taste in ripe grapes.

Nothing more can be said, though, about the union of truth with goodness in the senses that are under the control of the intellectual side. The secrets are too deep to grasp. It is absolutely necessary to first have knowledge about the state of spiritual heavenliness, about these senses, and about the state of the earthly plane when the union takes place.

[2] The symbolism of grapes as the goodness of a spiritual person and therefore as neighborly love becomes clear from many places in the Word. In Isaiah, for instance:

> My beloved had a *vineyard* on a horn of the offspring of oil; he waited for it *to produce grapes,* but it produced *wild grapes.* (Isaiah 5:1, 2, 4)

The vineyard stands for a spiritual religion. "He waited for it to produce grapes" means waiting for it to produce the goodness of neighborly love. "But it produced wild grapes" means that it produced the evils of hatred and revenge. [3] In the same author:

> This is what Jehovah has said: "Just as *new wine* is found *in the cluster,* and they say, 'Do not spoil it, because there is a blessing in it,' . . ." (Isaiah 65:8)

5117

The new wine in the cluster stands for truth on the earthly plane growing out of goodness. [4] In Jeremiah:

> "I will utterly destroy them," says Jehovah. "There are *no grapes on the grapevine* and no figs on the fig tree." (Jeremiah 8:13)

No grapes on the grapevine stands for no inner, rational goodness. No figs on the fig tree stands for no outer, earthly goodness. The grapevine means the intellect, as shown just above in §5113, and when truth and goodness unite in the intellect, the grapevine means rationality, since rationality comes from that union. For the meaning of a fig tree as goodness in the earthly, outer self, see §217. [5] In Hosea:

> Israel was like *grapes in the wilderness* when I discovered him. Your ancestors were like first fruit on a young fig tree when I saw them. (Hosea 9:10)

Grapes in the wilderness stand for rational goodness that has not yet become spiritual, and the first fruit on the fig tree stands for earthly goodness not yet spiritual. Israel stands for the ancient spiritual church at its beginning. The ancestors here and elsewhere are not Jacob's children but the people among whom the ancient church was first established. [6] In Micah:

> Is there a *cluster* to eat? An early fruit is what my soul has desired. The godly person has perished off the earth, and an upright person does not exist among humankind. (Micah 7:1, 2)

The cluster to eat stands for neighborly kindness in its rudiments; the early fruit, for religious truth too at that stage. [7] In Amos:

> Look! The days are coming in which the one who plows will overtake the one who reaps, and the one *treading grapes* [will overtake] the one trailing seed; and the mountains will shower down *new wine,* and all the hills will stream down. And I will bring my people back from captivity, so that they may rebuild the devastated cities, and sit down and *plant vineyards,* and *drink wine from them,* and *make clusters* and eat fruit from them. (Amos 9:13, 14)

This speaks about and depicts the establishment of a spiritual religion. The fact that the one who plows will overtake the one who reaps depicts the union of spiritual goodness with its truth; and the fact that the one treading grapes will overtake the one trailing seed depicts the union of spiritual truth with its goodness. The fact that the mountains will shower down new wine and that the hills will stream down symbolizes the loving, charitable goodness that will result. Bringing the people back from captivity stands for delivering them from falsity. Rebuilding the devastated cities stands for rectifying the falsified teaching of truth. Sitting down and planting vineyards stands for cultivating the ground covered by a spiritual religion. Drinking wine from them stands for adopting the truth that such a religion gleans from neighborly love, and making clusters and eating fruit from them stands for adopting the resulting goodness. Anyone can see that building cities, planting vineyards, drinking wine, making clusters, and eating fruit from them are mere earthly activities, which would have nothing divine in them if they had no spiritual meaning. [8] In Moses:

> He washed his clothing *in wine* and his robe in the *blood of grapes.* (Genesis 49:11)

This is about the Lord. The wine stands for spiritual goodness resulting from divine love; the blood of grapes, for heavenly goodness resulting from it. [9] In the same author:

> . . . the butter of the herd and the milk of the flock, together with the fat of lambs and of rams—the sons of Bashan—and of goats, together with the fat of the kidneys of wheat; and the *blood of the grape* you drink as unmixed wine. (Deuteronomy 32:14)

This is about the ancient church and depicts its loving, charitable goodness. Every item symbolizes a specific type of goodness. The blood of the grape symbolizes spiritual-heavenly goodness, which is a name for a divine quality in heaven that emanates from the Lord. Wine is being referred to as the blood of grapes because both symbolize holy truth emanating from the Lord—but wine is mentioned in connection with a spiritual religion, and blood, with a heavenly religion. This being so, wine was commanded for the Holy Supper. [10] In the same author:

> *From the grapevine of Sodom comes their grapevine,* and from the fields of Gomorrah. *Its grapes are grapes of gall; clusters of bitterness are theirs.* (Deuteronomy 32:32)

This is about the Jewish religion. "From the grapevine of Sodom comes their grapevine, and from the fields of Gomorrah" means that their intellectual side is overrun with falsities growing out of a hellish love. "Its grapes are grapes of gall; clusters of bitterness are theirs" means that the same is true of the will on their intellectual side. Since a grape in a positive sense symbolizes neighborly love, it relates to the will, but to the will as it exists in the intellectual part of the mind; and the same in a negative sense. All truth belongs to the intellect and all goodness to the will. [11] In John:

> The angel said, "Send in the sharp sickle and *harvest the earth's clusters,* because *its grapes have ripened.*" (Revelation 14:18)

Harvesting the earth's clusters stands for destroying every bit of neighborly love. [12] In Matthew:

> By their fruits you will know them. *Do people ever gather grapes from thorns,* or figs from thistles? (Matthew 7:16)

And in Luke:

> Every tree is known by its own fruit, for they do not gather figs from thorns *or harvest a grape from a bramble.* (Luke 6:44)

Since this verse is about charity for one's neighbor, it says that people will be known by their fruits, which are good actions done out of neighborly love. Neighborly goodness on the inside is meant by grapes, and on the outside, by figs.

[13] One law laid down in the Jewish religion was this:

> When you come into your companion's vineyard, you shall eat *grapes* as your soul urges, to your fill, but you shall not put them into your container. (Deuteronomy 23:24)

This involves the idea that in relation to others with a different theology and religion, we can learn about and welcome the good that they do out of neighborly love but not absorb it and unite it with the truth we know. Since the vineyard means a church, it is a place of theology, or religion. The grapes mean charitable goodness, and the container means truth in the church.

5118   *And Pharaoh's cup was in my hand* symbolizes the inflow of the inner earthly plane into the outer, and the start of its acceptance, as the following shows: *Pharaoh* represents the inner earthly plane, as noted above at §§5080, 5095. The cupbearer represents the outer earthly plane, as discussed at §§5077, 5082, and *in my hand* means with him. The *cup* symbolizes something that contains and also that which is contained, as discussed below in §5120. Because of this, and because of the train of ideas in the inner meaning, *Pharaoh's cup was in my hand* symbolizes the inflow of the inner earthly plane into the outer, and the start of its acceptance there.

The inner and outer earthly planes have already been defined. The inner earthly plane is the one that communicates with the rational plane and receives its inflow. The outer earthly plane is the one that communicates with the senses, or through the senses with the world, so it is the plane that receives the world's inflow.

[2] To focus on spiritual inflow, it travels in an unbroken stream from the Lord through the rational plane to the inner earthly plane and through this to the outer earthly plane. However, the inflows alter and change in accord with the way they are received. In the unregenerate, goodness turns into evil on the earthly level, and truth into falsity. In the regenerate, goodness and truth reveal themselves there in a kind of mirror. The earthly level is exactly like a face representing the spiritual qualities of the inner self, and this face develops the ability to represent such qualities when our outside corresponds to our inside.

This shows to some extent what is meant by the inflow of the inner earthly plane into the outer, and the start of its acceptance there.

And I took the grapes and squeezed them into Pharaoh's cup symbolizes a reciprocal inflow into the goodness from a spiritual origin there, as the following shows: *Grapes* symbolize good that is done out of neighborly love, as discussed directly above in §5117, so they symbolize goodness from a spiritual origin. All the goodness of genuine charity comes from a spiritual source. And *squeezing them into Pharaoh's cup* symbolizes a reciprocal inflow. **5119**

Reciprocal inflow does not mean an inflow of the outer earthly level into the inner, because this is impossible. What is outside can never flow into what is within. To say the same thing another way, what is lower or subsequent can never flow into what is higher or prior. Rather, the rational mind calls on the contents of the inner earthly plane, and through this on the contents of the outer earthly plane. Not that it calls on the actual contents, but on the conclusions we draw from them. That is what reciprocal inflow is.

[2] It looks as though objects in the world flow in toward our inner reaches through our senses, but this is a delusion of the senses. Our inner reaches flow into our outer surface, and we perceive objects because of that inflow. I have discussed these matters with spirits several times,

and personal experience has shown me that the inner self sees and perceives in the outer self what is going on outside the outer self. There is no other source for our sensory life—that is, for our ability to sense things, or for sensations themselves.

The delusion is so persuasive and strong, though, that our earthly self cannot dispel it. Not even our rational self can, unless it can think independently of our senses.

These remarks have been intended to show what a reciprocal inflow is.

5120 *And I put the cup on Pharaoh's palm* symbolizes adoption by the inner earthly plane. This is established by the symbolism of *putting a cup* [in someone's hand], which means giving wine to drink, as adopting (drinking means adopting truth; see §3168), and by the representation of *Pharaoh* as the inner earthly plane (noted at §§5080, 5095, 5118).

As the preceding sections show, the current theme is the rebirth of the senses that are under the control of the inner self's intellectual side, as symbolized by the cupbearer. Consequently, the theme is the inflow of truth and goodness and its acceptance on the outer earthly plane. These concepts are somewhat out of reach, though, for people who have no clear idea of the rational and earthly levels or of spiritual inflow, so I will dispense with further explanation.

[2] Moreover, the Word often mentions a cup, or goblet, and in a positive sense it symbolizes spiritual truth, or religious truth springing from charitable goodness, which is the same meaning wine has. In a negative sense it symbolizes both the falsity that leads to evil and the falsity that comes from evil. A cup has the same symbolism as wine because a cup is a container and what it holds is wine. They make a unit, then, and accordingly the one means the other.

This symbolism of a cup in the Word is plain from the following passages. [3] In David:

Jehovah, you will arrange before me a table in the presence of my enemies and enrich my head with oil; *my cup will overflow.* (Psalms 23:5)

Arranging a table and enriching someone's head with oil stands for giving someone the gift of a charitable, loving goodness. "My cup will overflow" means that the earthly level will be filled with spiritual truth and goodness as a result. In the same author:

What shall I return to Jehovah? *I will take the cup of salvation,* and I will call on Jehovah's name. (Psalms 116:12, 13)

Taking the cup of salvation stands for making faith-inspired goodness one's own. [4] In Mark:

> Any who *give you a cup of water to drink* in my name because you are Christ's—truly, I say to you, they will not lose their reward. (Mark 9:41)

"Giving someone a cup of water to drink in my name" stands for training people in religious truth from a meager supply of neighborly love. [5] In Matthew:

> Next, *taking the cup* and giving thanks, he gave it to them, saying, "Drink from it, all of you, because this is my blood, the blood of the new testament." (Matthew 26:27, 28; Mark 14:23, 24; Luke 22:20)

The word used is "cup" rather than "wine" because wine is mentioned in connection with a spiritual religion, and blood in connection with a heavenly religion. Both symbolize a holy influence of truth streaming from the Lord, but in a spiritual religion it is the holy influence of a faith that grows out of charity for one's neighbor, while in a heavenly religion it is the holy influence of a charity that grows out of love for the Lord. The difference between a spiritual and a heavenly religion is that a spiritual religion is devoted to charity for one's neighbor, and a heavenly one to love for the Lord. The Holy Supper was established to represent and symbolize the Lord's love for the entire human race and the love we give back to him.

[6] Since "cup" means a container and "wine" the contents, a cup symbolizes people's outer level, and wine symbolizes what they have inside them. That is why the Lord said:

> Doom to you, scribes and Pharisees—hypocrites! Because you cleanse the *outside of the cup* and plate, but the insides are full of plunder and excess. Blind Pharisee, cleanse first the *inside of the cup* and plate, and the outside will also become clean. (Matthew 23:25, 26; Luke 11:39)

Here too the cup in an inner sense means religious truth. To cultivate the truth taught by faith without the goodness taught by faith is to cleanse the outside of the cup, especially when the insides are full of hypocrisy, deceit, hatred, vengefulness, and cruelty. Under these circumstances, we have the truth taught by faith only in our outer self and none at all in our inner self. Cultivating and absorbing the goodness taught by faith unites truth with goodness in our outer self, but even then delusions are taken for truth, and this is symbolized by "cleansing first the inside of the cup and the outside will also become clean." [7] Likewise in Mark:

> There are many other things that the Pharisees and Jews received, to hold to: *baptizings of cups* and crockery and bronze dishes and beds. Abandoning the command of God, you hold to the tradition of humans— you carry out *baptisms of crockery* and *of cups* and many other similar things. You reject God's command in order to hold to your tradition. (Mark 7:4, 8, 9)

[8] The following passages show that in a negative sense a cup symbolizes falsity that leads to evil and falsity that comes from evil. In Jeremiah:

> This is what Jehovah, God of Israel, has said to me: "*Take* this *cup of the wine of anger* from my hand and make all the nations to which I am sending you *drink* it, so that they will drink and stagger and run mad because of the sword that I will send among them." So I took the *cup* from Jehovah's hand and made all the nations to which Jehovah sent me drink. (Jeremiah 25:15, 16, 17, 28)

The cup of the wine of anger stands for falsity that leads to evil. The reason for the symbolism is that falsity causes drunkenness and insanity in the same way wine does. Spiritual inebriation is nothing but the madness that results when people who believe only what they can grasp argue about the correctness of various beliefs, which leads to falsity, and from falsity to evil (§1072). That is why the passage says, "so that they will drink and stagger and run mad because of the sword that I will send." A sword means falsity engaged in battle against truth (§§2799, 4499). [9] In Lamentations:

> Rejoice and be glad, daughter of Edom, living in the land of Uz; *the cup will also pass to you.* You will become drunk and be exposed. (Lamentations 4:21)

Becoming drunk from the cup stands for going insane from falsity. Being exposed or laid bare without feeling shame stands for the resulting evil (§§213, 214). [10] In Ezekiel:

> "In the way of your sister you have walked; *therefore I will put her cup into your hand.*" This is what the Lord Jehovih has said: "*The cup of your sister you will drink, deep and wide.* You will become a laughingstock and a mockery, ample as you are in what you can hold. With

drunkenness and sorrow you will be filled, with the *cup* of devastation and ruin. The *cup of your sister* Samaria you will both drink and drain, and its shards you will pulverize." (Ezekiel 23:31, 32, 33, 34)

This is about Jerusalem, which symbolizes a spiritual quality in a heavenly religion. The cup stands for falsity derived from evil. Because this falsity devastates or destroys a religion, it is called the cup of devastation and ruin. In Isaiah:

Wake up! Wake up! Arise, Jerusalem, who drank from Jehovah's hand the *cup of his anger;* the dregs of the *cup of trembling* you have drunk. (Isaiah 51:17)

In Habakkuk:

Drink [wine] yourself, too, so that your foreskin may end up exposed; the *cup of Jehovah's right hand* will come around to you so that there may be shameful vomit on your glory. (Habakkuk 2:16)

In David:

A cup is in the hand of Jehovah. And he has mixed it with wine, filled it with the mixture, and poured out from it. But its dregs all the ungodly of the earth suck up [and] will drink. (Psalms 75:8)

[11] In these places too the cup stands for insanity driven by falsity and its resulting evil. It is called the cup of Jehovah's anger and of Jehovah's right hand because the Jewish nation (like the lower classes) believed that Jehovah was the only source of evil and of the punishment for evil and falsity—although these really come from us and the hellish horde with us. This manner of speaking in accord with appearances and with beliefs based on appearances occurs many times, but the inner meaning teaches how to understand it and what to believe. On this subject, see §§245, 592, 696, 1093, 1683, 1874, 1875, 2335, 2447, 3605, 3607, 3614.

[12] Since in a negative sense a cup (like wine) symbolizes falsity that leads to evil and falsity that comes from evil, it also symbolizes trial. Times of trial happen when falsity fights truth and evil consequently fights goodness. A cup is mentioned in relation to trials, and stands for a trial, in Luke:

Jesus prayed, saying, "If you want this *cup* to pass by me, . . . Still, let your will be done, not mine." (Luke 22:42; Matthew 26:39, 42, 44; Mark 14:36)

The cup stands for a time of trial. Likewise in John:

> Jesus said to Peter, "Put the sword into the sheath. Am I not to drink the *cup* that my Father gave me?" (John 18:11)

In Mark, too:

> Jesus said to James and John, "You do not know what you are asking. *Can you drink the cup that I myself drink* and be baptized with the baptism with which I myself am baptized?" They said, "We can." But Jesus said to them, "*Yes, the cup that I myself drink you will drink,* and you will be baptized with the baptism with which I myself am baptized." (Mark 10:38, 39; Matthew 20:22, 23)

Clearly, then, a cup means trials, because trials occur when evil uses falsity to combat goodness and truth. Baptism symbolizes rebirth, and since rebirth is accomplished through spiritual struggle, baptism too symbolizes trials.

[13] In a still more negative sense, a cup symbolizes falsity rising out of evil in profaners, or people who violate neighborly love on the inside but feign piety on the outside. It appears in this sense in Jeremiah:

> Babylon was a *cup of gold* in Jehovah's hand, intoxicating the whole earth. Of *her wine* all the nations drank, therefore the nations go mad. (Jeremiah 51:7)

Babylon stands for people with a reverent exterior, and profanation inside (§§1182, 1326). The falsity that they cover with a veil of sanctity is the cup of gold. Intoxicating the whole earth stands for leading people in the church (the "earth") into error and insanity. The profane intention that they hide under a veneer of piety is simply to be the most important and richest of all and to be worshiped as the divine owners of heaven and earth. This enables them to tyrannize others, soul and body, through the pretense of what is divine and devout. Their outer self, then, looks like an angel, but their inner self is a devil. [14] John speaks of Babylon the same way:

> The woman was dressed in red-violet and scarlet and was gilded with gold and precious stone and pearls, *having a golden cup in her hand,* full of abominations and the uncleanness of her whoredom. (Revelation 17:4)

In the same author:

> Babylon the Great fell, fell, and became a dwelling place for demons, because she has given *some of the wine* of her whoredom's *fury* to all the nations to drink, and the monarchs of the earth whored with her. I heard a voice from heaven saying, "Repay her as she repaid you; in the *cup* in which she mixed, mix double to her." (Revelation 18:2, 3, 4, 6)

In the same author:

> The great city was made into three parts, and the cities of the nations caved in. Babylon the Great was remembered before God, *to have the cup of the fury of God's anger given to her.* (Revelation 16:19)

In the same author:

> A third angel said in a loud voice, "If any worship the beast and its image, *they will drink of the wine of God's anger, mixed with pure wine in the cup of his anger,* and will be tortured with fire and sulfur." (Revelation 14:9, 10)

And Joseph said to him, "This is its interpretation," symbolizes revelation gleaned from a perception by heavenliness on the earthly plane, showing what [the senses subject to the intellectual side] contained, as the following shows: In Scripture narrative, *saying* symbolizes a perception, as discussed at §§1791, 1815, 1819, 1822, 1898, 1919, 2080, 2619, 2862, 3395, 3509. Here it symbolizes revelation gleaned from a perception, because the topic is a dream and its interpretation. All revelation comes either from dialog with angels through whom the Lord speaks or from perception, as discussed below. *Joseph* represents heavenliness on the earthly plane, as mentioned above at §§5086, 5087, 5106. And an *interpretation* symbolizes the content, as also discussed above, at §§5093, 5105, 5107. *Joseph said to him, "This is its interpretation,"* then, symbolizes revelation gleaned from a perception by heavenliness on the earthly plane, showing what [the senses subject to the intellectual side] contained.

5121

[2] Here is some important information regarding the idea that revelation comes either from perception or from dialog with angels through whom the Lord speaks: People intent on goodness and therefore on truth—and especially on the goodness that comes from loving the Lord—have revelation from perception. People not intent on goodness and therefore on truth can have revelation but not from perception, only through a living voice they hear inside them, that is, through angels from the Lord. Audible

revelation is outward; revelation from perception is inward. Angels, especially heavenly ones, have perceptive revelation. So did the people of the earliest church and some in the ancient church, but hardly anyone today does. Many people—even those lacking goodness—have received revelations through speech without perception, and through visions and dreams as well. [3] Most of the revelations received by the prophets of the Jewish religion were like this. The prophets heard a voice, saw a vision, or dreamed a dream, but since they lacked perception, they merely heard or saw the revelation without perceiving what it meant.

Genuine perception comes into being through heaven from the Lord. It touches our intellect in a spiritual way, leading us to conscious thinking that accords with reality. It also leads us to inner assent, though we do not know where this comes from. We suppose it is innate and results from the coherence of the idea, but it is an inner dictate from the Lord through heaven. This dictate flows into the inner depths of our thoughts, and concerns matters that transcend the earthly level and the senses—that is, matters belonging to the spiritual world, or heaven.

These remarks show what a revelation gleaned from perception is.

However, the perceptive revelation that belonged to the Lord (represented here by Joseph), which is the current theme of the inner meaning, came from his divine side and therefore from himself.

5122   *The three shoots are three days* symbolizes continuing developments, right to the end. This is established by the symbolism of *three* as a single period and its continuous span from beginning to end (discussed in §§2788, 4495); from that of *shoots* as outgrowths (discussed in §5114); and from that of *days* as states (discussed in §§23, 487, 488, 493, 893, 2788, 3462, 3785, 4850). From this it follows that *the three shoots are three days* symbolizes a state of rebirth for these senses (represented by the cupbearer) from the beginning of the state to its end. Its sequential developments are symbolized by the shoots.

[2] The state of rebirth for each of the senses, and for every attribute on the earthly plane, and for every attribute on the rational plane as well, has its progression from beginning to end. When it reaches the end, it starts all over, beginning with the final stage reached in the earlier state and continuing to a further goal—and so on. Eventually the pattern switches, and what had been last becomes first. For instance, when both our rational and our earthly planes are being regenerated, the phases of our first state advance from truth that leads to faith to good

that is done out of charity. The truth that brings faith seems to play the leading role, and good that is done out of charity a supporting role, because religious truth looks to charitable goodness as its goal. These phases continue until we have been reborn. Charity, which had been the goal, then becomes the starting point, where new states commence, heading in two directions: deeper within and further outside. The new states move deeper within toward love for the Lord and further outside toward religious truth, continuing beyond that toward earthly and even sensory truth. This last kind of truth is then gradually reduced to correspondence with goodness from charity and love on the rational plane, and the process brings them into heavenly order.

[3] That is what is meant by continuing advances and developments right to the end. These advances and developments are unending in people who are being reborn, stretching from their infancy all the way to the end of their life in the world and beyond to eternity. Yet the process can never regenerate us to the point where we may be called perfect in any way. The elements needing rebirth on our rational and earthly planes are numerous and even limitless, and each of them has unlimited offshoots, or advances and developments, reaching both deeper inside and further outside.

We are completely unaware of this, but the Lord knows absolutely all of it and provides for it every moment. If he let up for just a second, all development would be disrupted. What comes first looks to what comes next in an unbroken chain and produces a series of consequences to eternity. Divine foresight and providence clearly covers the very smallest details, then. If it did not, or if it took only a general sort of care, the human race would perish.

In another three days symbolizes something new at that point. This can be seen from the symbolism of *three* as something continuing right to the end and therefore as something complete (discussed at §§2788, 4495), and from the symbolism of *days* as states (mentioned above at §5122). Three days consequently symbolizes a complete state, so *in three days* or three days later symbolizes a new state (§4901). After all, when one state is complete, a new one begins.   **5123**

Pharaoh will lift your head symbolizes what would be provided and therefore decided. This can be seen from the symbolism of *lifting someone's head* as deciding, and on the highest level, as providing. Divine decision, and execution of the decision, is providence.   **5124**

Among the ancients, "lifting someone's head" was a standard figure of speech for judgment, used when captives or prisoners were judged worthy of either life or death. When they were judged worthy of life, lifting their head was spoken of, as occurs in 2 Kings:

> Evil-merodach, king of Babylon, in the year he became king, *lifted the head of Jehoiachin,* king of Judah, *out of the prison house,* and spoke kindly with him and put his throne over the thrones of the monarchs who were with him in Babylon. (2 Kings 25:27, 28)

Likewise in Jeremiah:

> Evil-merodach, king of Babylon, in the year of his kingship, *lifted the head of Jehoiachin,* king of Judah, and brought him *out of the prison house.* (Jeremiah 52:31)

When they were judged worthy of death, on the other hand, lifting their head *off them* was spoken of, as in the statement about the baker later on:

> In another three days Pharaoh will *lift your head off you.* (Genesis 40:19)

[2] This judicial turn of speech arose among the ancients (who thought in representational terms) from the representation of captives in a prison or pit. Such captives represented spirits going through spiritual devastation in the underground realm (§§4728, 4744, 5038), so lifting their head symbolized freeing them. When they are freed, you see, they are raised or lifted out of devastation and taken to heavenly communities (see §§2699, 2701–2704). Being lifted or raised means advancing to a more interior level, since loftiness or height is mentioned in connection with inner levels (§§2148, 4210). Because it means advancing to an inner level, it means advancing toward heaven, heaven being within. That is what lifting someone's head symbolizes.

To lift the head *off* someone meant receiving a death sentence because spirits above the ones undergoing devastation in the "pit" were then taken up to heaven, while the ones in the pit were sent lower. Because this judicial phrase symbolizes such things, it was used in the Word.

The symbolism of *lifting someone's head* as a decision can be seen from these considerations. And since it symbolizes a decision, on the highest level it symbolizes a provision, because what the Divine decides, the Divine provides for.

5125   *And return you to your position* means that sensations subject to the intellectual side would be reduced to order, so as to come last, as the following shows: The cupbearer (the person being spoken of here) represents the senses that are under the intellectual side's control, as discussed in §§5077, 5082, and therefore represents the impressions we have gathered from those senses on the outer earthly plane. It is not our senses themselves that are reduced to order but what has entered through our senses into our delusional thinking. And *returning one to one's position* means reducing something to order. Sense impressions—what has entered from the world through the outer senses—come last, and they come last when they aid or serve something deeper, so this idea too is being symbolized.

What is more, sense impressions come last in regenerate people but first in the unregenerate (see §§5077, 5081, 5084, 5089, 5094).

[2] You can easily tell whether your senses come first or last, if you pay attention. If you affirm everything your senses urge or crave, and dismiss everything your intellect dictates, your senses come first. You are motivated by your appetites and are totally sense-oriented. People like this are not far from the fate of irrational animals, whose motivations are exactly the same. In fact, the fate of such people is even worse than that of animals if they misuse their intellectual ability, or their rational mind, to justify the evil and falsity that their senses urge and long for. However, if you do not affirm these things but see with your inner eye that they are detours into falsity and goads to evil; if you work to chasten them and reduce them to obedience—in other words, to bring them under the control of your inner self's intellectual and volitional sides—then you are reducing your senses to order by putting them in last place.

When our senses come last, happiness and bliss from our inner self permeate our sensory pleasures and make them a thousand times better than they were before. Sense-oriented people do not understand or believe this, do not sense any other kind of pleasure, and do not think a higher kind exists. As a consequence, they regard the inner happiness and bliss within sensory pleasures as worthless. When we are ignorant of something, we do not believe it exists.

And you will put Pharaoh's cup into his hand means where they could serve the inner earthly plane, as the following shows: *Putting a cup* to drink [in someone's hand] means adopting, as noted above at §5120. Obviously, it means serving as well. And *Pharaoh* represents the inner earthly plane, as noted at §§5080, 5095, 5118.

There is an inner and an outer earthly plane. The outer earthly plane comprises what enters the earthly mind (specifically, its memory and imagination) from the world directly through the senses. See §5118.

5126

[2] I need to say a few words defining the outer and inner earthly levels (which belong to the outer self) and therefore the rational level (which belongs to the inner self). From infancy to adolescence we are purely sensory beings. We take in only earthly, bodily, and worldly information through our physical senses, and this information forms the basis of our thoughts and ideas. The connection with our inner self is not yet open, beyond the minimum needed for grasping and retaining information. The innocence we have at that stage is all outward, not inward, because true innocence resides in wisdom. The Lord uses this superficial innocence to bring into order what enters through our senses. Without the inflow of innocence from the Lord at that first stage of life, a foundation would never emerge on which to build an intellect, or rational mind—the true mark of a human.

[3] From adolescence to early adulthood a line of communication with our inner earthly plane is opened up by lessons in decency, civility, and integrity learned both from our parents and teachers and from our own studies.

Throughout early adulthood a line of contact between our earthly and rational planes is opened up by learning what is true and good in public and private life and most of all in spiritual life, from hearing and reading the Word. So far as we then steep ourselves in goodness through truth— that is, so far as we act on the truth we learn—our rational level opens up. So far as we do not steep ourselves in goodness through truth—so far as we fail to act on the truth—our rational level does not open up. Our thoughts stay on the earthly level, in our memory, and therefore on the threshold outside the house, so to speak. [4] At that stage and the next, so far as we undermine, deny, and violate goodness and truth, believing what is false and doing what is evil instead, our rational level shuts down, as does our inner earthly level. In the Lord's divine providence, we keep enough contact with the higher levels that we can still grasp what is good and true and understand it a little, but we cannot adopt it as our own, unless we repent belatedly and then spend a long time wrestling with falsity and evil.

The opposite happens in people who let themselves be reborn, though. Their rational plane gradually opens up, step by step; their inner earthly plane comes under its control; and their outer earthly plane comes under the control of their inner earthly plane. The main period during which this happens is in early and full adulthood, then progressively to the end of their life, and afterward in heaven to eternity.

This shows what the inner [earthly] plane is in us and what the outer [earthly] plane is.

According to your former custom means in keeping with the laws of order. This can be seen from the symbolism of *your former custom* as the laws of order. It is a law of order that outer traits be subordinate to inner traits—that is, that lower traits be subordinate to higher ones—and serve them as domestic help, so to speak. Outer, lower traits are nothing but servants, while inner, higher traits are comparative masters. The reason *according to your former custom* symbolizes this is that the cupbearer had previously acted as a servant to his master Pharaoh, in keeping with the rules of subordination. The senses represented by the cupbearer, then, had previously acted as a servant to the inner earthly level represented by Pharaoh, in keeping with the laws of order.

[2] Sense-oriented people know absolutely nothing of the law that lower, outer attributes ought to serve higher, inner ones. People wholly taken up with their senses do not know what inner depths are, so they also do not know what is relatively shallow. They know that they think and speak, will and act, so they imagine that thinking and willing are internal and that speaking and acting are external. They do not realize, though, that to think only from one's senses and act on one's appetites belongs to the outer self. Their thinking and willing is restricted to the outer earthly plane, then, especially when they think what is false and will what is evil. Because their line of communication with deeper levels is closed off, they do not know what inner thought and inner will are. If you tell them that inner thinking is thinking based on truth, and that inner willing is action based on goodness, they do not comprehend it at all. Still less do they grasp that the inner self is distinct from the outer self, and so distinct that the inner self can "look down" from a vantage point and see what is happening in the outer self. In fact, the inner self has the ability and power to chastise the outer self and to refuse to will and think what the outer self hallucinates and craves.

[3] As long as the outer self of sense-oriented people is in command and control, they cannot see any of this. Outside of that state, however (as, for instance, when they are suffering with bad luck or illness), they can see and understand it, because their outer self then loses control. The Lord always preserves in us the ability or power to understand. Of course, the faculty is quite dim in people who subscribe to falsity and evil and always grows clearer as falsity and evil are put to sleep. The Lord's divinity is constantly flowing into us, enlightening us, but where there is

5127

falsity and evil—in other words, the opposite of truth and goodness—the divine light is deflected, smothered, or corrupted. Only enough is let in through the cracks (so to speak) to enable us to think and speak from our senses, even on spiritual topics, using stock phrases engraved on our earthly or bodily memory.

5128 *When you were his cupbearer* means as sensations of that kind are used to doing. This is established by the symbolism of a *cupbearer* as sensations, or the sensations under the control of the intellectual side (discussed at §§5077, 5082). The fact that they are used to doing so is symbolized by the phrase *when you were.*

The idea that the senses have to be subject and subordinate to rational thinking was discussed just above [§§5125–5127]. Since that subjection and subordination is the current theme of the inner meaning, more needs to be said in explanation.

[2] A person in whom the senses are subordinate could be called a rational person, but one in whom they are not subordinate could be called a sense-oriented person. It is hard for others to tell whether a person is rational or sense-oriented, but we can tell about ourselves if we examine our inner dimension, or our willing and thinking.

Others cannot tell from our words or deeds whether we are sense-oriented or rational, because the living energy of thought in our words and the living energy of will in our deeds is not apparent to any of the physical senses. All that other people hear are sounds, and all they see are gestures, accompanied by an emotion that cannot be definitively identified as pretended or genuine. In the other world, though, people with goodness can tell clearly what is present in our words and deeds. So they can tell what the living energy in the words and deeds is like and where it comes from.

Still, in the world there are several signs indicating to some extent whether the senses are under the control of the rational mind or the other way around—that is, whether a person is rational or merely sense-oriented. These are the signs:

If you notice that someone's premises are false, and if the person does not allow her- or himself to be enlightened, but completely rejects the truth, and obstinately and irrationally defends falsity, it is a sign that the person is sense-oriented rather than rational. The rational mind in that person is too tightly shut to let heaven's light in.

[3] People who have persuaded themselves that falsity is true are even more dominated by their senses, because persuasive lies totally seal off the

rational mind. Starting with false premises is one thing; adopting false persuasions is another. People who convince themselves of falsity have some light on their earthly level, but only winterlike light. In the other life this light looks snowy-white among them, but as soon as heavenly light falls on their wintry light, it fades. Depending on the severity and nature of the conviction, it turns black as night. The same thing is evident in them when they live in the world, where they cannot see any truth at all. In fact, in the midnight darkness of their falsity, truth seems worthless to them, and they laugh at it. To the uneducated they sometimes seem rational, because by means of their snow-white winter light, through rational argument, they can defend falsity so skillfully that it looks true. This kind of persuasion ensnares the educated more than any others, since they prove falsity to themselves by syllogisms, by philosophy, and lastly by a wealth of facts. The ancients referred to people like them as snakes in the tree of knowledge (§§195, 196, 197). Today they can be described as profoundly sense-oriented and lacking in rationality.

[4] The most important sign indicating whether people are rational or merely sense-oriented is their life. By their life I do not mean their life as it *appears* in their words and deeds but as it actually *exists* there. The life in one's speech comes from thought, the life in one's activity comes from the will, and both come from the intent or aim. Consequently the nature of the intent or aim in one's speech and actions determines the nature of one's life. Words without any inner life are just sounds, and deeds without any inner life are just motions. The life that reflects one's intent is the kind meant in the assertion that our life awaits us after death. If we are rational, we speak from good thinking and act from goodwill. That is, we speak from faith and act from neighborly love. If we are not rational, we can pretend to act and speak like rational people, but we have no life from rationality inside us. A life of evil closes off every path or line of communication with the rational mind and restricts us to what is earthly and sensory.

[5] There are two things that not only block this path of communication but also rob us of the capacity of ever becoming rational, and they are deceit and profanation. Deceit is like a subtle poison that infects our inner depths, and profanation is what mingles falsity with truth, and evil with goodness. Both vices completely destroy rationality. In each of us the Lord stores up good desires and true ideas from the time we are babies, and the Word refers to these good desires and true ideas as a remnant, [or survivors]. (To learn about it, see §§468, 530, 560, 561, 661, 1050, 1738,

1906, 2284.) Deceit infects them, and profanation mingles them [with evil and falsity]. (For a definition of profanation, see §§593, 1008, 1010, 1059, 1327, 1328, 2051, 2426, 3398, 3402, 3479, 3898, 4289, 4601.)

These signs give some indication of who is rational and who is sense-oriented.

[6] When our senses are subordinate to our rational mind, the sense impressions that form our early imagination are lit by light coming through heaven from the Lord. They are also arranged in order so that they can take in the light and correspond. In this condition, sense impressions no longer prevent us from acknowledging and seeing the truth. We immediately remove anything that clashes and embrace anything that harmonizes. Harmonious sense impressions then take the center, and those that clash move to the edge. The ones in the center are raised up toward heaven, and the ones at the edges hang down, so to speak. The ones in the center receive light through the rational plane, which makes them visible in the other world. They then look like twinkling stars that scatter light right out to the edges all around, the light dimming with the distance. Such is the pattern in which earthly and sensory information is arranged when the rational plane is in charge and sense impressions are under its control. This happens when we are being reborn, and because of it, we come into the fullest possible state of seeing and acknowledging truth.

When the rational plane is subordinate to the senses, on the other hand, the opposite happens. Falsity is then in the middle, or center, and truth is at the edges. What is in the center stands in a kind of glimmer there, but in the glimmer of swamp light, or the kind of light that rises from a coal fire; this glimmer has light flowing into it on all sides from hell. It is what is called darkness, because as soon as any light from heaven flows into it, it turns to darkness.

5129 Genesis 40:14, 15. *"But remember me within yourself when it is well with you, and may you please show mercy on me and remind Pharaoh of me and bring me out of this house. Because I was treacherously stolen from the land of the Hebrews, and even here I have not done anything that they should put me in the pit."*

But remember me within yourself symbolizes an acceptance of faith. *When it is well with you* means when there is correspondence. *And may you please show mercy on me* symbolizes an acceptance of love for one's neighbor. *And remind Pharaoh of me* symbolizes communication with the inner earthly level. *And bring me out of this house* symbolizes deliverance from evil. *Because I was treacherously stolen* means that heavenly qualities were banished, owing to evil. *From the land of the Hebrews* means by the church. *And even here I have not done anything* symbolizes innocence. *That they should put me in the pit* symbolizes being rejected as false.

But remember me within yourself symbolizes an acceptance of faith, as the following shows: Joseph, who says this about himself, represents the Lord and the heavenly quality he had on his earthly plane (noted in §§5086, 5087, 5106). And *remember me within yourself* symbolizes an acceptance of faith. When we remember and recall the Lord, it is at the call of faith, so "remember me within yourself" urges the acceptance of faith.

Regarding faith, people who accept it and hold on to it have the Lord constantly in mind. This is so even when they are thinking or talking about something else or are performing their public, private, or domestic duties. Even then they have the Lord in mind, although they may be unaware of it. In people of faith, remembrance of the Lord prevails in everything, and what prevails in everything goes unnoticed except when our attention is drawn to it.

[2] A human being furnishes many examples. When we love something, whatever it is, we are constantly thinking about it and everything connected with it, even when thinking, saying, or doing something else. This is plain to see in the other world from the spiritual auras around everyone. Auras alone identify us there, revealing what we believe and what we love, even if we think and say something very different (§§1048, 1053, 1316, 1504–1520, 2489, 4464). What prevails everywhere in us produces the aura and puts our life on display for others.

This shows what it means to say that we always ought to be thinking about the Lord, salvation, and life after death. Everyone with a faith that results from neighborly love does this. That is why such people do not think bad thoughts about their neighbors but exhibit justice and fairness toward them in every single thought, word, and deed. After all, what prevails universally influences all the particular elements, guiding and governing them. The Lord anchors the minds of such people in matters of charity and the resulting faith, and in this way arranges the details so that they conform. An aura of faith rising out of charity is the aura that reigns supreme in heaven, because the Lord flows in with love and through love with charity. As a consequence, he flows in with the truth composing faith. That is why heaven's inhabitants are said to be in the Lord.

[3] The text immediately following deals with the rebirth of the senses subordinate to the intellectual side, as represented by the cupbearer, and

since it deals with the rebirth of these senses, it deals with the acceptance of faith. The sensory level of the mind, like the rational level, is reborn through faith, but through a faith into which charity is flowing. If charity does not flow into faith and give it life, faith can never prevail universally. What we love is what dominates, not what we merely know and hold in our memory.

5131   *When it is well with you* means when there is correspondence. This can be seen from the symbolism of *being well with you* as correspondence, when the theme is the rebirth or regeneration of the outer earthly level, or the sensory level, since things are not well with that level until it corresponds.

For a definition of correspondence, see the ends of the chapters. Sensory elements correspond with earthly ones, earthly elements correspond with spiritual ones, spiritual ones correspond with heavenly ones, and heavenly ones correspond with the Lord's divinity. So there is a chain of correspondence from the divine plane down to the outermost earthly plane.

[2] People who have not previously known anything about correspondence have a hard time forming an idea of its nature, so a brief explanation is in order. Philosophy teaches that a goal is prerequisite to any means, and means are prerequisite to an effect. If goal, means, and effect are to follow one another and form a unit, the effect has to correspond to the means, and the means to the goal. Still, a goal cannot be mistaken for a means, nor a means for an effect. In order for the goal to produce a means, it has to reach into the realm where the means exist, procure the necessary tools, and use them to create the means. And for the means to produce an effect, they also have to reach into the realm where the effect exists, procure the necessary tools, and use them to create the effect. These tools are what correspond, and because they correspond, the goal can exist in the means and bring them about, and the means can exist in the effect and bring it about. Therefore, the goal through the means can bring about the effect.

It is different when there is no correspondence. Then the goal has no means to lodge in, let alone an effect. Instead, the goal alters and changes in the means and eventually in the effect, according to the form created by the tools being used.

[3] Everything in the human being and in fact everything in the physical world follows in a series the way goal, means, and effect do. When it

all corresponds, it forms a single whole, because the goal is then the all-in-all of the means, and through the means it is the all-in-all of the effect.

For example, when heavenly love is the goal, then the will is the means, and action is the effect. If they correspond, heavenly love flows into the will, and the will flows into the action. In this way they form a unit, so that through correspondence, action essentially *is* love. Or for another example, when faith born of charity is the goal, then thought is the means, and speech is the effect. If they correspond, faith born of charity flows into the thought, which flows into the speech. In this way they form a unit, so that through correspondence, speech essentially *is* the goal. However, in order for the goal (love or faith) to produce a means (the will and thought), it has to procure the necessary tools in the rational mind, and these have to correspond. Without tools that correspond, there can be no reception of the goal (the love or faith), even if it flows in from the Lord through heaven.

Clearly, then, our inner and outer dimensions—our rational, earthly, and sensory dimensions—need to be reduced to correspondence so that we can accept the divine inflow and consequently so that we can be reborn. Until then, it is not well with us.

This now is the reason that *when it is well with you* symbolizes correspondence.

And may you please show mercy on me symbolizes an acceptance of love for one's neighbor. This can be seen from the symbolism of *mercy* as love (discussed at §§3063, 3073, 3120, 5042). Here it symbolizes neighborly love, or charity, because the acceptance of faith was spoken of above (§5130). Faith and charity have to form a unit on the level of the senses when this level is being reborn.

The reason mercy symbolizes charity is that everyone with charity has mercy. In other words, people who love their neighbors show mercy on them. As a result, the exercise of charity is portrayed as acts of mercy in the Word. In Matthew, for instance:

> I was hungry and you gave me something to eat, I was thirsty and you gave me a drink, I was a foreigner and you gathered me in, naked and you clothed me, I was sick and you visited me, I was in jail and you came to me. (Matthew 25:35, 36)

Other passages portray it as an obligation to do good to the poor, afflicted, widowed, and orphaned.

[2] In its essence, charity is wishing our neighbor well, feeling drawn to what is good, and acknowledging goodness as our neighbor. Acknowledging that goodness is our neighbor means acknowledging that people committed to goodness are our neighbor, with differences, depending on the strength of their commitment. Since charity loves goodness, then, it loves mercy toward people in misery. Charitable goodness contains this quality because it descends from the Lord's love for the entire human race, which consists in mercy because the entire human race is established in misery.

Mercy sometimes seems to exist in evil people who lack neighborly love, but it is actually pain over their own sufferings. They exercise it toward friends who are closely aligned with them and whose sufferings cause them to suffer themselves. This mercy is not the mercy of neighborly love but the mercy of self-centered friendship. Regarded in itself, it is merciless, because it brings us to despise or hate anyone besides ourselves and therefore anyone besides friends who make common cause with us.

5133 *And remind Pharaoh of me* symbolizes communication with the inner earthly level. This can be seen from the symbolism of *reminding* someone as communicating, and from the representation of *Pharaoh* as the inner earthly level (mentioned in §§5080, 5095).

Communication with the inner earthly level means connection through correspondence. The inner earthly level is the level that receives ideas of truth and goodness from the rational plane and stores them up for use. Accordingly, it is the level that communicates directly with the rational plane. The outer earthly level is the one that receives images and therefore ideas of things from the world through the senses. [2] Unless these ideas have light shed on them by the contents of the inner earthly level, they create illusions, which are called illusions of the senses. When we are prey to such illusions, we believe only what agrees with them, only what they confirm, and this happens when there is no correspondence. Correspondence in turn does not exist unless we are steeped in charity. Charity is a uniting medium, because the goodness in a person contains life from the Lord. This life arranges truth in an orderly pattern, allowing the form of charity to emerge—in other words, allowing charity to exist in an image. This form is visible to the eye in the other world and is the actual form of an angel. All angels are consequently forms of charity. The beauty of this form comes from the truth composing faith, and the life within the beauty comes from the goodness belonging to charity.

And bring me out of this house symbolizes deliverance from evil. This **5134** can be seen from the symbolism of *bringing out* as delivering and from that of a *house* as goodness (discussed in §§710, 1708, 2048, 2233, 3128, 3652, 3720, 4982) and therefore in a negative sense as evil. From this it is clear that *bring me out of this house* symbolizes deliverance from evil. This interpretation also follows in order from the preceding explanations.

When faith is accepted (§5130) on the outer earthly level (the current focus of discussion), and correspondence develops (5131), and love for one's neighbor is accepted (5132), and contact with the inner earthly level results (5133), that inner level is then delivered from evil. Evil banished the heavenly quality represented by Joseph (5086, 5087, 5106), and this banishment is symbolized by his being treacherously stolen, as discussed just below.

The earthly level is also delivered from evil when it is regenerated through neighborly love and faith, because the evil is then detached and removed. It is cast from the center, where it used to be, out to the edges, where the light of truth radiating from goodness does not reach. In human beings, evil is detached in this way but still retained, because it cannot be entirely erased. In the Lord, though, who made the earthly level in himself divine, evil and falsity were totally cast out and erased. Divinity cannot have anything in common with evil and falsity or rest on them, as humans do, because the Divine is the vital core itself of goodness and truth, which stands estranged at an infinite distance from evil and falsity.

Because I was treacherously stolen means that heavenly qualities were **5135** banished, owing to evil. This can be seen from the representation of Joseph, who says this about himself, as heavenliness on the earthly plane (noted at §§5086, 5087, 5106) and consequently as heavenly qualities there, and from the symbolism of being *stolen* as being banished, owing to evil. Stealing means banishing. Theft means evil that banishes, and it also means evil that confiscates for itself what is there. Theft symbolizes banishment in relation to the seat evil occupies, from which it ejects goodness and truth and which it fills with evil and falsity. Theft symbolizes the confiscation of what belongs to others when evil ascribes to itself the goodness and truth found in that seat and makes them its own, and when it applies them to evil and falsity.

To show what theft means in a spiritual sense, I need to explain the situation with evil and falsity when they invade and occupy a seat and also when they usurp the goodness and truth that are there.

[2] From childhood to adolescence, and sometimes into the beginning of adulthood, we absorb goodness and truth through instruction by our parents and teachers. At that stage we seize on what they teach us and believe it in simplicity. A state of innocence promotes these things and inserts them into our memory but places them on the first threshold. You see, the innocence of childhood and youth is not a deep innocence that touches the rational mind but a superficial innocence that touches only the outer earthly mind (§§2306, 3183, 3494, 4563, 4797). When we grow up, though, and start to think for ourselves rather than relying on our parents and teachers as before, we go back and ruminate on our earlier lessons and beliefs. Then we confirm them, have doubts about them, or deny them. If we confirm them, it is a sign that we are engaged in goodness. If we deny them, it is a sign that we are engaged in evil. If we have doubts about them, it is a sign that at the next stage of life we will turn either affirmative or negative.

[3] The ideas we seize on or believe at the first stage, as children, and later confirm, doubt, or deny are mainly these: God exists, and he is one. He created everything. He rewards people who do good and punishes those who do evil. There is life after death, and the evil go to hell, while the good go to heaven, so heaven and hell exist. Life after death is eternal. We ought to pray every day, with humility. We should keep the Sabbath holy, honor our parents, and refrain from adultery, murder, and theft. And so on. These are concepts we learn and absorb in childhood. When we start to think for ourselves and lead ourselves, we might confirm them for ourselves, add other principles that go even deeper, and live according to them. If so, it is well with us. On the other hand, we might start to break such rules and eventually deny them. If so, then no matter how closely we adhere to them in our external life because of secular law and social norms, we are ruled by evil. [4] This evil is what theft symbolizes because it resembles a thief in occupying the seat where goodness used to sit, and because in many people it steals the goodness and truth previously there and uses them to justify evil and falsity.

As much as possible, the Lord then removes childhood's goodness and truth from that seat and draws them deep inside, storing them up on the inner earthly level for later use. This goodness and truth stored up on the inner earthly level is symbolized in the Word by the remnant (as discussed in §§468, 530, 560, 561, 660, 661, 1050, 1738, 1906, 2284). If evil steals the goodness and truth there, though, and uses it to justify evil and falsity, especially if it does so in a deceitful way, it consumes that remnant, because it is mingling evil with goodness, and falsity with truth. It mixes them up so thoroughly that they cannot be separated, and then it is all over with us.

[5] This symbolism of theft can be seen simply by applying the idea of theft to matters of spiritual life. The only riches in spiritual life are concepts of what is good and true, and the only property and inheritance is a happy life stemming from goodness and from truth based on goodness. To steal these, as I said above, is theft in a spiritual sense. As a result, theft in the Word has no other symbolism on an inner level. In Zechariah, for instance:

> I raised my eyes and looked, when there! A scroll flying! And he said to me, "This is the curse issuing over the face of the whole earth, for *everyone stealing* from now on is as innocent as [the curse], and everyone swearing falsely is as innocent as it. I hurled it out so that it would *enter the house of the thief* and the house of the one swearing falsely in my name for a lie. And let it remain all night in that one's house and consume [the house], both its wood and its stones." (Zechariah 5:1, 2, 3, 4)

Evil that makes off with any remnant of goodness is symbolized by one stealing and by the house of the thief, and falsity that makes off with any remnant of truth is symbolized by one swearing falsely and by the house of the one swearing falsely. The face of the whole earth stands for the entire church. That is why it says the curse will consume the house, both its wood and its stones. The house means the earthly mind and the person in whom it exists (§§3128, 3538, 4973, 5023). Wood means the goodness there (§§2784, 2812, 3720, 4943), and stones mean the truth (§§643, 1298, 3720).

[6] Profanation and the resultant commandeering of goodness and truth is symbolized on a spiritual level by what Achan did. He took items that had been devoted to destruction—a coat from Shinar, two hundred shekels of silver, and a tongue of gold—and hid them underground in the middle of his tent. On that account he was stoned and all the objects were burned. Here is what is said about it in Joshua:

> Jehovah to Joshua: "Israel sinned; they went against my compact that I commanded them and took from what was devoted to destruction. *They stole,* lied, and put it among their vessels." (Joshua 7:11, 21, 25)

The objects devoted to destruction symbolized falsity and evil, which were never to be mingled with anything holy. In a spiritual sense, the coat from Shinar, shekels of silver, and tongue of gold are varieties of falsity. Hiding them underground in the middle of a tent symbolized mingling them with what was holy—a tent meaning holiness (see §§414, 1102, 1566, 2145, 2152, 3312, 4128, 4391, 4599). That is what was symbolized by the Israelites' stealing, lying, and putting it among their vessels—vessels meaning holy truth (§§3068, 3079, 3316, 3318). [7] In Jeremiah:

> Esau's end I will bring on him at the time I visit him. If grape harvesters come to you, won't they leave bunches to glean? *If thieves [come] in the night,* won't they ruin the ample supply? I myself will strip Esau naked, I will expose his secret places, so that he cannot hide. His seed has been laid waste, and his kin, and his neighbors, and he is no more. (Jeremiah 49:8, 9, 10)

Esau stands for the evil of self-love, with falsity connected to it (§3322). The way this evil consumes any remnant of goodness or truth is symbolized by "thieves in the night ruin the ample supply" and "his seed has been laid waste, and his kin, and his neighbors, and he is no more." Seed stands for the truth espoused by a faith that comes of neighborly love (§§1025, 1447, 1610, 1940, 2848, 3038, 3310, 3373). Kin, [or brothers,] stands for the goodness embraced by neighborly love (§§367, 2360, 2508, 2524, 3160, 3303, 3459, 3815, 4121, 4191). Neighbors stand for connected and related truth and goodness belonging to [neighborly love]. [8] Obadiah says something similar about Esau:

> If *thieves come to you,* if *overthrowers [come] by night,* how will you be cut off? *Won't they steal enough for themselves?* If grape harvesters come to you, won't they leave bunches? (Obadiah verse 5)

The grape harvesters stand for falsity that does not come of evil. This falsity does not consume the goodness and truth that the Lord stores up on our inner earthly plane, or our remnant. What destroys it is falsity that does come of evil. This falsity steals truth and goodness and also misuses them to confirm evil and falsity. [9] In Joel:

> A great, strong people: like heroes they will run, like men of war they will climb the wall, and they will each continue on their ways. In the city they will dash about; on the wall they will run; onto houses they will climb; *through windows they will enter like a thief.* (Joel 2:7, 9)

The people great and strong stands for falsity that is fighting against truth (§§1259, 1260). Because they fight hard to destroy truth, they are called heroes and are said to be like men of war. The city in which they are said to dash about stands for doctrinal truth (402, 2268, 2449, 2712, 2943, 3216). The houses they will climb onto stand for the goodness they destroy (710, 1708, 2048, 2233, 3128, 3652, 3720, 4982). The windows through which they will enter stand for intellectual matters and consequently for rationalizations (655, 658, 3391). Therefore they are compared to a thief, because they occupy what was formerly the seat of truth and goodness. [10] In David:

> Since you hate correction and cast my words behind you, *if you see thieves, you run with them,* and with adulterers is your portion. Your mouth you open for evil, and with your tongue you concoct deceit. (Psalms 50:17, 18, 19)

This is about the ungodly. Running with thieves stands for banishing truth from oneself through falsity. [11] In Revelation:

> They did not repent of their murders or of their spells or of their whoredoms *or of their thefts.* (Revelation 9:21)

Murders stand for evil that destroys goodness; spells for consequent falsity that destroys truth; whoredoms for truth that is falsified; and thefts for goodness that is therefore banished. [12] In John:

> Truly, truly, I say to you: whoever is not entering through the door into the sheepfold but climbs in from another place, that person is a *thief* and *robber.* But whoever enters through the door is the shepherd of the sheep. I myself am the doorway; if any come in through me, they will be saved, and go in and out, and find pasture. *The thief does not come except to steal* and slaughter and destroy. (John 10:1, 2, 8, 9, 10)

Here too the thief stands for the evil of taking credit, because those who take from the Lord what is his and claim it for themselves are called thieves. Because this evil closes the route by which goodness and truth would otherwise flow in from the Lord, it is said to slaughter and destroy. *You must not steal* in the Ten Commandments (Deuteronomy 5:19) has the same symbolism (§4174).

This discussion shows what is symbolized in a spiritual sense by the laws on theft laid down in the Jewish religion, as in Exodus 21:16;

22:1, 2, 3, 4; Deuteronomy 24:7. Since all laws in that religion traced their origin to the spiritual world, they correspond to the laws of order in heaven.

5136   *From the land of the Hebrews* means by the church—that is, heavenly qualities were banished by the church, owing to evil. This can be seen from the symbolism of the *land of the Hebrews* as the church. The land of the Hebrews here is the land of Canaan, since that is where Joseph was taken from.

The reason the land of Canaan in the Word means the church is that the church had been there since very ancient times. First there was the earliest church, which came before the Flood, then the ancient church, which came after the Flood, then the second ancient church, called the Hebrew church, and finally the Jewish religion. In order for the Jewish religion to be established there, Abram was commanded to go there from Syria, and there he received the promise that his descendants would be given that land as an inheritance. That is why land in the Word symbolizes the church. For the same reason, the whole earth (a phrase that occurs in many places) symbolizes the whole church, and a new heaven and new earth symbolize a new inner and outer church.

[2] Here is why the church maintained its presence there from earliest times: The people of the earliest church, who were heavenly, were the kind who saw a representation of the Lord's kingdom in each and every object in the world and on earth. To them, worldly and earthly objects were means of thinking about heavenly subjects. This was the source of all the representative and symbolic lore later possessed by the ancient church, because the people meant by Enoch gathered it together and preserved it for the use of later generations (§§519, 521, 2896). A consequence was that in the land of Canaan, where the earliest people lived, individual places, including individual mountains and rivers, came to represent something. So did all the surrounding nations. The Word could be composed only with the use of representation and symbolism—involving places, among other things—so it was for this purpose that the church was preserved in a series of forms in the land of Canaan. After the Lord's Coming, though, it was transferred elsewhere, because those representations were then done away with.

Plainly, then, the land of Canaan (here called the land of the Hebrews) symbolizes the church.

[3] However, see the evidence offered previously on these topics. The earliest church, which came before the Flood, existed in the land

of Canaan: 567, 3686, 4447, 4454. Part of the ancient church, which came after the Flood, was located there (3686, 4447), as was the second ancient church, called the Hebrew church (4516, 4517). That is why Abram was ordered to go there and why it was given to his descendants: 3686, 4447. For this reason the land of Canaan represented the Lord's kingdom: 1607, 3038, 3481, 3705, 4240, 4447. Consequently in the Word the land symbolizes the church: 566, 662, 1066, 1068, 1262, 1413, 1607, 1733, 1850, 2117, 2118 at the end, 3355, 4447, 4535.

And even here I have not done anything symbolizes innocence, as can be seen without explanation, since *not doing anything* bad is innocent.   **5137**

That they should put me in the pit symbolizes being rejected as false.   **5138**
This can be seen from the symbolism of a *pit* as falsity (discussed at §§4728, 4744, 5038).

The focus above was on evil—namely, that heavenly qualities were banished through evil (§§5134, 5135). The focus here is on falsity. Where the Word speaks of one, it also speaks of the other; where it speaks of evil, it also speaks of falsity. That is because where it speaks of goodness, it also speaks of truth, for the sake of a marriage in every detail of the Word. The heavenly marriage is a marriage of goodness and truth, but the hellish marriage is a marriage of evil and falsity. Where evil exists, falsity exists. Falsity attaches itself to evil as a wife attaches herself to her husband. And where goodness exists, truth exists, because truth unites with goodness as a wife unites with her husband. Our lives therefore reveal what our faith is like, because goodness is a matter of life, and truth is a matter of faith. The same in turn for evil and falsity.

On there being a marriage in every detail of the Word, see §§683, 793, 801, 2173, 2516, 2712, 4137 at the end.

Genesis 40:16, 17, 18, 19. And the chief of the bakers saw that he had given a good interpretation, and he said to Joseph, "I too was in my dream and look: three baskets with holes in them on my head! And in the top basket, some of every food of Pharaoh's, the work of a baker, and birds eating it from the basket on my head." And Joseph answered and said, "This is its interpretation: The three baskets are three days. In another three days Pharaoh will lift your head off you and hang you on wood, and birds will eat your flesh off you."   **5139**

And the chief of the bakers saw symbolizes an intuition of the senses under the control of the will side. *That he had given a good interpretation* means as to what would happen. *And he said to Joseph* symbolizes a perception by heavenliness on the earthly plane. *I too was in my dream* symbolizes a prediction. *And look: three baskets!* symbolizes successive forms of the will. *With holes in them on my head* means without a resting place anywhere in the middle. *And in the top basket* symbolizes the inmost level of the will. *Some of every food of Pharaoh's* means full of heavenly goodness for nourishing the earthly plane. *The work of a baker* means in supporting all the useful functions performed by the senses. *And birds eating it from the basket on my head* means that falsity rising out of evil would destroy it. *And Joseph answered and said* symbolizes revelation gleaned from a perception by heavenliness on the earthly plane. *This is its interpretation* means showing what [the senses subject to the will side] contained. *The three baskets* symbolizes successive forms of the will. *Are three days* means right to the last. *In another three days* means that at the last. *Pharaoh will lift your head off you* means there would be a decision based on foresight. *And hang you on wood* symbolizes rejection and damnation. *And birds will eat your flesh off you* means that falsity rising from evil will destroy what is gained through those senses.

5140   *And the chief of the bakers saw* symbolizes an intuition of the senses under the control of the will side. This is established by the symbolism of *seeing* as understanding and intuiting (discussed in §§2150, 2807, 3764, 4723) and by that of the *chief of the bakers* as the senses under the control of the will side, in general, and accordingly as the evidence of those senses (discussed in §§5078, 5082).

5141   *That he had given a good interpretation* means as to what would happen. This can be seen from the symbolism of *giving an interpretation* as the content, or what was inherent (discussed above at §§5093, 5105, 5107, 5121), and therefore as what would happen, too.

It is an intuition of the senses that things would go well, and the intuition of the senses is relatively obscure.

There are actually three kinds of intuition: that of the senses, or the outer earthly level; that of the inner earthly level; and that of the rational level. When a desire moves us to think deeply, and we take our mind off our senses and our person, we experience rational intuition. Baser concerns or the concerns of our outer self die down, and we are almost conscious in our spirit. When worldly stimuli cause us to think more shallowly, our intuitions come from our inner earthly plane. Our rational plane does flow into them but without providing any emotional vitality. But when we are awake to sensual pleasures and the gratifications of materialism and self-love, our intuitions come from our senses.

We then live life on the surface, or in our body. We accept only enough of deeper influences to keep us from erupting into violations of honor and decency.

The shallower an intuition is, the vaguer it is, because the outer dimension is relatively general. Countless inward elements appear as a single whole on the outward plane.

And he said to Joseph symbolizes a perception by heavenliness on the earthly plane. This can be seen from the symbolism of *saying* in the Word's narratives as a perception (mentioned many times before) and from the representation of *Joseph* as heavenliness on the earthly plane (discussed at §§5086, 5087, 5106).

5142

I too was in my dream symbolizes a prediction. This can be seen from the discussion in §§5092, 5104, 5112 of the symbolism of a *dream* as a prediction of an outcome.

5143

And look: three baskets symbolizes successive forms of the will. This is indicated by the symbolism of *three* as completion and continuing developments, right to the end (discussed in §§2788, 4495, 5114, 5122), and therefore as a succession, and by the symbolism of *baskets* as forms of the will. The reason baskets mean forms of the will is that they are containers for food, and food symbolizes heavenly and spiritual goodness, which is the province of the will. All goodness relates to the will, and all truth to the intellect. As soon as anything comes from the will, it is perceived as being good.

5144

The preceding verses dealt with the senses subject to the intellectual side, as represented by the cupbearer. The current verses deal with the senses subject to the will side, as represented by the baker. See §§5077, 5078, 5082. A succession or series of developments in the intellect was represented by the grapevine and its three shoots, flowers, clusters, and grapes, leading finally to truth in the intellect, represented by the cup (§5120). [2] Successive forms of the will, though, are represented by the three baskets on the baker's head, the top one of them containing some of every food of Pharaoh's, the work of a baker.

Successive forms of the will mean a succession from the deepest core of a person to the outermost surface, where the senses are. You see, there are different levels, or steps on the ladder, so to speak, from the deepest core to the outermost surface (§5114). Goodness from the Lord flows into the deepest level, which flows through the rational level into the inner earthly level and from there into the outer earthly level, or the level of the senses. It flows into each step of the ladder individually, and is modified by the way it is received at each step. More will be said later, however, to explain this inflow and its successive forms [§§5145, 5147, 5150].

[3] Baskets symbolize forms of the will, so far as forms of the will contain what is good. This is so elsewhere in the Word too, such as in Jeremiah:

> Jehovah showed me, when look! *two baskets of figs* set up before Jehovah's Temple. *In one basket,* very good figs, like the figs of [plants] bearing first fruits. *But in the other basket,* very bad figs, which could not be eaten for their badness. (Jeremiah 24:1, 2, 3)

This passage in the original language uses another word for basket, symbolizing the will on the earthly level. The figs in one basket mean earthly goodness, but those in the other basket mean earthly evil. [4] In Moses:

> When you come into the land that Jehovah your God will give you, you must take some of the first fruits of every fruit of the land that you bring from your ground and *put them in the basket* and go to the place that Jehovah chooses. Then the priest must take the *basket* from the person's hand and stand it before the altar of Jehovah your God. (Deuteronomy 26:1, 2, 3, 4)

Here too the basket is represented by another word, symbolizing a new will in the intellectual part of the mind. The first fruits of the fruit of the land mean the good that results. [5] In the same author:

> To consecrate Aaron and his sons, Moses was to take a loaf of unleavened bread, and cakes of unleavened bread mixed with oil, and wafers of unleavened bread anointed with oil; of wheat flour he was to make them. And he was to *put them in one basket* and bring them close *in the basket.* "Aaron and his sons shall *eat the flesh of the ram* and *the bread in the basket* at the doorway of the meeting tent." (Exodus 29:2, 3, 32)

This passage uses the same word for a basket as the current chapter does. It symbolizes a will holding in it the goodness symbolized by the bread, cakes, oil, wafers, flour, and wheat. "A will" means something that works as a container, because goodness from the Lord flows into our inward forms as its vessels. If these forms are disposed to accept what flows in, they are baskets containing that goodness. [6] In the same author, when a Nazirite was to be ordained:

> He or she shall take a *basket of unleavened loaves* of flour, cakes mixed with oil, and wafers of unleavened bread anointed with oil, with their minha and their libations. A ram he or she shall also offer as a sacrifice of peace offerings to Jehovah, besides the *basket of unleavened loaves*. And the priest shall take the cooked flank of a ram and one unleavened cake *from the basket* and one wafer of unleavened bread and put them onto the hand of the Nazirite and wave them in a wave offering before Jehovah. (Numbers 6:15, 17, 19, 20)

Again the basket stands for the will as a container. The cakes, wafers, oil, minha, and cooked flank of a ram are the heavenly kinds of goodness that were being represented—a Nazirite representing a heavenly person (§3301).

[7] At that time people used baskets for carrying similar items for worship, as Gideon did with the kid of the goats that he took out to the angel under the oak (Judges 6:19). People used baskets because baskets represented a kind of container, and what was in them represented the contents.

With holes in them on my head means without a resting place any-where in the middle, as the following shows: *With holes in them* means open from top to bottom and therefore not closed, so it means without a resting place anywhere in the middle. And a *head* symbolizes the inner depths, particularly in matters of the will. The starting points for all the substances and forms [of the body] are in the head, so all sensation moves toward the head and presents itself in the head, and all action descends and derives from the head. Of course our mental faculties of intellect and will are situated there. As a consequence, the head symbolizes what is inside. The baskets represented what is in the head.

[2] The focus is now on the senses under the control of the will side, and the baskets with holes on the baker's head mean that inner depths had no resting place anywhere in the middle. Therefore the impressions of those senses were rejected and damned, as discussed later [§5157]. How-ever, I need to say what is meant by the lack of a resting place anywhere in the middle.

Our inner dimensions are separated into levels and on each level reach a boundary that divides them from the next level down, going from inmost to outermost. The inner rational plane constitutes the first level, and that is the level of heavenly angels, or of the third and inmost heaven. The outer rational plane makes the second level, the level of spiritual angels, or of the second and middle heaven. The inner earthly plane makes the third level, the level of good spirits, or of the first and outermost heaven. The outer earthly plane, or the sensory plane, makes the fourth level, the level of people on earth.

[3] These levels are quite distinct in us. That is why, if we live a good life, we are a heaven in its smallest form as to our inner reaches. In other words, our inner reaches correspond to the three heavens. It is also why after death, if we have lived a life of charity and love, we can be brought all the way to the third heaven. To be this kind of person, though, all the levels in us have to be well defined and consequently set off from each other by their boundaries. When they are well defined or clearly distinguished by their boundaries, each of them is a platform where goodness flowing in from the Lord rests and is received. Without these levels as platforms, goodness is not received but flows on through as it would through a sieve or through a basket with a hole till it reaches the sensory level. There, because it has not been steered in any direction along the way, it turns into something sordid that appears good to the people immersed in it. That is, it turns into the pleasure that comes with self-love and materialism. So it turns into the pleasure of hatred, revenge, cruelty, adultery, and greed, or into mere self-indulgence and luxury. That is what happens if matters of the will in a person lack a resting place anywhere in the middle, or if they have holes.

[4] It is possible to tell whether there are resting places and therefore platforms in a person. Perceptions of what is good and true and forms of conscience are the indicators. In individuals who perceive what is good and true, such as heavenly angels, there are resting places on every level from first to last. Without resting places on every level, such perceptions cannot exist. (Concerning these perceptions, see §§125, 202, 495, 503, 511, 536, 597, 607, 784, 865, 895, 1121, 1383, 1384, 1387, 1919, 2144, 2145, 2171, 2515, 2831.) In individuals who have a conscience, such as spiritual angels, there are also resting places, but only on levels from the second or third to the last. The first level is closed to them. I say from the second or third level because there are two kinds of conscience, inner and outer. Inner conscience has to do with spiritual goodness and truth; outer conscience, with justice and fairness. Conscience itself is an inner platform where divine goodness flows in and comes to rest. Individuals without any conscience

have no inner platform to receive the inflow, though. With them, goodness flows right through to the outer earthly level, or the physical senses, where (to repeat) it turns into sordid pleasures. Sometimes these people seem to feel a pang of conscience, but it is not conscience. The pang comes from being deprived of something they enjoy, such as position, wealth, reputation, their life, sensual pleasures, or the friendship of people like themselves. That is because these kinds of enjoyment are the resting places in them. Such considerations show who is symbolized on a spiritual level by the baskets with holes in them.

[5] In the other world it is especially easy to recognize whether matters of the will had resting places in a person or not. People who had such resting places possess a zeal for spiritual goodness and truth, or else for justice and fairness. They did what is good for the sake either of goodness or of truth, and they did justice for the sake of justice or fairness, not for the sake of wealth, position, and so on.

Everyone whose inner depths of will had resting places is taken up to heaven, because a divine inflow can guide such a person. Everyone whose inner depths of will lacked resting places steers toward hell, because divine inflow passes on through and turns hellish, like the sun's warmth falling on rotting manure and creating a terrible stench.

Everyone who had a conscience, then, is saved, but people who lacked all conscience cannot be saved.

[6] Matters of the will are described as having a hole (or lacking resting places) when people have no desire for goodness and truth or for justice and fairness. Instead, they view goodness and truth, justice and fairness as relatively contemptible or worthless, or else value such qualities only as a means of winning riches or high position. Desire is what creates a stopping point and closure, so it is called a restraint. A desire for goodness and truth is an internal restraint, while a desire for evil and falsity is a superficial restraint (§3835). If a desire for evil and falsity did not restrain us, we would go crazy (§4217). Insanity is nothing but the loosening of such restraints and therefore a lack of boundaries in people with a desire for evil and falsity. However, since they have no inner restraints, they are inwardly crazy in their thoughts and feelings. Superficial restraints—their desire for wealth, status, and the resulting prestige, and therefore fear of the law and fear for their life—control their craziness and keep it from breaking out into the open.

This was represented in the Jewish religion by the rule that in the house of a dead person every open vessel on which there was no cover strap was unclean (Numbers 19:15). [7] The same thing is also symbolized by "open work," [or porous fabric,] in Isaiah:

> Those producing silk linen and those weaving *open work* will blush. And its foundations will be crushed. All of them are making pools of the soul their wage. (Isaiah 19:9, 10)

And by holes in Ezekiel:

> The Spirit brought the prophet in at the gate of the courtyard, where he looked, and here, a *hole in the wall!* And [the Spirit] said to him, "*Come, make a hole in the wall,*" so he made a hole in the wall, and here, a doorway! Then [the Spirit] said to him, "Go in and see the abominations that they make here." When he went in and saw, here, every likeness of creeping thing and animal (an abomination) and all the idols of the house of Israel were painted on the wall all around. (Ezekiel 8:7, 8, 9, 10)

5146   *And in the top basket* symbolizes the inmost level of the will. This can be seen from the symbolism of a *basket* as a form of the will (discussed above at §5144) and from the meaning of *top* as inmost (discussed at §§2148, 3084, 4599).

Top means inmost because to people on earth, living a spatial existence, anything inside looks higher, and anything outside looks lower. When the idea of space is discarded, as it is in heaven and in our deeper thinking, the idea of high and low is also discarded, because high and low come from the idea of space.

In fact, the inner heaven lacks the concept of inner and outer too, because even this concept has something spatial clinging to it. It is replaced with the idea of a fuller, more perfect state, and a less full or perfect state. Inner levels exist in a more perfect or complete condition than outer levels do, because inner levels are closer to the Divine and outer levels are more distant. That is why topmost means inmost.

[2] However, no one can grasp what the inner realm is in relation to the outer without knowing about levels (see the discussion at §§3691, 4154, 5114, 5145). People's concept of what is inward and therefore more perfect is simply that of something constantly becoming purer as it is more finely divided. However, one and the same level can range from pure to coarse, depending on how expansive or compressed a thing is, how well-defined it is, and whether compatible or incompatible elements are added to it. Since people think of our inner reaches this way, they cannot help picturing that the outer dimension is continuous with the inner,

so that the two are completely unified. Anyone who forms a true idea of levels, though, can grasp how distinct the inner and outer realms are from each other—so distinct that the inner realm can come into being and continue to exist without the outer realm but not the other way around. Such a person can also grasp how outer objects display correspondence with inner attributes and can represent them.

This is the reason that scholars cannot discuss the interaction of soul and body except in a hypothetical way. In fact, many of them believe that life inheres in the body, so that when our body dies, anything inside us must also die, since it is continuous with our body. The reality is, though, that only the outer level dies. The inner level survives and remains alive.

Some of every food of Pharaoh's means full of heavenly goodness for nourishing the earthly plane, as established by the symbolism of *food* as heavenly goodness (discussed below) and by the representation of *Pharaoh* as the inner earthly plane (discussed at §§5080, 5095). Pharaoh also represents the earthly plane as a whole, because the inner and outer earthly planes form a unit when they correspond. And since food is for nourishment, *some of every food of Pharaoh's* means full of heavenly goodness for nourishing the earthly plane.

5147

The text says this food was in the top basket, which means that the inmost level of the will was full of heavenly goodness. Goodness flows in from the Lord through our inmost core and from there down the levels, or the steps of the ladder, to our outer surface. The core is in a state of complete perfection, relatively speaking, so it can receive goodness directly from the Lord, whereas lower levels cannot. If lower levels received goodness directly from the Lord, they would either cloud or corrupt it, since they are relatively imperfect.

[2] Regarding the inflow of heavenly goodness from the Lord and its reception, you need to know that our will receives goodness, and our intellect receives truth. The intellect can never receive truth in such a way as to adopt it unless the will at the same time receives goodness, and the reverse. Each flows into the other and makes it receptive. Intellectual matters can be compared to constantly varying forms, and matters of the will can be compared to harmonies that result from the variation. Truth, then, can be compared to variations, and goodness to the pleasure they give. Truth and goodness actually and preeminently *are* variation and its pleasure, too, so it is clear that neither can exist without the other or be brought into existence except through the other.

[3] Food symbolizes heavenly goodness because angels have no other food than good that is done out of love and charity. Not only does it keep them alive, it refreshes them. To act on or exercise that goodness is the main thing that revitalizes them, because it is what they wish for. It is well known that actually obtaining our wishes refreshes us and brings us life.

These kinds of things serve to nourish our spirit when we take food to nourish our body, as demonstrated by the fact that food lacking in appeal does little good, whereas food eaten with pleasure is nourishing. Pleasure is what opens the channels or ducts that receive the nutrients and transfer them to the blood, while unpleasantness closes them. For angels, this pleasure is good that is done out of love and charity, which is spiritual food corresponding to earthly food, as the discussion shows.

Just as food means goodness, drink means truth.

[4] The Word mentions food in many places. People who do not know the inner meaning cannot help thinking regular food is meant there, but it is spiritual food that is meant. In Jeremiah, for instance:

> All the people are groaning, *looking for bread;* they have exchanged what is pleasant to them *for food to revive their soul.* (Lamentations 1:11)

In Isaiah:

> Everyone who is *thirsty,* come to the water, and whoever does not have silver, come, buy and *eat,* and come, without silver and without the price buy *wine* and *milk!* (Isaiah 55:1)

In Joel:

> The day of Jehovah is near, and it will come as devastation from the Thunderer. *Hasn't food been cut off before our eyes?* Gladness and joy [cut off] from the house of our God? The *seeds* have rotted under their clods, the *barns* have been devastated, the *granaries* have been destroyed, because the *grain* has shriveled. (Joel 1:15, 16, 17)

In David:

> *Our barns* are full, supplying us *from food to food;* our flocks number a thousand, and ten thousand in our streets; there is no outcry on our roads. Fortunate is the people for whom it is thus. (Psalms 144:13, 14, 15)

In the same author:

> They all wait for you *to give them their food in its season.* You give to them; they gather. You open your hand; *they receive abundant goodness.* (Psalms 104:27, 28)

[5] Where physical food is meant in the literal sense of these passages, heavenly and spiritual food is meant in the inner sense. This shows how the inner and outer levels of the Word—that which belongs to the Word's spirit and that which belongs to its literal text—correspond to each other. It also shows that when we take such things at their literal value, the angels with us take the same things at their spiritual value. So Scripture was composed to serve not only the human race but heaven as well. As a result, all the words in it symbolize heavenly qualities; all the people, places, and things in it represent those qualities; and this is true down to the smallest jot.

[6] The Lord also teaches openly that food in a spiritual sense means goodness. In John:

> Work, not for the *food* that perishes, but for the *food* that lasts to eternal life, which the Son of Humankind will give you. (John 6:27)

In the same author:

> My flesh is truly *food,* and my blood is truly drink. (John 6:55)

The flesh means divine goodness (§3813), and the blood means divine truth (§4735). And in the same author:

> Jesus said to the disciples, "*I have food to eat* that you do not know of." The disciples said to each other, "Has someone brought him something to eat?" Jesus said to them, "*My food is* to do the will of him who sent me, and I will finish his work." (John 4:32, 33, 34)

To do the will of the Father and finish his work is to act on or exercise divine goodness, which is food in its genuine sense, as noted above.

The work of a baker means in supporting all the useful functions performed by the senses. This can be seen from the meaning of *work* as supporting all the useful functions (explained below) and from the symbolism of a *baker* as the senses under the control of the will side (discussed in §§5078, 5082).

5148

The reason *work* means useful functions is that the term is being applied to the will, or to the senses that are subject to the will side of the mind. Whatever the will does that can be called work is, necessarily, useful activity. All works of neighborly love are just that, because they are deeds done with a will, which are useful services.

And birds eating from the basket on my head means that falsity rising out of evil would destroy it, as the following shows: A *bird* symbolizes matters

5149

of the intellect and thoughts, so it symbolizes the results of thought, which in a positive sense are truth of every kind, and in a negative sense, falsity. This symbolism is discussed in §§40, 745, 776, 778, 866, 988, 3219. *Eating* means destroying—and "destroy" is a meaning of the word *eat* in the original language. A *basket* symbolizes the will, as discussed in §§5144, 5146, and here it symbolizes evil coming out of the will, because the basket had a hole (§5145). It follows, then, that *birds eating from the basket on my head* means that falsity rising out of evil would destroy [that goodness].

[2] Falsity has two origins: doctrine and evil. Falsity originating in doctrine does not consume what is good, because we can subscribe to false doctrine but still be devoted to goodness. That is why people of every theology are saved, including non-Christians. Falsity originating in evil is what consumes goodness. Evil itself opposes goodness, although on its own it does not actually consume goodness. Instead, it uses falsity, because falsity attacks the truth that accompanies goodness. Truth is like a bulwark sheltering what is good, and falsity assails it. Once the bulwark has been assailed, goodness is massacred.

[3] Anyone who fails to realize that *birds* symbolize intellectual matters cannot help assuming that the birds mentioned in the Word either mean birds or are being used as a metaphor, as they are in everyday conversation. Birds mean that which pertains to the intellect, such as thoughts, ideas, rationalizations, and assumptions, and therefore truth or falsity, but no one can see this except from the inner meaning. In Luke, for example:

> The kingdom of God is like a mustard seed that a person, taking it, threw into the garden; and it grew and turned into a large tree, *so that the birds of the sky lived in its branches.* (Luke 13:19)

A bird of the sky stands for truth. [4] In Ezekiel:

> It will turn into a majestic cedar, and *every bird of every wing whatever will live under it;* in the shade of its branches they will live. (Ezekiel 17:23)

The bird of every wing whatever stands for truth of every kind. In the same author:

> Assyria, a cedar in Lebanon—in its branches *all the birds of the heavens* nested, and under its branches every animal of the field gave birth, and in its shade all the great nations lived. (Ezekiel 31:6)

The birds of the heavens again stand for truth. [5] In the same author:

> On its wreckage will live *every bird of the heavens,* and on its branches
> will be every wild animal of the field. (Ezekiel 31:13)

The bird of the heavens stands for falsity. In Daniel:

> Nebuchadnezzar was seeing in a dream: here, a tree in the middle of the
> earth! Under it the animal of the field found shade, and *in its branches
> lived the birds of the sky.* (Daniel 4:10, 12, 14, 21)

Here too the birds of the sky stand for falsity. [6] In Jeremiah:

> I looked, when there! Not a human! And *every bird of the sky* had flown
> away. (Jeremiah 4:25)

"Not a human" stands for no goodness (§4287). The birds of the sky that
flew away stand for truth that had been done away with. In the same
author:

> *From the bird in the heavens* to the beast, they have flown away, they
> have left. (Jeremiah 9:10)

The meaning is the same here. In Matthew:

> A sower went out to sow, and some fell on the hard path, and *the birds
> came and ate it.* (Matthew 13:3, 4)

This time the birds of the sky stand for skewed reasoning and for falsity.
    Likewise in many other places.
    And Joseph answered and said symbolizes revelation gleaned from a
perception by heavenliness on the earthly plane. This can be seen from
the symbolism of *answering and saying* as revelation gleaned from a perception (discussed above in §5121) and from the representation of *Joseph*
as heavenliness on the earthly plane (discussed in §§5086, 5087, 5106).
Joseph means heavenliness on the earthly plane here because the earthly
plane is what the chapter is talking about.
    A word about heavenliness and spirituality: Heavenliness itself and
spirituality itself, which flow into heaven from the Lord's divinity, reside
mainly on our inner rational plane, the forms that exist on that plane
being more perfect and suited to receiving the inflow. However, heavenliness and spirituality also flow from the Lord's divinity into our outer
rational plane, and into our earthly plane as well. What is more, they

5150

flow in both indirectly and directly—indirectly through the inner rational dimension, and directly from the Lord's divinity itself. What flows in directly is an organizing force, and what flows in indirectly is what is organized. Such is the case on the outer rational level, and such is the case on the earthly level.

From this you can see what heavenliness on the earthly plane is.

[2] What is heavenly comes from divine goodness, and what is spiritual comes from divine truth, both of them from the Lord. When they are present on the rational plane, they are called heavenliness and spirituality on the rational plane, and when they are present on the earthly plane, they are called heavenliness and spirituality on the earthly plane.

By the rational and earthly planes is meant the person him- or herself, so far as he or she is formed to receive what is heavenly and spiritual. By the rational plane is meant the person's inner part, and by the earthly plane, the outer part. People are called heavenly or spiritual based on divine inflow and how they receive it. They are called heavenly if they receive the Lord's divine goodness in their volitional side, and spiritual if they receive it in their intellectual side.

5151   *This is its interpretation* means showing what [the senses subject to the will side] contained. This is established by the symbolism of *interpretation* as the content, or what is inside (discussed above at §§5093, 5105, 5107).

5152   *The three baskets* symbolizes successive forms of the will. This is established by the discussion above in §5144 of the symbolism of *three baskets* as successive forms of the will.

5153   *Are three days* means right to the last. This is established by the symbolism of *three* as a single period and its continuous span from beginning to end, or right to the last (discussed in §§2788, 4495, 5122).

5154   *In another three days* means that at the last. This can be seen from the remarks just above in §5153 concerning the symbolism of *three*.

5155   *Pharaoh will lift your head off you* means [there would be] a decision based on foresight. This can be seen from the symbolism of *lifting someone's head* as what would be provided and therefore decided—in other words, as a decision based on providence (discussed above in §5124). Here it symbolizes a decision based on foresight because the text goes on to say that the baker would be hanged on wood, which symbolizes rejection and damnation.

The reason the clause symbolizes a decision based on foresight rather than providence is that providence pertains to what is good, but foresight, to what is evil. Everything good flows in from the Lord, so he provides it, but everything evil flows in from hell, or from human selfhood (which is in league with hell), so he foresees it. In regard to evil, providence's sole effort is to redirect it toward something less bad and so far as possible toward something good; but the evil itself is foreseen. In the current case, then, since the theme is the senses subordinate to the will side and their rejection on account of evil, foresight is what is being symbolized.

And hang you on wood symbolizes rejection and damnation. This can be seen from the symbolism of being *hanged on wood* as rejection and damnation. To be hanged on wood was a curse, and a curse means rejection by the Divine and therefore damnation. It can be seen in Moses that to be hanged on wood was a curse:

5156

> When there is in a man a crime judged worthy of death, and he is killed, *so that you hang him on wood,* his corpse shall not be left out overnight on the wood, but you shall unfailingly bury him on the same day, since *the hanged man is God's curse.* Because you shall not defile the land that Jehovah your God will give you as an inheritance. (Deuteronomy 21:22, 23)

The fact that the corpse was not to be left out overnight on wood symbolized permanent rejection. Day started over in the evening, so if hanging victims had not been disposed of before evening, it would have represented a failure to dispose of or reject evil, which would have meant that the land was not freed of the evil but defiled. That is why the passage adds, "You shall not defile the land that Jehovah your God will give you as an inheritance." (To see that victims were hanged until evening and not beyond, see Joshua 8:29; 10:26.)

The Jewish nation had two main punishments: stoning and hanging—stoning, on account of falsity, and hanging on wood, on account of evil. This was because a stone means truth (§§643, 1298, 3720), and in a negative sense, falsity, and wood means goodness (§§2784, 2812, 3720), and in a negative sense, evil. As a consequence, the prophetic part of the Word speaks several times of committing adultery with stone and wood, which symbolizes the corruption of truth, in other words, falsity, and the adulteration of goodness, in other words, evil.

And birds will eat your flesh off you means that falsity rising from evil will destroy what is gained through those senses, as the following shows: *Eating* means destroying, as discussed above in §5149. A *bird* symbolizes falsity, as also discussed above in §5149. *Flesh* symbolizes goodness, as discussed in

5157

§§3812, 3813 and therefore, in a negative sense, evil. Most words in Scripture also have a negative sense, which is known from their symbolism in a positive sense. And *off you* means from the impressions of the senses under the control of the will side, since that is what the baker represents (§§5078, 5082). Earlier comments make it plain that these sense impressions were evil and therefore needed to be rejected [§5084].

[2] The situation in all this—that the impressions of the senses under the control of the intellectual side, represented by the cupbearer, were kept, but the impressions of the senses under the control of the will side, represented by the baker, were rejected—is a secret that cannot be understood without enlightenment, but let the following remarks serve to clarify a little: "Sense impressions" means knowledge and pleasure instilled through the five outer, physical senses in our memory and among our cravings. They also constitute the outer earthly plane that causes us to be called sensory beings. The knowledge is under the control of our intellectual side, but the pleasure is under the control of our will side. In addition, knowledge relates to truth in the intellect, and pleasure relates to goodness in the will. The knowledge is what the cupbearer represents and was kept, but the pleasure is what the baker represents and was rejected. [3] The knowledge was kept because for the time being it could harmonize with intellectual matters, but the pleasure was rejected because it could not harmonize at all with the will.

From the time of the Lord's conception (and he is the subject of the highest inner meaning), his will was divine and was divine goodness itself. The will he had through birth from his mother was evil, though, and therefore had to be rejected. A new will to replace it had to be acquired from the divine will through the intellect, or from divine goodness through divine truth, and accordingly by the Lord's own power.

This is the secret being described in the inner meaning.

5158   Genesis 40:20, 21, 22, 23. *And it happened on the third day, the day on which Pharaoh had been born, that he made a banquet for all his servants and lifted the head of the chief of the cupbearers and the head of the chief of the bakers in the midst of his servants. And he returned the chief of the cupbearers to his position as cupbearer, and he put the cup on Pharaoh's palm. And the chief of the bakers he hanged, as Joseph had interpreted to them. And the chief of the cupbearers did not remember Joseph and forgot him.*

And it happened on the third day means at the last. *The day on which Pharaoh had been born* means when the earthly level was being regenerated. *That he made a banquet for all his servants* symbolizes being introduced to and united with the outer earthly level. *And lifted the head* means in accord with providence and foresight. *Of the chief of the cupbearers and the head of the chief of the bakers* means concerning the impressions of the senses subject to both sides, the intellectual and volitional. *In the midst of his servants* means which were among the contents of the outer earthly level. *And he returned the chief of the cupbearers to his position as cupbearer* means that the sense impressions on the intellectual side were accepted and put in a subordinate position. *And he put the cup on Pharaoh's palm* means and were serving the inner earthly level. *And the chief of the bakers he hanged* means that the sense impressions on the will side were rejected. *As Joseph had interpreted to them* symbolizes a prediction made by heavenliness on the earthly level. *And the chief of the cupbearers did not remember Joseph* means that there was not yet thorough union with heavenliness on the earthly plane. *And forgot him* symbolizes distance.

And it happened on the third day means at the last. This can be seen from the symbolism of the *third day* as the last part of a state. A *day* means a state (§§23, 487, 488, 493, 893, 2788, 3462, 3785, 4850), and *third* means complete and therefore last (§§1825, 2788, 4495). The last part of a state means when a previous state ends and a new one begins. A new state begins in a person being reborn when things turn upside down, which happens when inner attributes take control of outer attributes, and outer attributes start to serve inner ones, in the area both of the intellect and of the will. Regenerating people can tell this is happening when something inside them persuades them not to let sensual pleasures and bodily or earthly gratifications reign supreme, dragging intellectual matters onto their side to justify them. At this stage, the previous state is at its end, and a new state is in its beginnings. That is what *on the third day* symbolizes.

[2] In everyone, whether regenerating or not, states change and even turn upside down, but this happens one way in people who are regenerating, and another way in those who are not. In nonregenerating people, the changes or upheavals are triggered by their body and aim at purposes involving public life. The bodily triggers are the gain and loss of various appetites as they grow up and grow old, and thoughts about their physical health and their life span in this world. The aims in public life involve times when these people appear on the outside to rein in their appetites, mainly in order to win a reputation for seeming to be wise and to love what is just and good, although their real goal is to amass prestige and wealth.

5159

In regenerating people, the changes or upheavals aim at spiritual purposes, which rise out of genuine goodness and justice. When these qualities begin to appeal to people, they are then at the end of their previous state and the start of a new one.

[3] Not many can understand what all this means, though, so it needs to be illustrated by examples. People who do not allow themselves to be reborn love bodily advantages for the sake of the body and not for any other purpose. They love the world for its own sake, too, and do not venture any higher, because at heart they deny anything higher or deeper. People who are being reborn, on the other hand, equally love bodily and worldly advantages, but their purpose is higher or deeper. They love bodily advantages for the sake of a healthy mind in a healthy body, and they love their mind and its health for a still deeper purpose, which is to gain a wise appreciation of goodness and an intelligent understanding of truth. They also love worldly advantages as much as anyone does, but their goal is to use the world and worldly resources, possessions, and status to gain the means for putting goodness and truth, justice and fairness, into act.

[4] This example shows what each of the two types is like, and that they look alike on the outside but are totally different on the inside. The discussion also identifies and describes the causes and purposes of changes and upheavals in state in people who are not being reborn and people who are. From this it can also be seen that in the regenerate, the inner realm rules the outer, while in the unregenerate, the outer realm rules the inner. The goals we have are what govern, because our goals bring everything in us under their control and command. Our very life has no other source than our ultimate goal, because what we aim for is always what we love.

5160   *On the day on which Pharaoh had been born* means when the earthly level was being regenerated. This can be seen from the symbolism of *being born* as regenerating (discussed below) and from the representation of *Pharaoh* as the inner earthly plane (discussed at §§5080, 5095). In this case he represents the earthly plane as a whole, because correspondence makes a single unit out of the inner and outer earthly levels in regenerate people.

Being born means regenerating because the inner meaning is about spiritual things, and spiritual birth is regeneration, which is also called rebirth. Therefore, when the Word speaks of birth, heaven understands it only as the kind accomplished through "water and spirit," or through faith and neighborly love. It is being reborn or regenerated that makes us human and entirely different from animals, because that is when we become offspring and heirs of the Lord's kingdom.

For spiritual births being symbolized by births mentioned in the Word, see §§1145, 1255, 3860, 3868, 4070, 4668.

That he made a banquet for all his servants symbolizes being intro-   **5161**
duced to and united with the outer earthly level. This can be seen from the symbolism of a *banquet* as introduction to union (discussed in §3832), and also from its symbolism as union through love, and adoption (§3596), and from the symbolism of *servants* as the contents of the outer earthly plane. When we are being reborn, our lower levels become subject and subordinate to our higher levels, or our outer to our inner planes. The outer planes become servants, and the inner planes, masters. That is what servants symbolize in the Word; see §§2541, 3019, 3020. But the outer planes become the kind of servants that their master loves. Reciprocal love unites them and makes their service seem not like servitude but like heartfelt obedience. Goodness flows into them from within, making their duty a pleasure.

Banquets once took place for various reasons. They would symbolize the first steps into mutual love and the resulting union. They might also be given for people's birthdays, and then they represented being born anew, or regenerating. Rebirth is the union of our inside and our outside through love, and consequently the union of heaven with the world in us, since what is worldly or earthly in us then unites with what is spiritual and heavenly.

And lifted the head symbolizes providence and foresight. This can be   **5162**
seen from the symbolism of *lifting someone's head* as a decision based on providence and also on foresight, as discussed above in §§5124, 5155. It symbolizes providence in respect to the senses under the control of the intellectual side, which were held onto as something good and are represented by the cupbearer. It symbolizes foresight in respect to the senses under the control of the will side, which were rejected as something evil and are represented by the baker. Goodness is provided, and evil is foreseen, because everything good comes from the Lord, and everything evil from hell, or from human selfhood. Human selfhood is nothing but evil; see §§210, 215, 694, 874, 875, 876, 987, 1023, 1044, 1047, 1581, 3812, 4328.

Of the chief of the cupbearers and the head of the chief of the bakers   **5163**
means concerning the impressions of the senses subject to both sides, the intellectual and the volitional. This is established by the representation

of the *cupbearer* as the senses subject to the intellectual side (discussed at §§5077, 5082) and from that of the *baker* as the senses subject to the will side (discussed at §§5078, 5082).

5164   *In the midst of his servants* means which were among the contents of the outer earthly level. This stands to reason from the symbolism of *in the midst* as among, and from that of the *servants* as the contents of the outer earthly level (discussed just above at §5161).

"Servants" is the Word's term for everything lower down and accordingly for everything under the command and control of higher levels. This describes the contents of the outer earthly plane, or the sense impressions there, in relation to the inner earthly plane. The contents of the inner earthly plane are also called servants in relation to the rational plane. Each and every thing in a human being, whether inner or outer, is therefore called a servant in relation to the Divine, which is the highest of all.

[2] These servants, in whose midst Pharaoh, the monarch, passed judgment on the cupbearer and baker, were leading courtiers and nobles. Like other royal subjects of every station in life, they are called servants in relation to the monarch, as is also done in every modern kingdom, because royalty represents the Lord and his divine truth (§§2015, 2069, 3009, 3670, 4581, 4966, 5068). In relation to him, no matter what rank we hold, we are all equally servants. In fact, the inhabitants of the Lord's kingdom or heaven who are the greatest—that is, the inmost—are more subservient than others because they show the greatest obedience and have more humility than anyone else. They are the ones meant by the least who will be greatest, and the last who will be first:

> The first will be last, and *the last will be first.* (Matthew 19:30; 20:16; Mark 10:31; Luke 13:30)

> The one who emerges as *least* among you all, that one will be *great.* (Luke 9:48)

They are also meant by the great who will be attendants, and the first who will be servants:

> Anyone who wants to be *great* among you must be your *attendant.* And whichever of you wants to be *first* must be everyone's *servant.* (Mark 10:43, 44; Matthew 20:26, 27)

[3] They are called servants in respect to divine truth from the Lord, and attendants in respect to divine goodness from him. The reason the

last who will be first are more subservient than others is that they know, acknowledge, and perceive that all the life and therefore all the power they have comes from the Lord, and absolutely none from themselves. Anyone who does not perceive this because of not acknowledging it is also a servant but more by an acknowledgment of the lips than of the heart.

On the other hand, those who oppose the idea, although they also call themselves servants in relation to the Divine, want to be master. They grow angry and resentful if the Divine does not favor and essentially obey them. Eventually they turn against the Divine, and then they rob the Divine of all its power, attributing everything to themselves. Most people of this type are the ones in the church who deny the Lord and say they acknowledge a single Supreme Being.

And he returned the chief of the cupbearers to his position as cupbearer 5165 means that the sense impressions on the intellectual side were accepted and put in a subordinate position. This can be seen from the representation of the *chief of the cupbearers* as sensations subordinate to the intellectual side in general (discussed above [§§5077, 5082]) and from the symbolism of *returning one to one's position as cupbearer* as reducing something to order under the intellect. Returning one to one's position means reducing something to order so as to come last (see §5125). The wording here is "to his position as cupbearer" because cup bearing and the liquids a cupbearer provides—wine, new wine, strong drink, water—is mentioned in connection with matters of the intellect. So are the acts of giving a drink and drinking (§§3069, 3168, 3772, 4017). These comments show that *returning the chief of the cupbearers to his position as cupbearer* means reducing the sensations on the intellectual side to order and consequently accepting and subordinating them.

[2] Those sensations are accepted and put in a subordinate position when they minister to deeper levels and serve as a means both for bringing deeper levels into reality and for seeing inside. After all, we see something deeper in sensations belonging to the outer earthly level almost the same way we see emotions in a face and emotions that are deeper still in the eyes. Without an inner face of this kind, or a background of this kind, we cannot possibly think about anything above our senses while we are in our body. That is where we view higher things, as one person sees feelings and thoughts in another's face without noticing the face itself. It is also like hearing another speaking and paying attention to the meaning of the words rather than to the words themselves. The actual words being said

are a background for the meaning. It is the same with the outer earthly
plane. If this plane did not provide our deeper levels with a background
as a mirror in which they could see themselves, we could not think at all.
So this background needs to be formed first, in infancy. But all of this is
unknown, because what happens inside us does not make itself visible
unless we reflect deeply on it.

[3] The nature of our outer earthly plane reveals itself openly in the
other life, because the face of spirits and angels is formed from it and
in accord with it. Their inner attributes, particularly their intentions or
goals, shine through that face in heaven's light. If love for the Lord and
charity for their neighbor formed their inner reaches, this creates a glow in
their face, and their face is actually love and charity in a form. If self-love
and materialism and the consequent hatred, vengefulness, cruelty, and so
on formed their inner reaches, this creates something diabolical in their
face, and their face is actually hatred, vengefulness, and cruelty in a form.

This discussion shows what the outer earthly level is and what its use
is. The discussion also shows what that level is like when it is subordinate
to inner levels, and what that level is like when inner levels are subordinate to it.

5166   *And he put the cup on Pharaoh's palm* means and were serving the
inner earthly level. This can be seen from the remarks above at §5126,
where similar words occur.

5167   *And the chief of the bakers he hanged* means that the sense impressions
on the will side were rejected. This can also be seen from remarks above
where similar words occur, at §5156.

5168   *As Joseph had interpreted to them* symbolizes a prediction made by
heavenliness on the earthly level, as the following shows: *Interpreting*
means saying what the content is, or what is inherent, and what would
happen, as discussed at §§5093, 5105, 5107, 5141, so it means predicting.
And *Joseph* represents heavenliness on an earthly level, as discussed at
§§5086, 5087, 5106.

Concerning the situation in all this—that sensations on the intellectual side were kept, and sensations on the will side were rejected—see
above at §5157.

[2] The inner meaning of this chapter deals with the taming of the
outer earthly level, which needs to be brought under control in order to
serve as a background for the inner earthly plane (§5165). If it is not subordinate, inner truth and goodness have no medium in which they can be
represented. As a result, inner thoughts containing what is spiritual and

heavenly have no such medium, because the outer earthly level functions as a face or mirror in which they present themselves. Consequently, when there is no subordination people cannot have any inner thoughts. In fact, they cannot have any faith, because they have no comprehension of what is remote or lofty and therefore no awareness of such things.

The only agent that tames the earthly plane and reduces it to correspondence is goodness containing innocence, and the Word calls this goodness neighborly love. Sense impressions and empirical knowledge are just a medium for this goodness to flow into, revealing itself in a form and laying itself open for every possible use. Even if empirical knowledge were faith's truth itself, as long as it lacks this goodness it is nothing but husks on things in the garbage, which fall off.

[3] How is the outer dimension reduced to order and to correspondence with the inner dimension through goodness by means of knowledge and religious truth? The answer lies further beyond grasp now than it once did, for many reasons. The main reason is that today there is no longer any neighborly love within the church. These are the church's final days, so there is also no interest in learning about such topics. Consequently a certain amount of resistance immediately crops up when anyone says anything that goes deeper or higher than the senses and therefore when anyone brings out the kinds of ideas that go to make up angelic wisdom. However, since the inner meaning contains the kinds of ideas that are suited to angelic wisdom, and I am explaining the Word according to that meaning, I need to say these things anyway, no matter how distant they must seem from sensory experience.

And the chief of the cupbearers did not remember Joseph means that there was not yet thorough union with heavenliness on the earthly plane, as the following shows: *Remembering* Joseph symbolizes acceptance of faith (as discussed above in §5130) and therefore union, too, since union comes about by means of faith. *Not remembering,* then, means that there was not yet thorough union. The *chief of the cupbearers* represents sense impressions on the intellectual side. And *Joseph* represents heavenliness on the earthly plane, as noted above.

5169

And forgot him symbolizes distance. This can be seen from the symbolism of *forgetting* as distance, since "not remembering" means lack of union. The less union there is, the more distance. What we forget about grows remote.

5170

This is also true of sense impressions under the control of the intellectual side. They do not form a bond [with heavenliness on the earthly plane] just because they are retained, because they are not yet pure from fallacies. Rather, as they are purified they are united.

This subject will be explored in the next chapter, which tells how Joseph was recalled to the cupbearer's mind.

Correspondence with the Universal Human (Continued): Correspondence of the Internal Organs

5171   IN the other life it is possible to tell what areas various angelic communities belong to by their location relative to the human body and by their operation and inflow—since they operate and flow into that organ and limb in which they dwell. Their inflow and operation can be perceived only by inhabitants of the other world, though, and not by people on earth, except those whose inner depths have opened up to that world. Not even then is it possible unless the Lord enables them to reflect on incoming sensations and perceive something from them.

5172   There are certain upright spirits whose thinking is not very meditative and who therefore quickly say what comes to mind, more or less without thinking ahead. They have inner perception, but other spirits do more pondering and thinking about what they perceive, which renders their perceptions more visual than is the case with these spirits. As these spirits advance through life, they seem to learn spontaneously about the goodness inherent in things, and not so much about the truth involved.

I was told that these spirits belong to the area of the *thymus gland.* The thymus is a gland that performs its main use for children, in whom it is soft. These spirits also have something soft and childlike left in them into which the perception of goodness flows, and truth shines from the perception in a general way.

Such spirits can be surrounded by large mobs without feeling disturbed, as is also the case with the thymus gland.

5173   In the other world there are many ways in which spirits are tormented and many ways in which they are initiated into choral circles.

The torments are represented by the purification in the body of the blood, the serum or lymph, and the chyle—which itself is accomplished through various harsh processes of refinement. The initiation into choral circles is represented by the subsequent introduction of these fluids into their proper function.

It is very common in the next life for spirits who have been tormented to then be brought into a calm, pleasant state and accordingly into the communities that they are to be introduced to and connected with.

[2] The fact that the chastening and purifying of the blood, serum, and chyle and of food particles in the stomach correspond to these processes in the spiritual world must seem strange to people who think that earthly things contain only what is earthly. This is especially true for people who put faith in that thought, denying that anything spiritual exists or can exist within and be an active, governing force. In reality, each and every component of nature and its three kingdoms has something from the spiritual world inside that drives it. If it did not, absolutely nothing in the physical world would bring about a cause or effect. So nothing would be productive. The element of the spiritual world present in earthly things is referred to as a force inherent from the beginning of creation, but it is an impetus, and when the impetus stops, activity or motion stops. That is why the whole visible world is a theater representing the spiritual world.

[3] The situation resembles the movement of the muscles, which results in action. If the energy of human thought and will does not lie behind movement, the movement immediately stops. According to laws known to the scholarly world, motion stops when its impetus stops and the impetus has complete control over the direction the motion takes. The laws also show that nothing real exists in a motion except the impetus. This force or energy within the activity or motion is clearly the spiritual element within the physical, because thinking and willing is spiritual, but acting and moving is physical. Not even people who limit their thoughts to the physical realm can deny this, although they do not grasp it.

The element of will and therefore of thought that produces an effect does not have the same form as the action it produces. The action merely represents what the mind wills and thinks.

Food particles in the stomach undergo many harsh processes to draw out their inner nutrients so that these can be put to use by being turned into chyle and then into blood. This is known, as is the fact that food then also goes into the intestines. The rough treatment the food undergoes is **5174** represented by the spirits' first torments, which all depend on their life in the world. The torments are intended to separate out what is evil and gather what is good so that it can be put to use. Not long after departure or release from the body, then, souls or spirits can be said to enter the area of the "stomach" first, where they are pummeled and purified. Those in whom evil predominated, having undergone these rigors in vain, move on through the stomach into the intestines all the way to the last part, the colon and rectum, which excretes them into the latrine, or hell.

Those in whom goodness predominated, though, having endured some afflictions and purification, turn into chyle and become part of the blood. Some take a longer route, some take a shorter. Some are tormented harshly, some mildly, and some hardly at all. The ones who escape almost all torment are represented by the liquids in food, which are absorbed immediately by the veins and circulate to the brain and other parts of the body.

5175   When we die and enter the other world, our life resembles food that is gently taken in by the lips and then directed through the mouth, jaws, and esophagus into the stomach, depending on the character we acquired during bodily life through our deeds. Most of us are treated gently at first, being kept in the company of angels and good spirits. This is represented by the way food is first handled gently by the lips and then tasted by the tongue to discover its nature. Food that is soft and contains sugar, oil, or a volatile substance is immediately received by the veins and circulated. Food that is tough, though, and contains something bitter, foul, or nonnutritious is harder to break down. It is sent down through the esophagus to the stomach, where it is belabored and chastened in various ways. Food that is tougher, fouler, and more unproductive yet is propelled down into the intestines and eventually into the rectum (where the first hell is located) and is finally eliminated, turning into excrement.

Our life after death matches this situation. At first we are kept in superficialities, and having lived a well-mannered, ethical life on the surface, we coexist with angels and upright spirits. Superficialities are later taken away from us, however, and then it becomes obvious what we have been like inside in regard to our thoughts, our feelings, and in the end our aims. It is in accord with our aims that our life awaits us.

5176   As long as we are in this state, in which we resemble nutrients or food in the stomach, we are not part of the universal human but are being introduced into it. When we representatively enter the bloodstream, on the other hand, we are then in the universal human.

People who have worried a lot about the future, especially if they have **5177** become grasping and greedy on that account, appear in the area of the stomach. I saw many there.

The aura their life gives off can be compared to a sickening stench wafting from the stomach, and to the lead weight of indigestion. People who were like this linger a long time in the area, because worry about the future, reinforced by one's actions, seriously blunts and slows the inflow of spiritual life. They attribute what is actually the work of divine providence to themselves, and people who do this block the inflow, keeping a life of goodness and truth at arm's length.

Since concern over the future is what creates anxiety in people, and **5178** since spirits that cause anxiety appear in the area of the stomach, anxiety affects the stomach more than any other organ.

In fact, I was allowed to sense how these anxieties waxed and waned in accord with the presence or withdrawal of such spirits. Some anxieties seemed deeper, some shallower, some higher, and some lower, depending on differences in the source, development, and focus of the worries.

For the same reason the area around our stomach tightens when these anxieties invade our mind, and we sometimes feel pain there. The anxiety even seems to well up out of our stomach. It is also why the area around our stomach relaxes and expands and we start to enjoy ourselves when we stop worrying about the future, or when everything turns out well for us, removing any fear of misfortune.

I once felt some anxiety in the pit of my stomach, which showed me **5179** that these spirits were present. I spoke with them, saying, "It would be better if you went away, because the aura around you generates anxiety, and it doesn't harmonize with the aura of the spirits around me."

Then I talked with them about auras in these terms: People on earth have a great many spiritual auras around them, but they do not know it and do not want to know it, because they deny anything that is called spiritual. Some of them deny anything they cannot see and touch. People therefore have around them a number of auras from the spiritual world that mirror their life and connect them to spirits with similar desires. These auras produce many effects, but humankind, which attributes everything to nature, either denies them or ascribes them to the more mysterious forces of nature. Take, for instance, what people ascribe to luck. Some have been thoroughly convinced by experience that there is a hidden factor at work called luck, though they do not know where it comes from. Such events result from a spiritual aura and constitute the outermost level of providence, as I will testify elsewhere from experience [§§6493–6494], with the Lord's divine mercy.

5180 There are demons and spirits who apply to one's head a kind of suction or pull, so that the site of the pulling or suction feels great pain. I experienced a very clear feeling of suction, as if a membrane were being sucked out while my senses were fully awake. Whether others could endure the pain of it, I am unsure, but because I grew used to it, I learned to bear it often, without suffering. The suction started at the top of my head and spread from there toward the area of my left ear and toward the area of my left eye. The suction reaching toward my eye came from spirits, and that reaching toward my ear came from demons. Both groups consist of those who belong to the region of the *cisterna chyli* and *chyle ducts,* to which chyle is drawn from all directions (although it is also propelled there).

There were others as well who acted inside my head, in almost the same way but without so much sucking power. I was told that they are the ones to whom purified *chyle* corresponds. This chyle travels toward the brain, where it mixes with fresh animal spirit, to be channeled down toward the heart.

The ones who acted on the outside first appeared to me in the front part [of my head], slightly to the left. Later they appeared higher up there, so that their region was observed to reach from the level of the nasal septum up toward the level of the left ear.

[2] The [spirits] constituting this region are of two kinds. Some are fairly modest, and others are insolent. The modest ones are those who wanted to know what people were thinking in order to attract and attach them to themselves. When we know others' thoughts, we know something private and intimate about them, which brings us close to them. The goal is social contact and friendship. They want to know only the good things, and that is what they look into. Anything else they find they put a good interpretation on.

The insolent ones, though, understand and pursue many methods of fishing out others' thoughts with the aim either of material advantage for themselves or of harm to their victims. Since this is their passion and preoccupation, they detain their victim's mind on the subject they want to know about, refusing to back off. They even side with the person sympathetically and in this way draw out even the person's secret thoughts. They do the same in the communities of the other world, and with even greater skill. There too they do not allow their victims to wander off topic but fan the fire and in this way extract what they seek. As a result, they then have their victims in chains and exercise power over them, because they are aware of their evils.

But these spirits among others are vagabonds and are often punished.

To some extent an observer can tell from their choral circles what region spirits and angels belong to in the universal human and (by correspondence) in the body. The circles of those belonging to the region of the *lymphatic system* are thin and rapid like a gently flowing liquid, so that hardly any circular movement can be detected.

5181

The spirits belonging to the lymphatic system later go to places that they said resemble the *mesentery*. I was told that there are labyrinths of a kind there, and that the spirits are later taken to various other places in the universal human to serve a purpose, as chyle does in the body.

There are choral circles that newly arrived spirits have to be initiated into so that they can interact with others and both speak and think in unison with them. In the other life everything has to be harmonious and unanimous so that it can all be one. Just as everything large and small in the human being differs throughout but still forms a single whole, through unanimity, so likewise in the universal human. To this end, an individual's thoughts and words have to harmonize with others'.

5182

There is a basic need for the thought and speech of each member of a community to be internally harmonious. Otherwise bystanders sense dissonance as a harsh, disturbing noise that assaults their minds. All dissonance creates rifts and is an impurity that ought to be rejected. This impurity resulting from dissonance is represented by impurities of and in the blood, which need to be removed from it. The removal is accomplished through harsh rigors (which are actually trials of various kinds) and afterward through initiations into choral circles. The first initiation into these circles is to make it possible for spirits to fit in. The second is to bring their thoughts into harmony with their words. The third is to attune the spirits to each other in thought and feeling. The fourth is to attune them in truth and goodness.

I was given the opportunity to perceive the choral circles of those who belong to the region of the *liver* for the space of an hour. Their circles were gentle, swirling around in different ways, in accord with the activity of that organ. They gave me great pleasure. Their activity varies but generally moves spherically.

5183

The wide range of their activity is represented in the functions of the liver, which are also diverse. The liver collects blood, separates it, pours the better kind into the veins, sends the middling kind to the hepatic duct, and leaves the worst for the gall bladder—at least in adults. In embryos, the liver takes blood from the mother's womb, purifies it, and releases the purer portion into the veins to take a shortcut to the heart. There it stands guard before the heart.

5184   Spirits belonging to the *pancreas* take a sharper, almost sawlike approach, which even makes a rasping sound to match. The rasp actually reaches spirits' ears in an audible way but not the ears of people on earth, unless they are in the spirit while in their body. The spirits' territory lies between the areas of the spleen and the liver and farther to the left.

Spirits in the region of the *spleen* are almost directly overhead, but their activity is directed down into the spleen.

5185   There are spirits who correlate with the *pancreatic, hepatic,* and *cystic ducts* and consequently with the different kinds of fluid they hold, which they secrete into the intestines.

These spirits are different from each other but work in harmony, according to the state of the [spirits] who are the focus of their efforts.

Most of all they help with discipline and punishment, which they would like to direct. The worst of them are so implacable that they never would voluntarily stop this unless they were deterred by fears and threats. They themselves are afraid of being punished, which inspires them to promise anything.

They are ones who doggedly clung to their opinions during bodily life, not so much because they had lived evil lives as because of a natural wickedness.

When they are in their earthly state, they think nothing. Thinking nothing means thinking vaguely about a lot of things all at once without a clear thought about any of it. Their delight is to do good by disciplining others, but they themselves do not abstain from what is filthy.

5186   Spirits constituting the region of the *gall bladder* are at the back. They are ones who in bodily life looked with contempt on integrity and to some extent on religious devotion, and also ones who took steps to discredit those qualities.

5187   A spirit once came to me asking whether I knew where he could stay a while. He seemed to me to be honest, and when I said maybe he could stay here, the harassing spirits from the region of the gall bladder came and tormented him miserably. It upset me, and I tried in vain to stop it.

I noticed then that I was in the region of the gall bladder. The harassing spirits were some of those who looked down on integrity and piety.

I had the chance to observe one type of torment there, which consisted in forcing spirits to talk faster than they were thinking. The harassing spirits accomplished this by disconnecting a victim's words from her or his thoughts and forcing her or him to keep up with their own rate of speech, which causes pain. Slow spirits are initiated into more rapid thought and speech by this kind of torment.

There are some in the world who do what they do through tricks **5188** and lies, with evil results. I was shown what they are like and how they act by the fact that they used the innocent as their advocates and that they pretended to have said so-and-so on a subject they never actually addressed. In short, they use evil means for achieving whatever they seek. Their means are frauds, lies, and tricks. Spirits like this relate to blemishes called *spurious growths* that usually develop on the pleura and other membranes. Where these take root, they spread blemishes far and wide until they finally make the whole membrane disintegrate.

[2] Such spirits are harshly punished. Their punishment is different from others'. It consists in wheeling around in a circle. They revolve from left to right in an orbit that seems flat at first but bulges as they circle. Then the bulge appears to be pressed down and become hollow, at which point the speed increases. Amazingly, the process mirrors the shape of the growths, or abscesses.

I observed that as they revolved they tried to draw others—especially the innocent—into their orbit and therefore into their ruin. In other words, they do not care if they involve everyone in their destruction while they seem to themselves to be perishing.

[3] I also observed that they have powerful vision, as if they were instantly scrutinizing and seizing on the most favorable material as their means. They are sharper eyed than anyone else, then. They can also be called fatal ulcers, wherever they appear in the chest cavity, whether in the pleura, the pericardium, the mediastinum, or the lungs.

I was shown that after these spirits are punished, they are sent away toward the back and down deep, where they lie with their face and belly down and little human life remaining. So they are deprived of their keen eyesight, which was the mark of their animal life.

Their hell is in a deep place under the right foot, a little out in front.

Some spirits came forward, and before they arrived I sensed the kind **5189** of atmosphere that is given off by the evil. As a result I thought the spirits about to come were evil, but they were enemies of the evil ones. This I discovered from the antagonism and enmity they inspired against the evil ones. When they came, they placed themselves over my head and addressed me, saying they were people.

"You are not the kind of people who have a body, the way people in the world do," I answered. "People in the world are used to calling themselves human because of their physical form. But you are people anyway, because a person's spirit is the true person." I did not sense any resistance to this idea, because they agreed.

They went on to say they were dissimilar individuals. Since this seemed impossible to me—that a community of unlike spirits should exist in the other world—I talked with them about it, saying that if a common cause united them they could still form a community, because they would then all have one goal.

They said that by nature they each speak differently but all think alike. They illustrated this by examples, which made it clear that they all have a single way of perceiving things but different ways of talking about them.

[2] Next they placed themselves at my left ear, saying that they were good spirits and that this was their manner of speaking. I heard that they come in a group and no one knows where they come from.

I perceived an aura extremely hostile to them that was given off by evil spirits, the evil spirits being subordinates whom they harass.

Their community, which drifts from place to place, was represented by a man and woman in a room, wearing clothing that turned into a simple garment of a blue color.

[3] I perceived that they related to the brain's *isthmus,* which lies between the cerebrum and cerebellum and has nerve fibers passing through it. The fibers run out from there in different directions and behave in different ways in the outer parts, wherever they go.

The spirits also relate to the *ganglia* in the body. A ganglion has a nerve flowing into it and branching out into many fibers, some of which run in one direction and some in another. The fibers act in different ways when they reach the surface, but they still extend from a single starting point. So to all appearances they act in different ways on the surface but in the same way when it comes to their purpose. It is recognized that a single driving force can vary in many ways on the outside, depending on the form it encounters there.

In addition, final purposes are represented by the elementary sub-stances composing the nerve fibers, as those substances exist in the brain. The thoughts resulting from the purposes are represented by the fibers consisting of those substances. And the actions resulting from the thoughts are represented by the nerves consisting of those fibers.

There will be more about correspondence with the universal human at the end of the next chapter [§§5377–5396a].

5190

[CONTINUED IN VOLUME 8]

Biographical Note

E MANUEL SWEDENBORG (1688–1772) was born Emanuel Swedberg (or Svedberg) in Stockholm, Sweden, on January 29, 1688 (Julian calendar). He was the third of the nine children of Jesper Swedberg (1653–1735) and Sara Behm (1666–1696). At the age of eight he lost his mother. After the death of his only older brother ten days later, he became the oldest living son. In 1697 his father married Sara Bergia (1666–1720), who developed great affection for Emanuel and left him a significant inheritance. His father, a Lutheran clergyman, later became a celebrated and controversial bishop, whose diocese included the Swedish churches in Pennsylvania and in London, England.

After studying at the University of Uppsala (1699–1709), Emanuel journeyed to England, the Netherlands, France, and Germany (1710–1715) to study and work with leading scientists in western Europe. Upon his return he apprenticed as an engineer under the brilliant Swedish inventor Christopher Polhem (1661–1751). He gained favor with Sweden's King Charles XII (1682–1718), who gave him a salaried position as an overseer of Sweden's mining industry (1716–1747). Although Emanuel was engaged, he never married.

After the death of Charles XII, Emanuel was ennobled by Queen Ulrika Eleonora (1688–1741), and his last name was changed to Swedenborg (or Svedenborg). This change in status gave him a seat in the Swedish House of Nobles, where he remained an active participant in the Swedish government throughout his life.

A member of the Royal Swedish Academy of Sciences, he devoted himself to studies that culminated in a number of publications, most notably a comprehensive three-volume work on natural philosophy and metallurgy (1734) that brought him recognition across Europe as a scientist. After 1734 he redirected his research and publishing to a study of anatomy in search of the interface between the soul and body, making several significant discoveries in physiology.

From 1743 to 1745 he entered a transitional phase that resulted in a shift of his main focus from science to theology. Throughout the rest of his life he maintained that this shift was brought about by Jesus Christ, who appeared to him, called him to a new mission, and opened his perception to a permanent dual consciousness of this life and the life after death.

He devoted the last decades of his life to studying Scripture and publishing eighteen theological titles that draw on the Bible, reasoning, and his own spiritual experiences. These works present a Christian theology with unique perspectives on the nature of God, the spiritual world, the Bible, the human mind, and the path to salvation.

Swedenborg died in London on March 29, 1772 (Gregorian calendar), at the age of eighty-four.